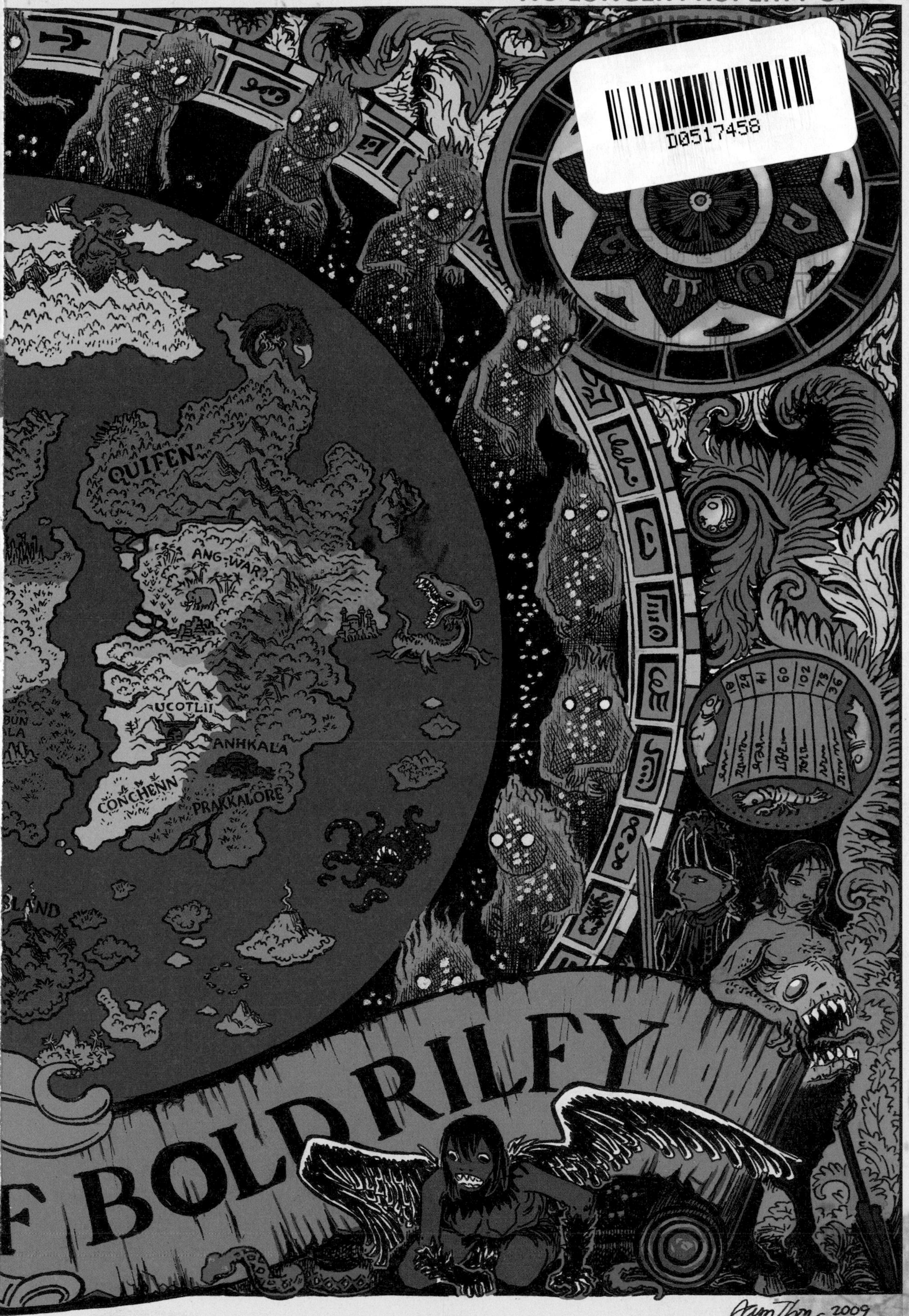
QUIFEN
ANG-WAR
UCOTLII
ANHKALA
CONCHENN
PRAKKALORE
F BOLD RILEY
2009

The Legend of Bold Riley

LEIA WEATHINGTON

MARCO AIDALA
VANESSA GILLINGS
KELLY McCLELLAN
KONSTANTIN POGORELOV
JASON THOMPSON

COVER ARTWORK BY BRINSON THIEME

FOREWORD BY JANE ESPENSON

Thank you...

My endless thanks go to Pancha Diaz, who spent countless nights listening to me ramble and then later on laid out the minicomics and did a sizable portion of the lettering as well. She is one of my good friends and a prized colleague. Liz Conley deserves thanks for helping staple all of those minicomics. Her insight into bookbinding and paper art is invaluable. I also want to thank Shaenon Garrity and Andrew Farago for their support and friendship. All four of them are fabulous creators and you can find them at **couscouscollective.com**. Go check them out.

Chloe Dalquist was our fantastic colorist on "The Strange Bath." I asked her to do the colors after seeing how great they looked on her own comic, Jamie the Trickster. You can read that at **jamiethetrickster.com**.

I have to thank Robert Revels, Chuck Pyle and Dan Cooney, three excellent professors at the Academy of Art University where Vanessa, Konstantin, Kelly and I met and studied. They were especially helpful in accepting "The Golden Trumpet Tree" as coursework for a full semester and giving me helpful critiques when I studied under them.

Last but not least, I want to thank everyone at Prism Comics and Northwest Press for being such a wonderful supportive community.

As well as you, for reading.

This book is dedicated to my father, Chris Weathington. Without his tireless support and encouragement, Bold Riley would never have happened.

Thanks for telling me stories whenever I couldn't sleep, Dad.

Leia Weathington,
Portland, 2012

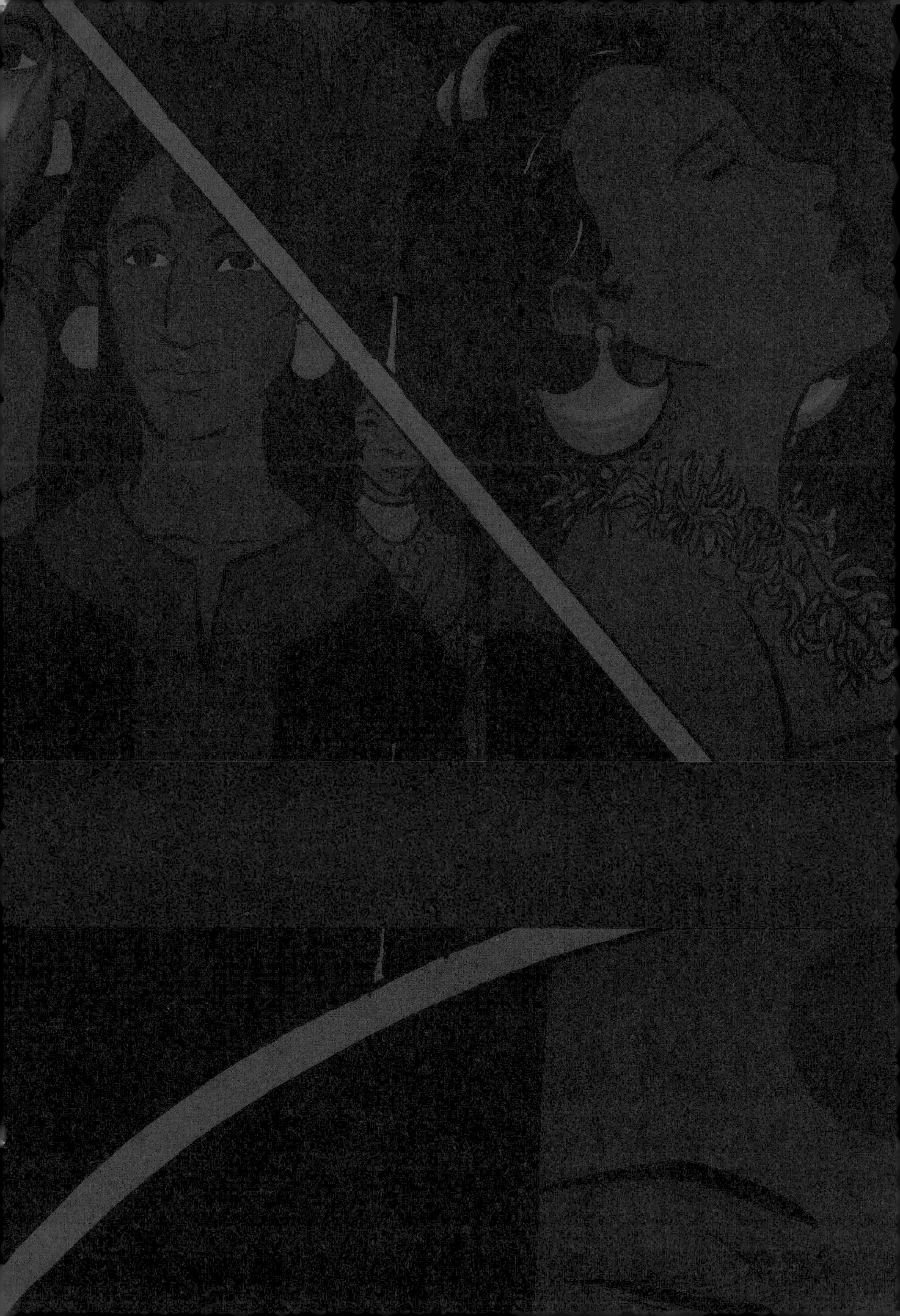

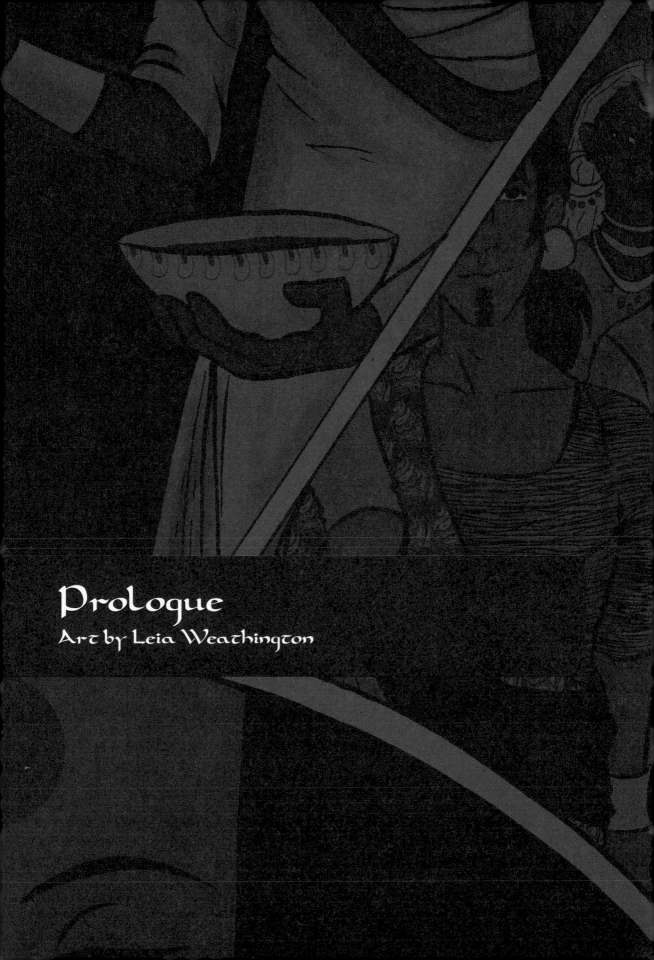

Prologue
Art by Leia Weathington

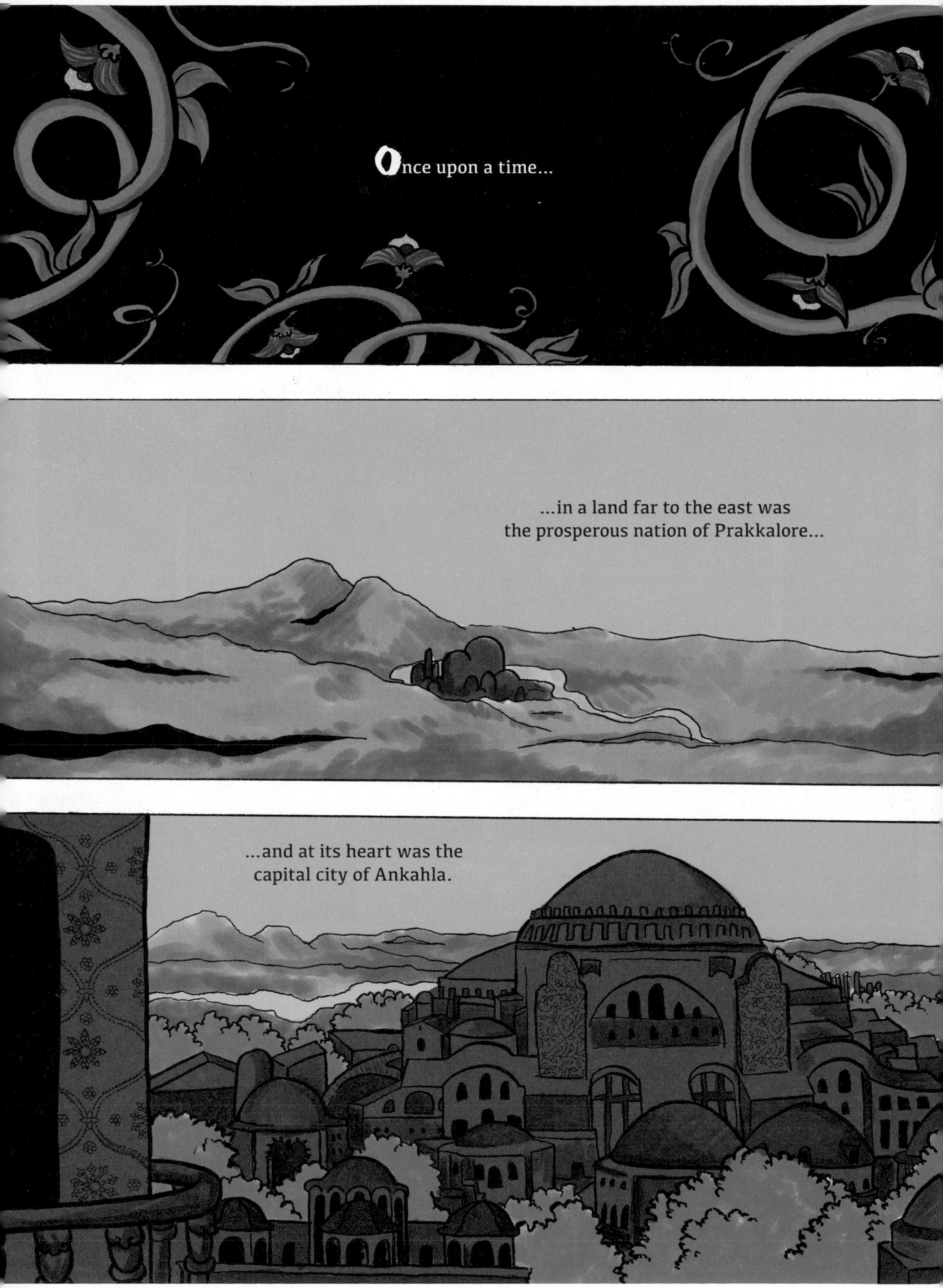
Once upon a time...
...in a land far to the east was the prosperous nation of Prakkalore...
...and at its heart was the capital city of Ankahla.

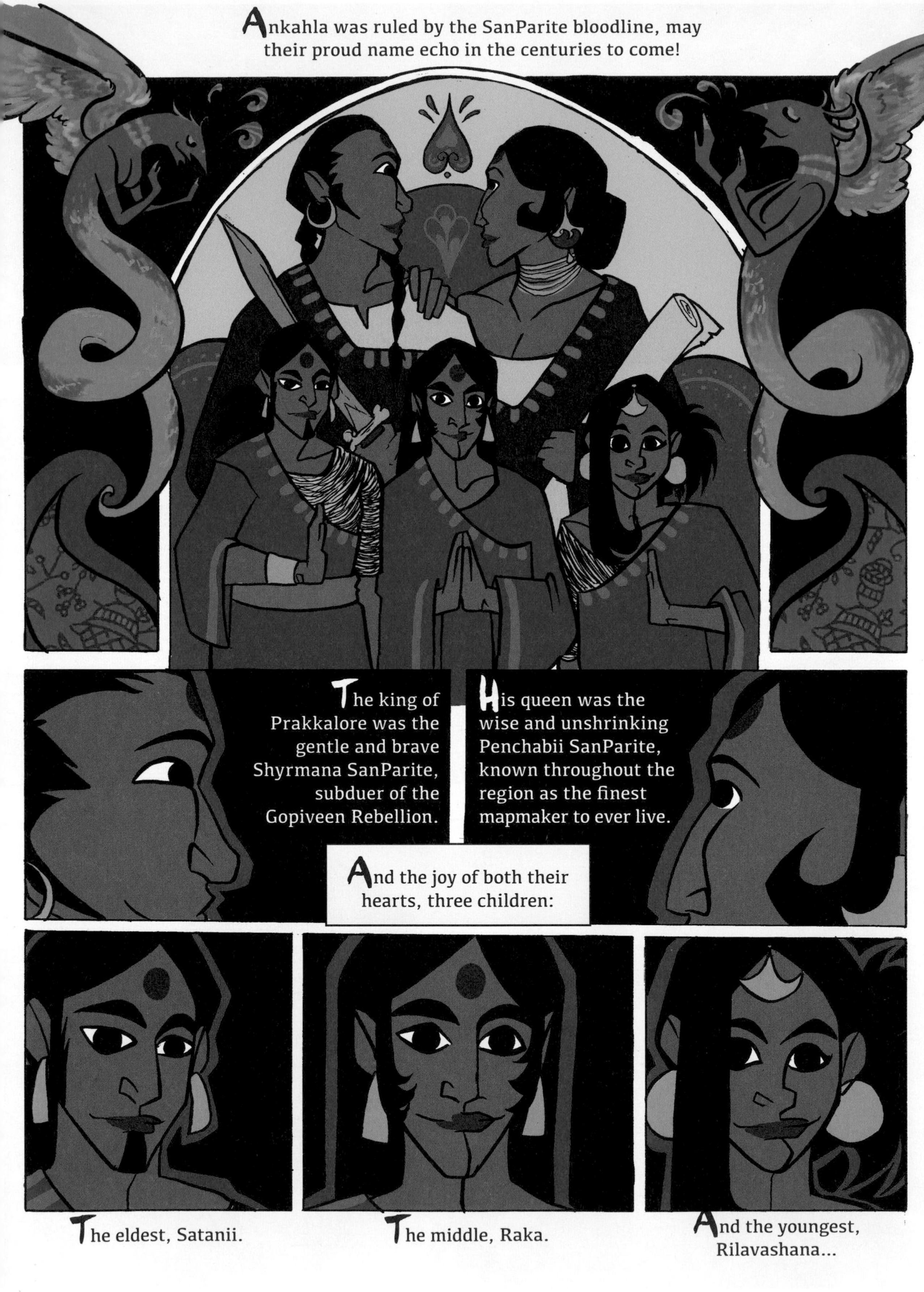
Ankahla was ruled by the SanParite bloodline, may their proud name echo in the centuries to come!
The king of Prakkalore was the gentle and brave Shyrmana SanParite, subduer of the Gopiveen Rebellion.
His queen was the wise and unshrinking Penchabii SanParite, known throughout the region as the finest mapmaker to ever live.
And the joy of both their hearts, three children:
The eldest, Satanii.
The middle, Raka.
And the youngest, Rilavashana...

All of the SanParite children would become persons of distinction, but it is with Rilavashana that these tales concern themselves.

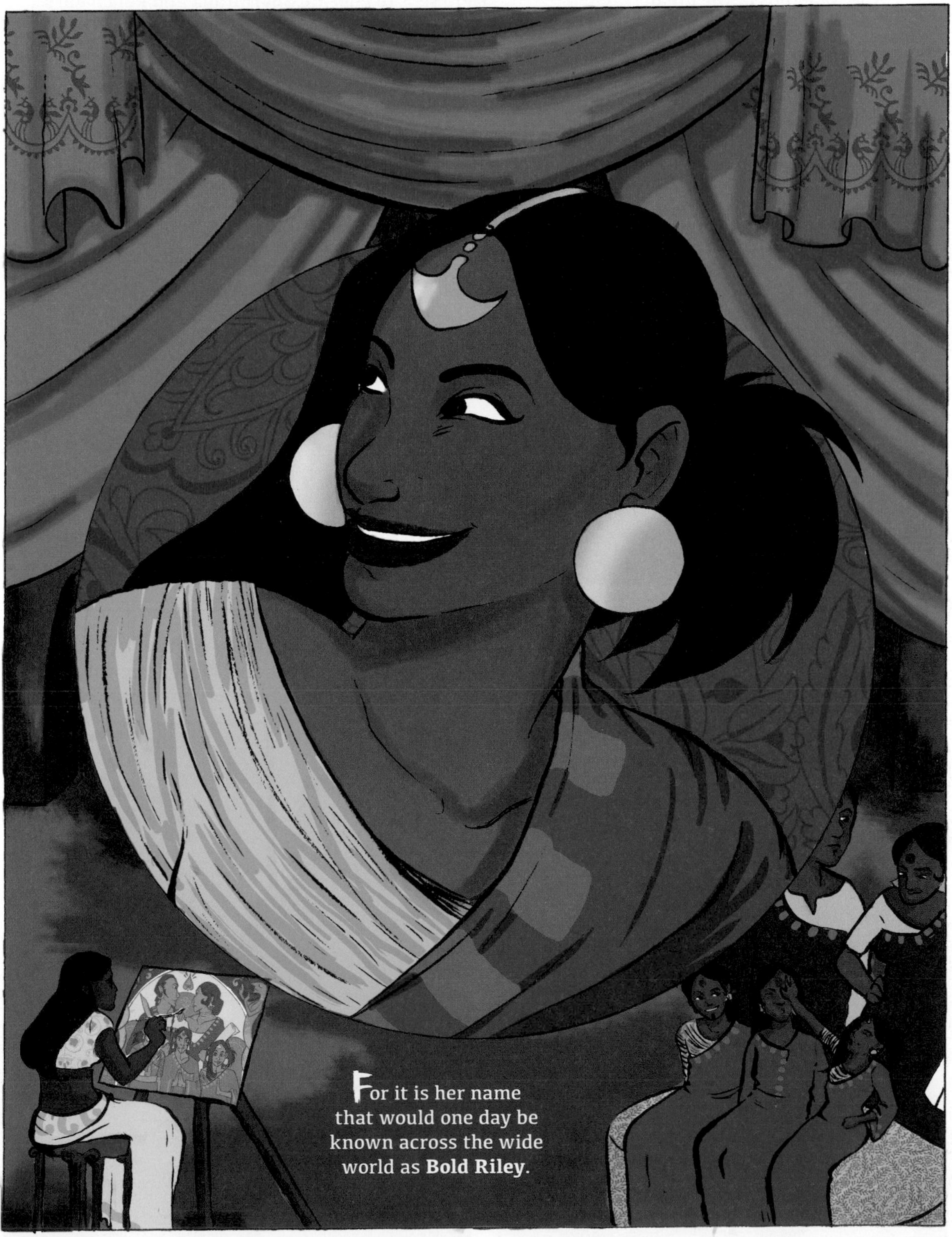
For it is her name that would one day be known across the wide world as **Bold Riley**.

Along with her brothers, she was raised to follow in the footsteps of the great monarchs of Prakkalore.

Swordplay, diplomacy, arithmetic, language, history, the sciences: from far and wide, tutors were sent to educate Shyrmrana and Penchabii's little darlings in the ways of the world.

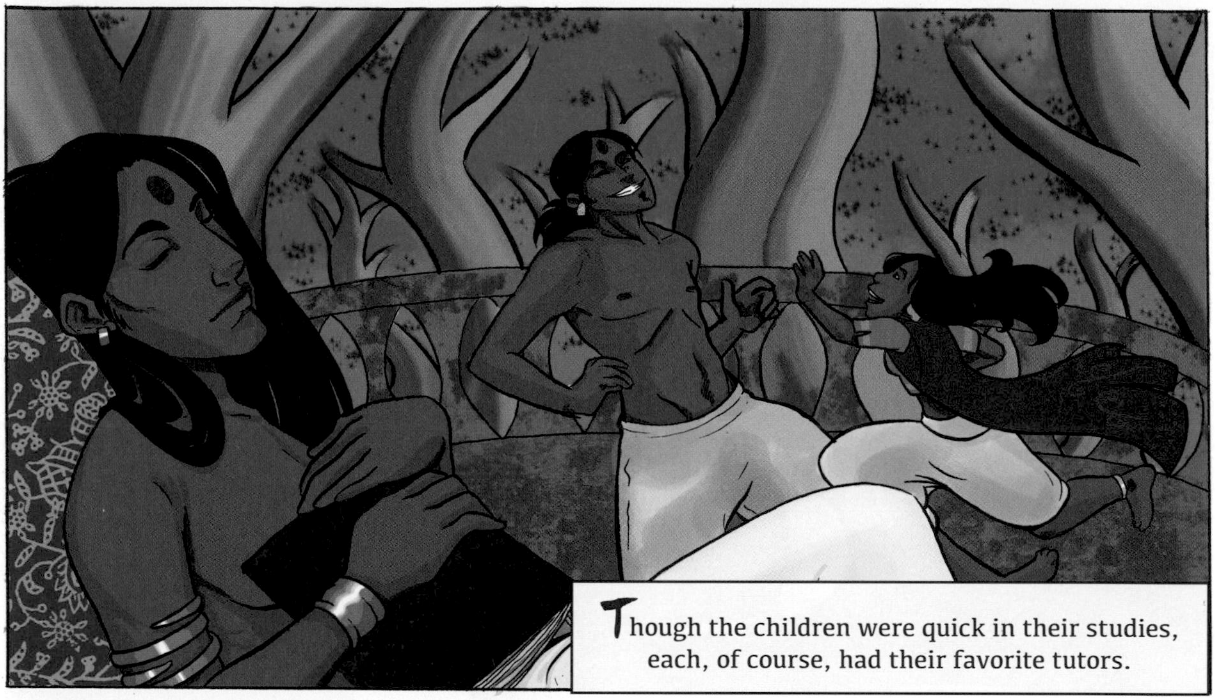
Though the children were quick in their studies, each, of course, had their favorite tutors.

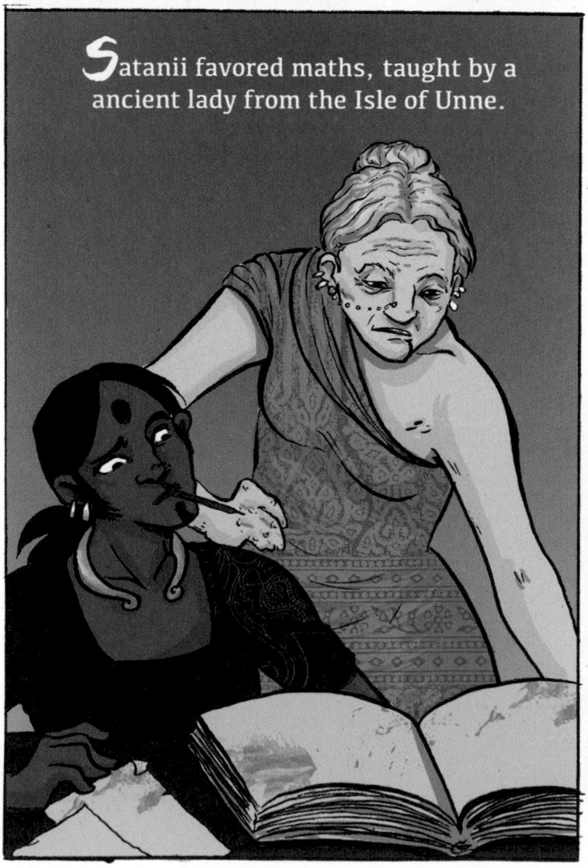
Satanii favored maths, taught by a ancient lady from the Isle of Unne.

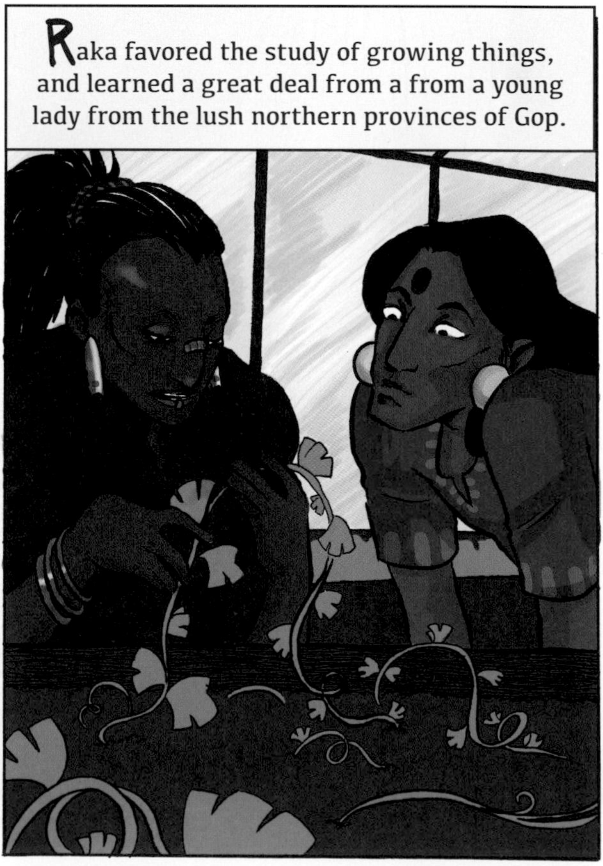
Raka favored the study of growing things, and learned a great deal from a from a young lady from the lush northern provinces of Gop.

And Rilavashana favored history, taught by a man who hailed from the distant west...

...a gentleman who had something of a difficulty with the Prakkaloran tongue.

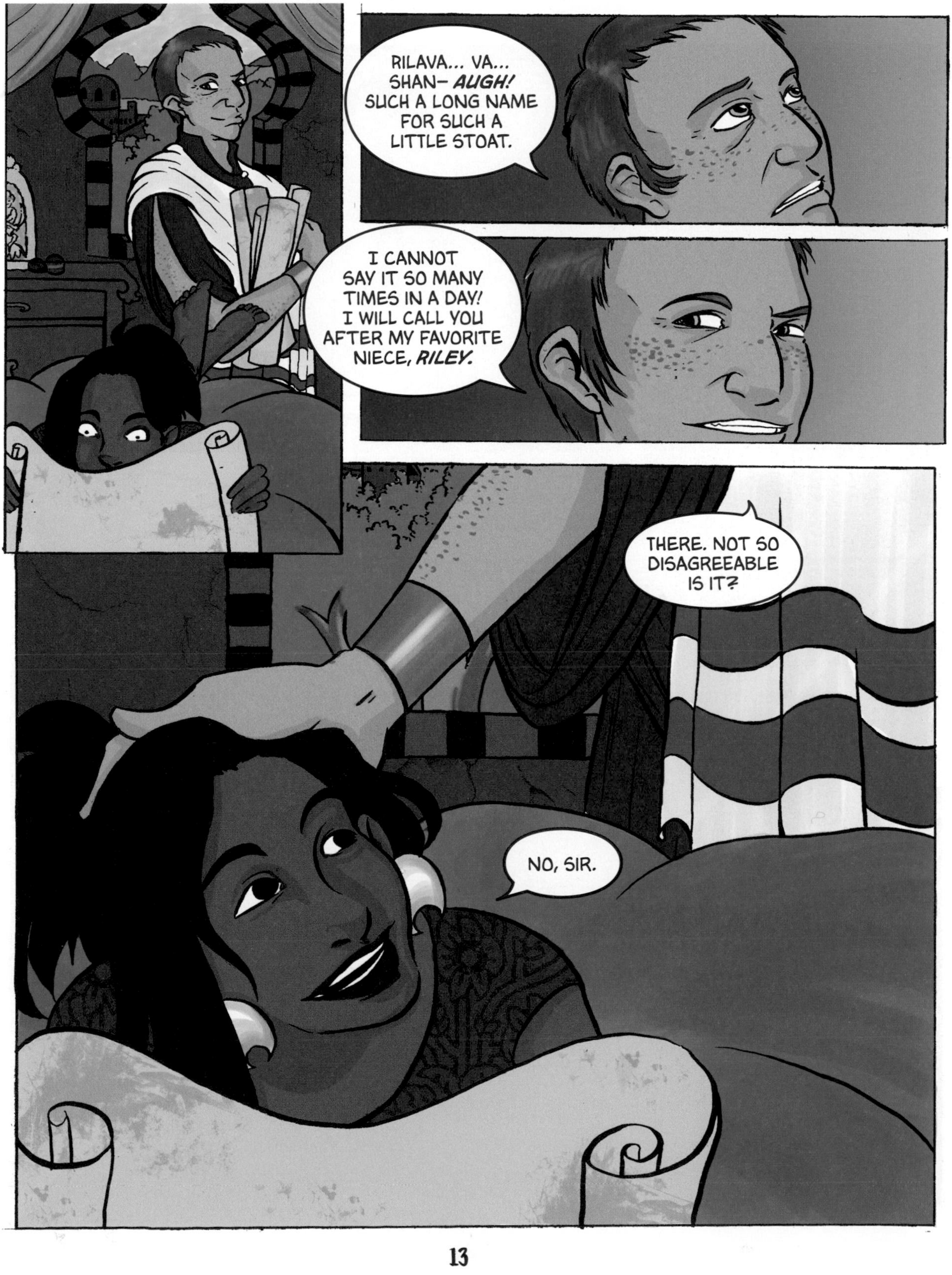

RILAVA... VA... SHAN- AUGH! SUCH A LONG NAME FOR SUCH A LITTLE STOAT.
I CANNOT SAY IT SO MANY TIMES IN A DAY! I WILL CALL YOU AFTER MY FAVORITE NIECE, RILEY.
THERE. NOT SO DISAGREEABLE IS IT?
NO, SIR.

Perhaps it was the long hot days spent in the gentleman's study hearing tales of distant peoples and strange lands...

Or perhaps it was sitting on her mother's knee as each new year's maps were drawn out and lovingly colored by Penchabii's own hand...

But in Rilavashana, the seed of restlessness had been sown.

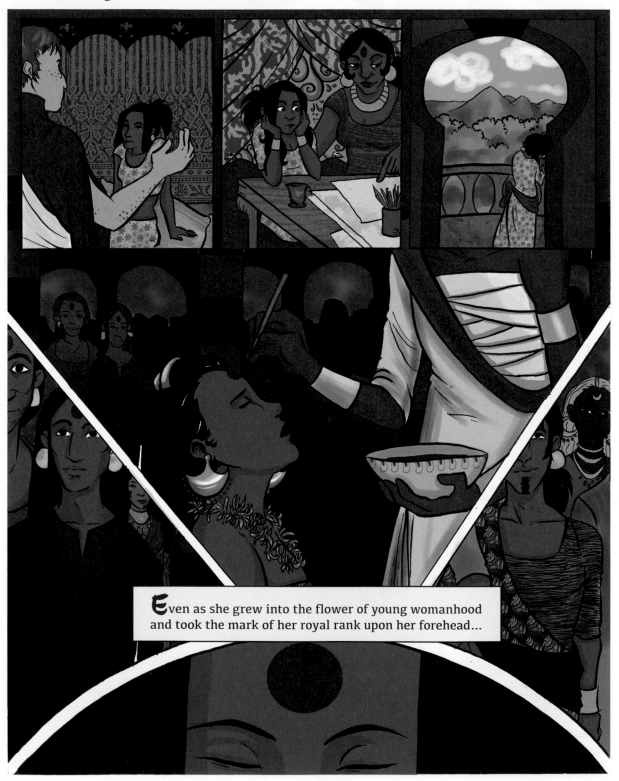

Even as she grew into the flower of young womanhood and took the mark of her royal rank upon her forehead...

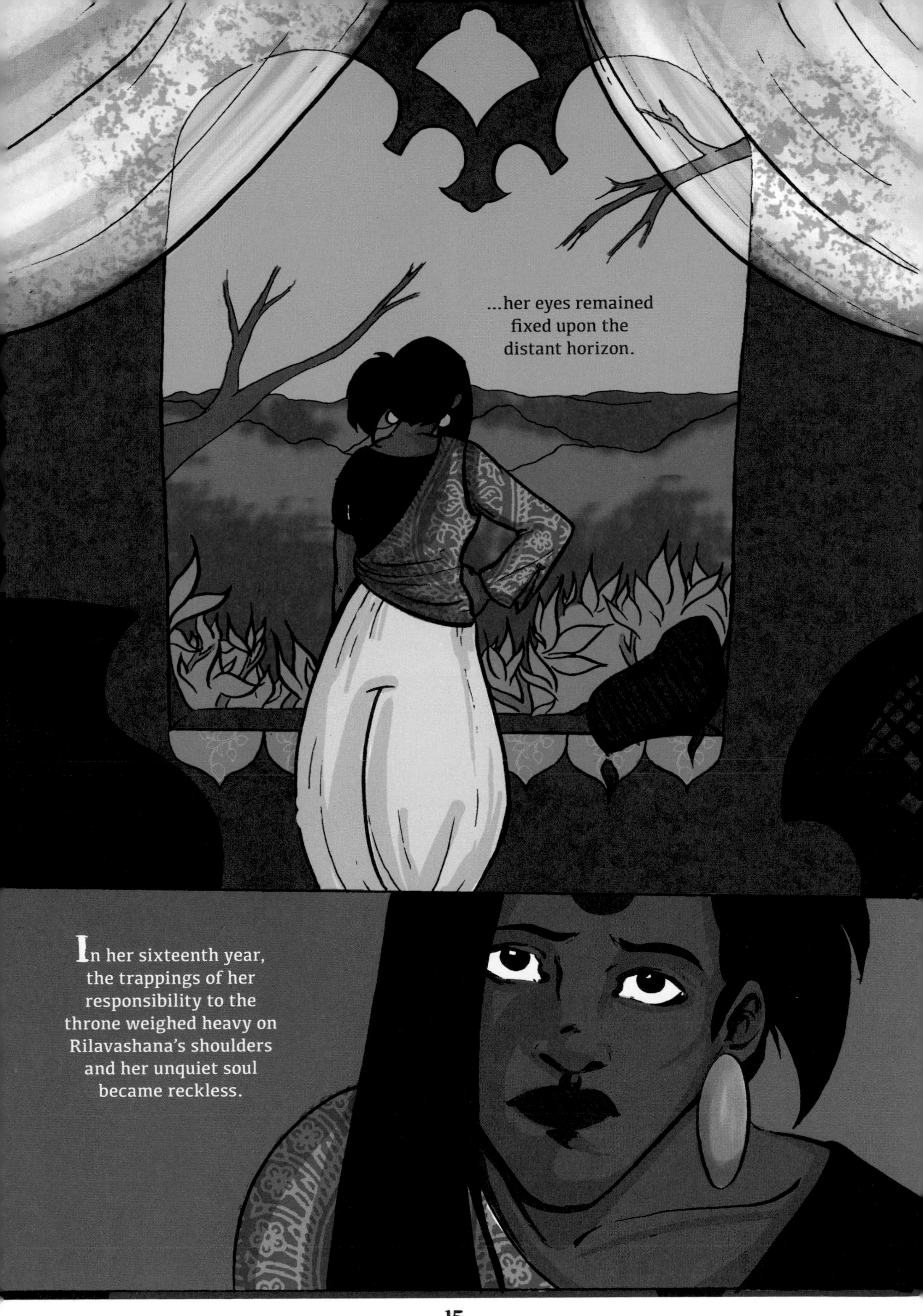
...her eyes remained fixed upon the distant horizon.
In her sixteenth year, the trappings of her responsibility to the throne weighed heavy on Rilavashana's shoulders and her unquiet soul became reckless.

She hunted the wildest of game with her brother Satanii from sunup to sundown, when she returned home bloodied.

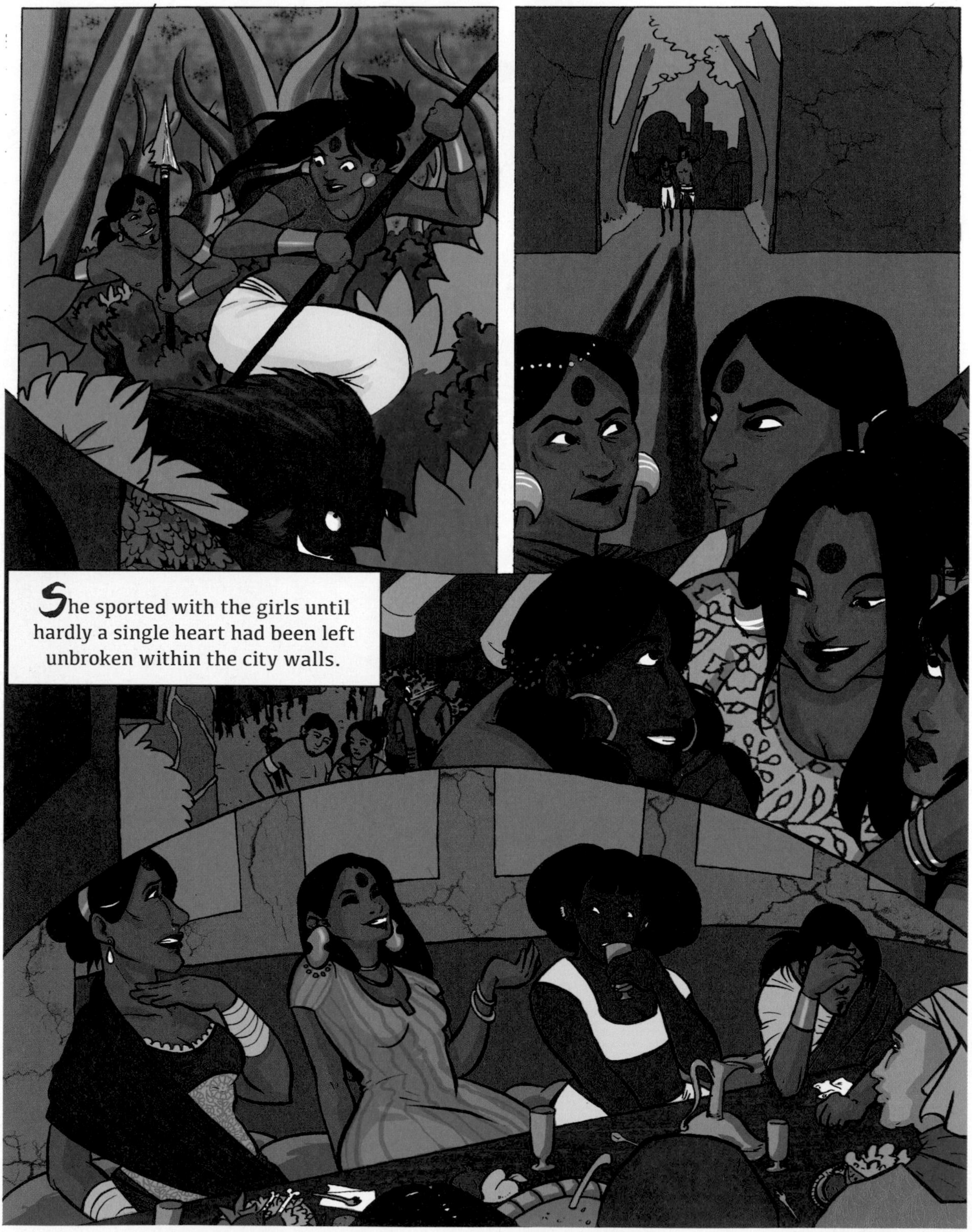
She sported with the girls until hardly a single heart had been left unbroken within the city walls.

She sipped wine with visiting dignitaries and made their wives blush with ribald tales most unbecoming from the lips of a young princess.

To her father and mother this behavior became most unbearable.

Her father called her before him.

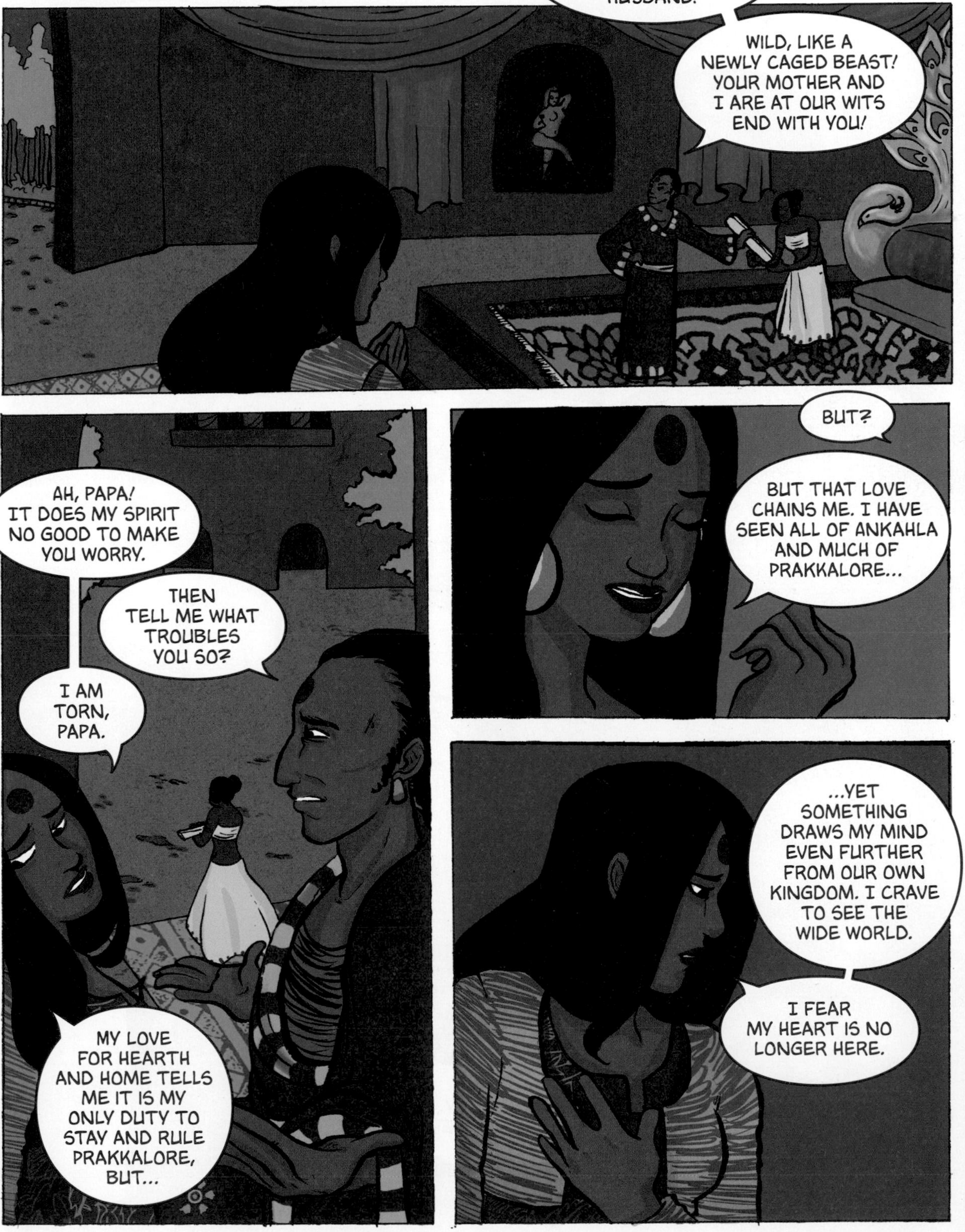

WHAT VEXES YOU SO, MY LITTLE JEWEL? YOU ARE SPITEFUL LIKE A WIFE WITH AN UNFAITHFUL HUSBAND!
WILD, LIKE A NEWLY CAGED BEAST! YOUR MOTHER AND I ARE AT OUR WITS END WITH YOU!
AH, PAPA! IT DOES MY SPIRIT NO GOOD TO MAKE YOU WORRY.
THEN TELL ME WHAT TROUBLES YOU SO?
I AM TORN, PAPA.
MY LOVE FOR HEARTH AND HOME TELLS ME IT IS MY ONLY DUTY TO STAY AND RULE PRAKKALORE, BUT...
BUT?
BUT THAT LOVE CHAINS ME. I HAVE SEEN ALL OF ANKAHLA AND MUCH OF PRAKKALORE...
...YET SOMETHING DRAWS MY MIND EVEN FURTHER FROM OUR OWN KINGDOM. I CRAVE TO SEE THE WIDE WORLD.
I FEAR MY HEART IS NO LONGER HERE.

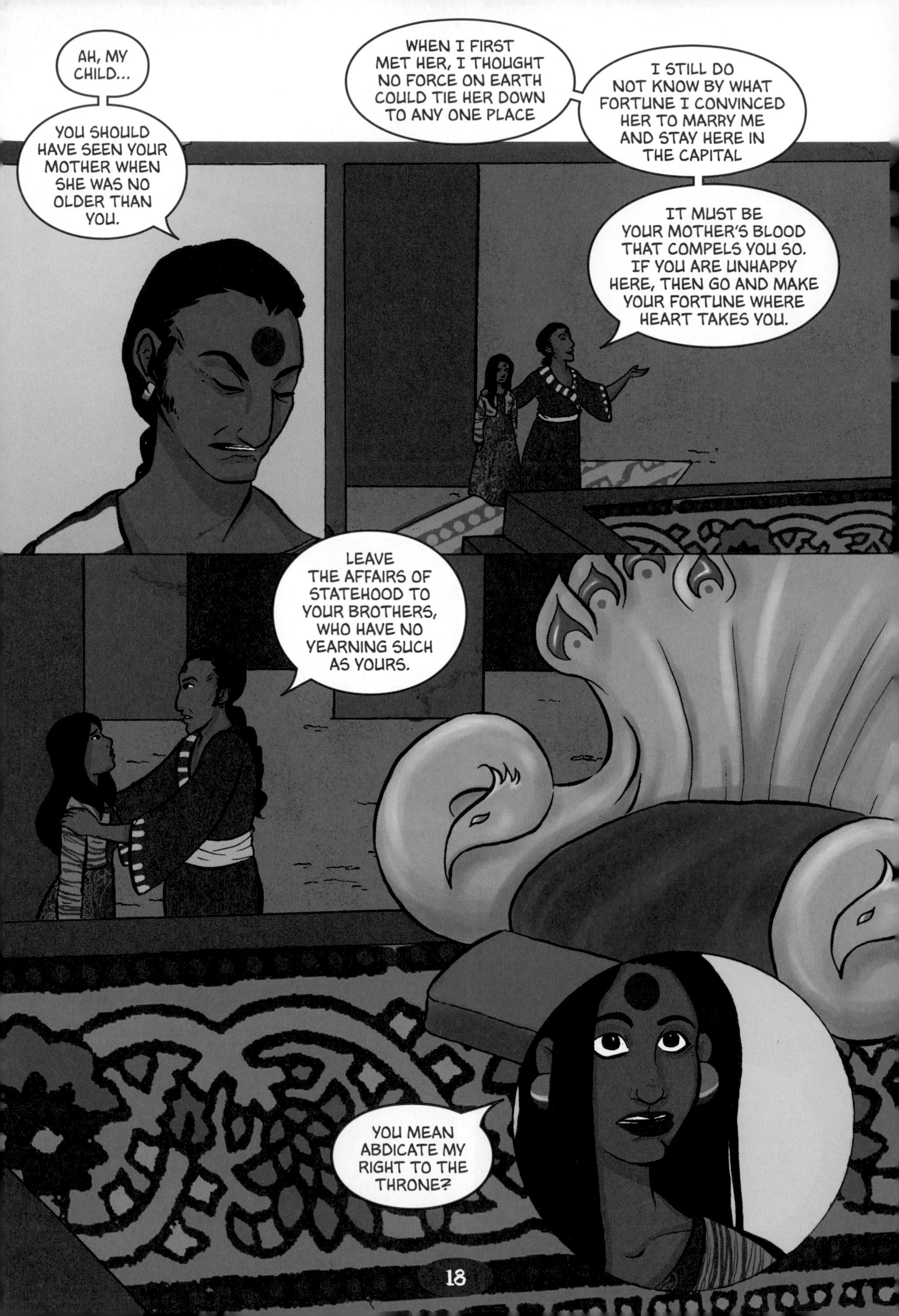
AH, MY CHILD...
YOU SHOULD HAVE SEEN YOUR MOTHER WHEN SHE WAS NO OLDER THAN YOU.
WHEN I FIRST MET HER, I THOUGHT NO FORCE ON EARTH COULD TIE HER DOWN TO ANY ONE PLACE
I STILL DO NOT KNOW BY WHAT FORTUNE I CONVINCED HER TO MARRY ME AND STAY HERE IN THE CAPITAL
IT MUST BE YOUR MOTHER'S BLOOD THAT COMPELS YOU SO. IF YOU ARE UNHAPPY HERE, THEN GO AND MAKE YOUR FORTUNE WHERE HEART TAKES YOU.
LEAVE THE AFFAIRS OF STATEHOOD TO YOUR BROTHERS, WHO HAVE NO YEARNING SUCH AS YOURS.
YOU MEAN ABDICATE MY RIGHT TO THE THRONE?

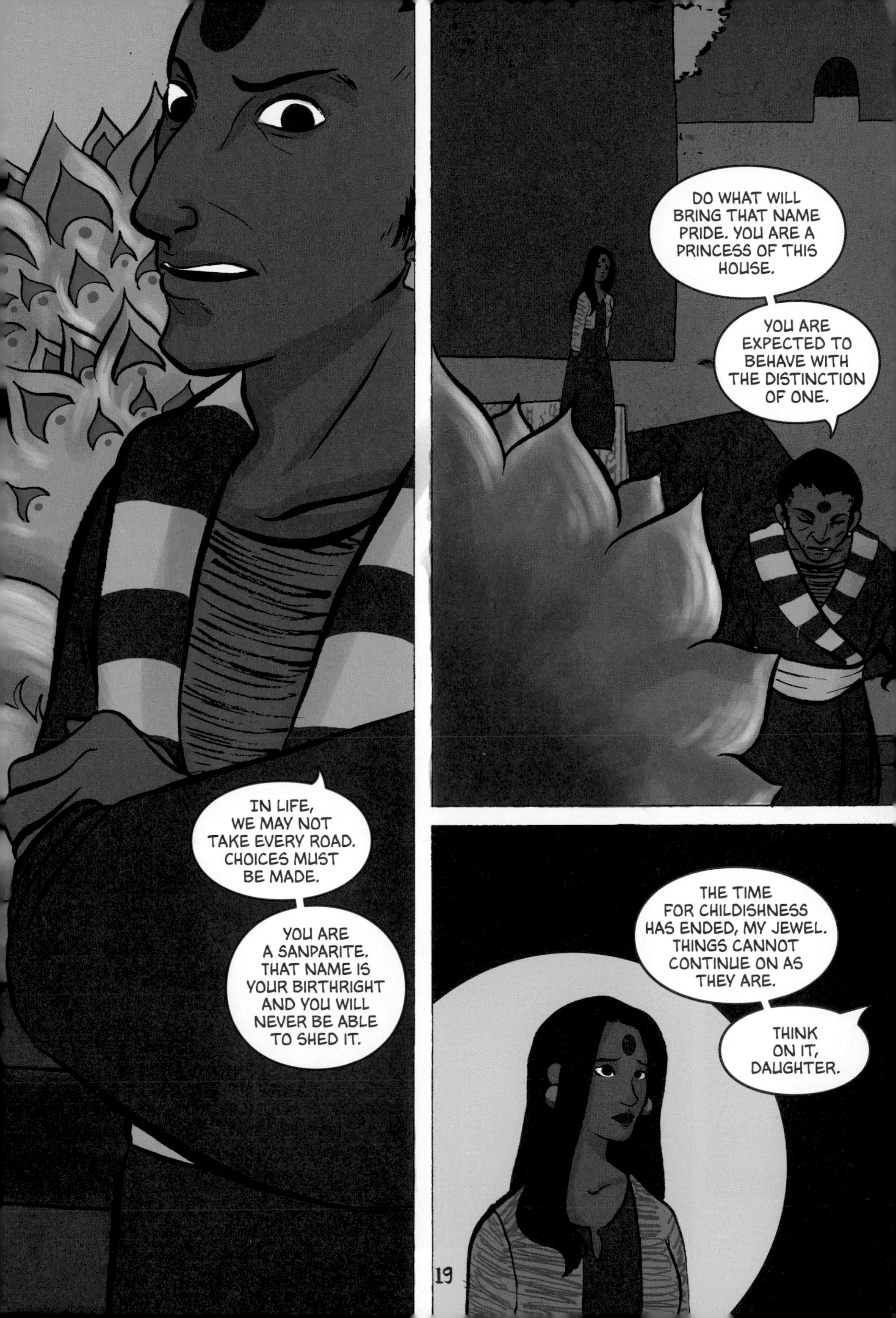
IN LIFE, WE MAY NOT TAKE EVERY ROAD. CHOICES MUST BE MADE.
YOU ARE A SANPARITE. THAT NAME IS YOUR BIRTHRIGHT AND YOU WILL NEVER BE ABLE TO SHED IT.
DO WHAT WILL BRING THAT NAME PRIDE. YOU ARE A PRINCESS OF THIS HOUSE.
YOU ARE EXPECTED TO BEHAVE WITH THE DISTINCTION OF ONE.
THE TIME FOR CHILDISHNESS HAS ENDED, MY JEWEL. THINGS CANNOT CONTINUE ON AS THEY ARE.
THINK ON IT, DAUGHTER.

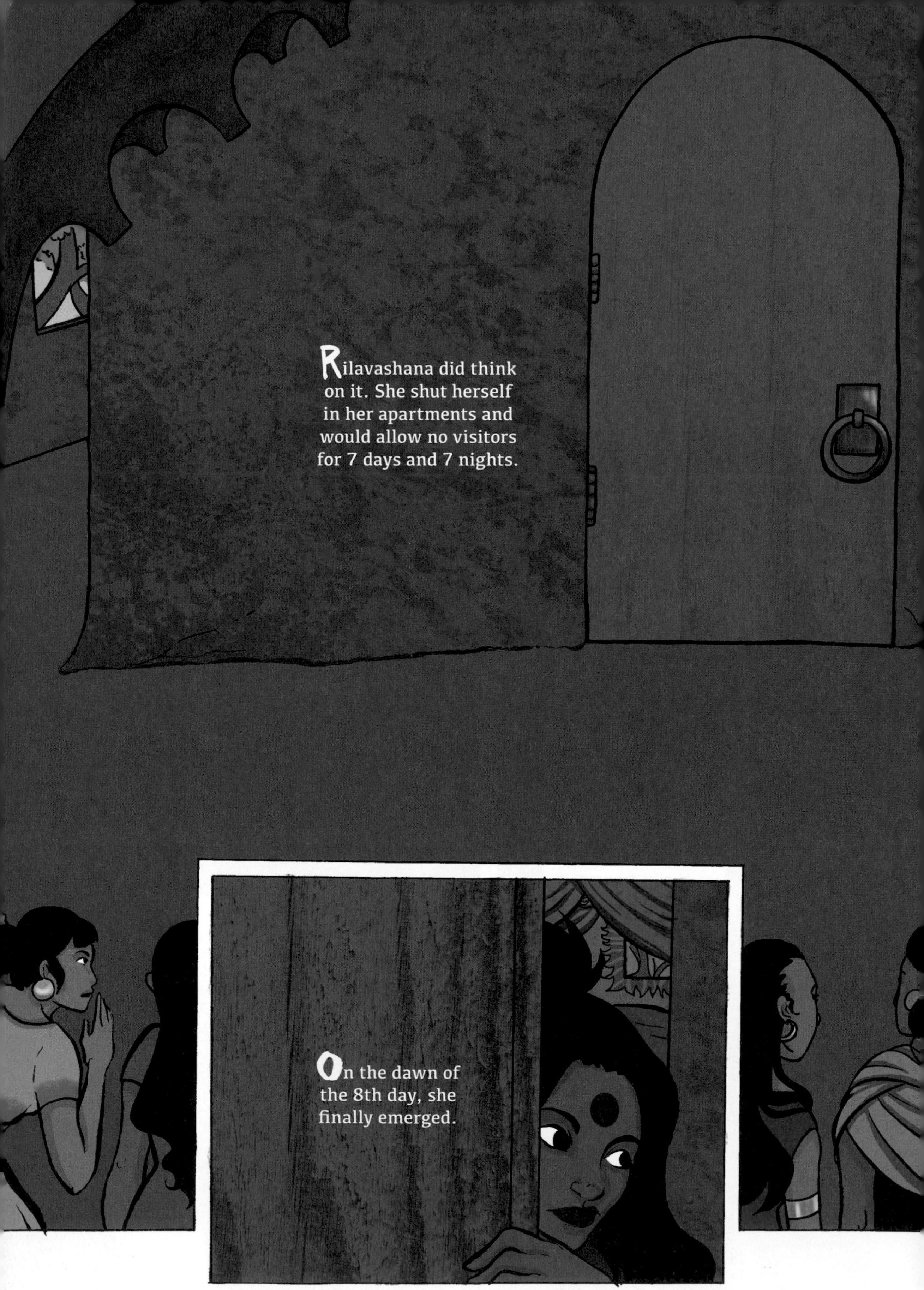
Rilavashana did think on it. She shut herself in her apartments and would allow no visitors for 7 days and 7 nights.
On the dawn of the 8th day, she finally emerged.

The fingers of dawn had only just begun to pry at the dark dome of the sky and a new sword hung heavy at Rilavashana's side, a great bay mare snorting at her back.

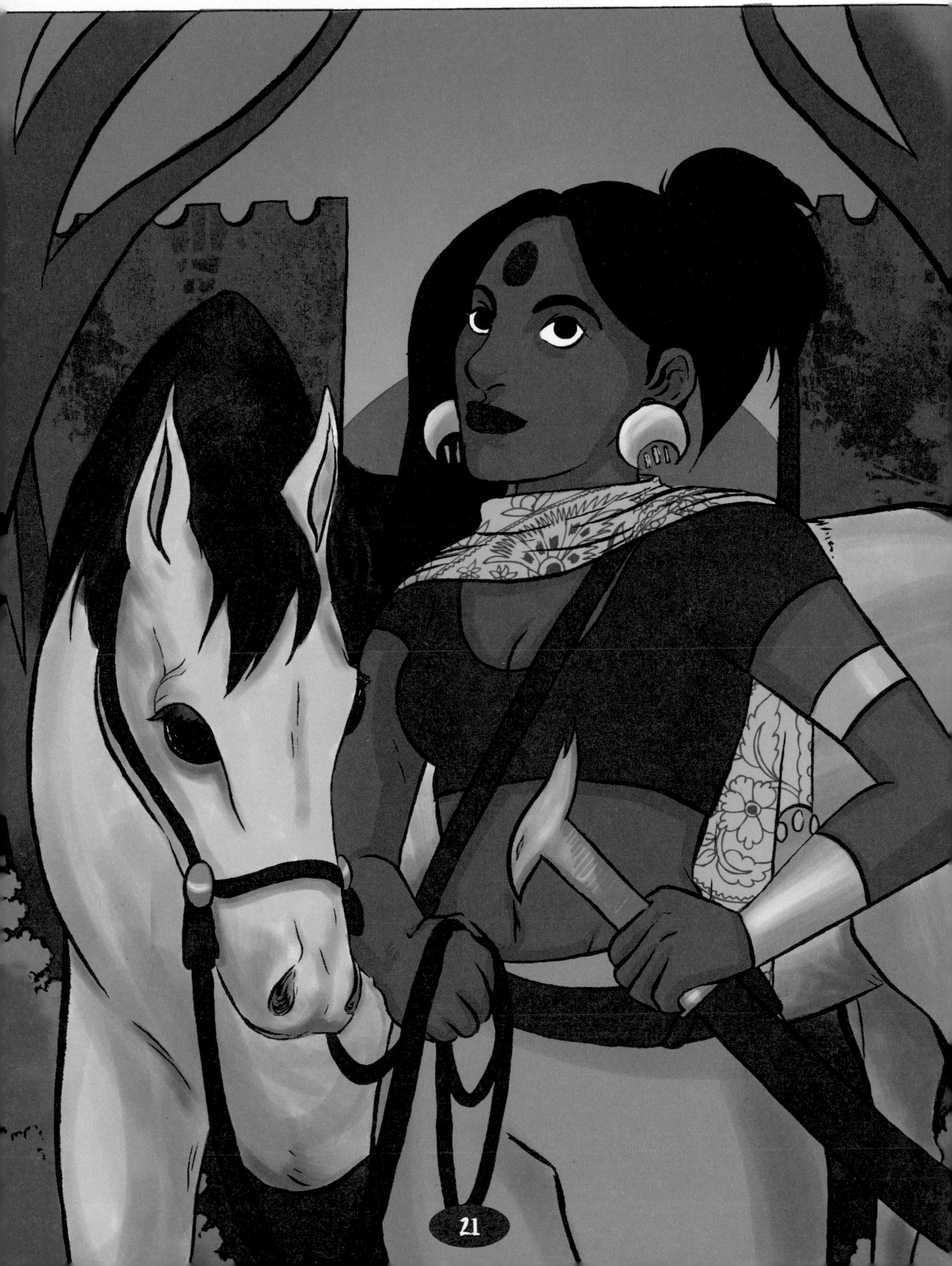

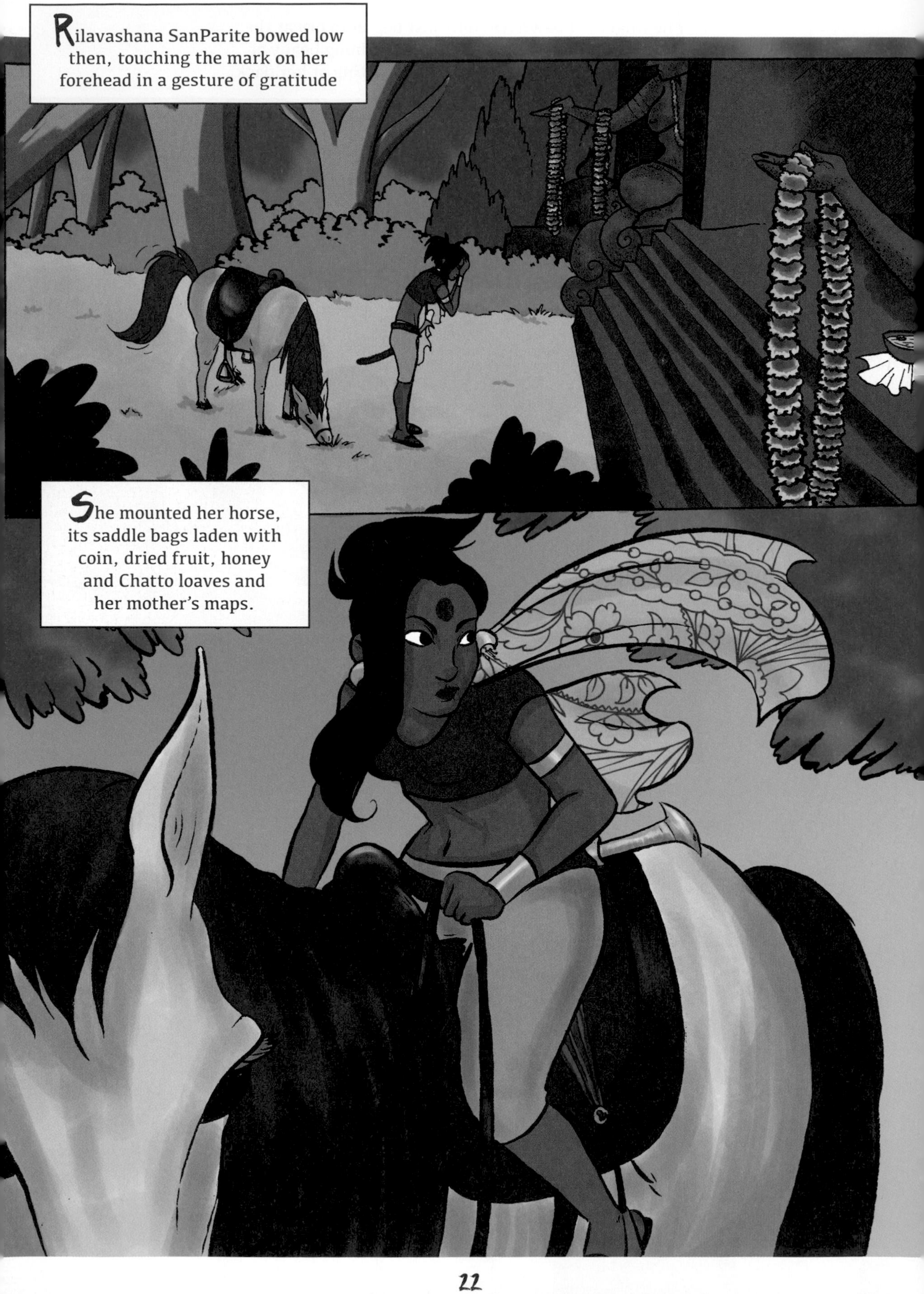
Rilavashana SanParite bowed low then, touching the mark on her forehead in a gesture of gratitude
She mounted her horse, its saddle bags laden with coin, dried fruit, honey and Chatto loaves and her mother's maps.

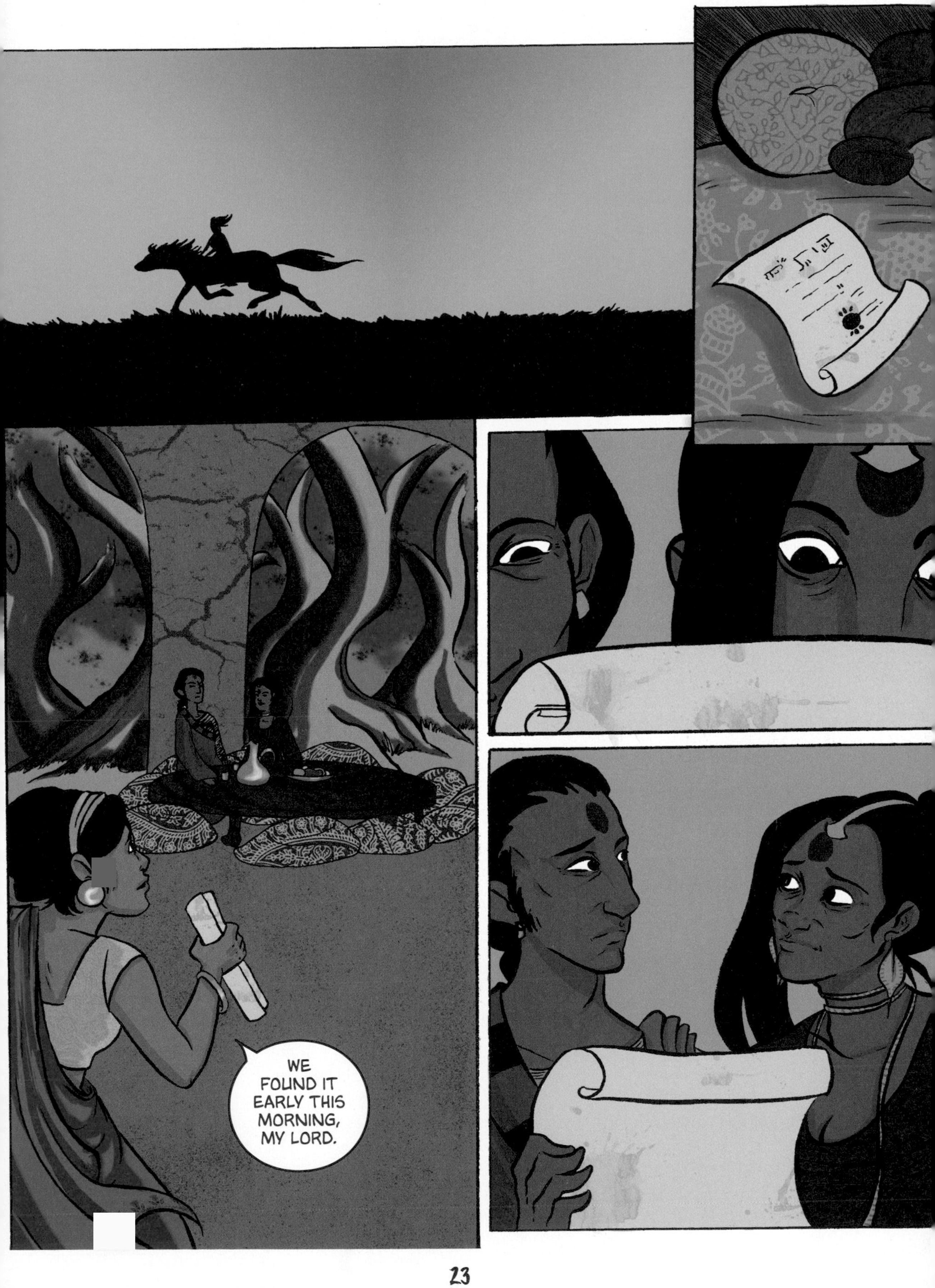
WE FOUND IT EARLY THIS MORNING, MY LORD.

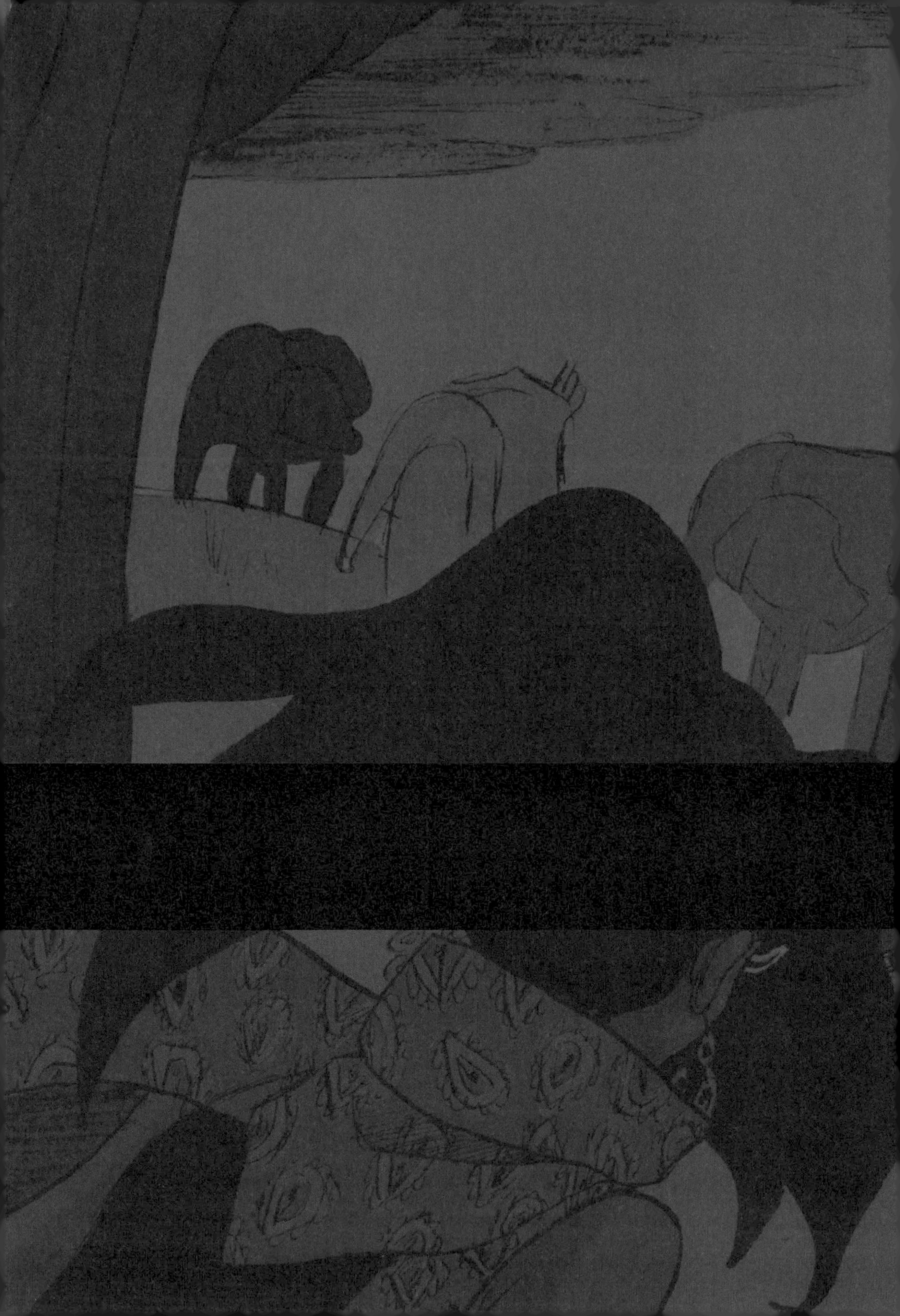

[redacted]

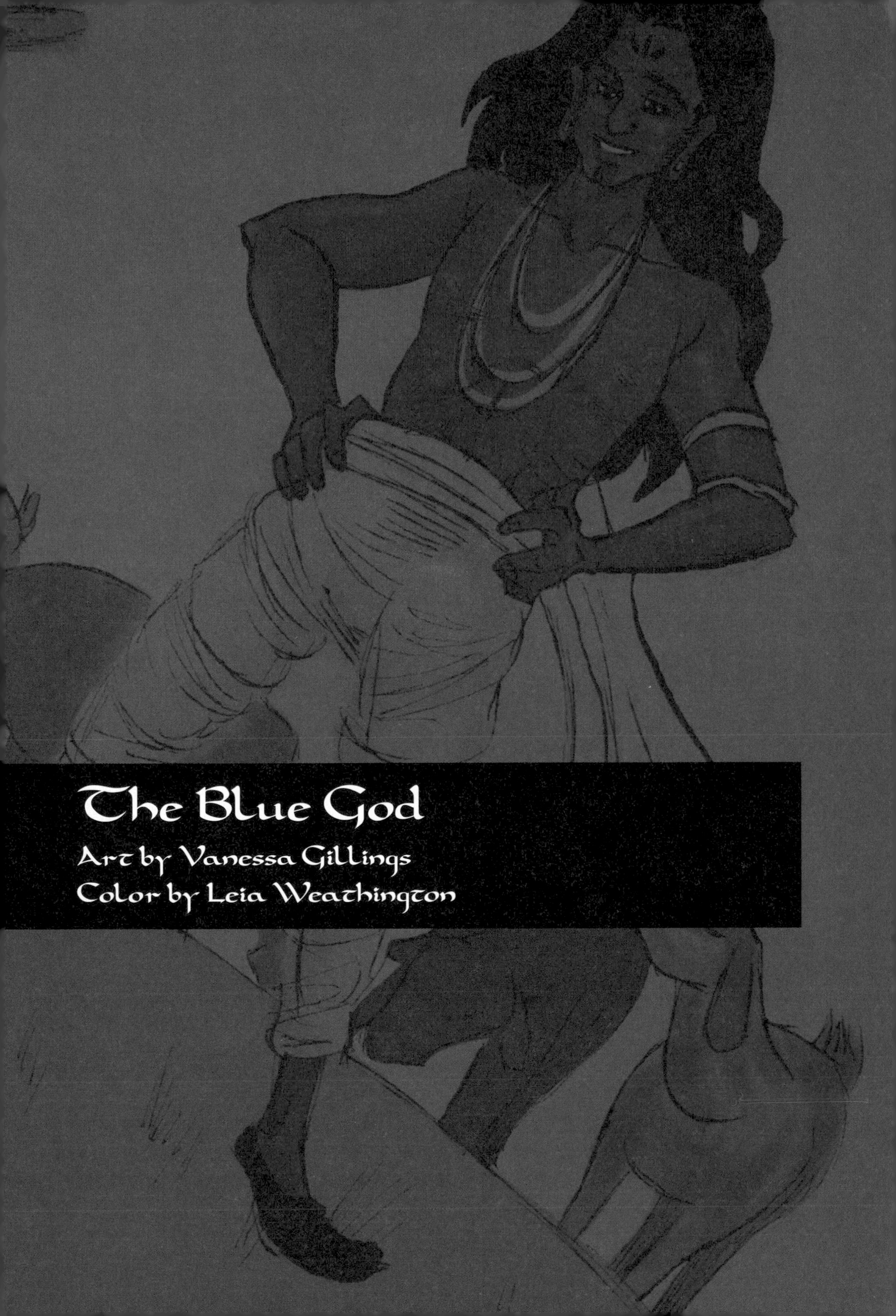

The Blue God

Art by Vanessa Gillings
Color by Leia Weathington

Princess Rilavashana SanParite, called **Bold Riley**, rode to the borders of her lands, finally in peace.

Word of her departure from the capital city of Ankahla had spread quickly through Prakkalore.

At her coming, the streets had filled with well-wishers draping her neck with flowers...

...waving children and joyous calls.

Grateful though she was for their kind words of good luck...

...Riley now welcomed being left alone with her thoughts.

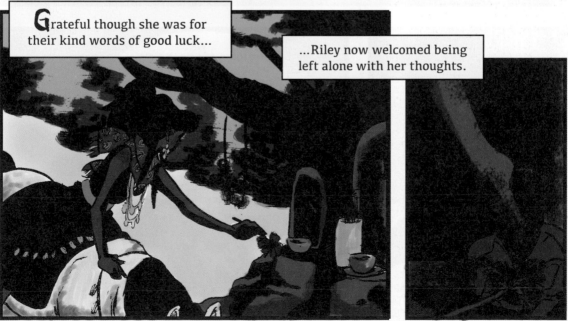

27

But soon, her solitude was broken by the sound of goat bells and shuffling feet.

HIGHNESS! HIGHNESS! OH PLEASE, A MOMENT, I BEG YOU!

OF COURSE, GOOD UNCLE. WHAT IS THE TROUBLE?

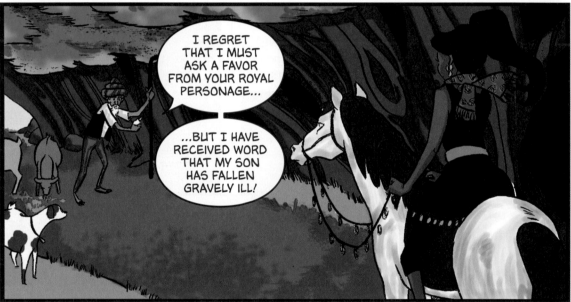

I REGRET THAT I MUST ASK A FAVOR FROM YOUR ROYAL PERSONAGE...

...BUT I HAVE RECEIVED WORD THAT MY SON HAS FALLEN GRAVELY ILL!

I MUST RETURN HOME WITH ALL HASTE!

I WAS TAKING MY GOATS TO PASTURE BUT THEY ARE CLUMSY CREATURES AND SLOW MY RETURN GREATLY.

WILL YOU PLEASE WATCH THEM FOR ME UNTIL I AM ABLE TO FETCH THEM BACK?

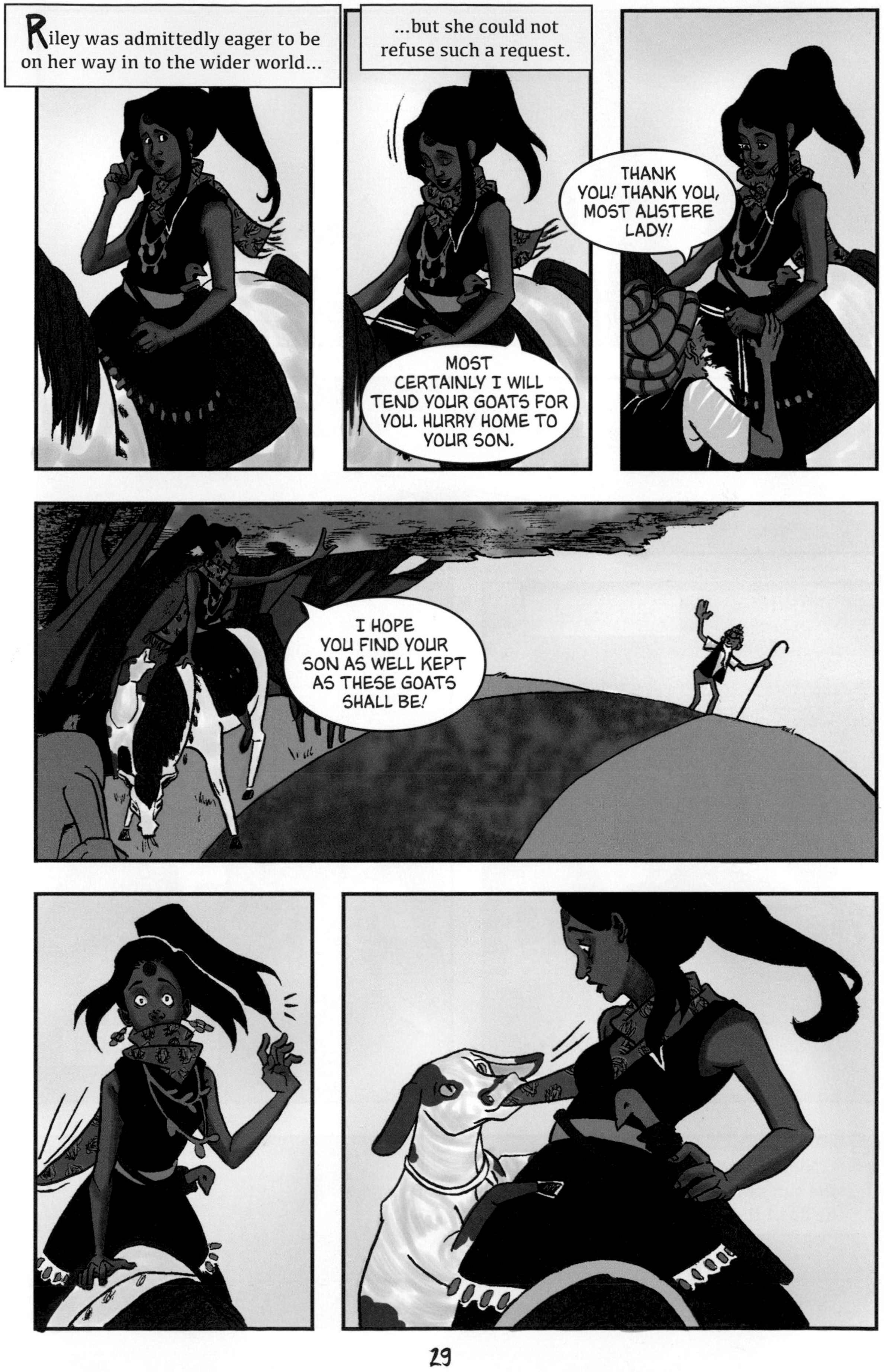
Riley was admittedly eager to be on her way in to the wider world...
...but she could not refuse such a request.
MOST CERTAINLY I WILL TEND YOUR GOATS FOR YOU. HURRY HOME TO YOUR SON.
THANK YOU! THANK YOU, MOST AUSTERE LADY!
I HOPE YOU FIND YOUR SON AS WELL KEPT AS THESE GOATS SHALL BE!

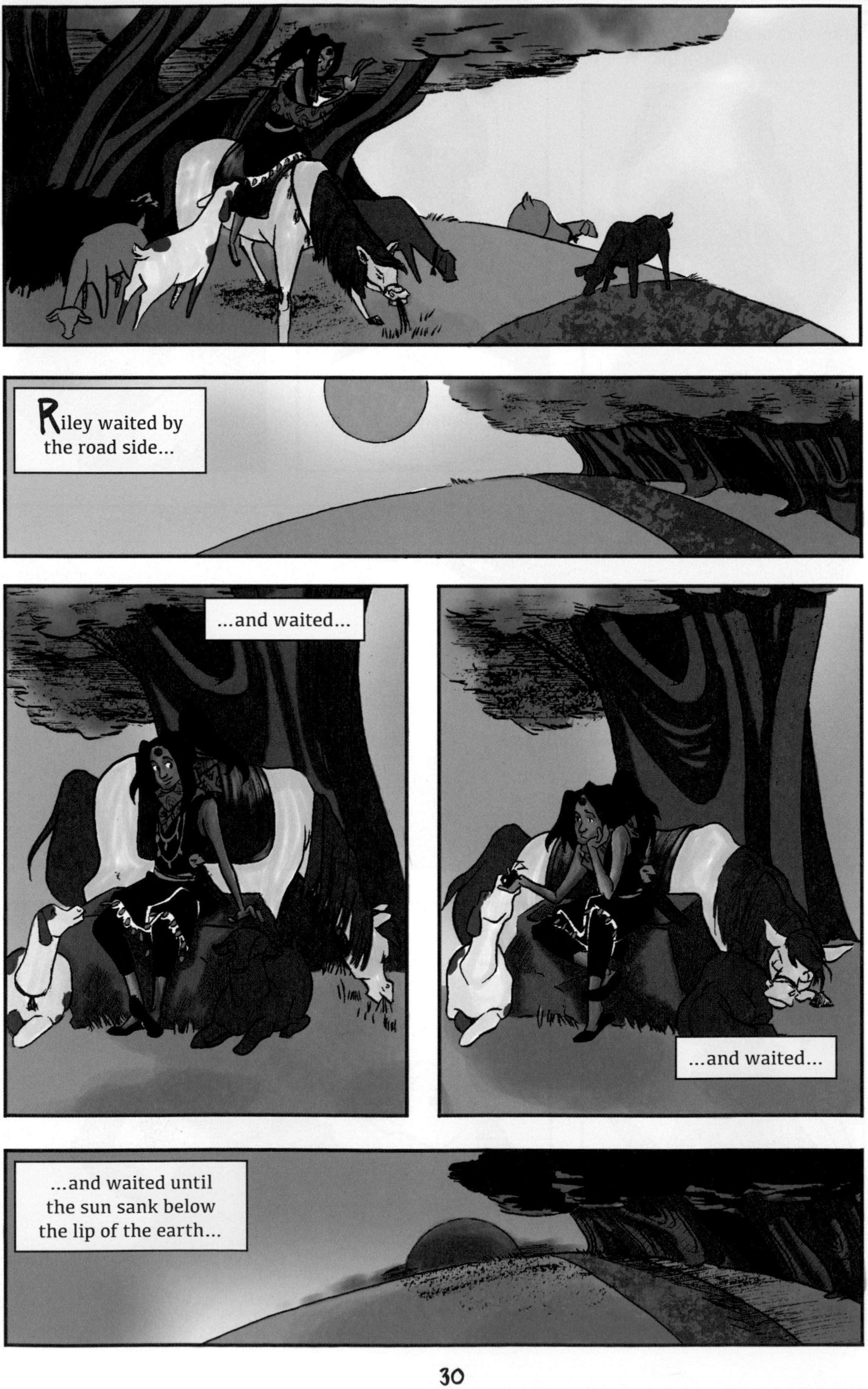
Riley waited by the road side...
...and waited...
...and waited...
...and waited until the sun sank below the lip of the earth...

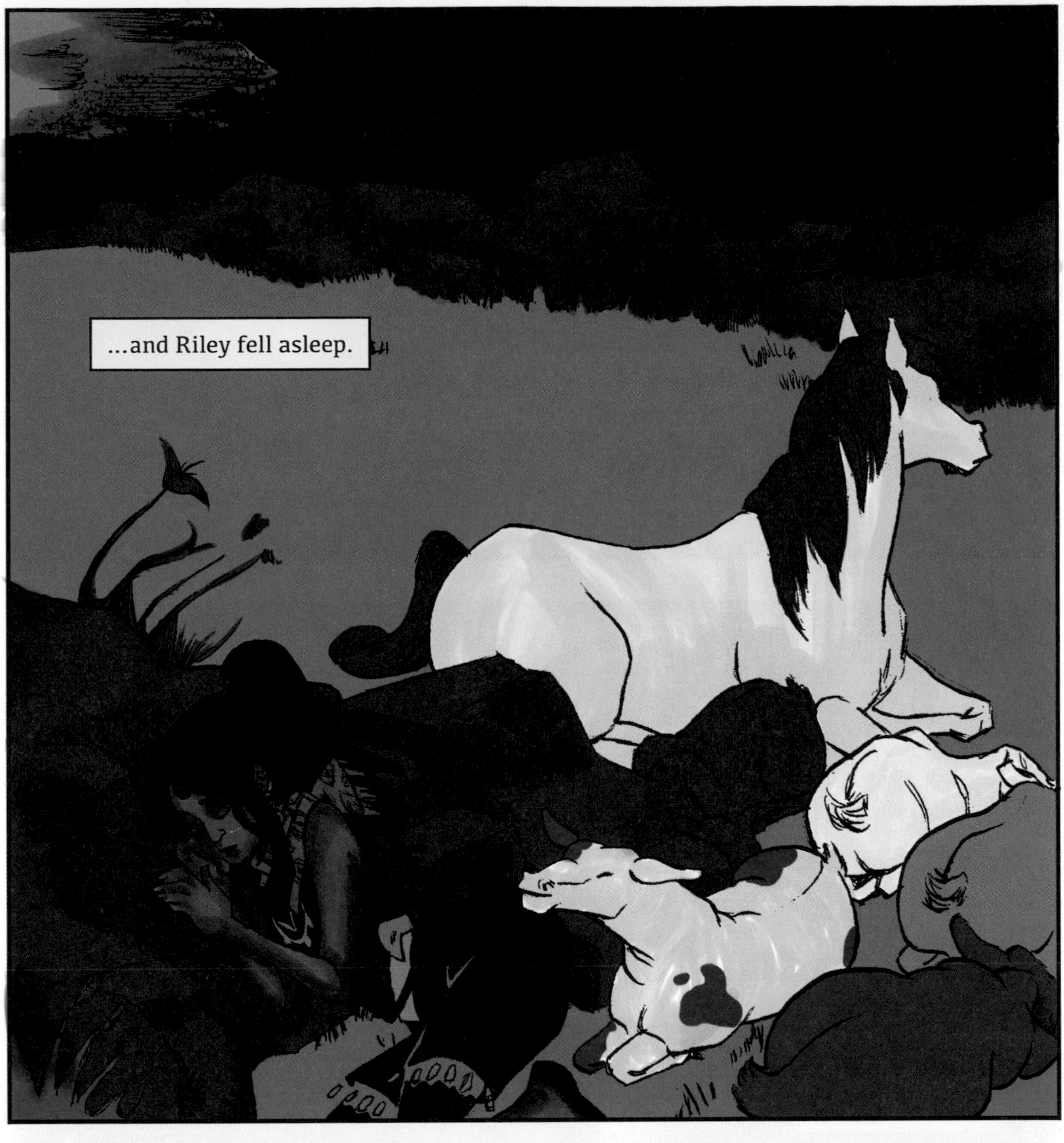
...and Riley fell asleep.

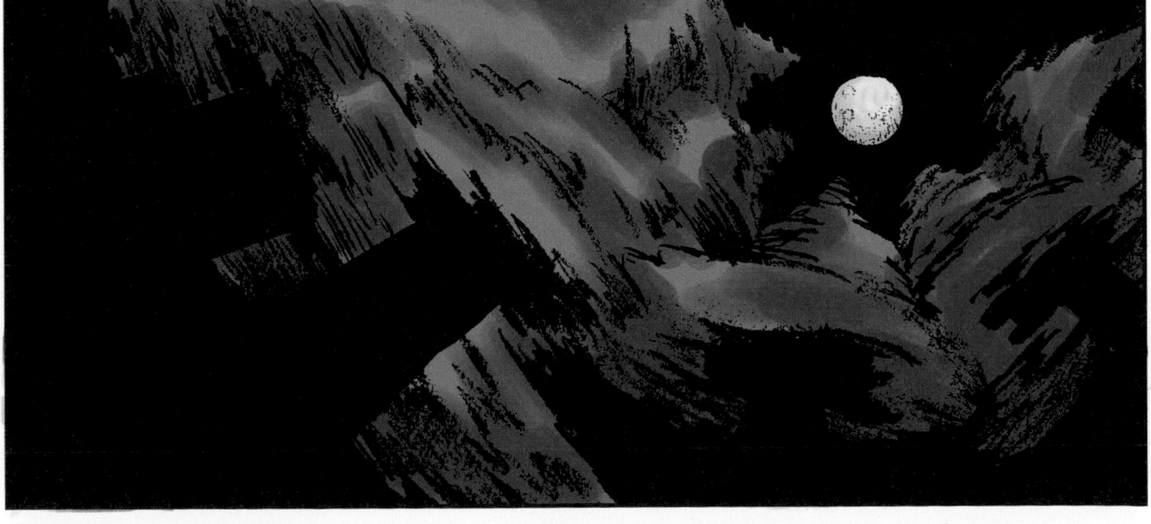

Deep in the night, when the moon's face peers down from its apogee...

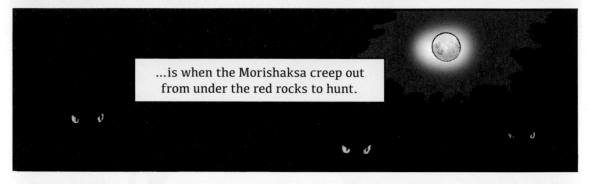

...is when the Morishaksa creep out from under the red rocks to hunt.

And they have spied their prey...

Six fat goats...

...and a little girl.

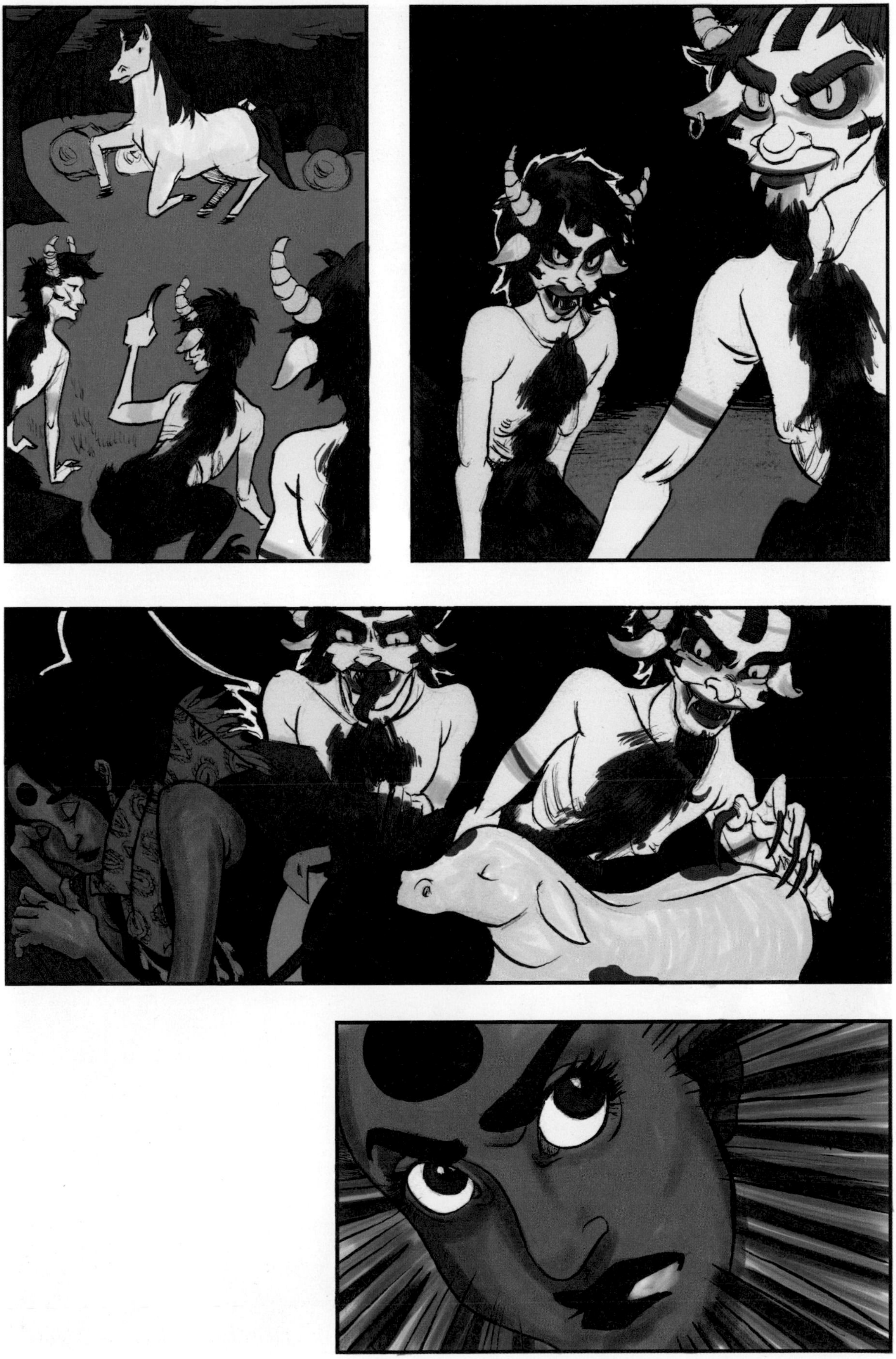

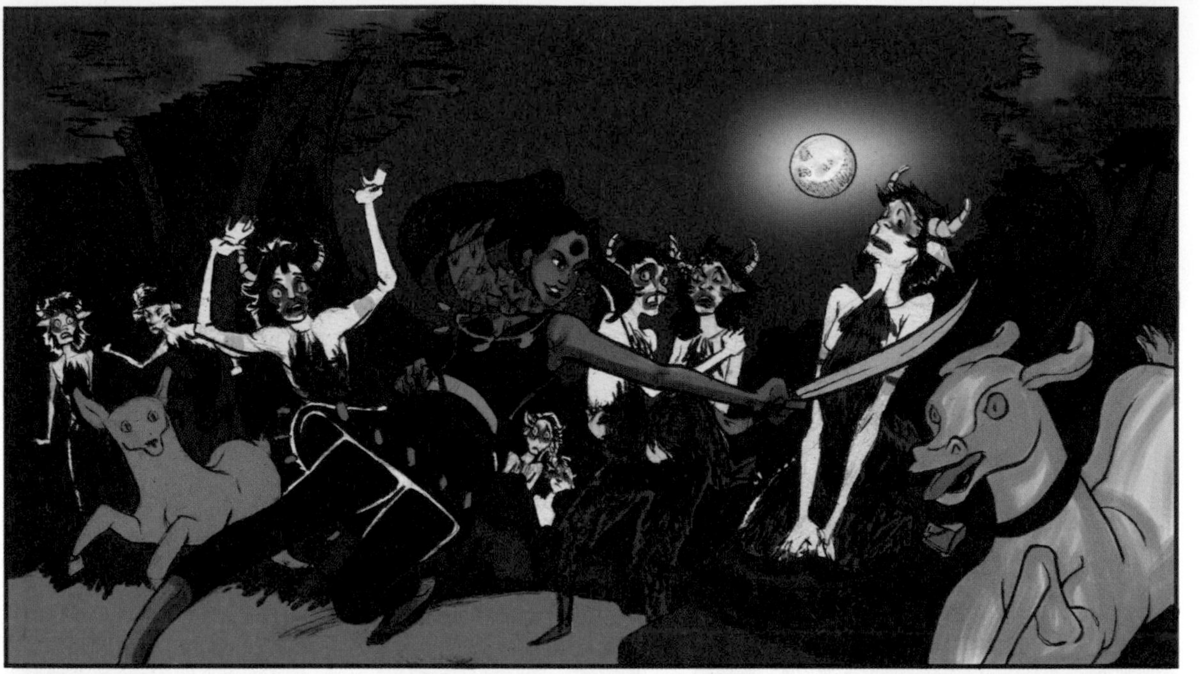

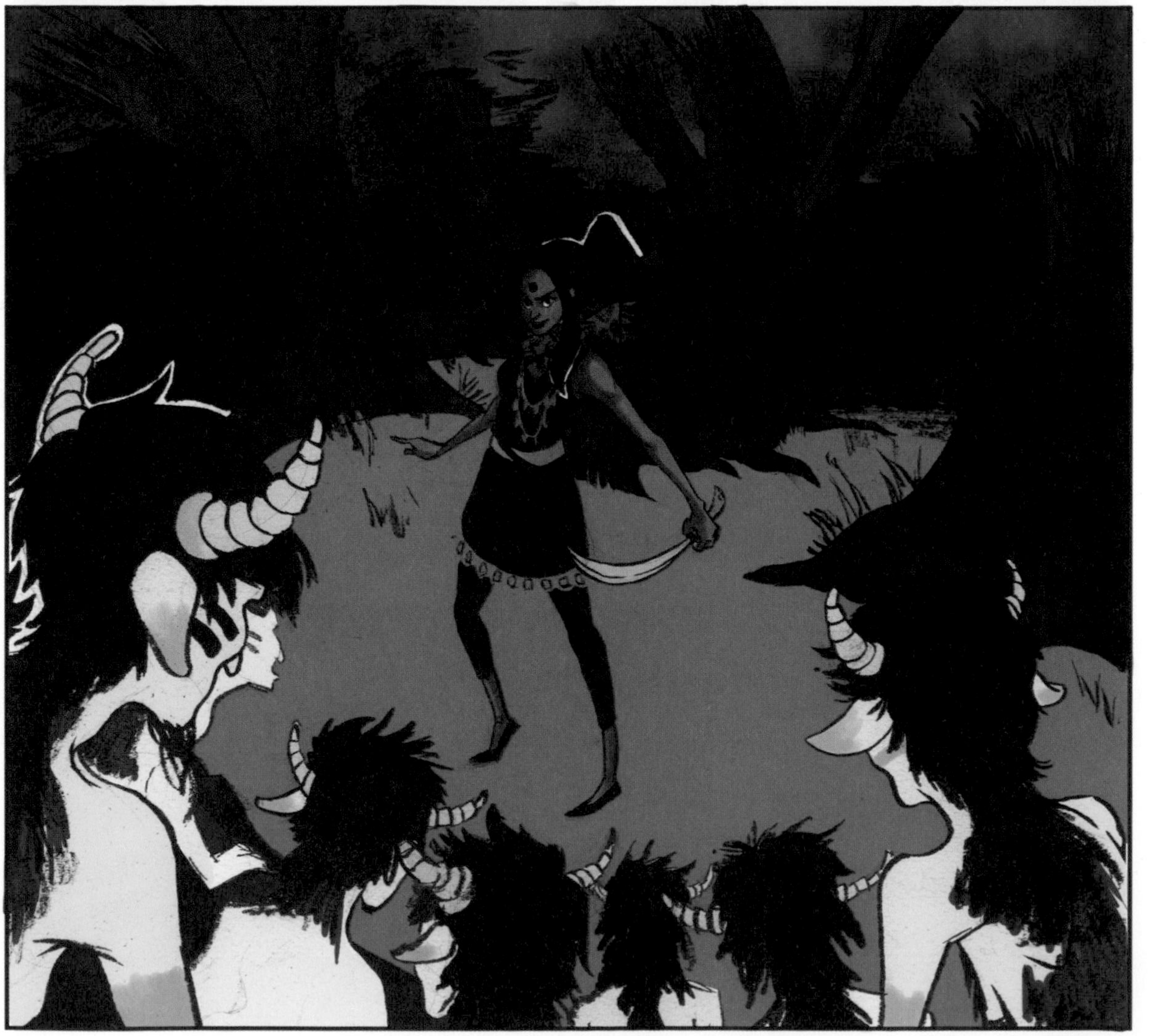

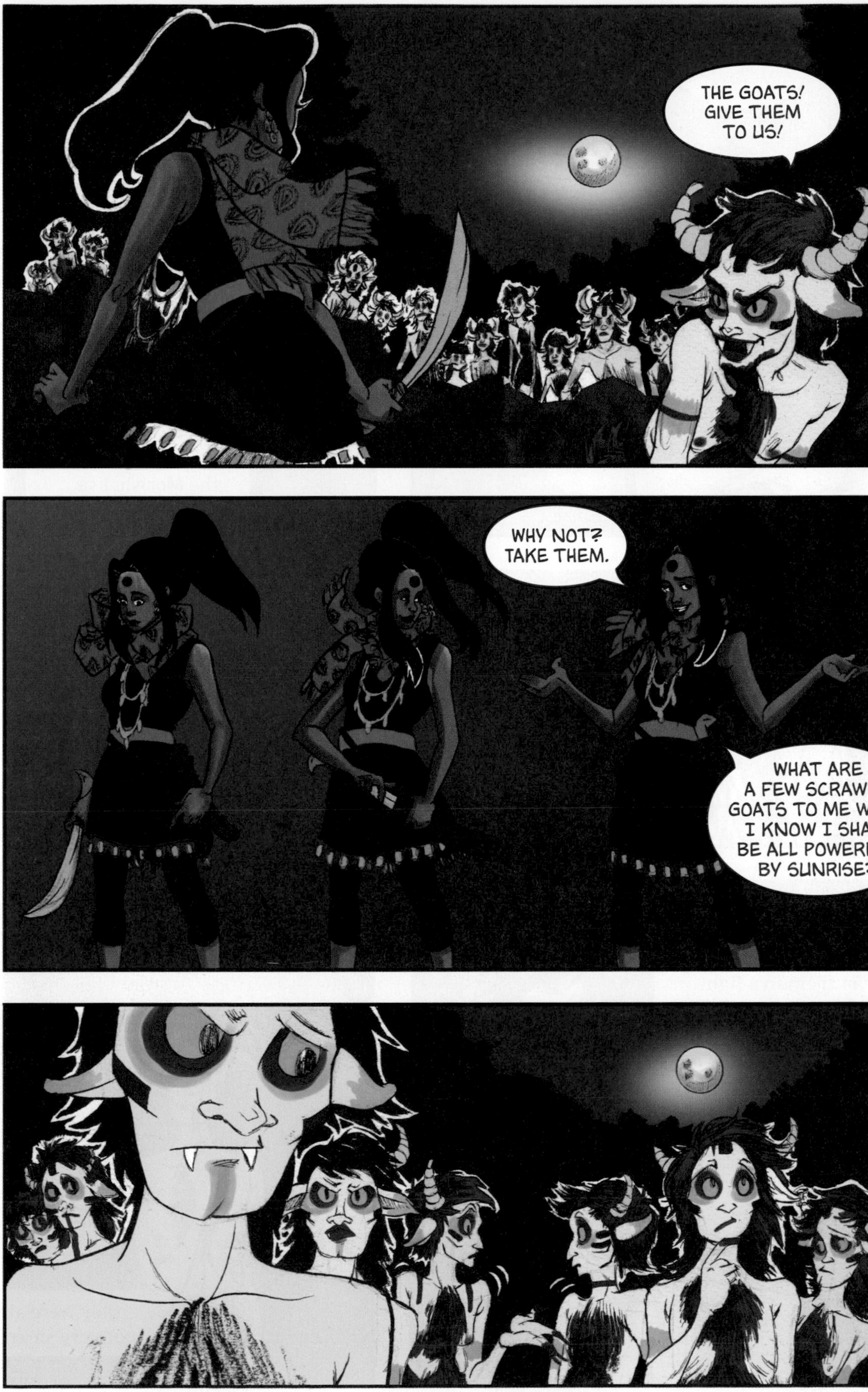
THE GOATS! GIVE THEM TO US!
WHY NOT? TAKE THEM.
WHAT ARE A FEW SCRAWNY GOATS TO ME WHEN I KNOW I SHALL BE ALL POWERFUL BY SUNRISE?

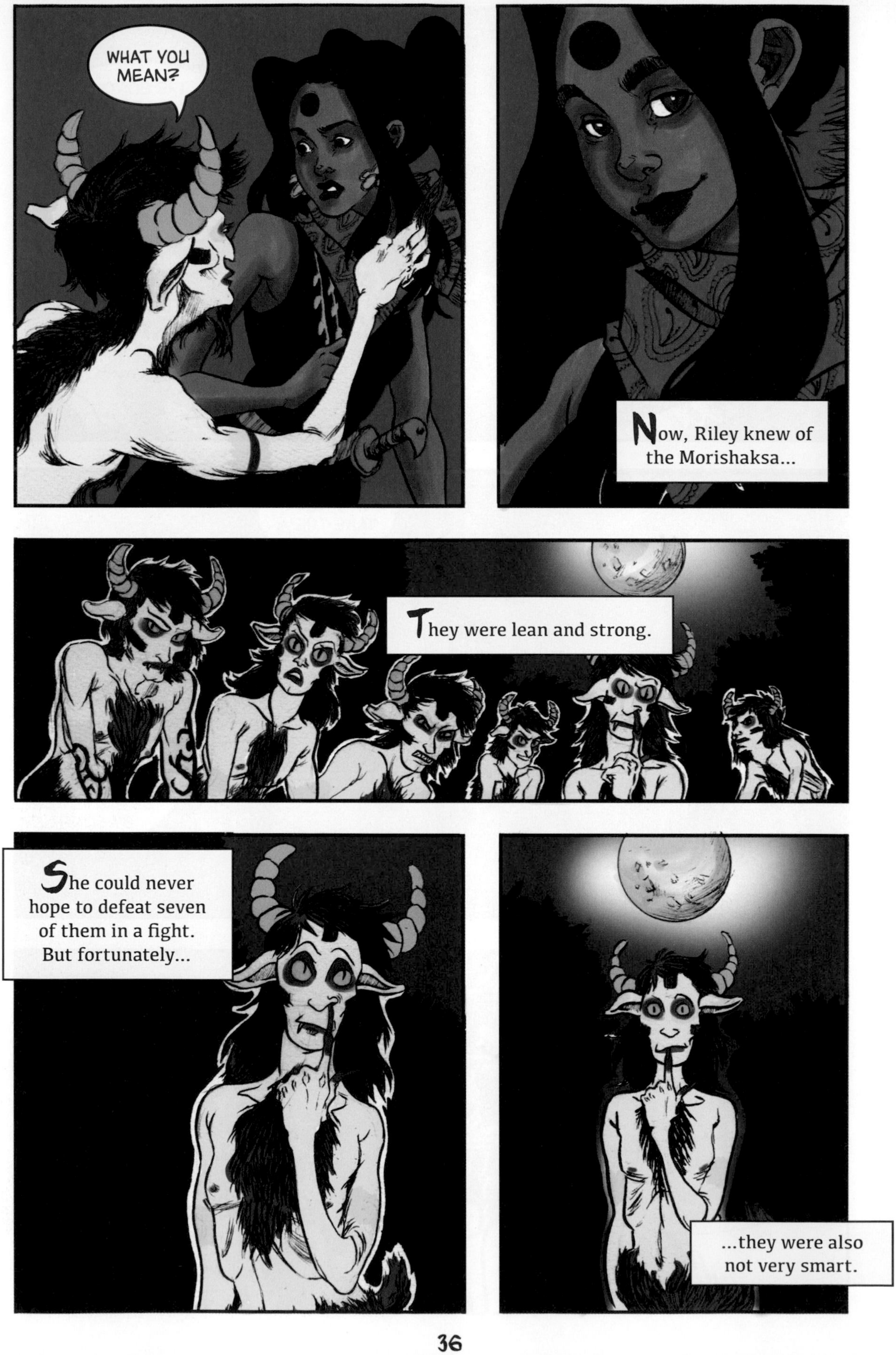

WHAT YOU MEAN?
Now, Riley knew of the Morishaksa...
They were lean and strong.
She could never hope to defeat seven of them in a fight. But fortunately...
...they were also not very smart.

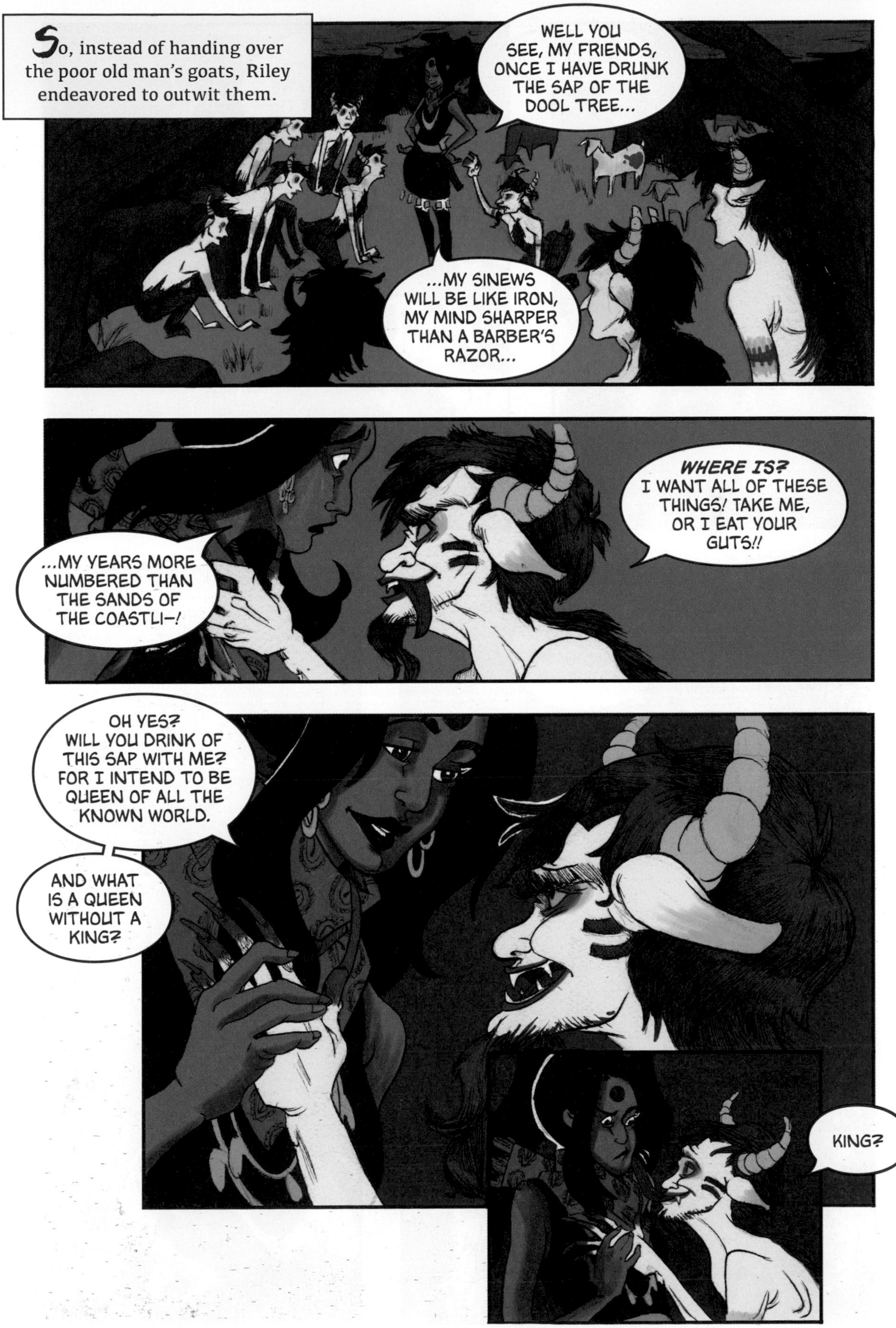
So, instead of handing over the poor old man's goats, Riley endeavored to outwit them.
WELL YOU SEE, MY FRIENDS, ONCE I HAVE DRUNK THE SAP OF THE DOOL TREE...
...MY SINEWS WILL BE LIKE IRON, MY MIND SHARPER THAN A BARBER'S RAZOR...
...MY YEARS MORE NUMBERED THAN THE SANDS OF THE COASTLI–!
WHERE IS? I WANT ALL OF THESE THINGS! TAKE ME, OR I EAT YOUR GUTS!!
OH YES? WILL YOU DRINK OF THIS SAP WITH ME? FOR I INTEND TO BE QUEEN OF ALL THE KNOWN WORLD.
AND WHAT IS A QUEEN WITHOUT A KING?
KING?

YES. KING.

THE GIRL WILL TAKE US TO THE DOOL TREE! WE WILL REIGN OVER THE LAND AS WELL WE SHOULD!

COME THEN, MY FRIENDS! MY BROTHERS!

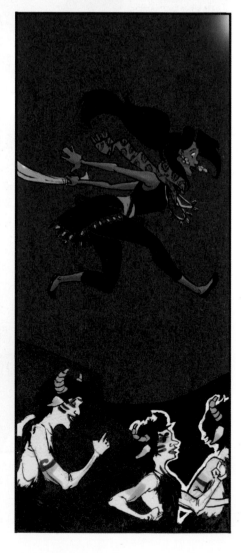

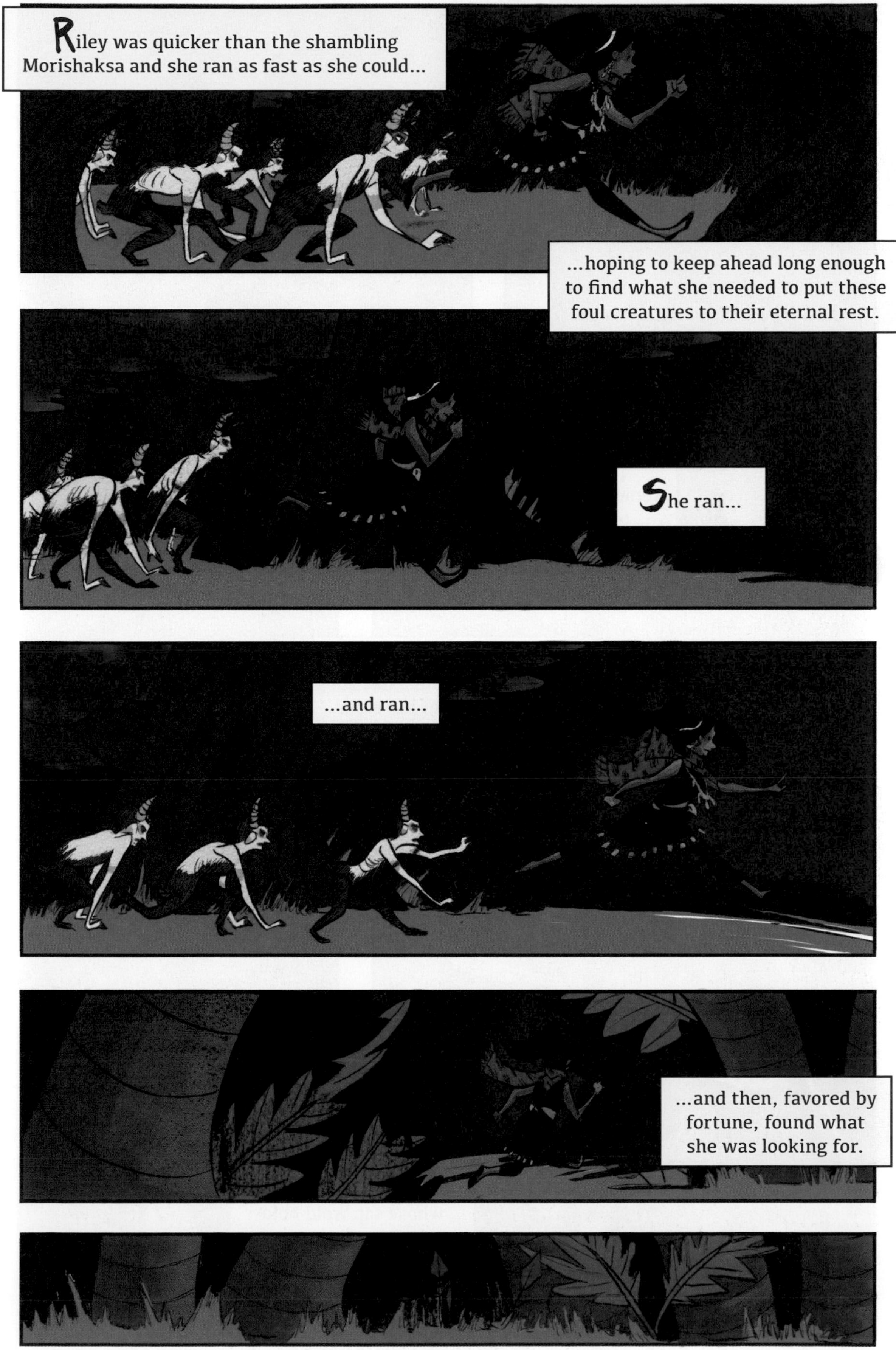
Riley was quicker than the shambling Morishaksa and she ran as fast as she could...
...hoping to keep ahead long enough to find what she needed to put these foul creatures to their eternal rest.
She ran...
...and ran...
...and then, favored by fortune, found what she was looking for.

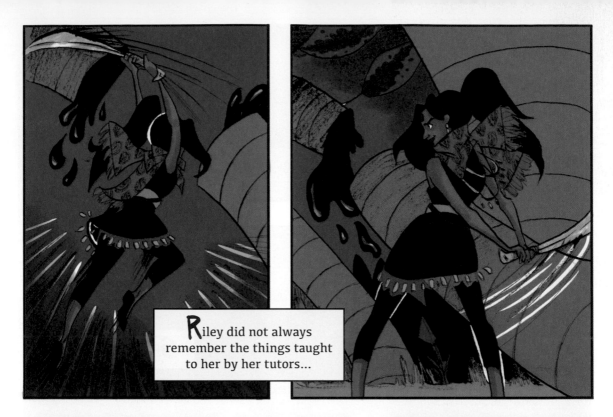

Riley did not always remember the things taught to her by her tutors...

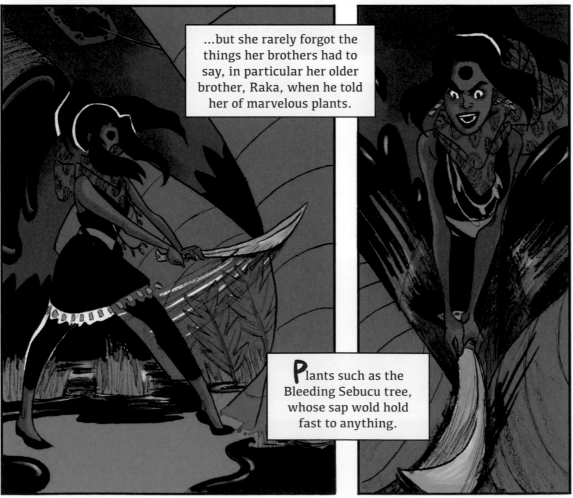

...but she rarely forgot the things her brothers had to say, in particular her older brother, Raka, when he told her of marvelous plants.

Plants such as the Bleeding Sebucu tree, whose sap wold hold fast to anything.

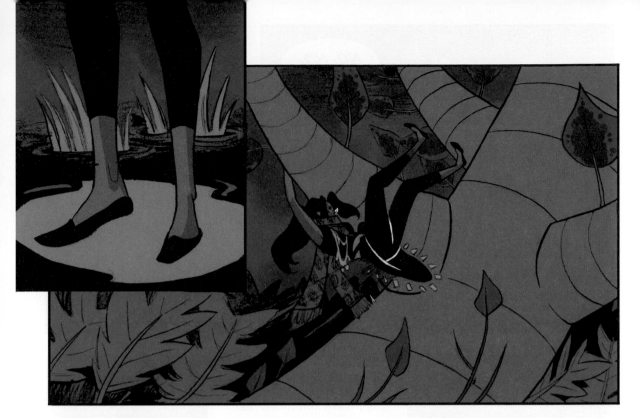

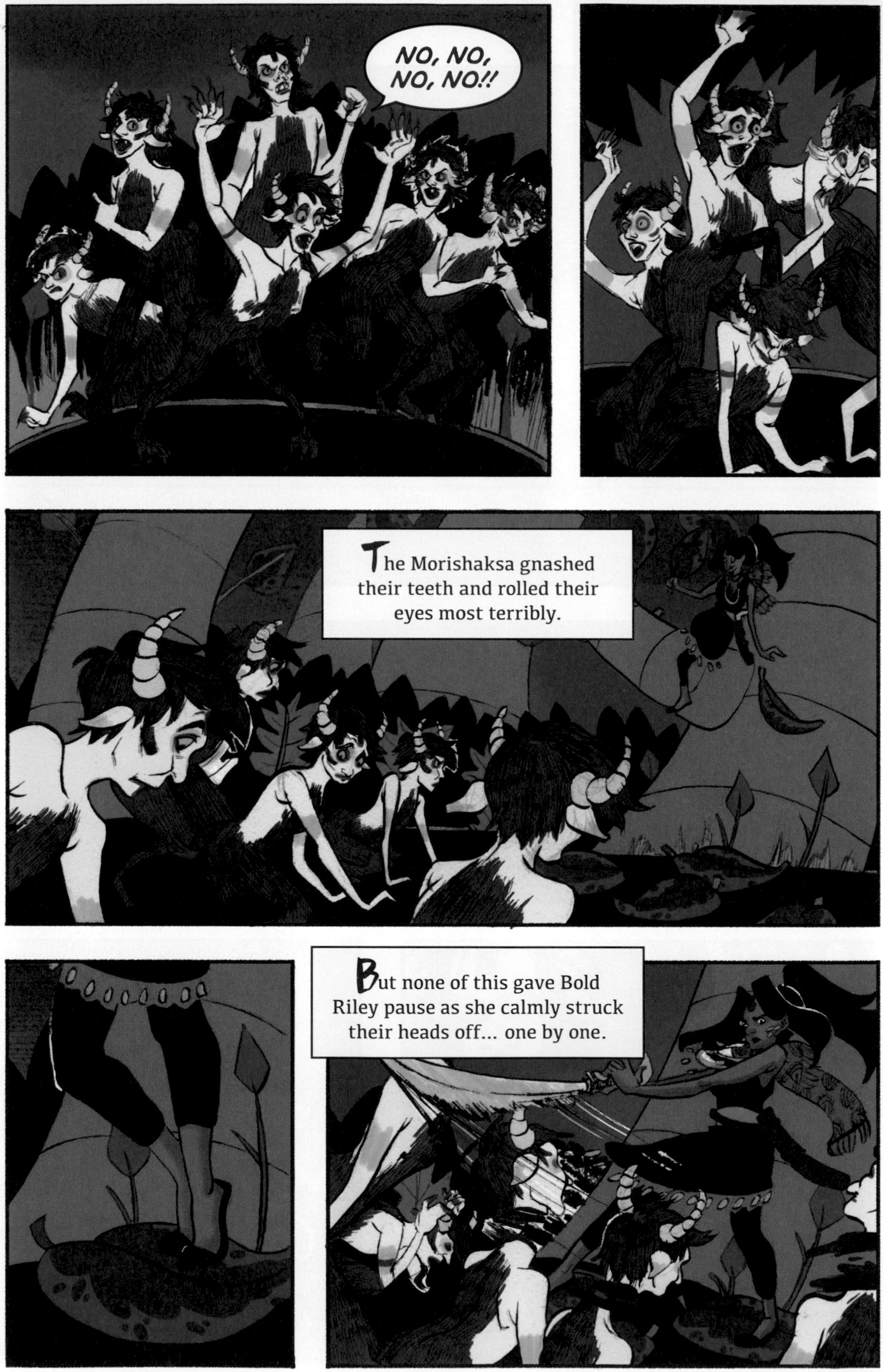
NO, NO, NO, NO!!
The Morishaksa gnashed their teeth and rolled their eyes most terribly.
But none of this gave Bold Riley pause as she calmly struck their heads off... one by one.

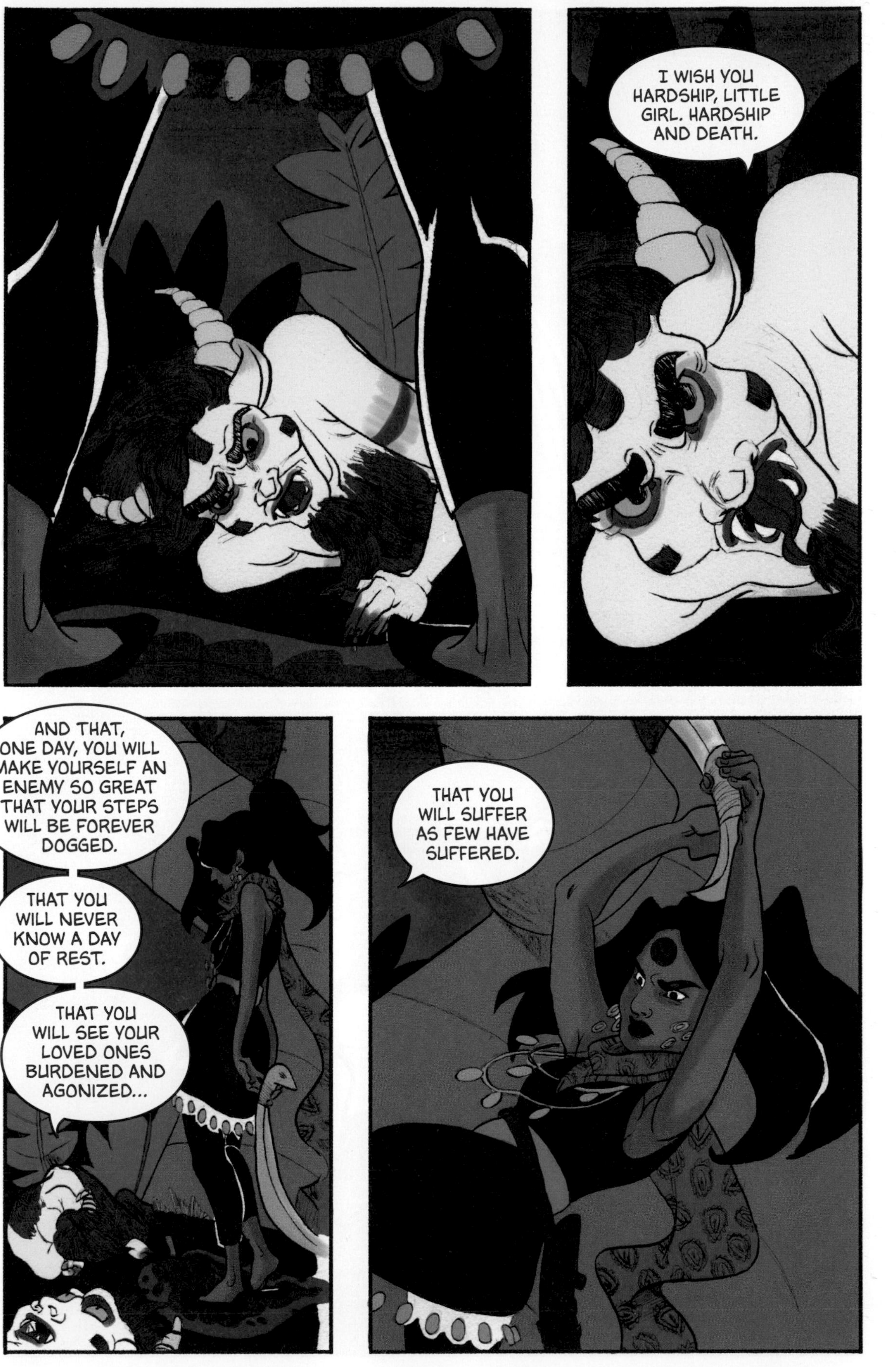
I WISH YOU HARDSHIP, LITTLE GIRL. HARDSHIP AND DEATH.
AND THAT, ONE DAY, YOU WILL MAKE YOURSELF AN ENEMY SO GREAT THAT YOUR STEPS WILL BE FOREVER DOGGED.
THAT YOU WILL NEVER KNOW A DAY OF REST.
THAT YOU WILL SEE YOUR LOVED ONES BURDENED AND AGONIZED...
THAT YOU WILL SUFFER AS FEW HAVE SUFFERED.

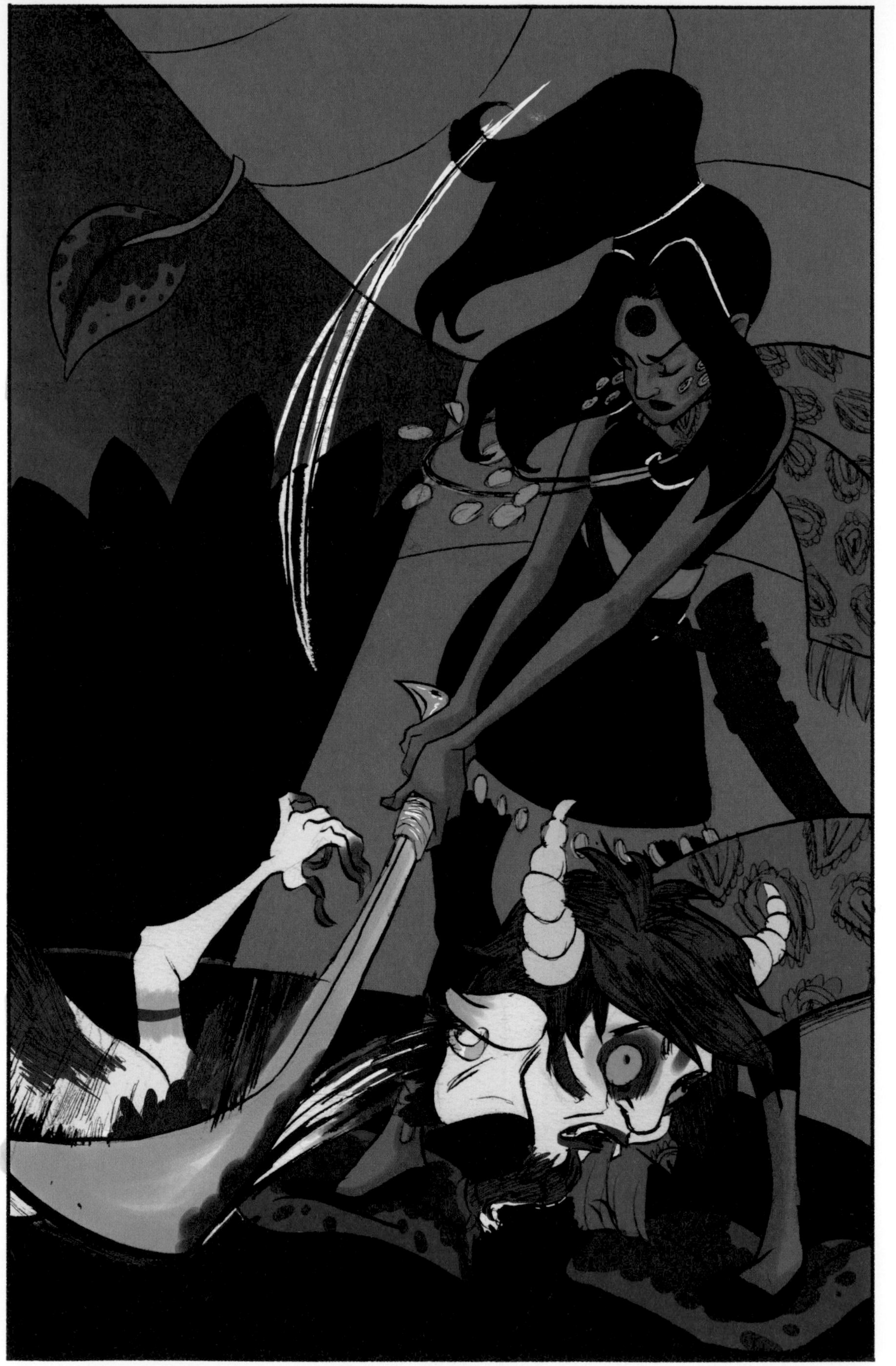

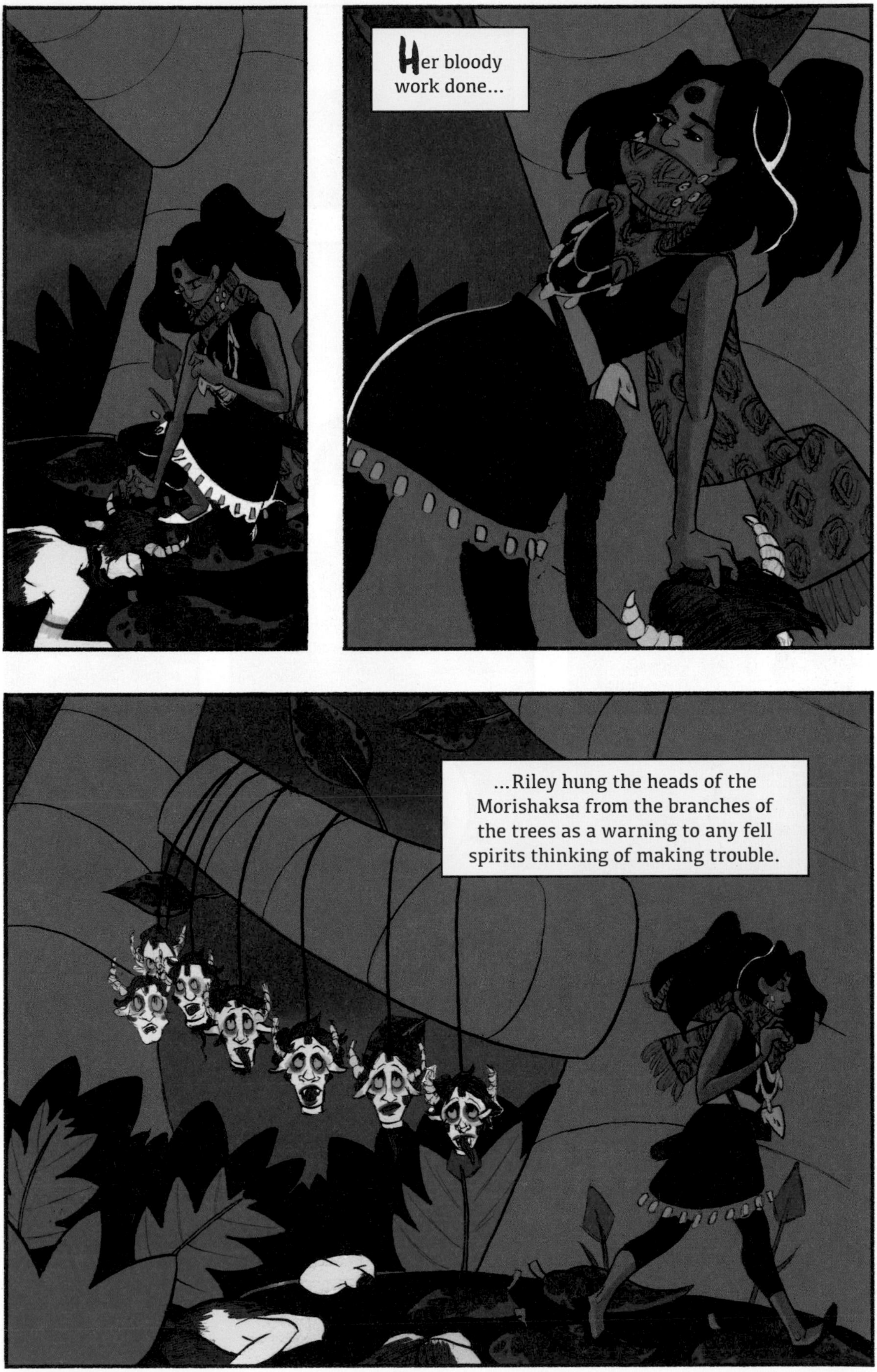
Her bloody work done...
...Riley hung the heads of the Morishaksa from the branches of the trees as a warning to any fell spirits thinking of making trouble.

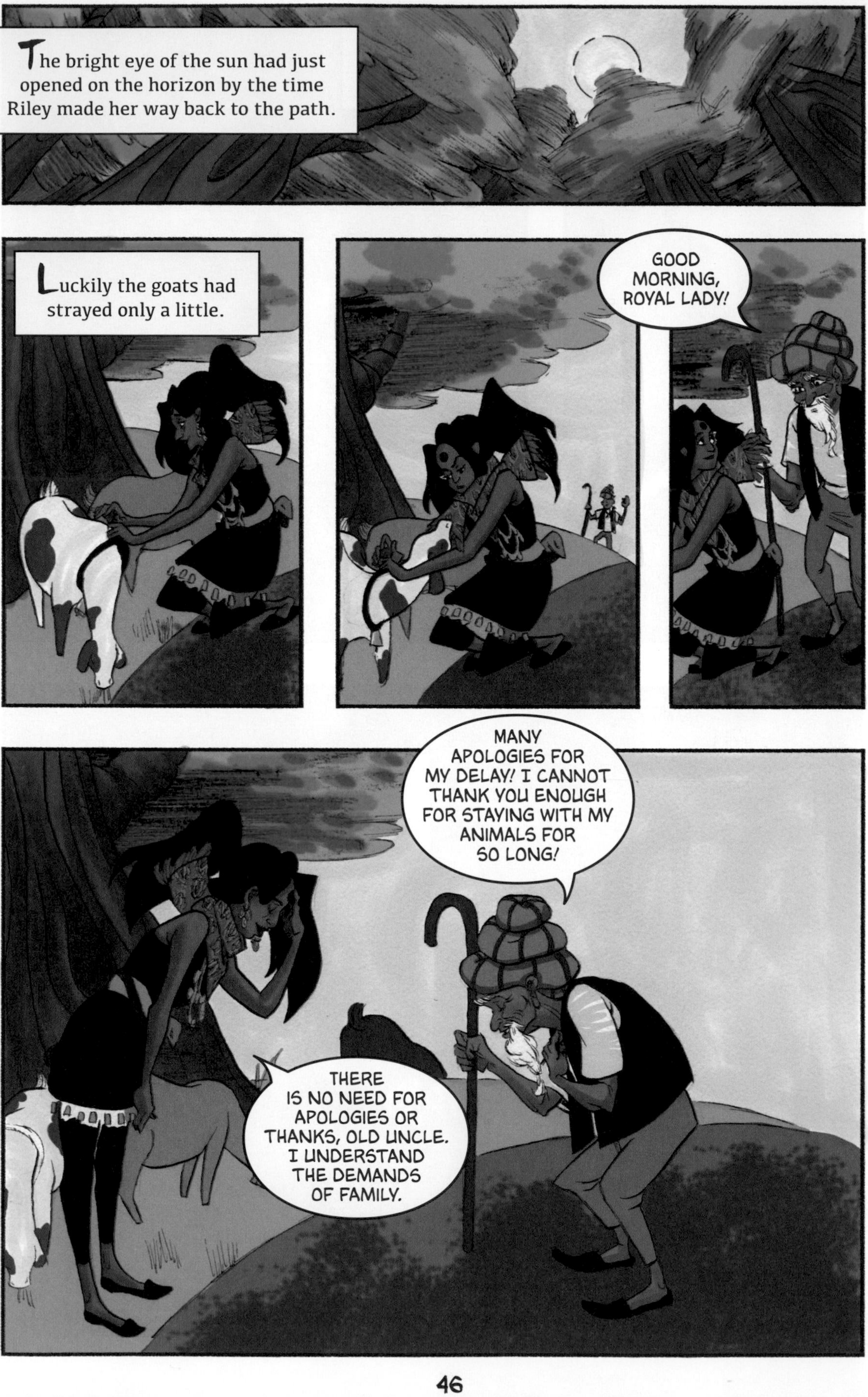
The bright eye of the sun had just opened on the horizon by the time Riley made her way back to the path.
Luckily the goats had strayed only a little.
GOOD MORNING, ROYAL LADY!
MANY APOLOGIES FOR MY DELAY! I CANNOT THANK YOU ENOUGH FOR STAYING WITH MY ANIMALS FOR SO LONG!
THERE IS NO NEED FOR APOLOGIES OR THANKS, OLD UNCLE. I UNDERSTAND THE DEMANDS OF FAMILY.

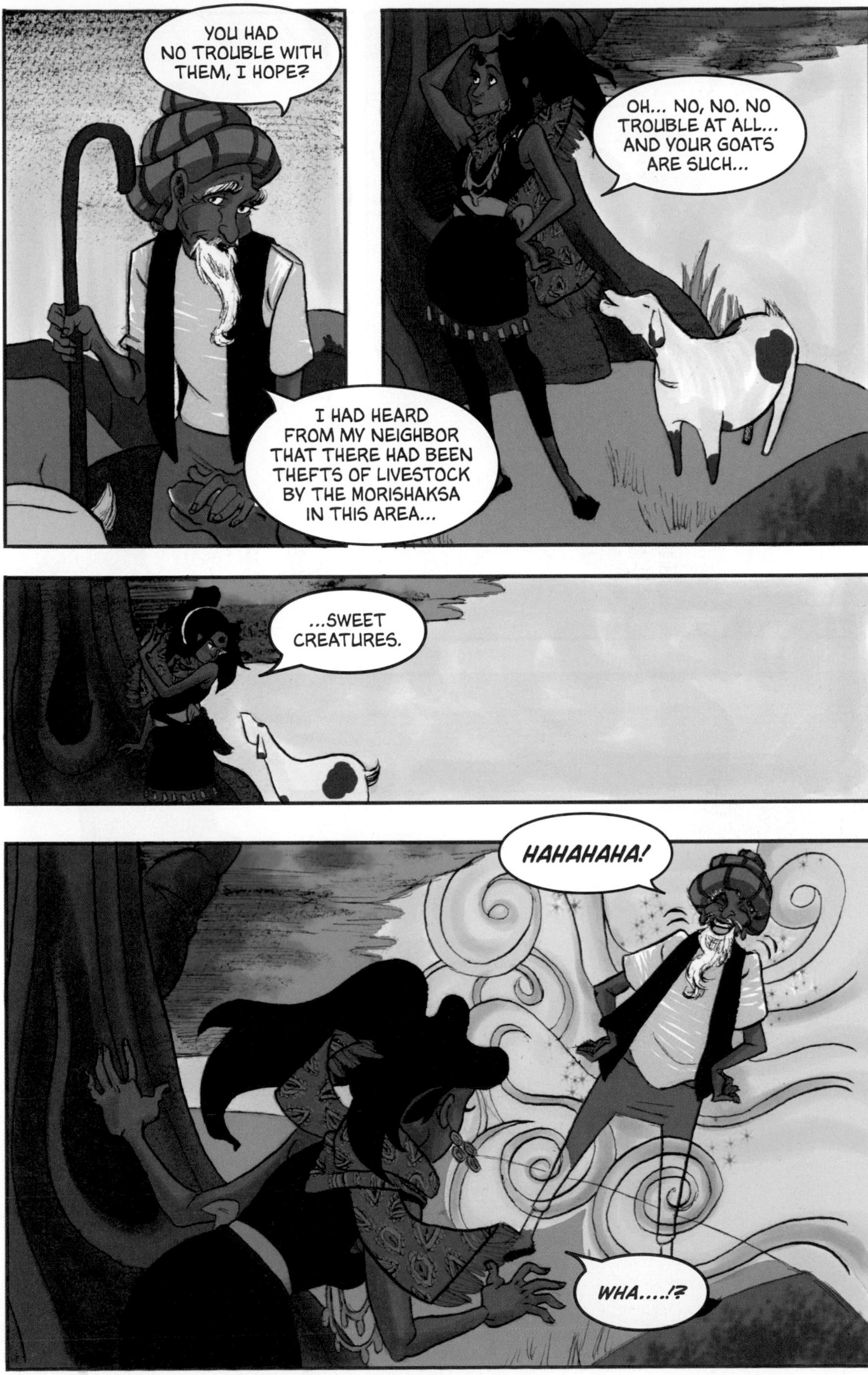
YOU HAD NO TROUBLE WITH THEM, I HOPE?
OH... NO, NO. NO TROUBLE AT ALL... AND YOUR GOATS ARE SUCH...
I HAD HEARD FROM MY NEIGHBOR THAT THERE HAD BEEN THEFTS OF LIVESTOCK BY THE MORISHAKSA IN THIS AREA...
...SWEET CREATURES.
HAHAHAHA!
WHA....!?

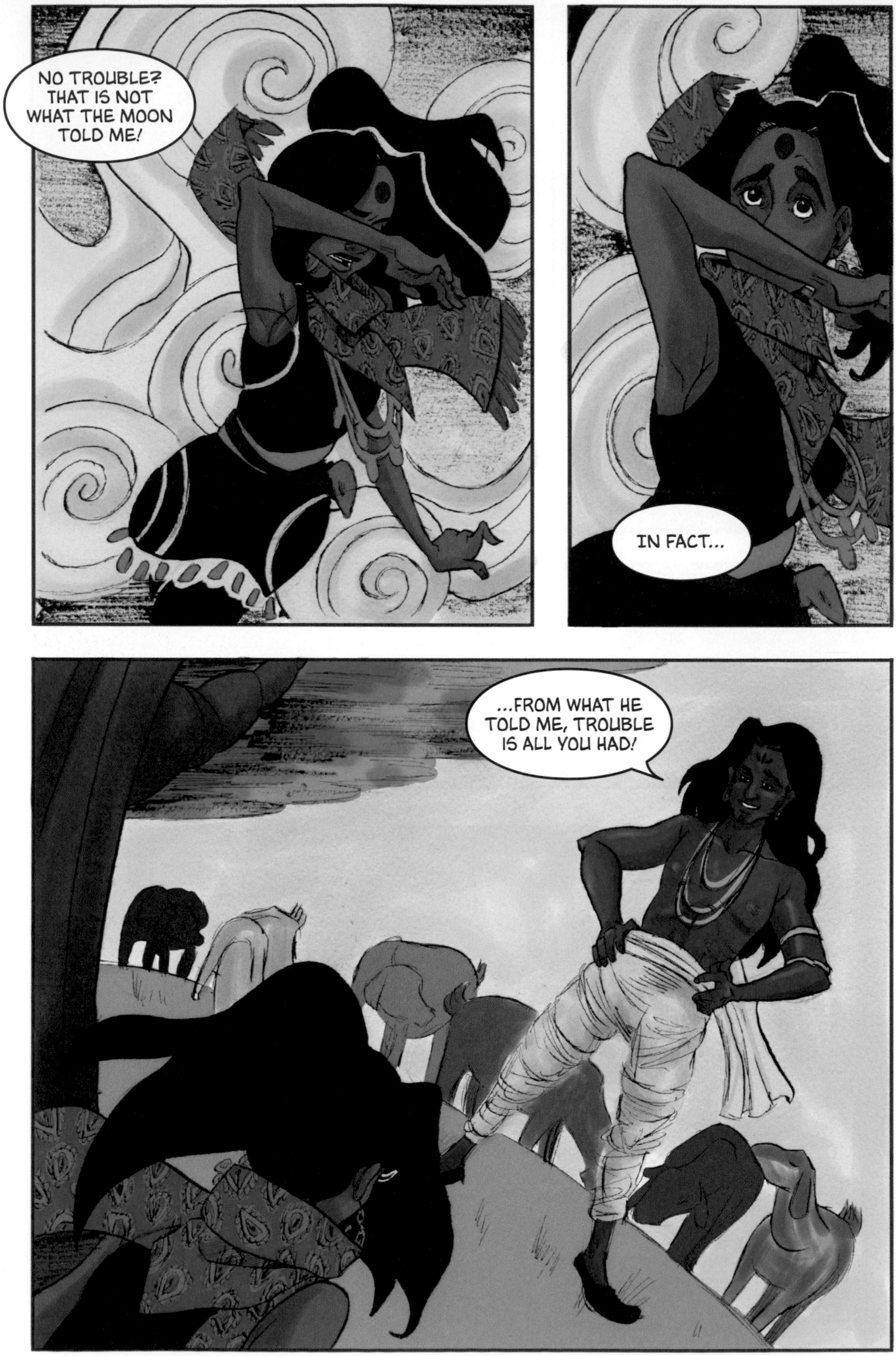
NO TROUBLE? THAT IS NOT WHAT THE MOON TOLD ME!
IN FACT...
...FROM WHAT HE TOLD ME, TROUBLE IS ALL YOU HAD!

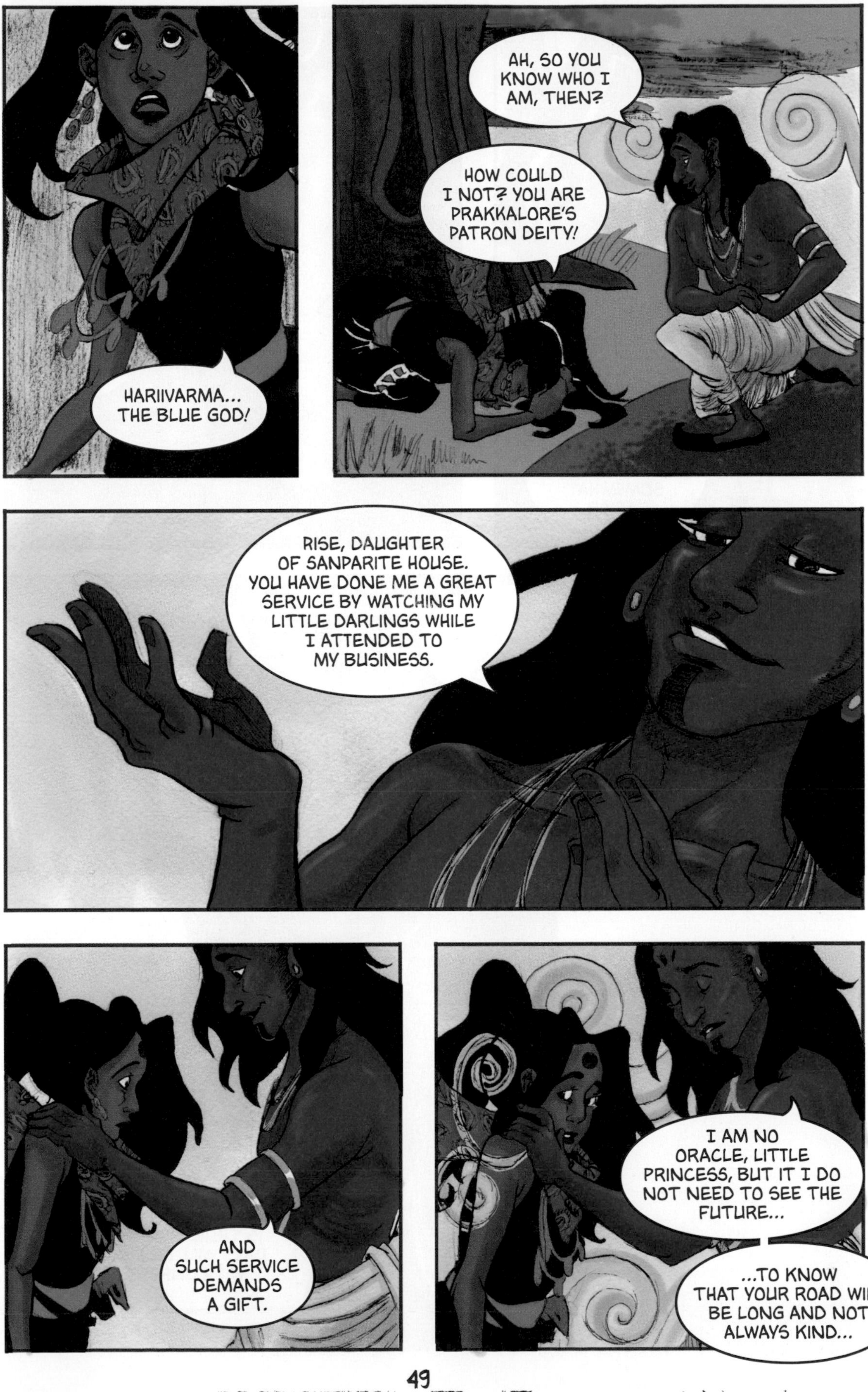
HARIIVARMA... THE BLUE GOD!
AH, SO YOU KNOW WHO I AM, THEN?
HOW COULD I NOT? YOU ARE PRAKKALORE'S PATRON DEITY!
RISE, DAUGHTER OF SANPARITE HOUSE. YOU HAVE DONE ME A GREAT SERVICE BY WATCHING MY LITTLE DARLINGS WHILE I ATTENDED TO MY BUSINESS.
AND SUCH SERVICE DEMANDS A GIFT.
I AM NO ORACLE, LITTLE PRINCESS, BUT IT I DO NOT NEED TO SEE THE FUTURE...
...TO KNOW THAT YOUR ROAD WILL BE LONG AND NOT ALWAYS KIND...

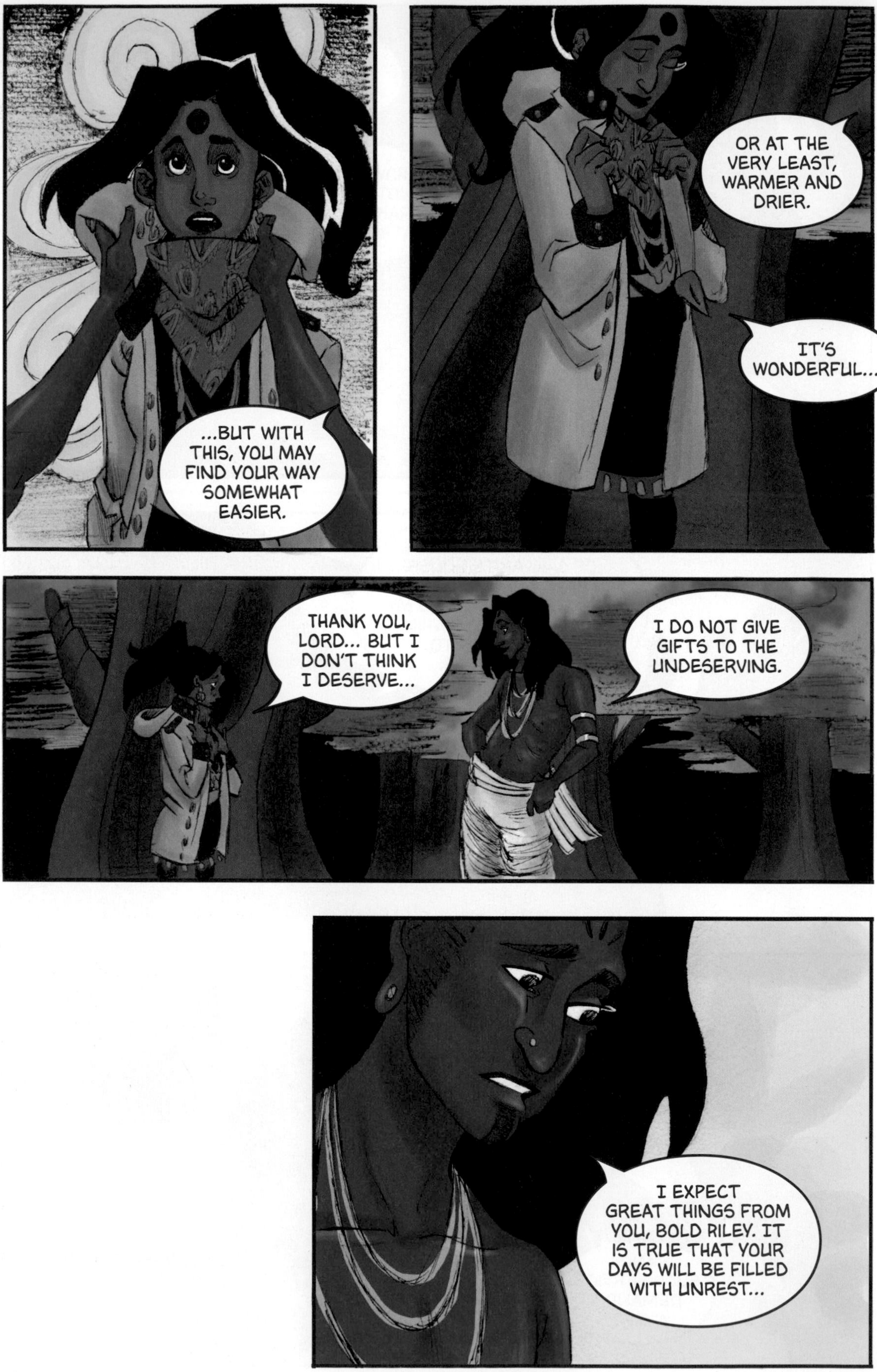
...BUT WITH THIS, YOU MAY FIND YOUR WAY SOMEWHAT EASIER.
OR AT THE VERY LEAST, WARMER AND DRIER.
IT'S WONDERFUL...
THANK YOU, LORD... BUT I DON'T THINK I DESERVE...
I DO NOT GIVE GIFTS TO THE UNDESERVING.
I EXPECT GREAT THINGS FROM YOU, BOLD RILEY. IT IS TRUE THAT YOUR DAYS WILL BE FILLED WITH UNREST...

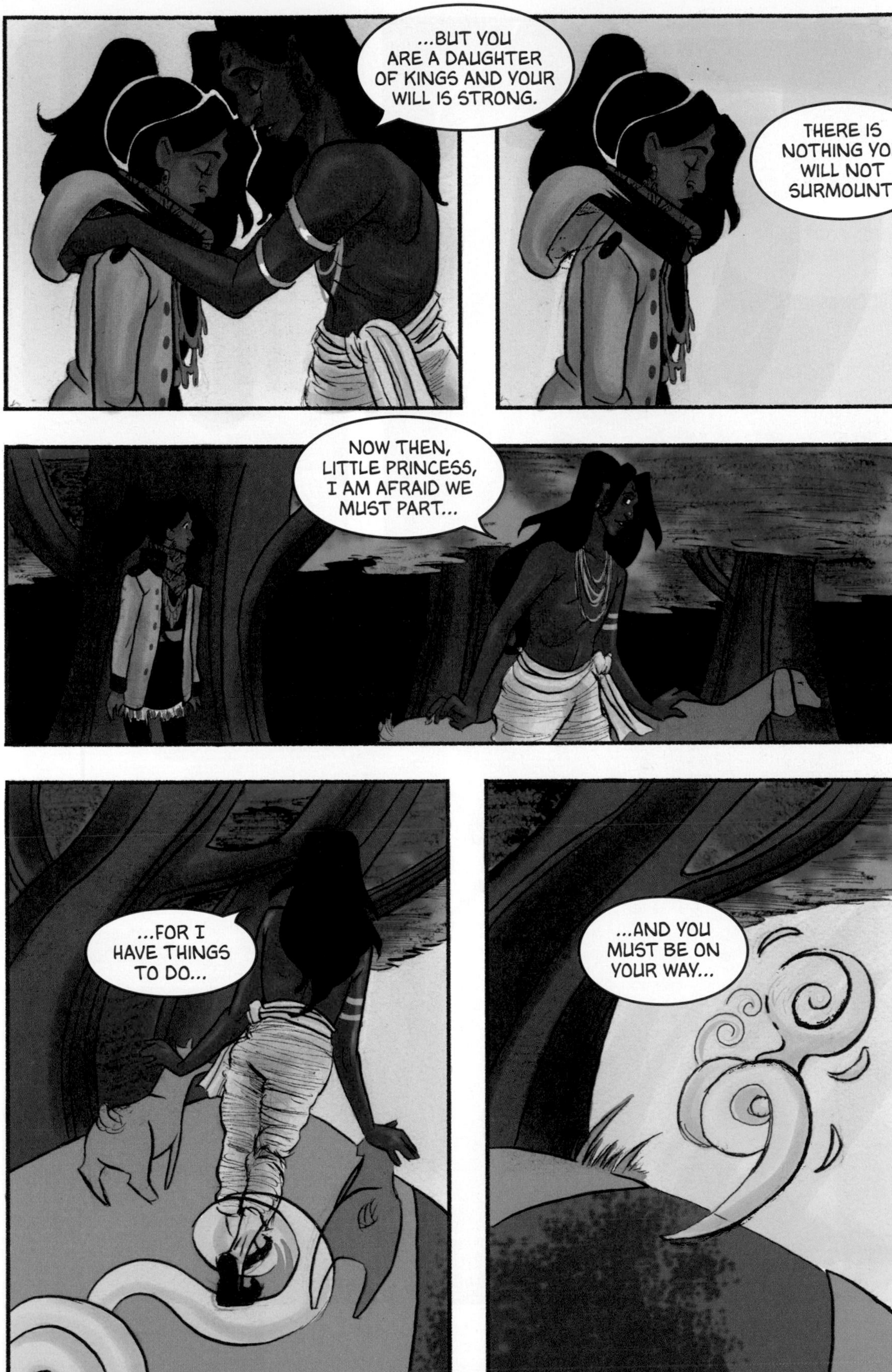
...BUT YOU ARE A DAUGHTER OF KINGS AND YOUR WILL IS STRONG.
THERE IS NOTHING YOU WILL NOT SURMOUNT.
NOW THEN, LITTLE PRINCESS, I AM AFRAID WE MUST PART...
...FOR I HAVE THINGS TO DO...
...AND YOU MUST BE ON YOUR WAY...

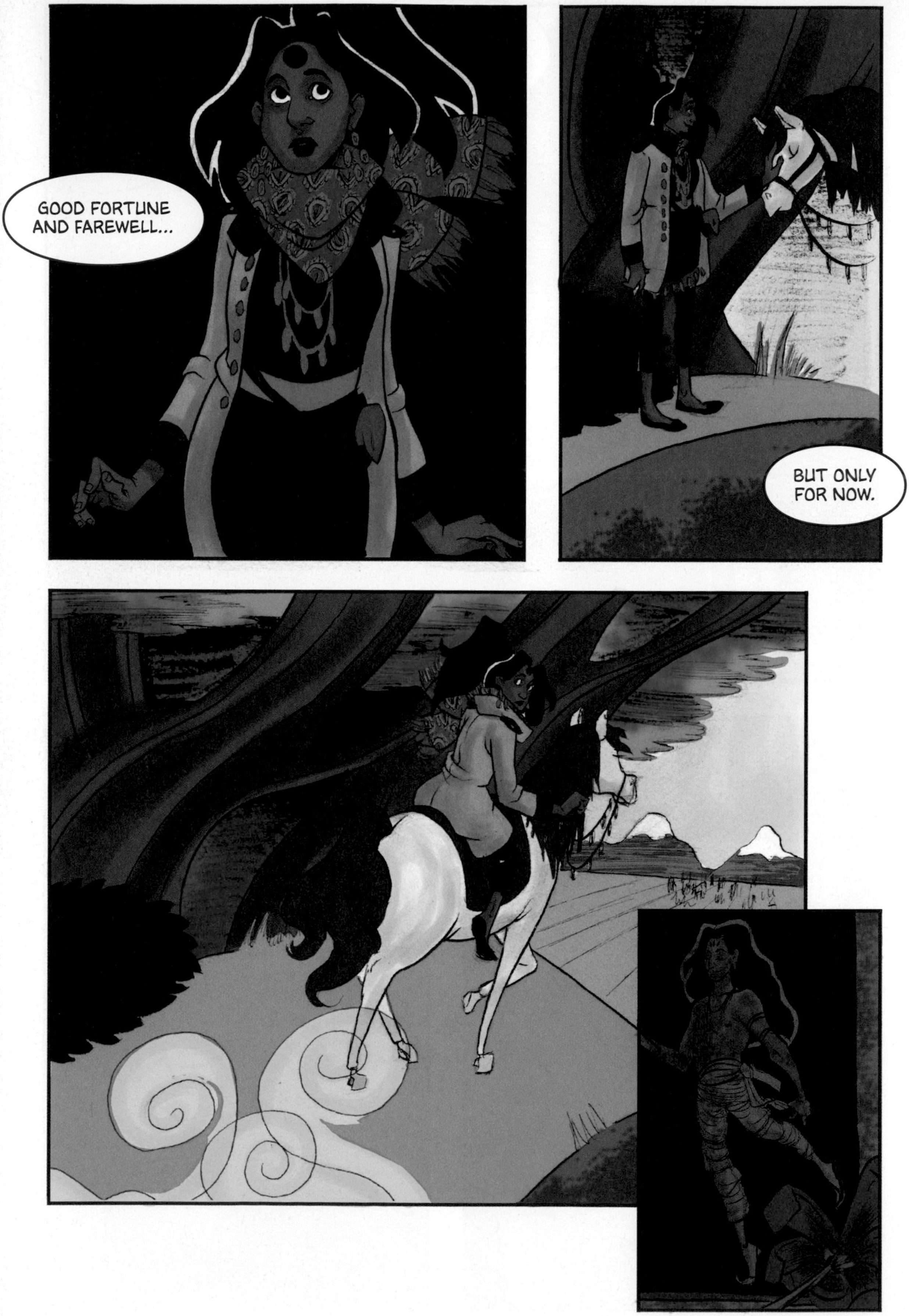
GOOD FORTUNE AND FAREWELL...
BUT ONLY FOR NOW.

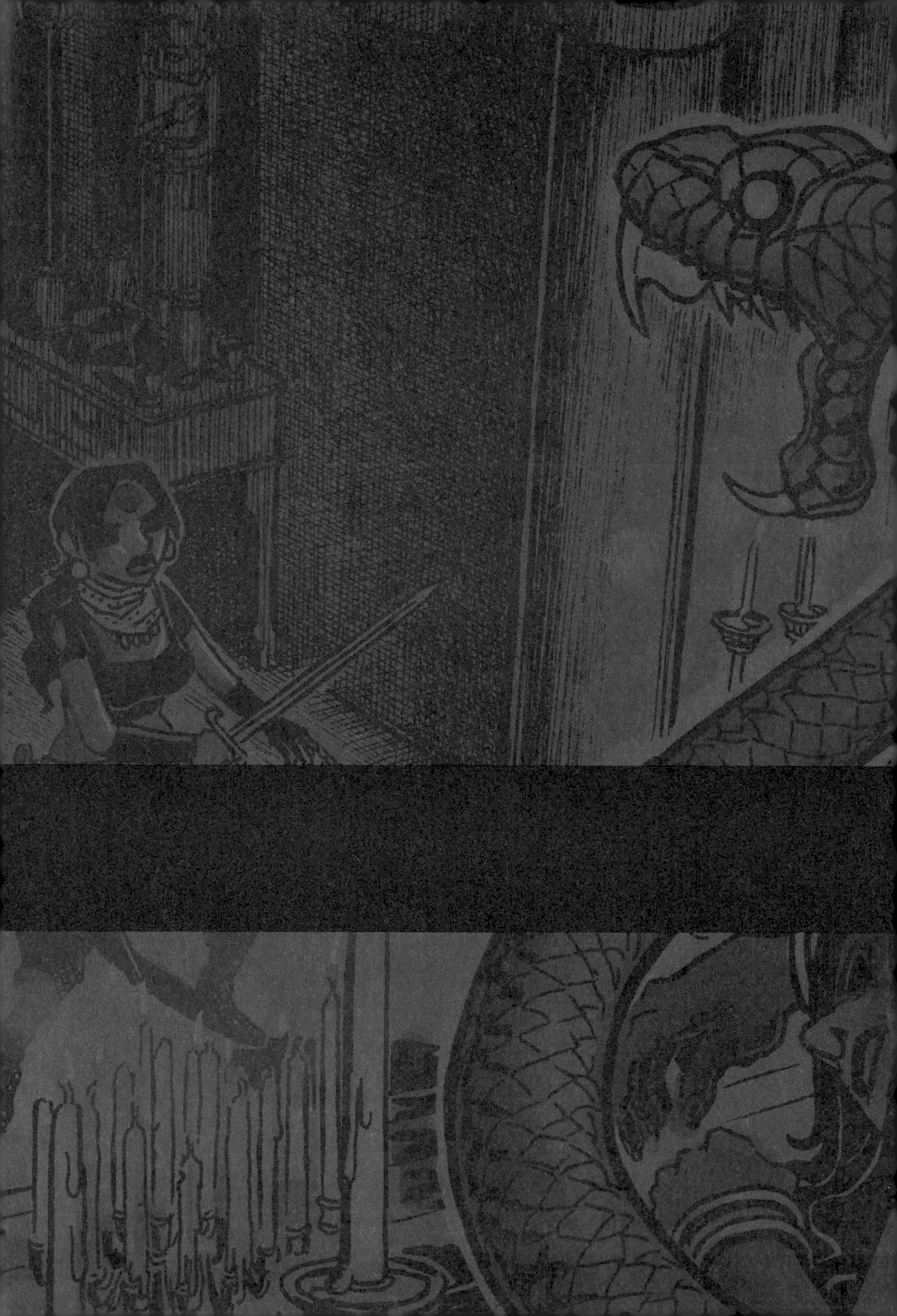

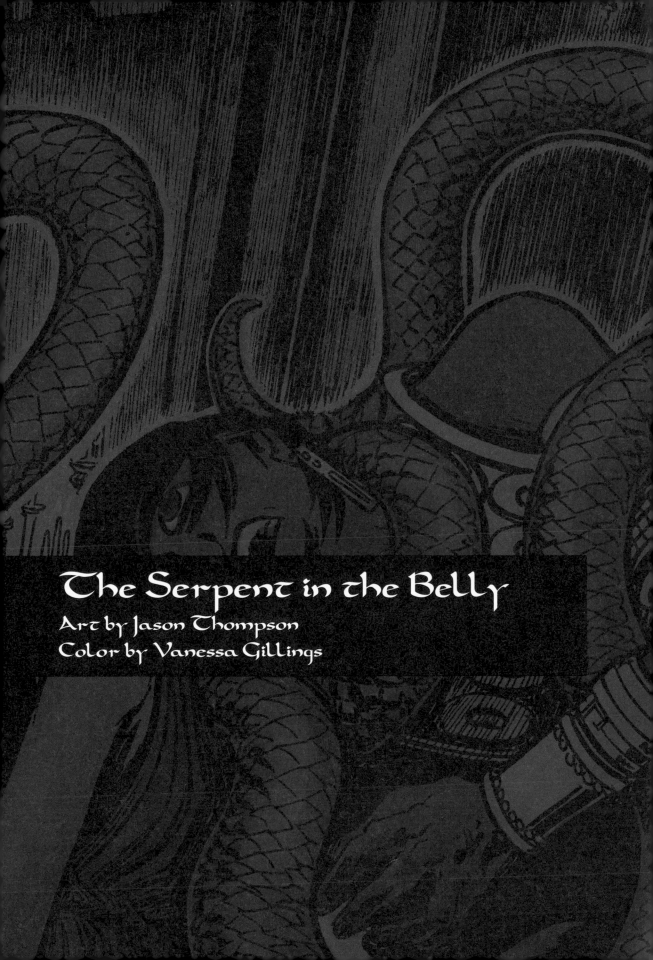

The Serpent in the Belly
Art by Jason Thompson
Color by Vanessa Gillings

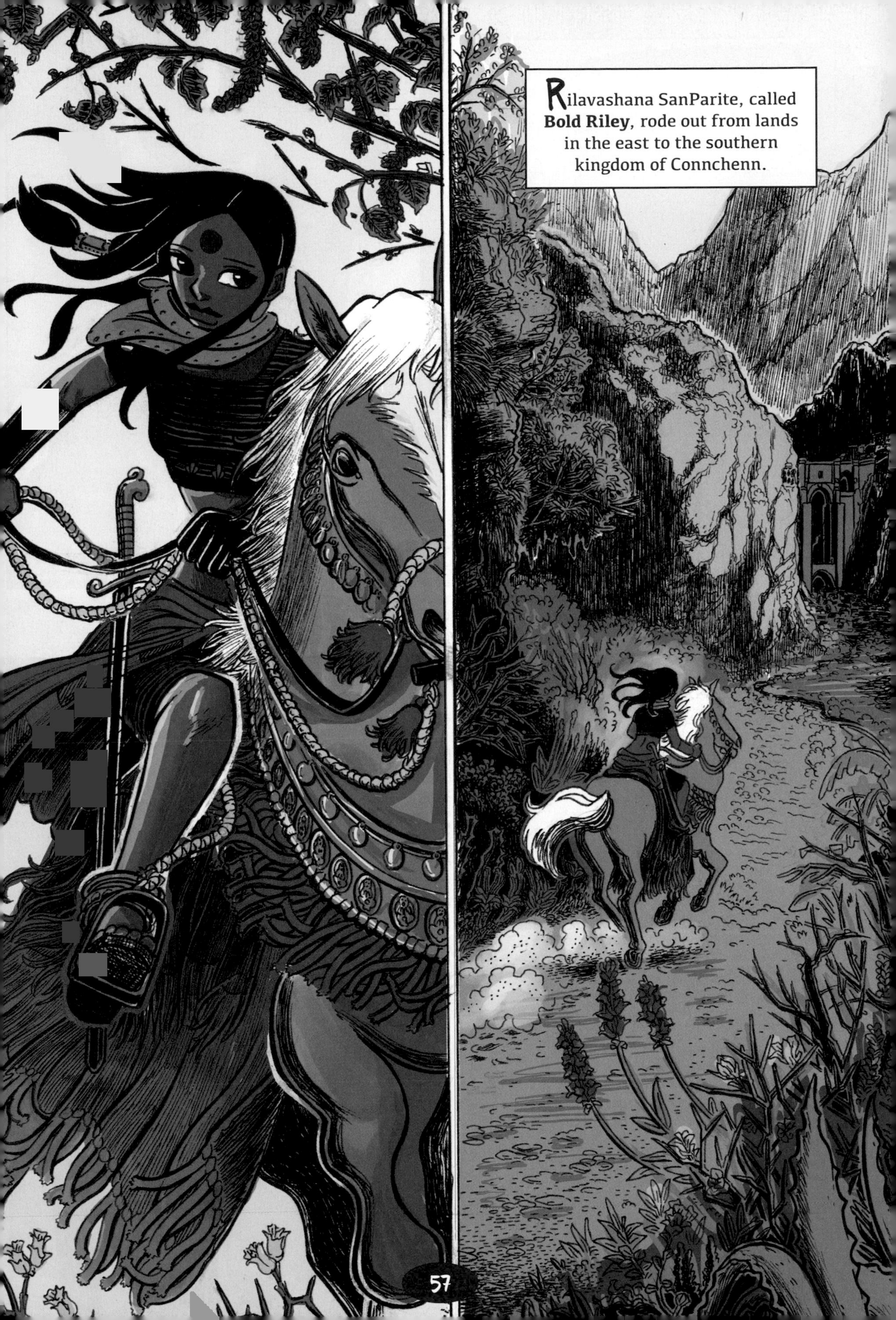
Rilavashana SanParite, called **Bold Riley**, rode out from lands in the east to the southern kingdom of Connchenn.

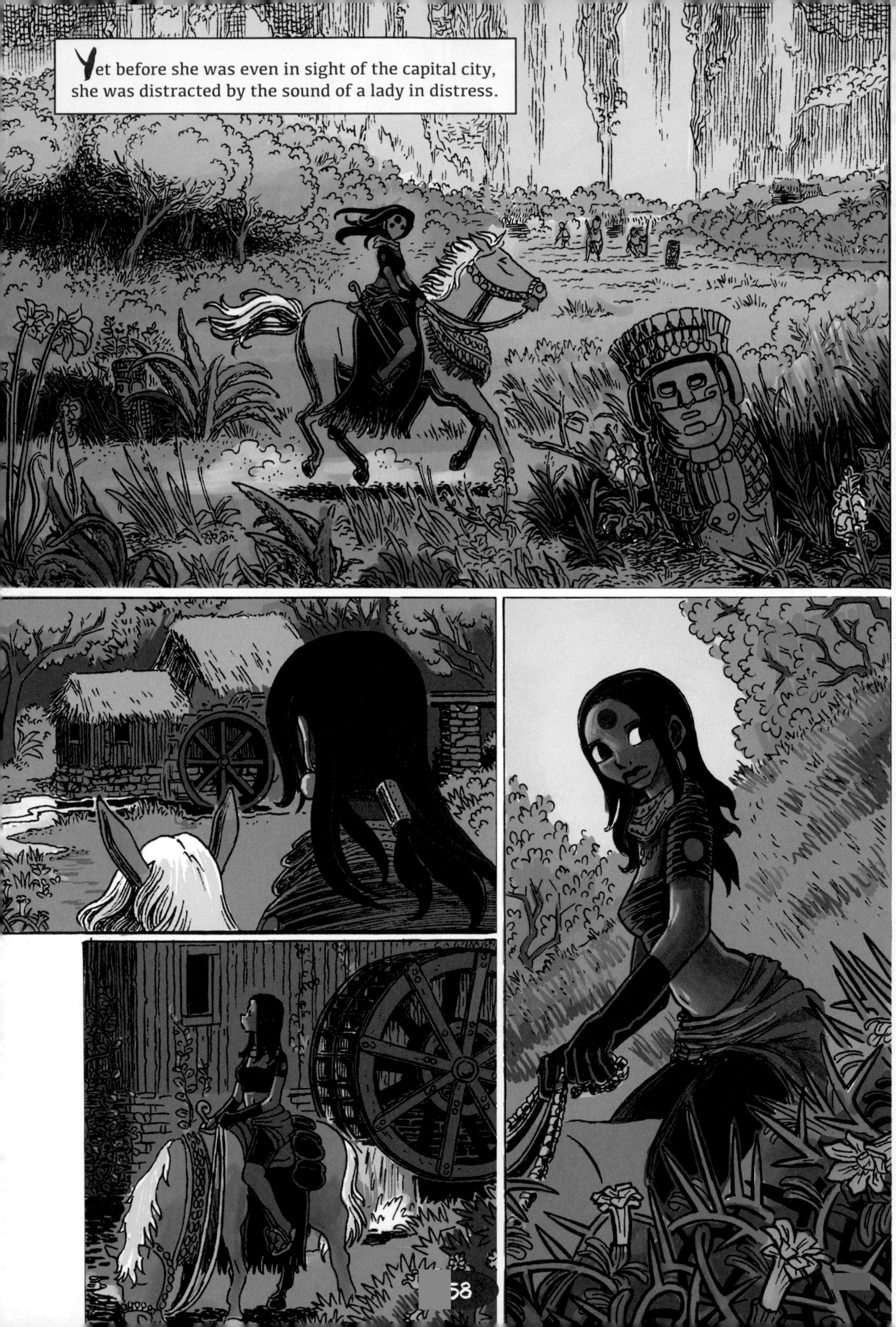
Yet before she was even in sight of the capital city,
she was distracted by the sound of a lady in distress.

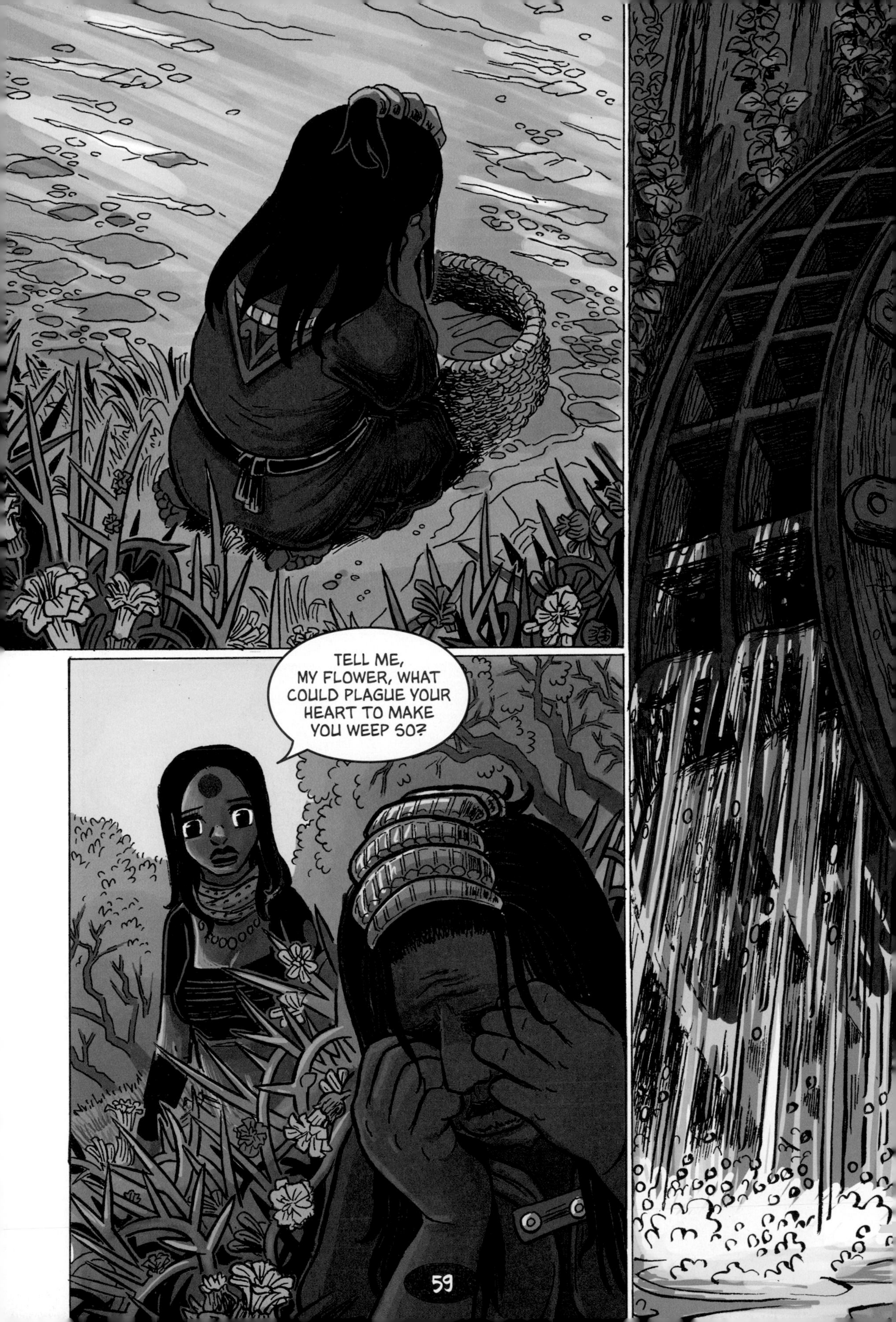
TELL ME, MY FLOWER, WHAT COULD PLAGUE YOUR HEART TO MAKE YOU WEEP SO?

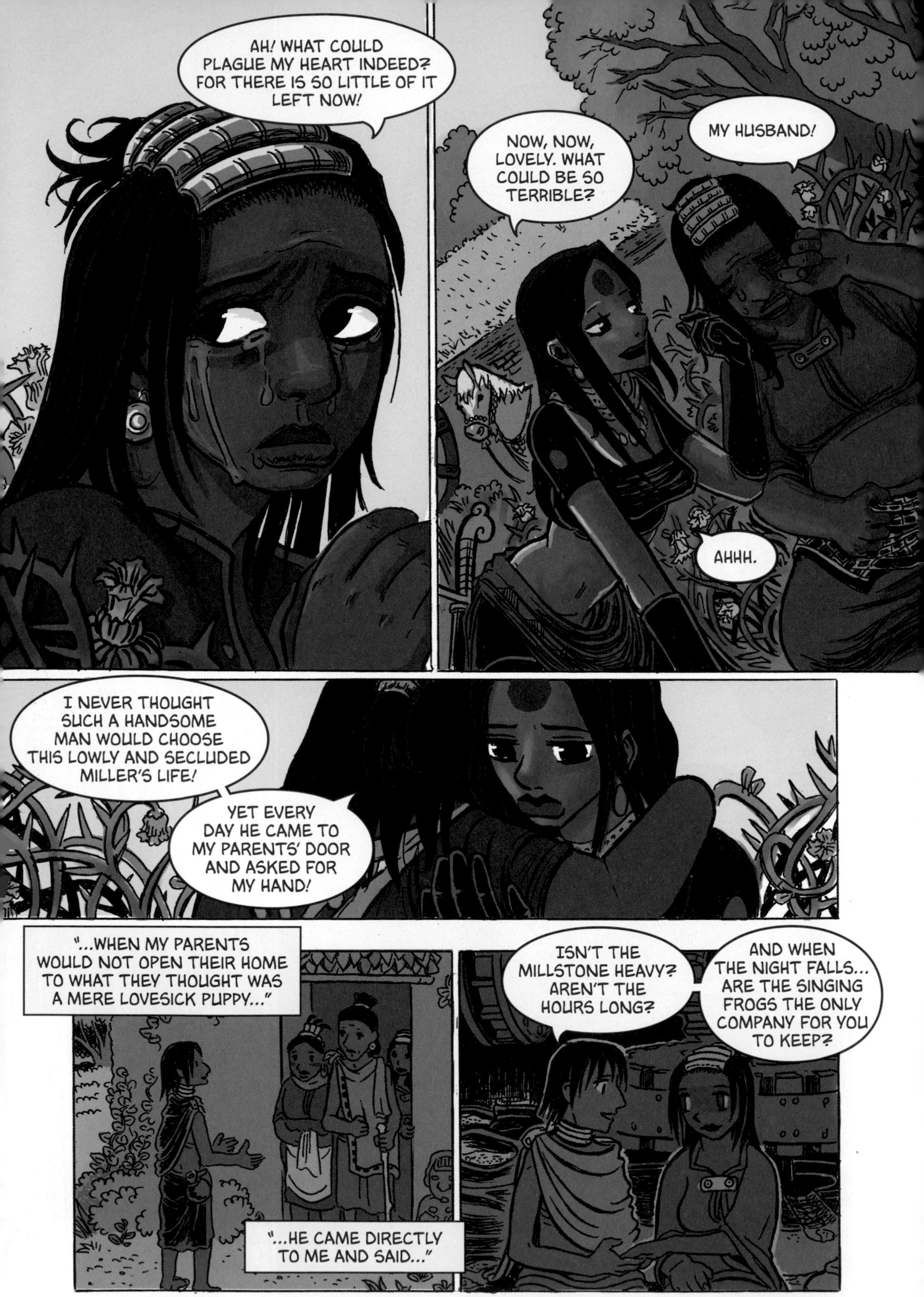
AH! WHAT COULD PLAGUE MY HEART INDEED? FOR THERE IS SO LITTLE OF IT LEFT NOW!
NOW, NOW, LOVELY. WHAT COULD BE SO TERRIBLE?
MY HUSBAND!
AHHH.
I NEVER THOUGHT SUCH A HANDSOME MAN WOULD CHOOSE THIS LOWLY AND SECLUDED MILLER'S LIFE!
YET EVERY DAY HE CAME TO MY PARENTS' DOOR AND ASKED FOR MY HAND!
"...WHEN MY PARENTS WOULD NOT OPEN THEIR HOME TO WHAT THEY THOUGHT WAS A MERE LOVESICK PUPPY..."
"...HE CAME DIRECTLY TO ME AND SAID..."
ISN'T THE MILLSTONE HEAVY? AREN'T THE HOURS LONG?
AND WHEN THE NIGHT FALLS... ARE THE SINGING FROGS THE ONLY COMPANY FOR YOU TO KEEP?

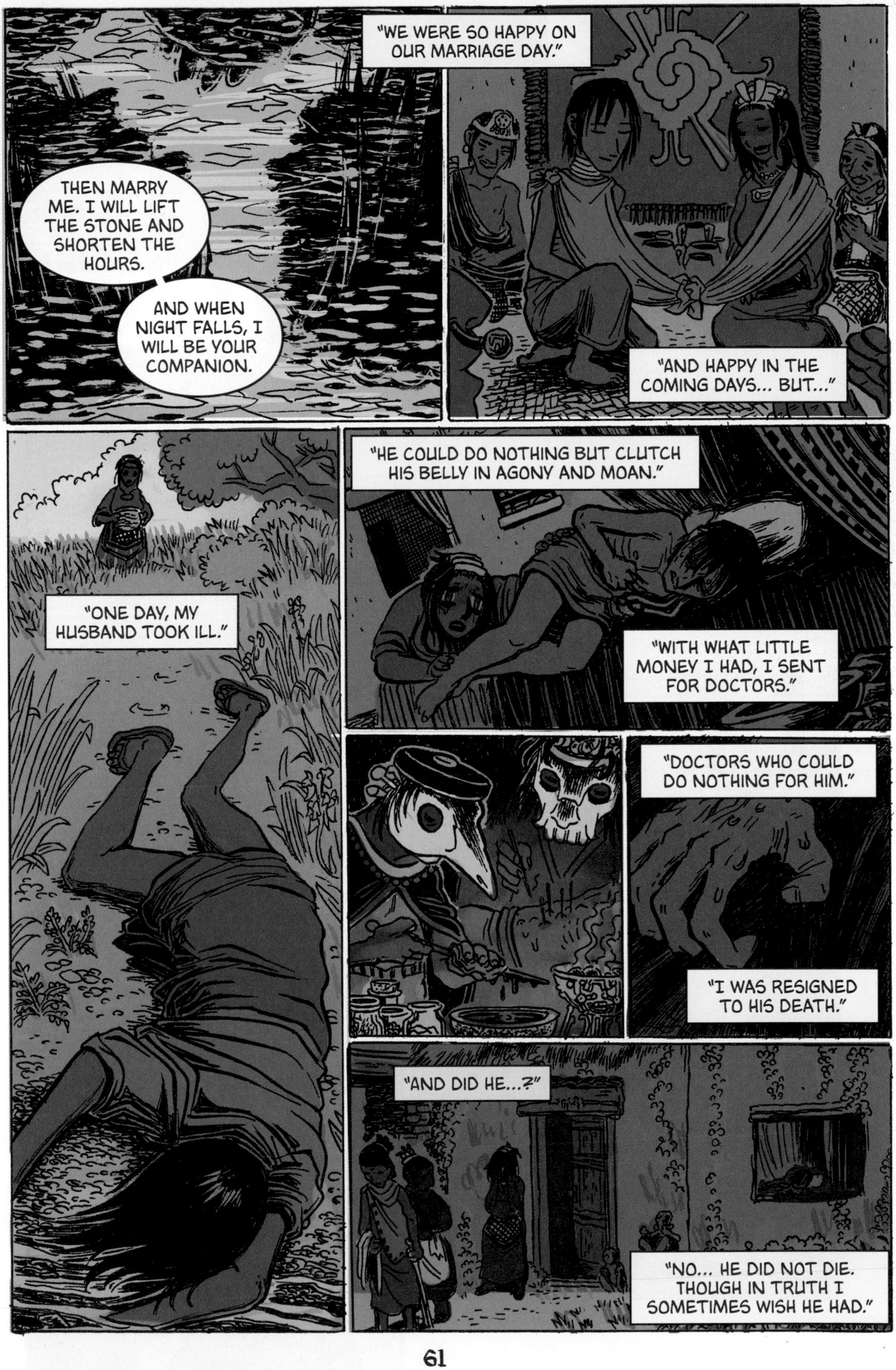
THEN MARRY ME. I WILL LIFT THE STONE AND SHORTEN THE HOURS.
AND WHEN NIGHT FALLS, I WILL BE YOUR COMPANION.
"WE WERE SO HAPPY ON OUR MARRIAGE DAY."
"AND HAPPY IN THE COMING DAYS... BUT..."
"ONE DAY, MY HUSBAND TOOK ILL."
"HE COULD DO NOTHING BUT CLUTCH HIS BELLY IN AGONY AND MOAN."
"WITH WHAT LITTLE MONEY I HAD, I SENT FOR DOCTORS."
"DOCTORS WHO COULD DO NOTHING FOR HIM."
"I WAS RESIGNED TO HIS DEATH."
"AND DID HE...?"
"NO... HE DID NOT DIE. THOUGH IN TRUTH I SOMETIMES WISH HE HAD."

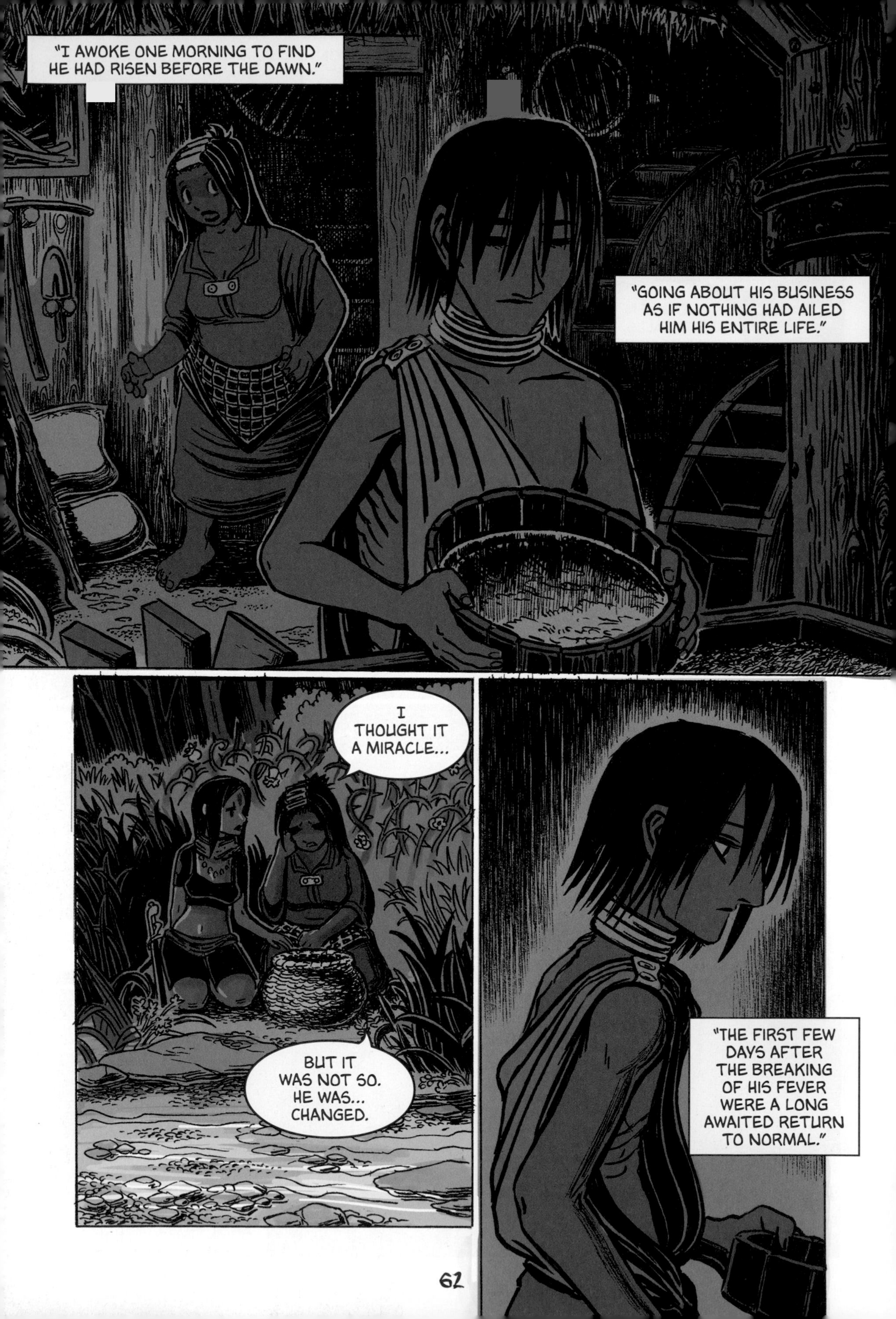
"I AWOKE ONE MORNING TO FIND HE HAD RISEN BEFORE THE DAWN."
"GOING ABOUT HIS BUSINESS AS IF NOTHING HAD AILED HIM HIS ENTIRE LIFE."
I THOUGHT IT A MIRACLE...
BUT IT WAS NOT SO. HE WAS... CHANGED.
"THE FIRST FEW DAYS AFTER THE BREAKING OF HIS FEVER WERE A LONG AWAITED RETURN TO NORMAL."

"BUT SOON AFTER, I REALIZED THAT ALL WAS NOT RIGHT."

"YET NOW I WOULD CATCH HIM COUNTING THE MEAGER COINS WE HAD SAVED, OVER AND OVER AGAIN AT A FEVERED PACE..."

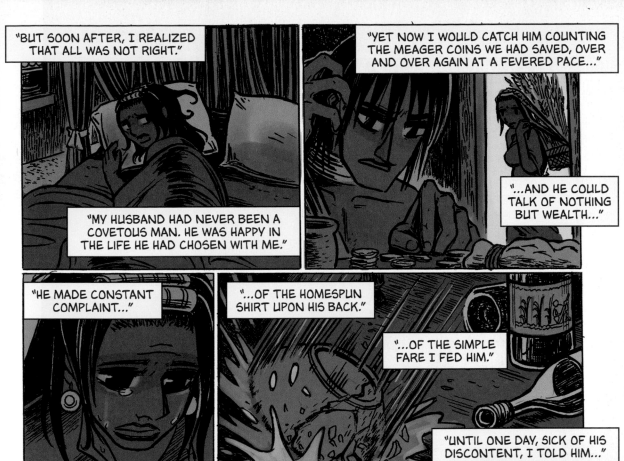

"MY HUSBAND HAD NEVER BEEN A COVETOUS MAN. HE WAS HAPPY IN THE LIFE HE HAD CHOSEN WITH ME."

"...AND HE COULD TALK OF NOTHING BUT WEALTH..."

"HE MADE CONSTANT COMPLAINT..."

"...OF THE HOMESPUN SHIRT UPON HIS BACK."

"...OF THE SIMPLE FARE I FED HIM."

"UNTIL ONE DAY, SICK OF HIS DISCONTENT, I TOLD HIM..."

ARE YOU SO UNHAPPY!?

IF YOU ARE SO MISERABLE WITH YOUR PATHETIC MILLHOUSE SHREW OF A WIFE...

...THEN WHY DON'T YOU FIND YOURSELF SOME MERCHANT'S DAUGHTER TO CONTENT YOURSELF WITH?

"HE LOOKED ME DEAD IN THE FACE THEN AND SAID..."

WHAT AN EXCELLENT SUGGESTION, MY DARLING.

FOR SURELY A MAN SUCH AS MYSELF DESERVES FAR BETTER THAN A LIFE IN A HOVEL WITH A SHREW.

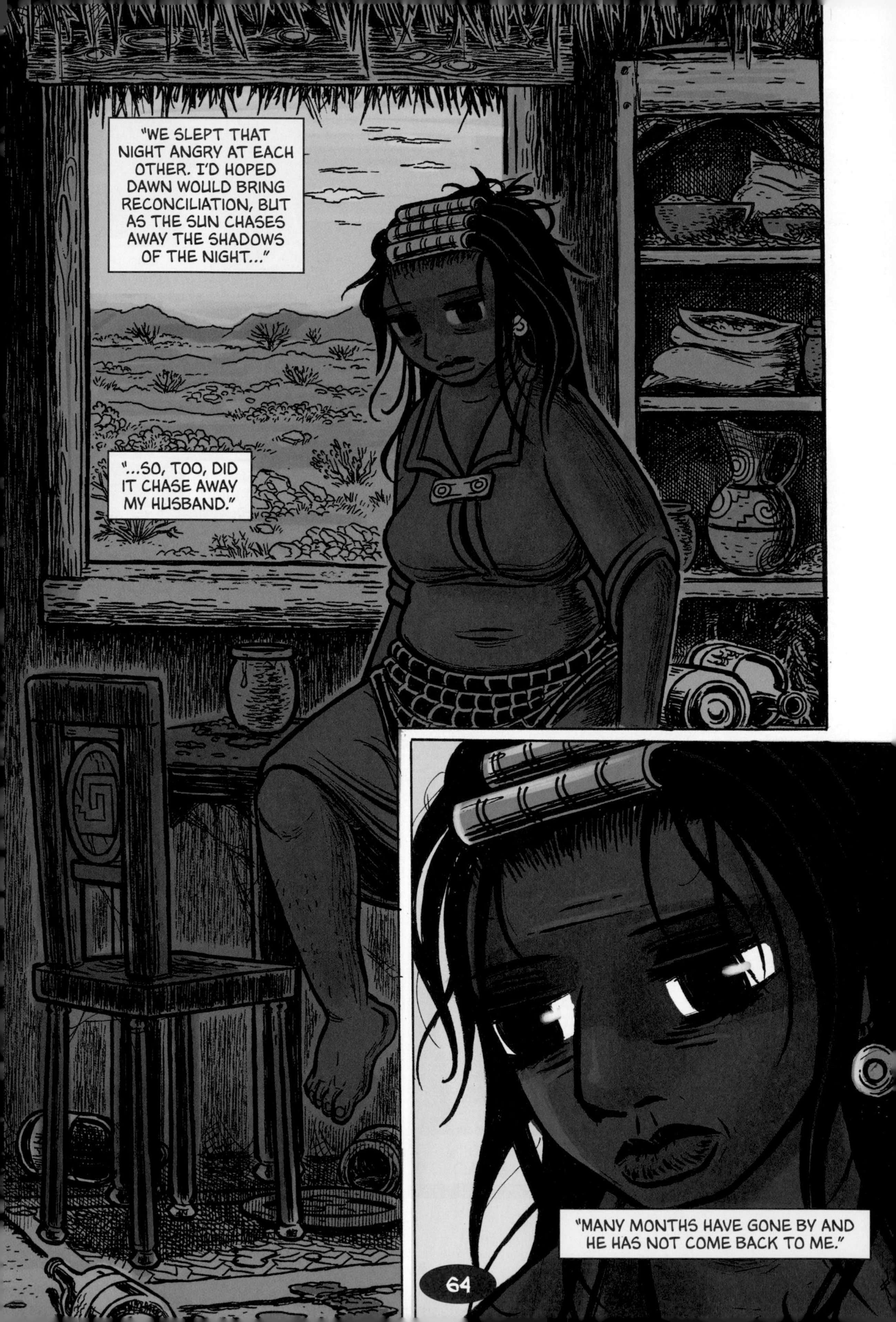
"WE SLEPT THAT NIGHT ANGRY AT EACH OTHER. I'D HOPED DAWN WOULD BRING RECONCILIATION, BUT AS THE SUN CHASES AWAY THE SHADOWS OF THE NIGHT..."
"...SO, TOO, DID IT CHASE AWAY MY HUSBAND."
"MANY MONTHS HAVE GONE BY AND HE HAS NOT COME BACK TO ME."

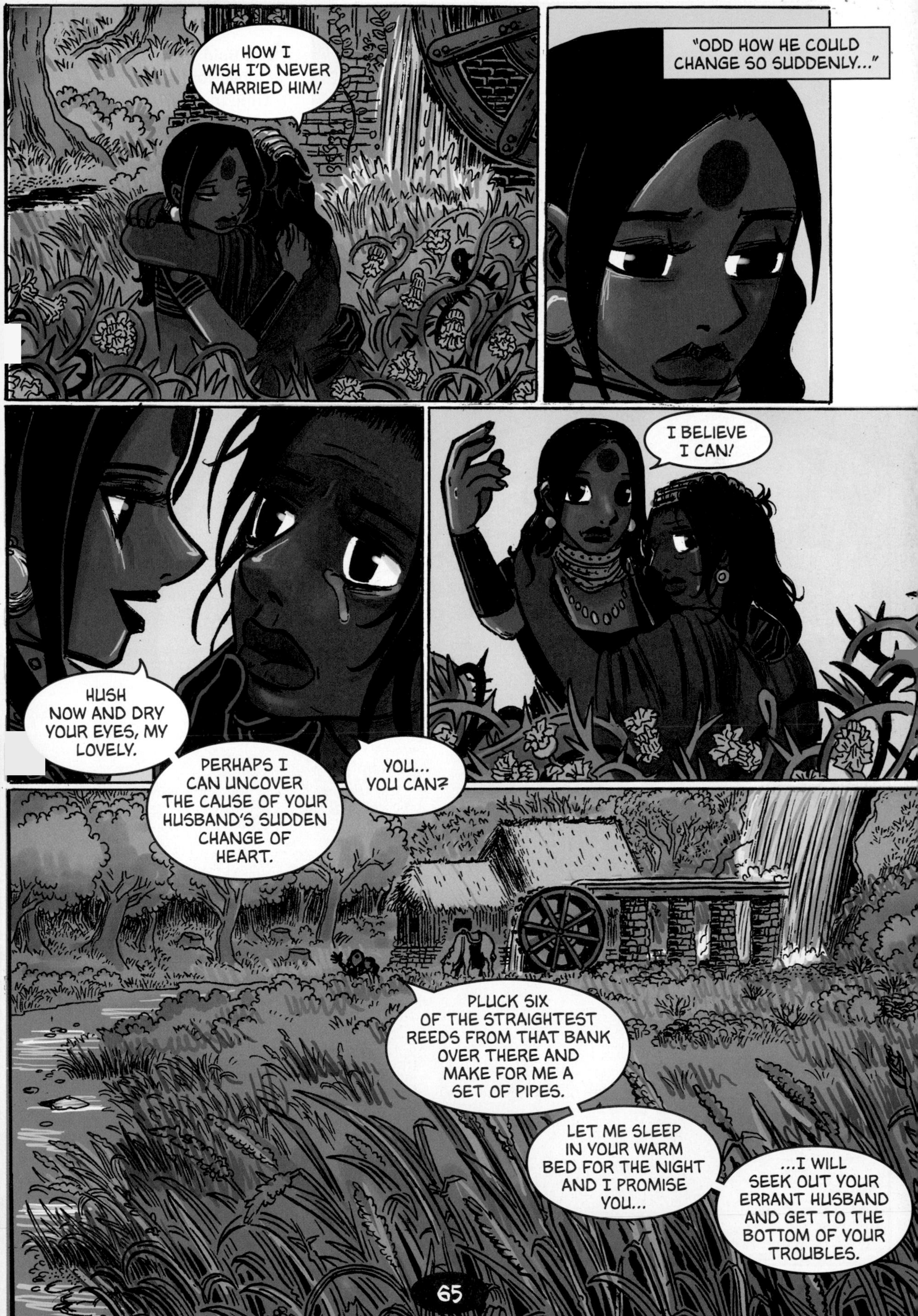
HOW I WISH I'D NEVER MARRIED HIM!
"ODD HOW HE COULD CHANGE SO SUDDENLY..."
HUSH NOW AND DRY YOUR EYES, MY LOVELY.
PERHAPS I CAN UNCOVER THE CAUSE OF YOUR HUSBAND'S SUDDEN CHANGE OF HEART.
YOU... YOU CAN?
I BELIEVE I CAN!
PLUCK SIX OF THE STRAIGHTEST REEDS FROM THAT BANK OVER THERE AND MAKE FOR ME A SET OF PIPES.
LET ME SLEEP IN YOUR WARM BED FOR THE NIGHT AND I PROMISE YOU...
...I WILL SEEK OUT YOUR ERRANT HUSBAND AND GET TO THE BOTTOM OF YOUR TROUBLES.

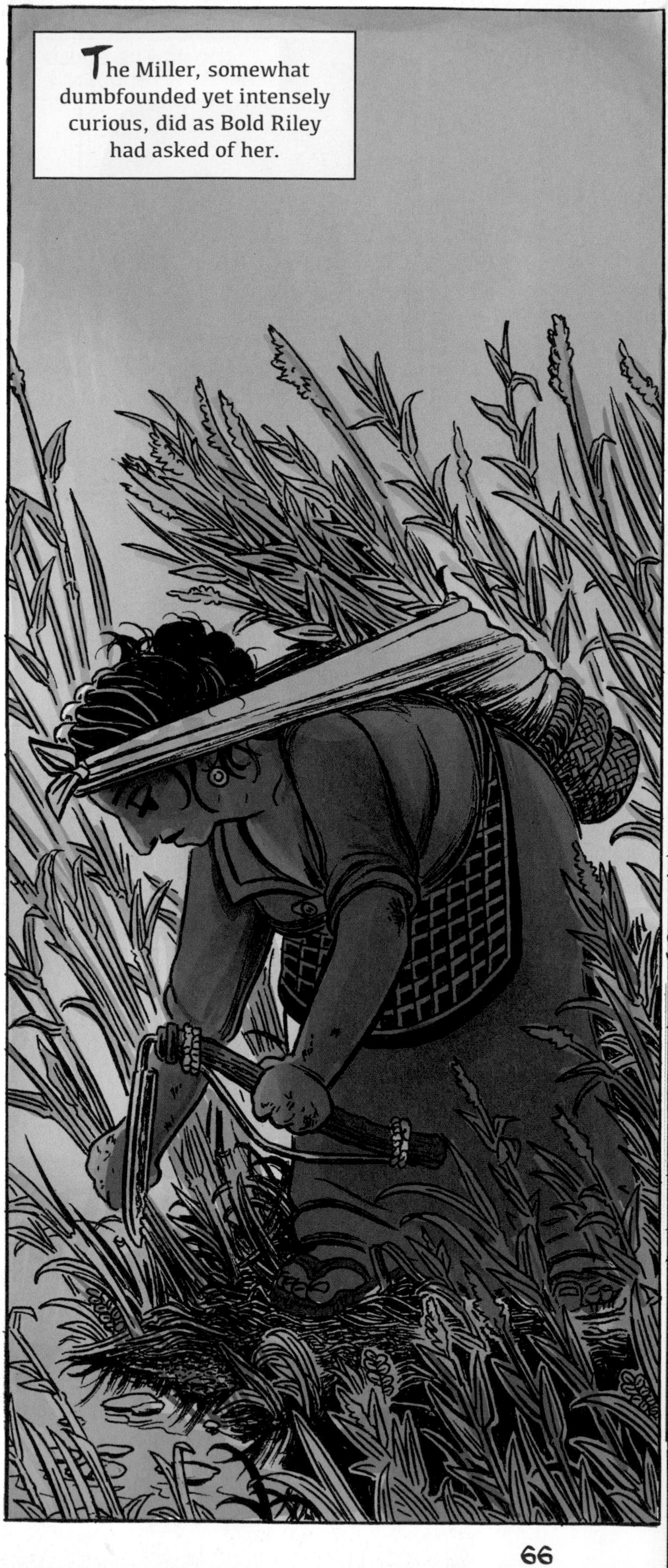
The Miller, somewhat dumbfounded yet intensely curious, did as Bold Riley had asked of her.

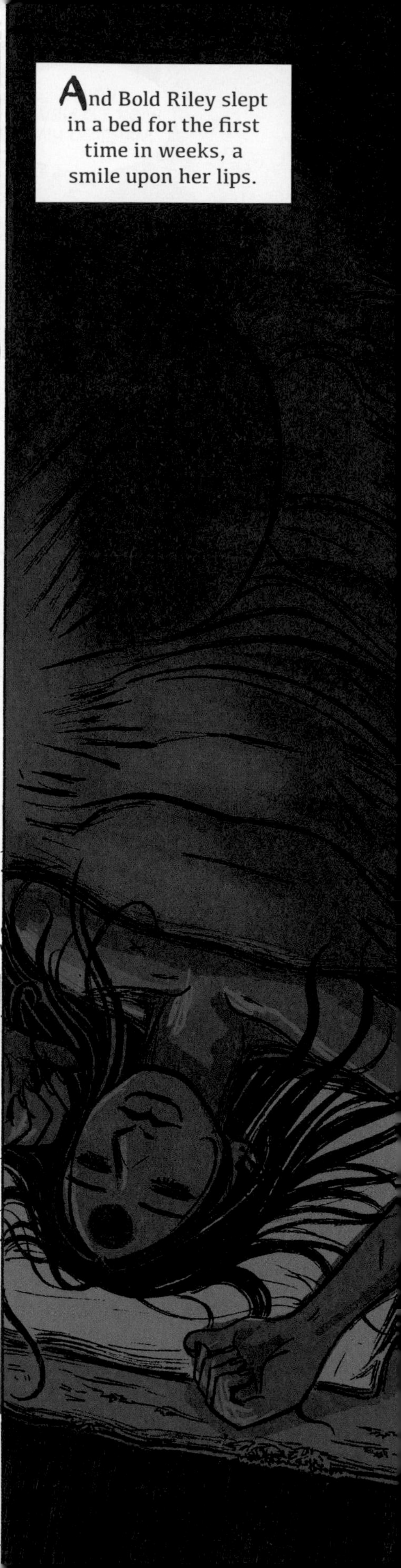
And Bold Riley slept in a bed for the first time in weeks, a smile upon her lips.

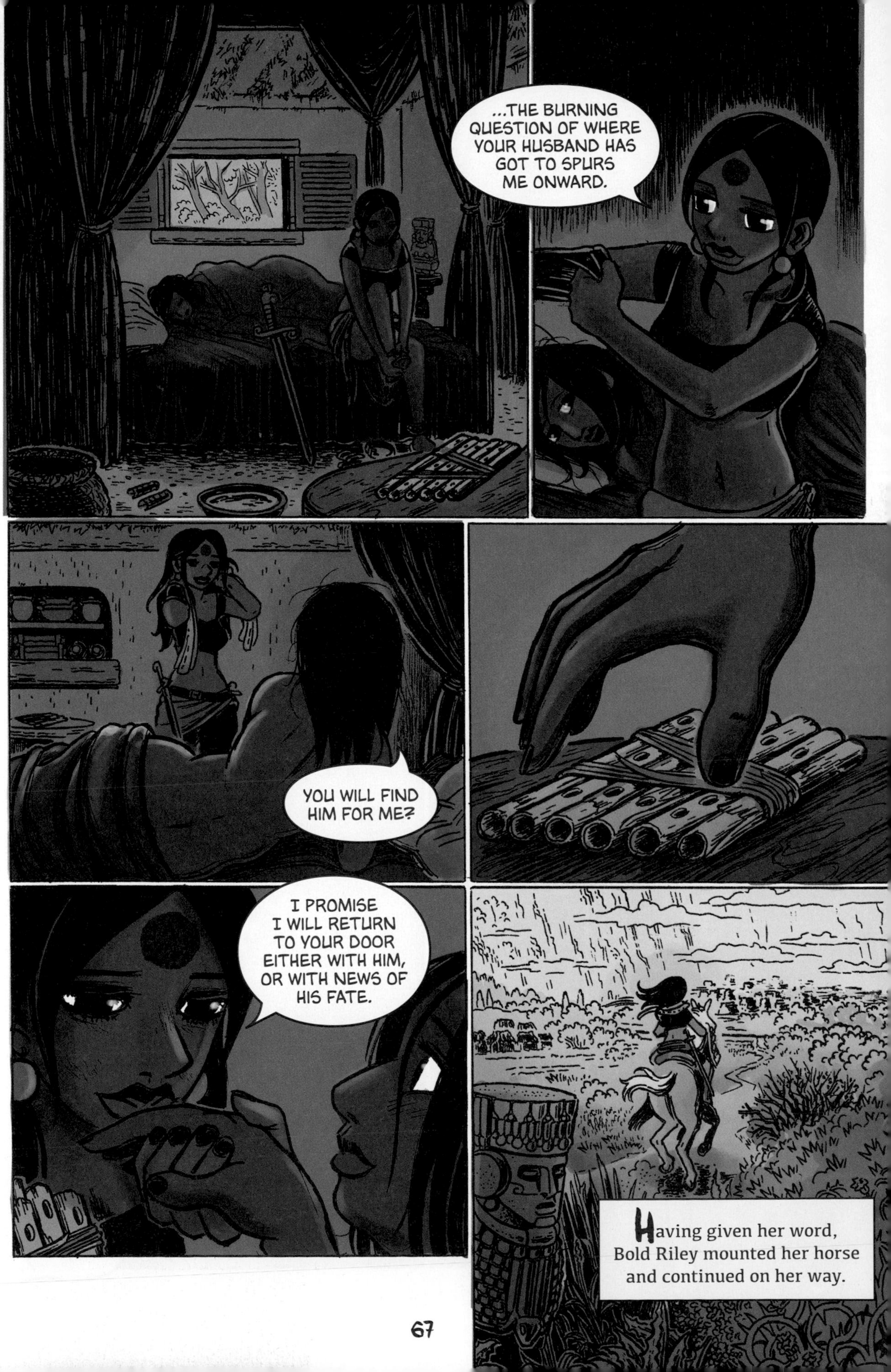
...THE BURNING QUESTION OF WHERE YOUR HUSBAND HAS GOT TO SPURS ME ONWARD.
YOU WILL FIND HIM FOR ME?
I PROMISE I WILL RETURN TO YOUR DOOR EITHER WITH HIM, OR WITH NEWS OF HIS FATE.
Having given her word, Bold Riley mounted her horse and continued on her way.

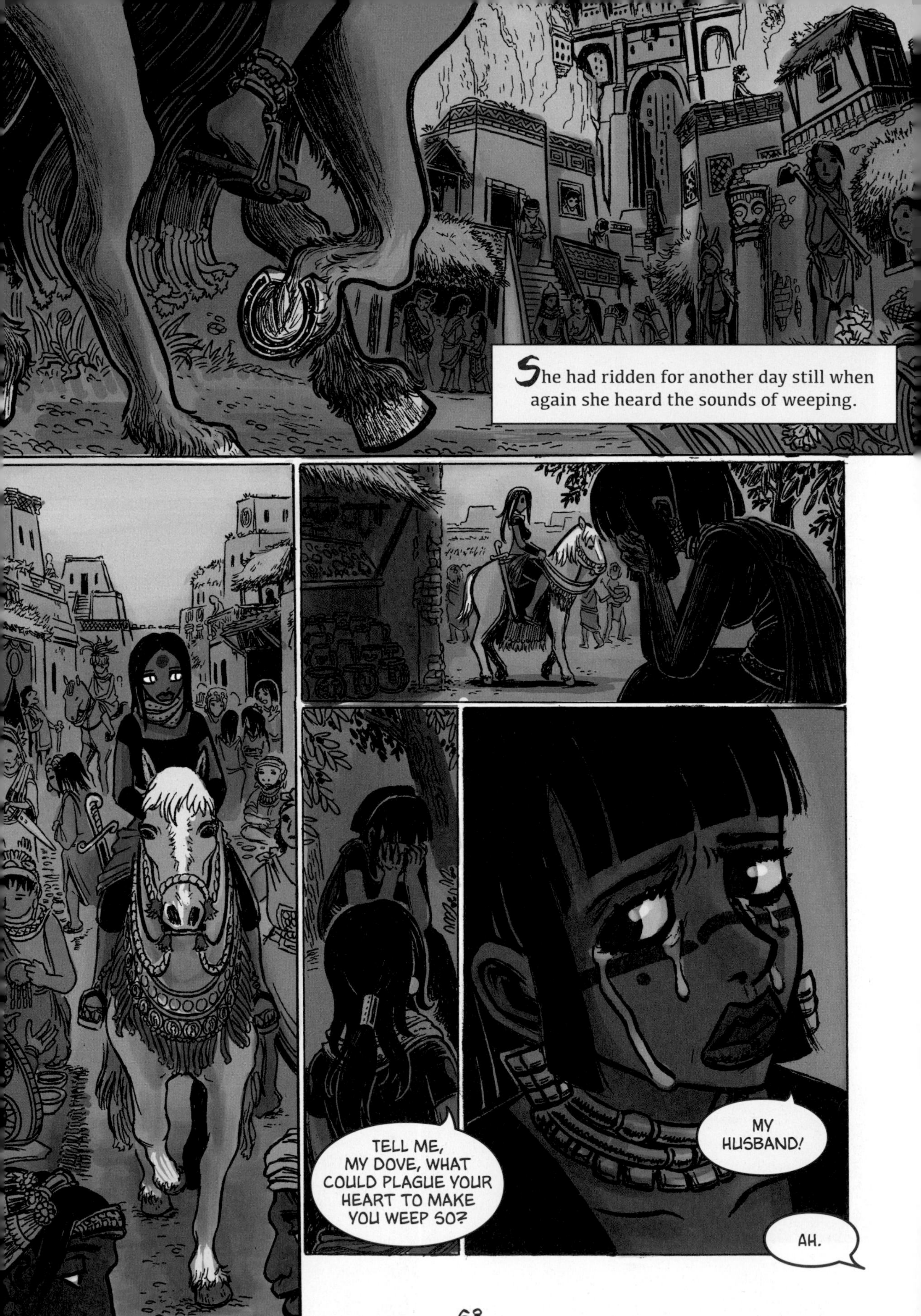
She had ridden for another day still when again she heard the sounds of weeping.
TELL ME, MY DOVE, WHAT COULD PLAGUE YOUR HEART TO MAKE YOU WEEP SO?
MY HUSBAND!
AH.

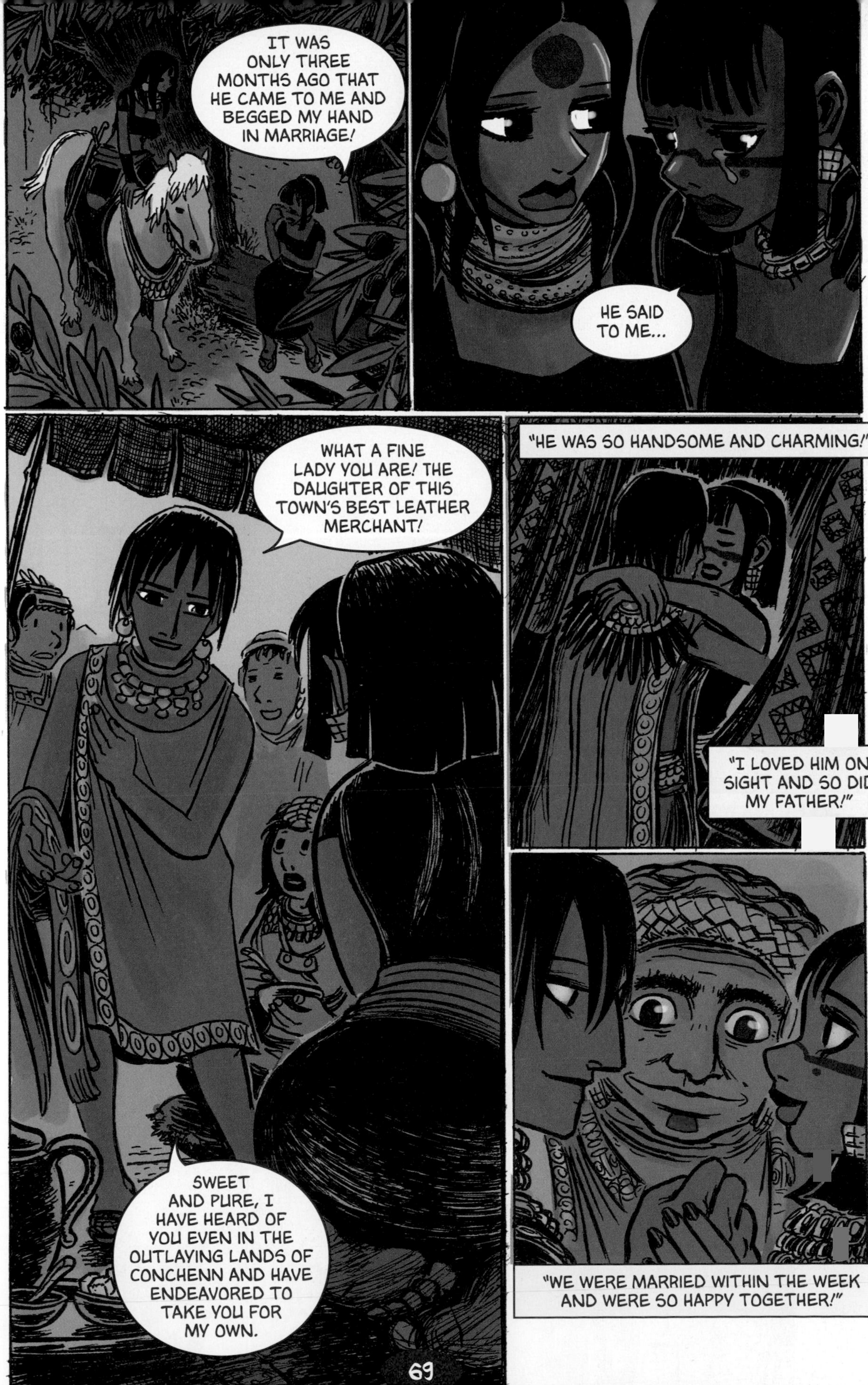
IT WAS ONLY THREE MONTHS AGO THAT HE CAME TO ME AND BEGGED MY HAND IN MARRIAGE!
HE SAID TO ME...
WHAT A FINE LADY YOU ARE! THE DAUGHTER OF THIS TOWN'S BEST LEATHER MERCHANT!
SWEET AND PURE, I HAVE HEARD OF YOU EVEN IN THE OUTLAYING LANDS OF CONCHENN AND HAVE ENDEAVORED TO TAKE YOU FOR MY OWN.
"HE WAS SO HANDSOME AND CHARMING!"
"I LOVED HIM ON SIGHT AND SO DID MY FATHER!"
"WE WERE MARRIED WITHIN THE WEEK AND WERE SO HAPPY TOGETHER!"

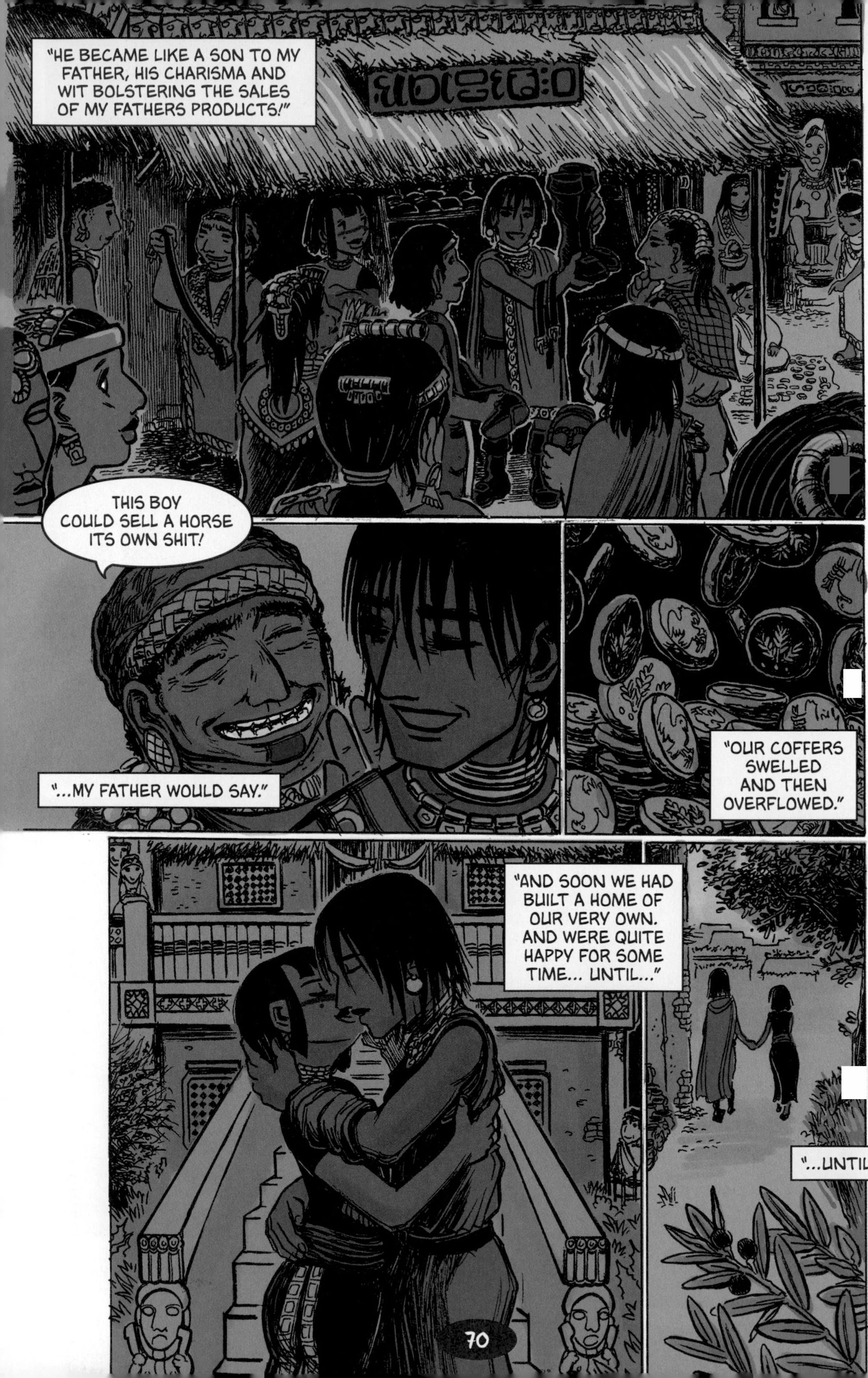
"HE BECAME LIKE A SON TO MY FATHER, HIS CHARISMA AND WIT BOLSTERING THE SALES OF MY FATHERS PRODUCTS!"
THIS BOY COULD SELL A HORSE ITS OWN SHIT!
"...MY FATHER WOULD SAY."
"OUR COFFERS SWELLED AND THEN OVERFLOWED."
"AND SOON WE HAD BUILT A HOME OF OUR VERY OWN. AND WERE QUITE HAPPY FOR SOME TIME... UNTIL..."
"...UNTIL..."

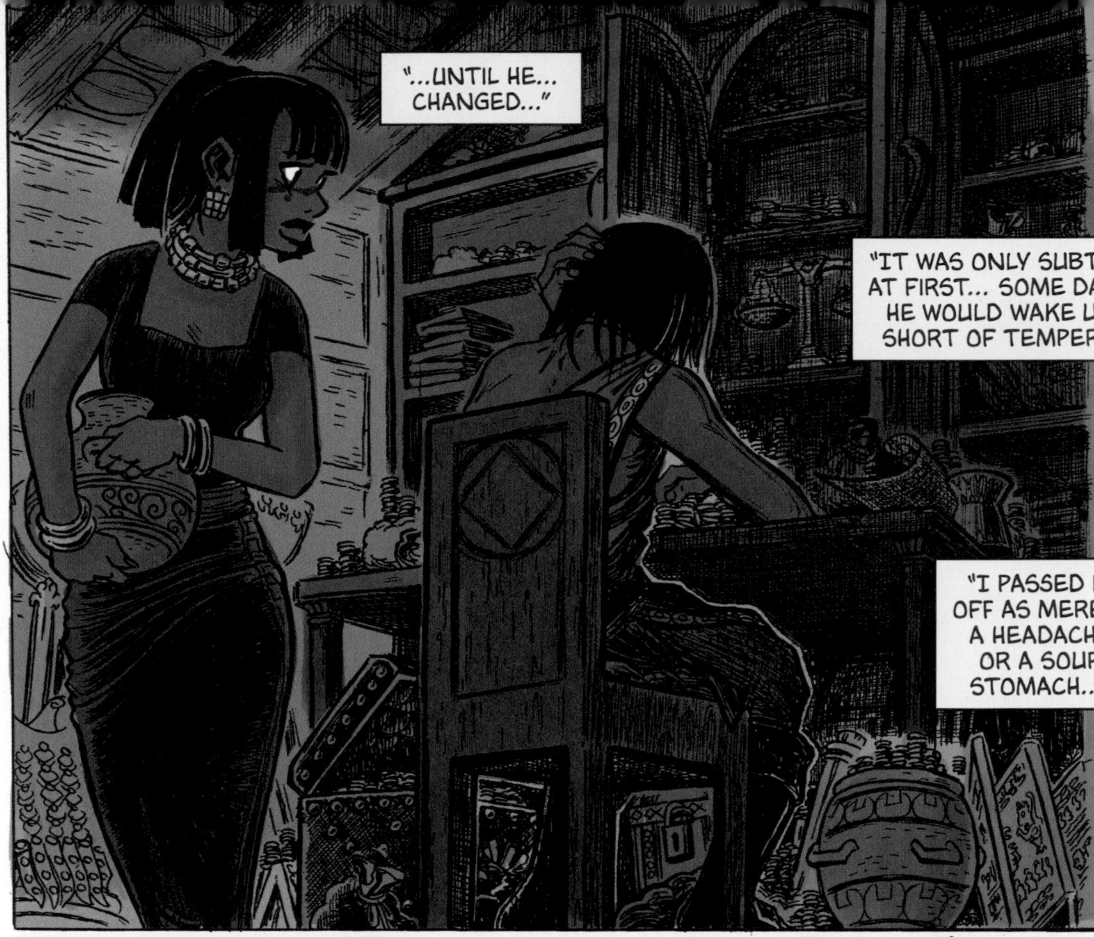
"...UNTIL HE... CHANGED..."
"IT WAS ONLY SUBTLE AT FIRST... SOME DAYS HE WOULD WAKE UP SHORT OF TEMPER."
"I PASSED IT OFF AS MERELY A HEADACHE OR A SOUR STOMACH..."

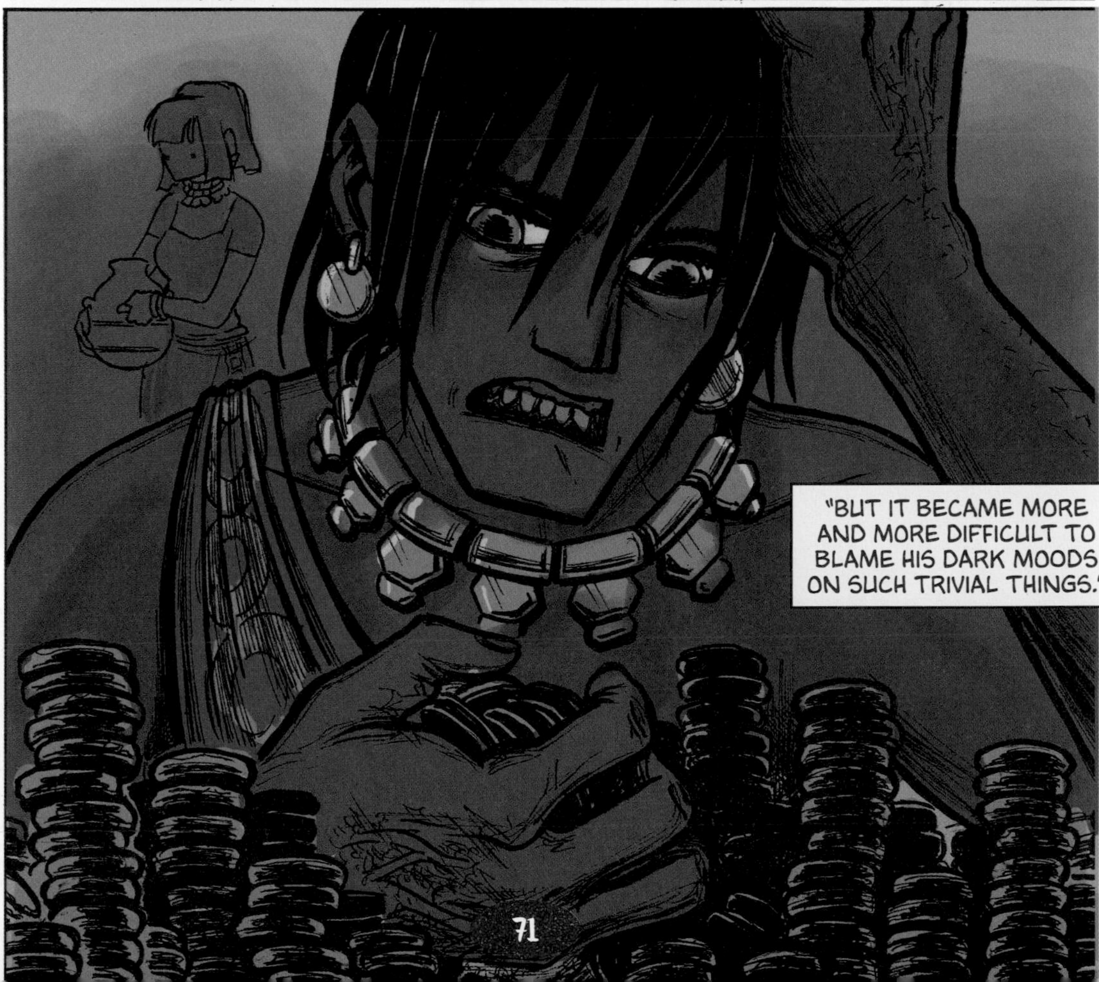
"BUT IT BECAME MORE AND MORE DIFFICULT TO BLAME HIS DARK MOODS ON SUCH TRIVIAL THINGS."

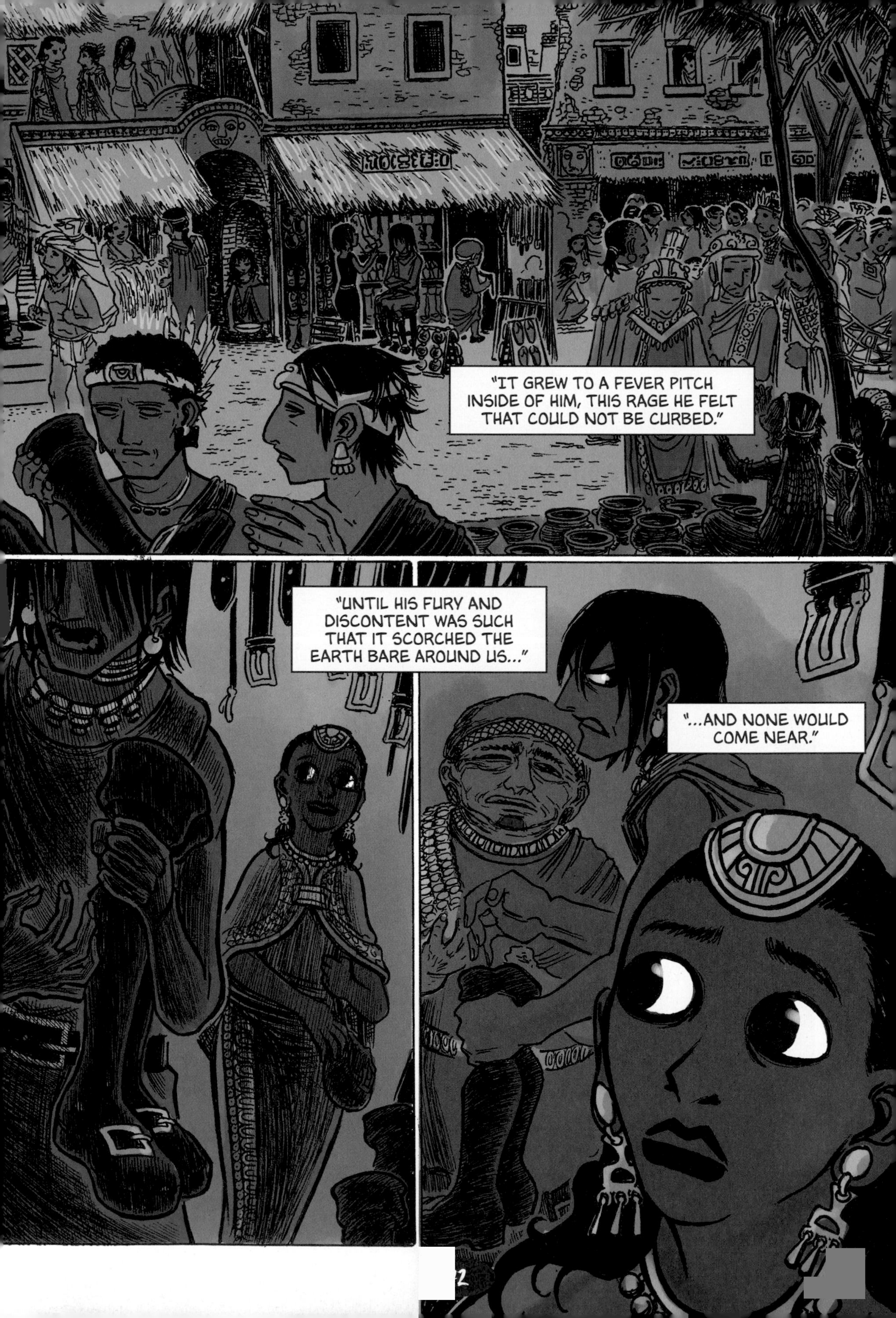
"IT GREW TO A FEVER PITCH INSIDE OF HIM, THIS RAGE HE FELT THAT COULD NOT BE CURBED."
"UNTIL HIS FURY AND DISCONTENT WAS SUCH THAT IT SCORCHED THE EARTH BARE AROUND US..."
"...AND NONE WOULD COME NEAR."

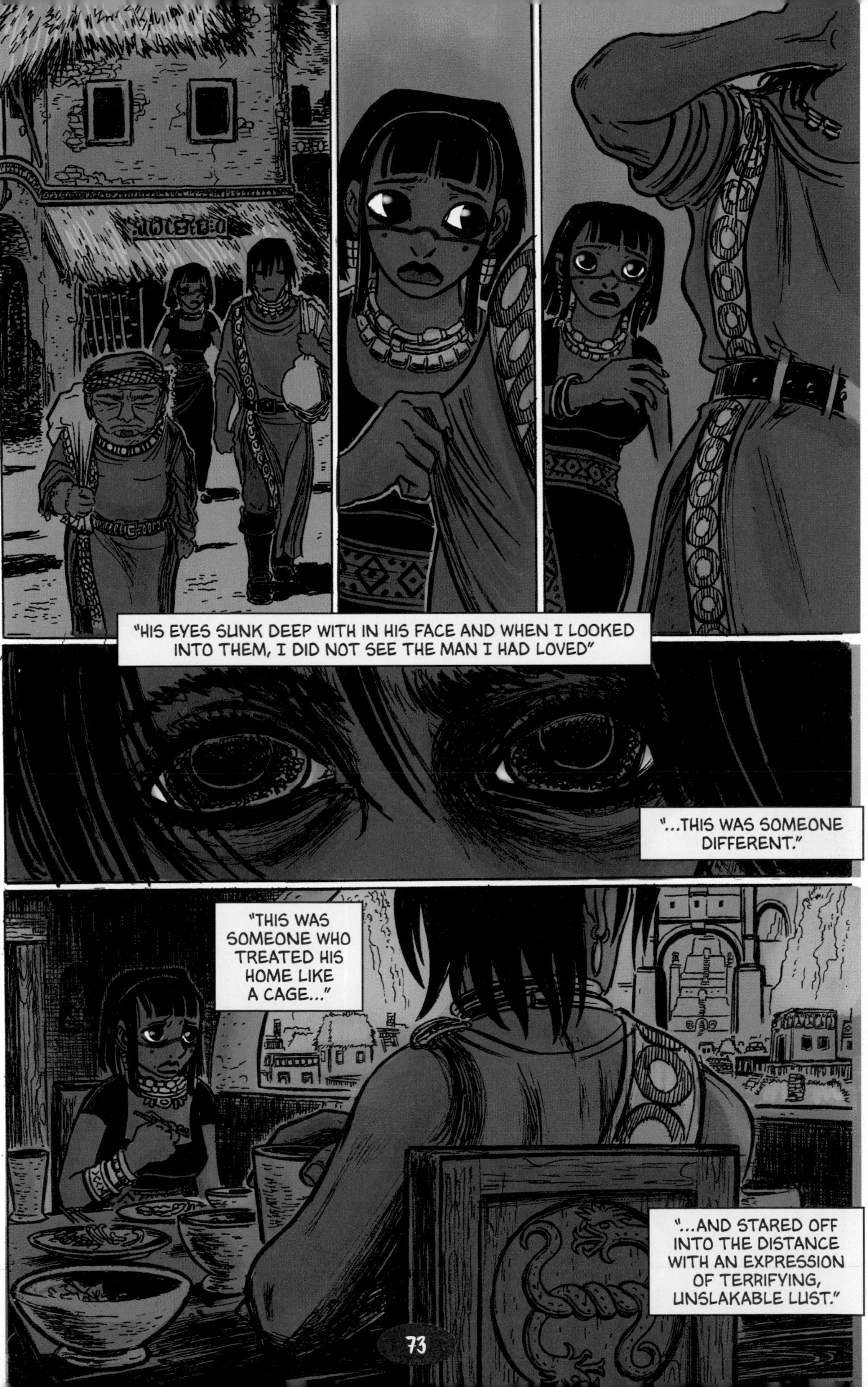
"HIS EYES SUNK DEEP WITH IN HIS FACE AND WHEN I LOOKED INTO THEM, I DID NOT SEE THE MAN I HAD LOVED"
"...THIS WAS SOMEONE DIFFERENT."
"THIS WAS SOMEONE WHO TREATED HIS HOME LIKE A CAGE..."
"...AND STARED OFF INTO THE DISTANCE WITH AN EXPRESSION OF TERRIFYING, UNSLAKABLE LUST."

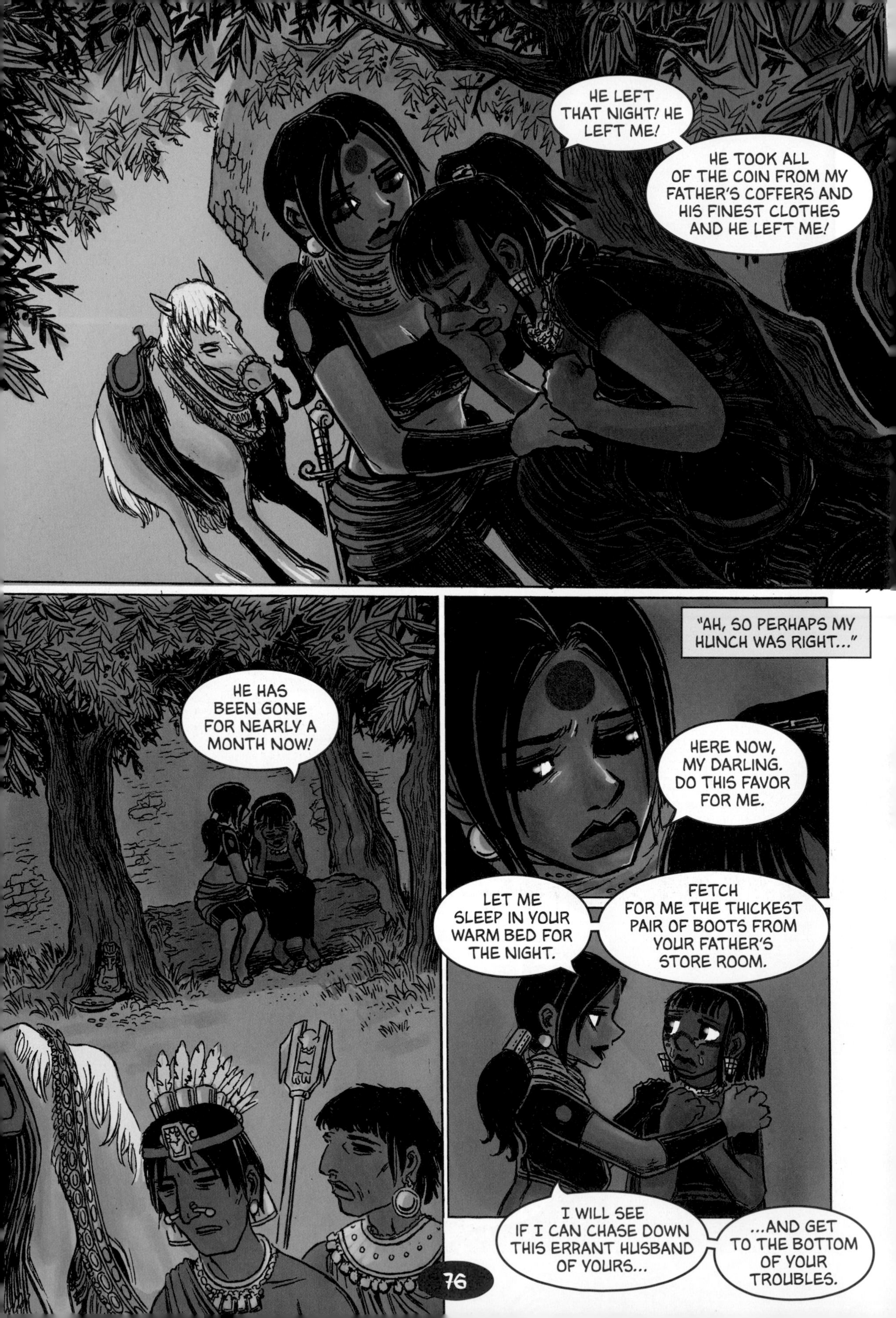
HE LEFT THAT NIGHT! HE LEFT ME!
HE TOOK ALL OF THE COIN FROM MY FATHER'S COFFERS AND HIS FINEST CLOTHES AND HE LEFT ME!
HE HAS BEEN GONE FOR NEARLY A MONTH NOW!
"AH, SO PERHAPS MY HUNCH WAS RIGHT..."
HERE NOW, MY DARLING. DO THIS FAVOR FOR ME.
FETCH FOR ME THE THICKEST PAIR OF BOOTS FROM YOUR FATHER'S STORE ROOM.
LET ME SLEEP IN YOUR WARM BED FOR THE NIGHT.
I WILL SEE IF I CAN CHASE DOWN THIS ERRANT HUSBAND OF YOURS...
...AND GET TO THE BOTTOM OF YOUR TROUBLES.

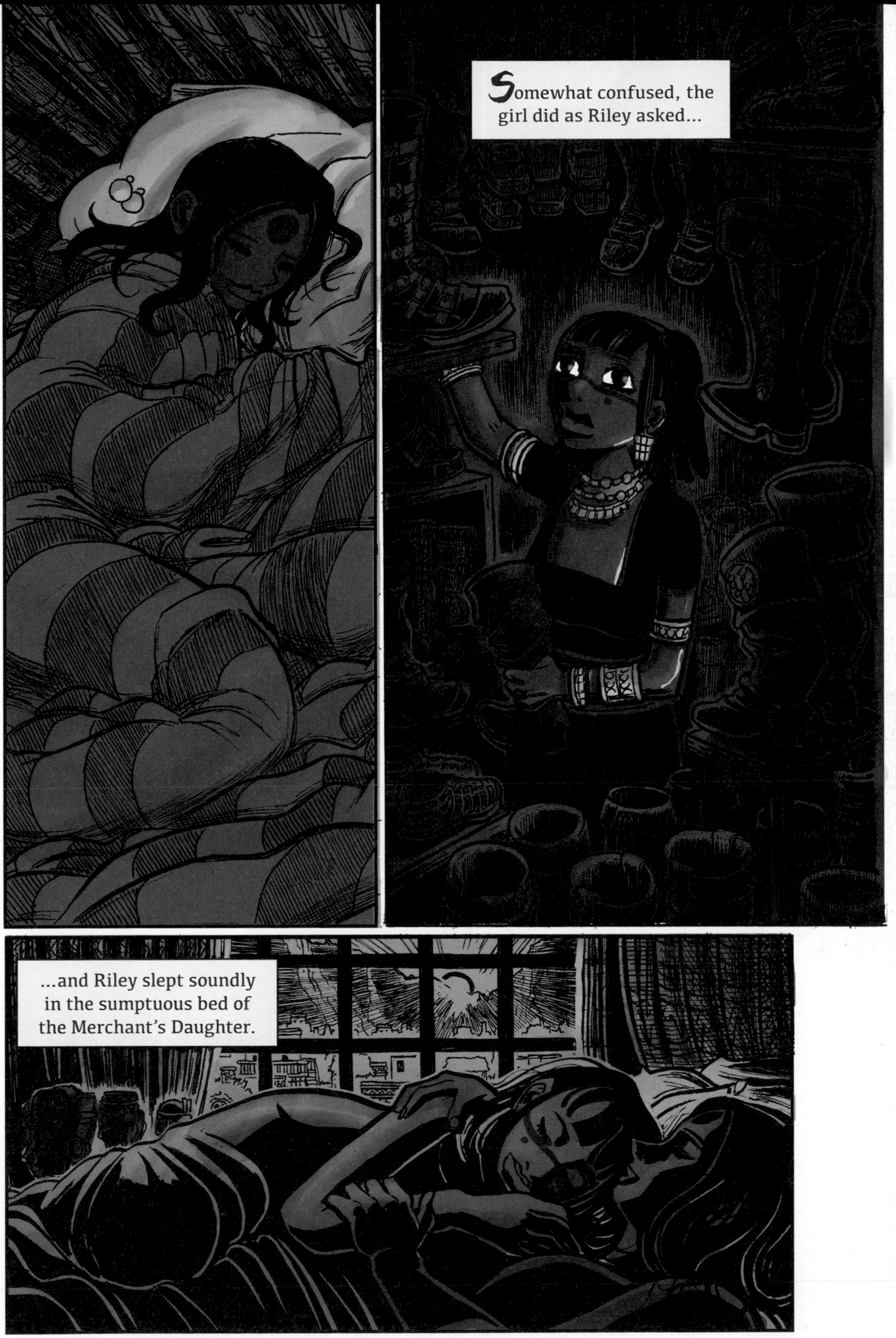
Somewhat confused, the girl did as Riley asked...
...and Riley slept soundly in the sumptuous bed of the Merchant's Daughter.

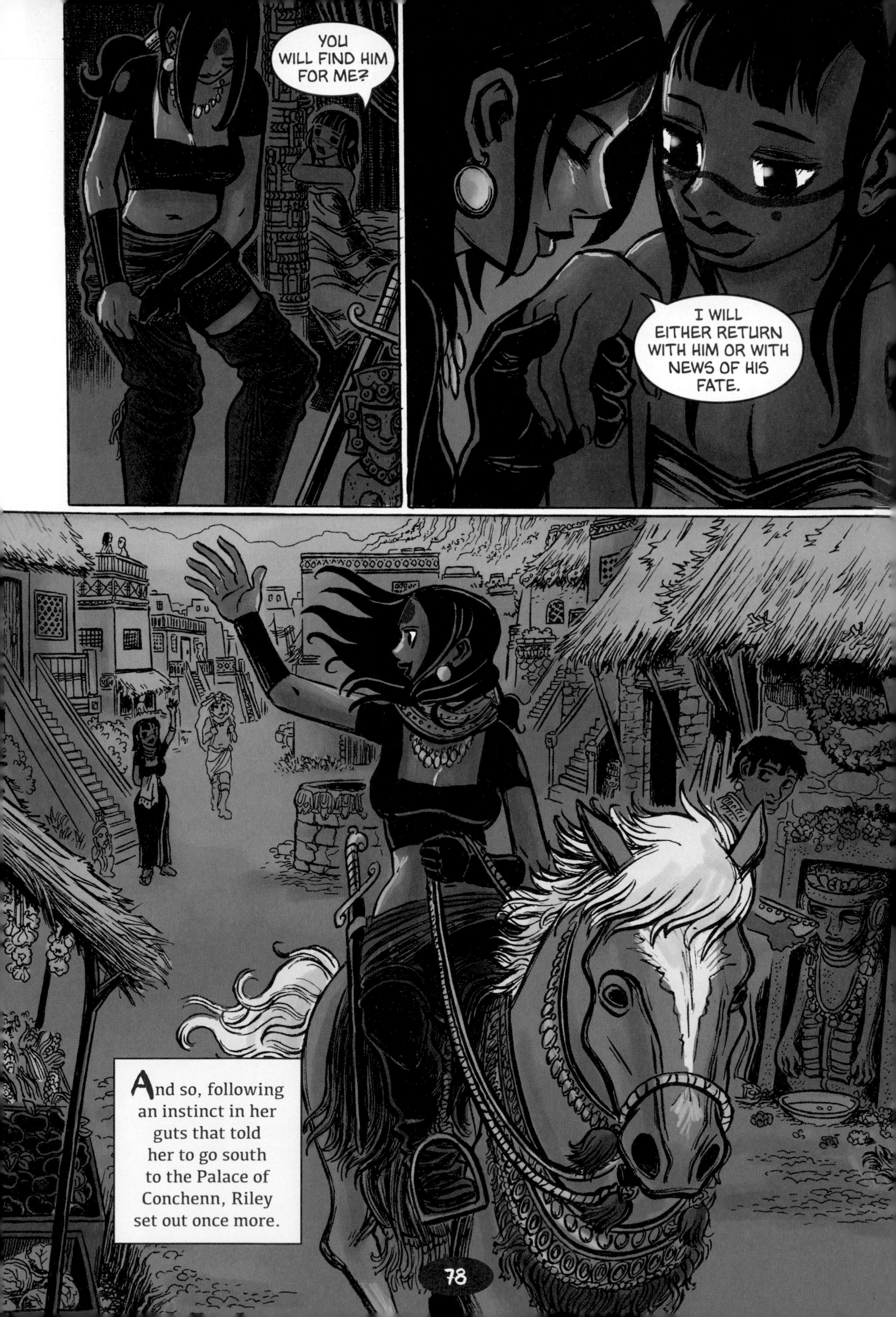
YOU WILL FIND HIM FOR ME?
I WILL EITHER RETURN WITH HIM OR WITH NEWS OF HIS FATE.
And so, following an instinct in her guts that told her to go south to the Palace of Conchenn, Riley set out once more.

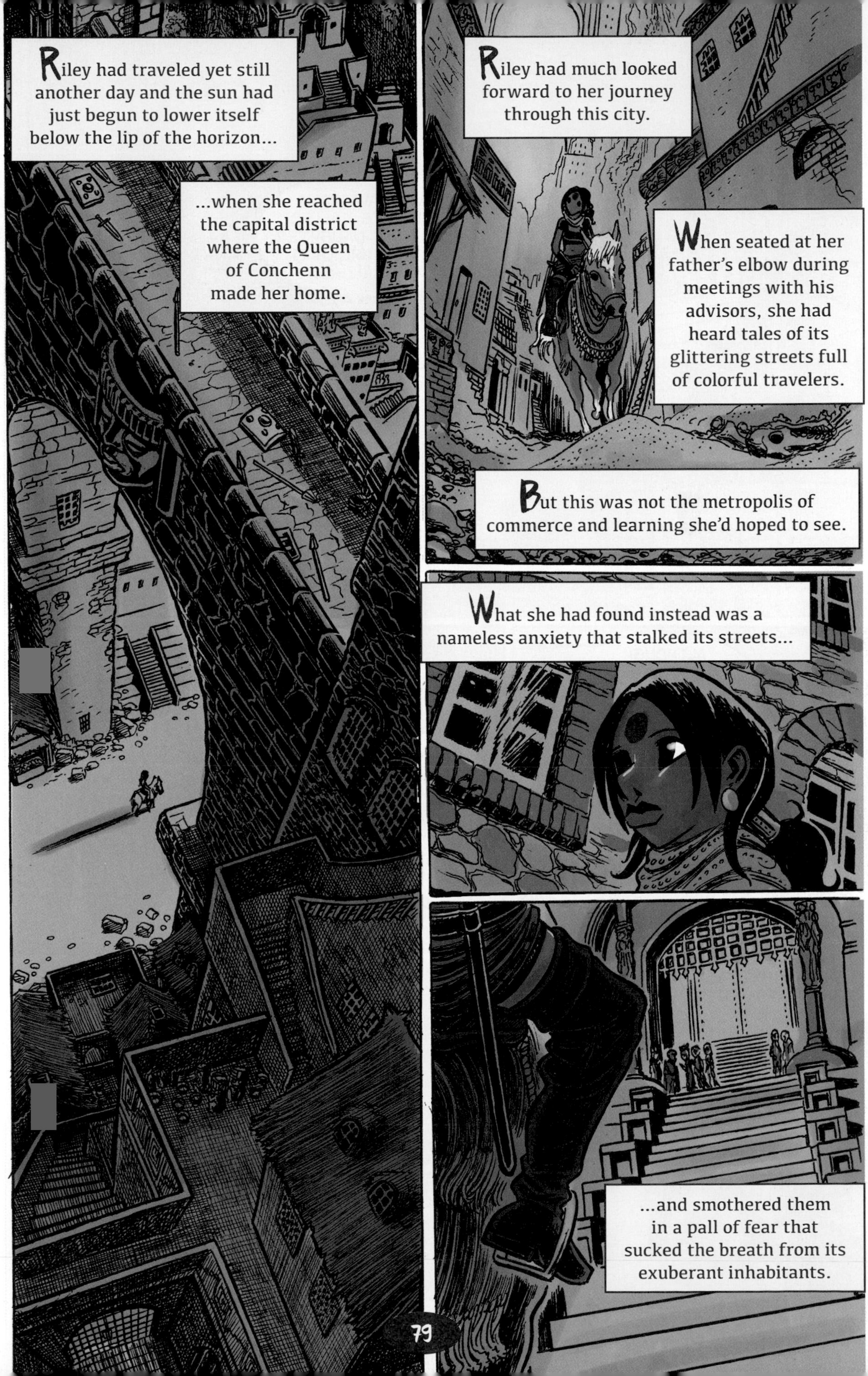
Riley had traveled yet still another day and the sun had just begun to lower itself below the lip of the horizon...
...when she reached the capital district where the Queen of Conchenn made her home.
Riley had much looked forward to her journey through this city.
When seated at her father's elbow during meetings with his advisors, she had heard tales of its glittering streets full of colorful travelers.
But this was not the metropolis of commerce and learning she'd hoped to see.
What she had found instead was a nameless anxiety that stalked its streets...
...and smothered them in a pall of fear that sucked the breath from its exuberant inhabitants.

I AM RILAVASHANA SANPARITE, CALLED BOLD RILEY, DAUGHTER OF THE THRONE IN PRAKKALORE.

COME TO SEE THE SPLENDOR OF YOUR LANDS AND CALL UPON YOUR MOST ESTEEMED QUEEN.

ALTHOUGH IT APPEARS I HAVE ARRIVED AT AN INCONVENIENT TIME.

"INCONVENIENT" IS THE GROSSEST OF UNDERSTATEMENTS, LADY.

OUR QUEEN HAS GONE MAD.

OH?

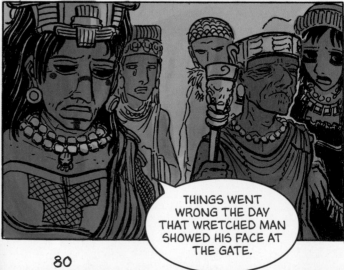

THINGS WENT WRONG THE DAY THAT WRETCHED MAN SHOWED HIS FACE AT THE GATE.

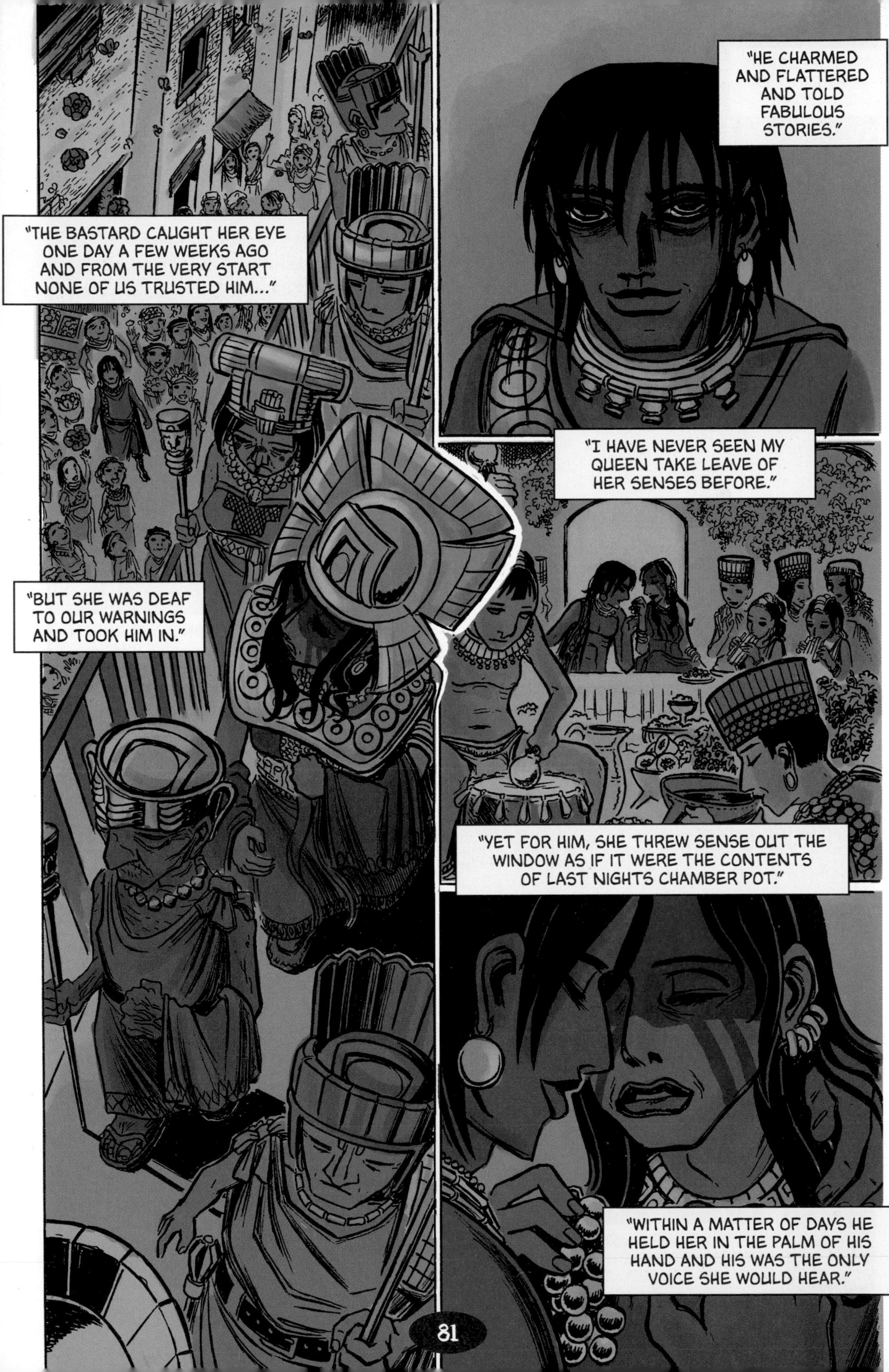
"THE BASTARD CAUGHT HER EYE ONE DAY A FEW WEEKS AGO AND FROM THE VERY START NONE OF US TRUSTED HIM..."
"BUT SHE WAS DEAF TO OUR WARNINGS AND TOOK HIM IN."
"HE CHARMED AND FLATTERED AND TOLD FABULOUS STORIES."
"I HAVE NEVER SEEN MY QUEEN TAKE LEAVE OF HER SENSES BEFORE."
"YET FOR HIM, SHE THREW SENSE OUT THE WINDOW AS IF IT WERE THE CONTENTS OF LAST NIGHTS CHAMBER POT."
"WITHIN A MATTER OF DAYS HE HELD HER IN THE PALM OF HIS HAND AND HIS WAS THE ONLY VOICE SHE WOULD HEAR."

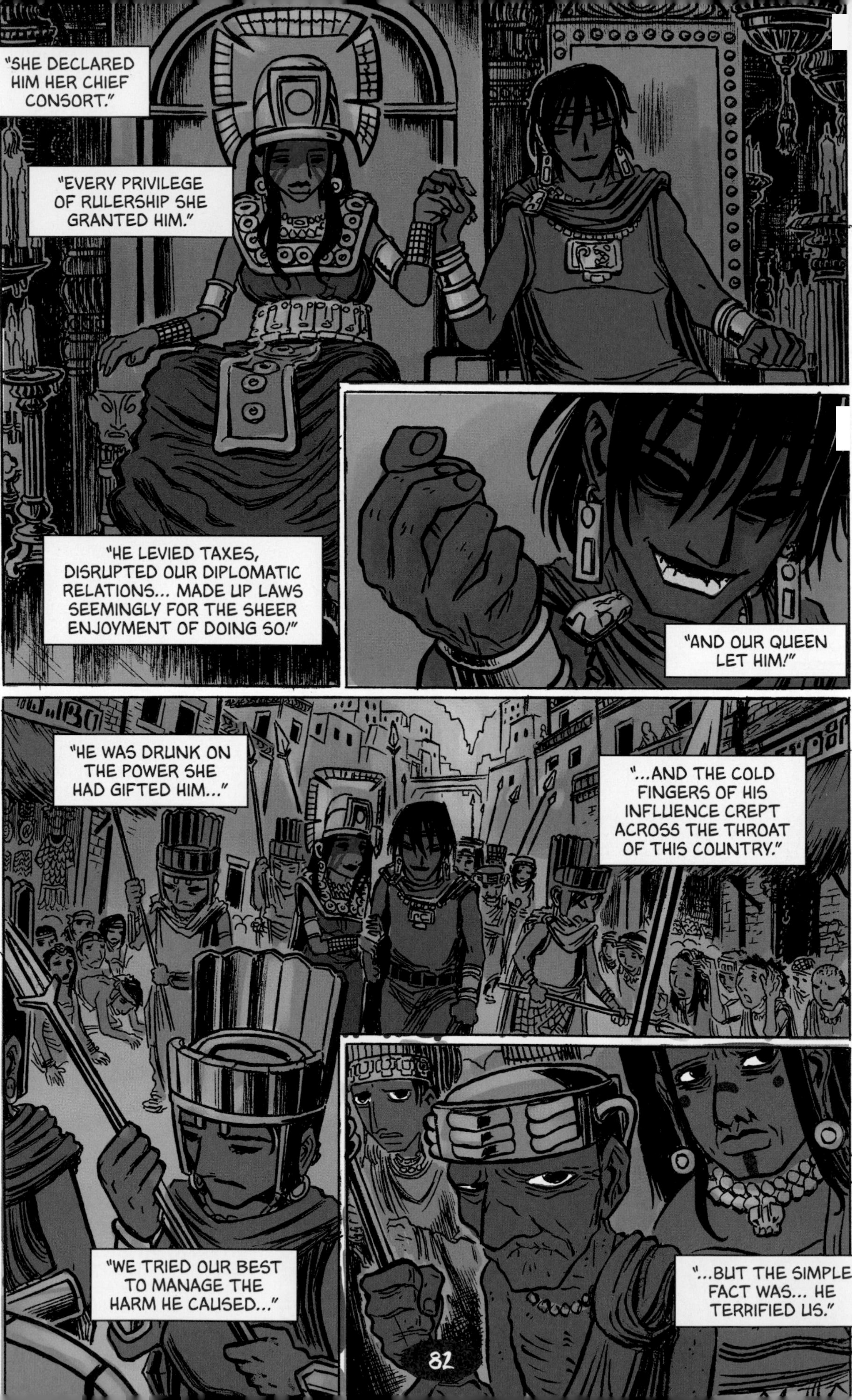
"SHE DECLARED HIM HER CHIEF CONSORT."
"EVERY PRIVILEGE OF RULERSHIP SHE GRANTED HIM."
"HE LEVIED TAXES, DISRUPTED OUR DIPLOMATIC RELATIONS... MADE UP LAWS SEEMINGLY FOR THE SHEER ENJOYMENT OF DOING SO!"
"AND OUR QUEEN LET HIM!"
"HE WAS DRUNK ON THE POWER SHE HAD GIFTED HIM..."
"...AND THE COLD FINGERS OF HIS INFLUENCE CREPT ACROSS THE THROAT OF THIS COUNTRY."
"WE TRIED OUR BEST TO MANAGE THE HARM HE CAUSED..."
"...BUT THE SIMPLE FACT WAS... HE TERRIFIED US."

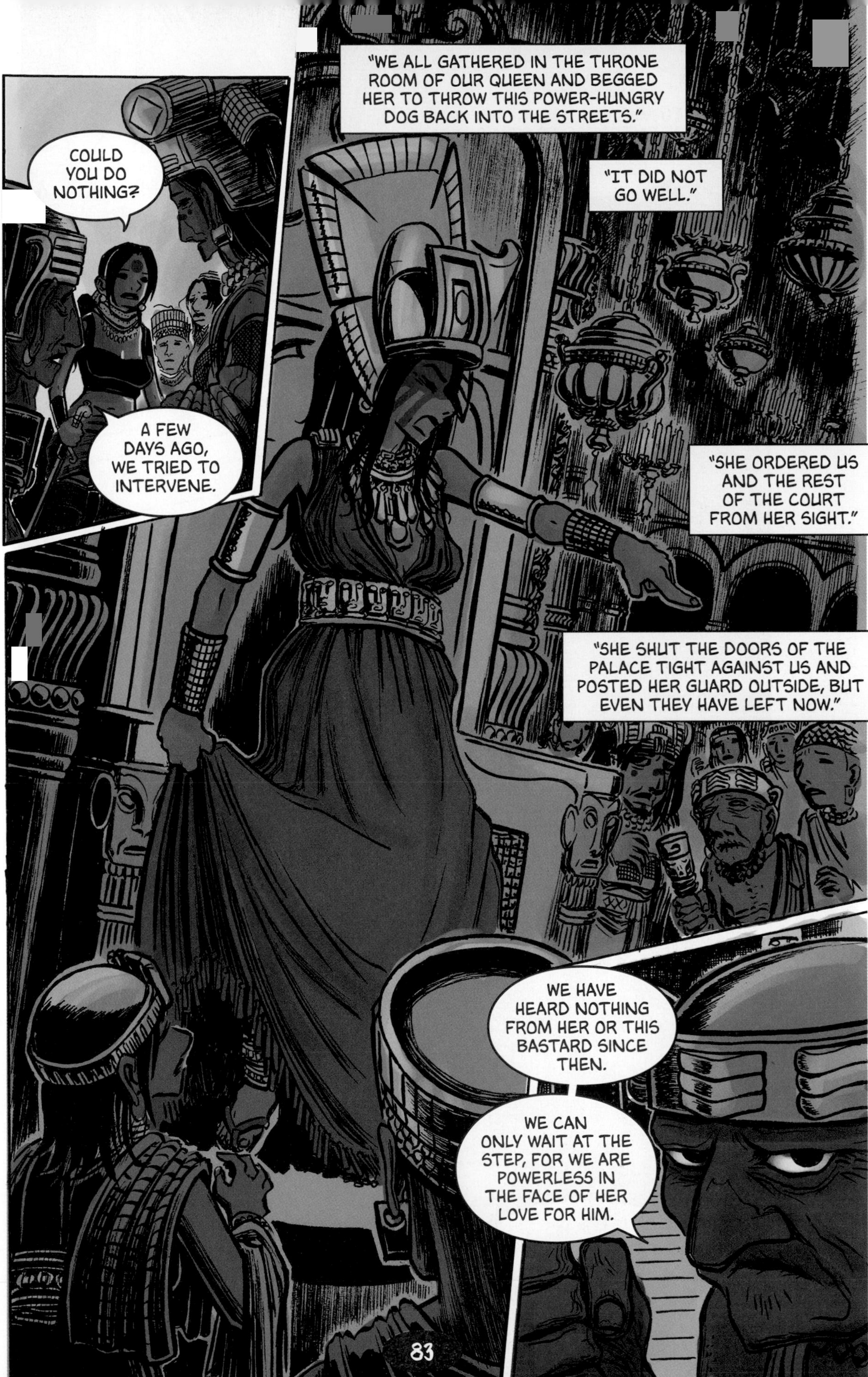
COULD YOU DO NOTHING?
A FEW DAYS AGO, WE TRIED TO INTERVENE.
"WE ALL GATHERED IN THE THRONE ROOM OF OUR QUEEN AND BEGGED HER TO THROW THIS POWER-HUNGRY DOG BACK INTO THE STREETS."
"IT DID NOT GO WELL."
"SHE ORDERED US AND THE REST OF THE COURT FROM HER SIGHT."
"SHE SHUT THE DOORS OF THE PALACE TIGHT AGAINST US AND POSTED HER GUARD OUTSIDE, BUT EVEN THEY HAVE LEFT NOW."
WE HAVE HEARD NOTHING FROM HER OR THIS BASTARD SINCE THEN.
WE CAN ONLY WAIT AT THE STEP, FOR WE ARE POWERLESS IN THE FACE OF HER LOVE FOR HIM.

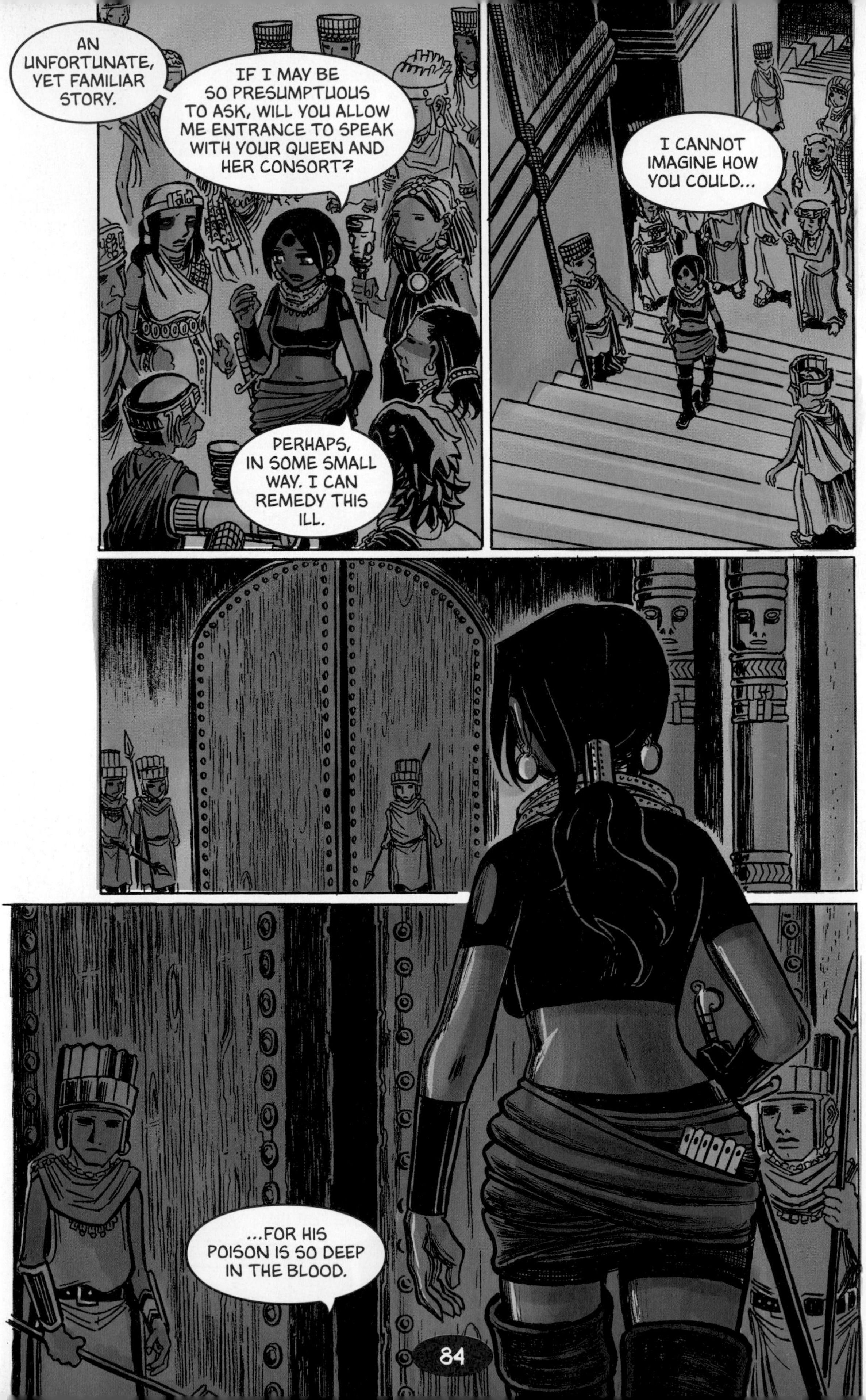
AN UNFORTUNATE, YET FAMILIAR STORY.
IF I MAY BE SO PRESUMPTUOUS TO ASK, WILL YOU ALLOW ME ENTRANCE TO SPEAK WITH YOUR QUEEN AND HER CONSORT?
PERHAPS, IN SOME SMALL WAY, I CAN REMEDY THIS ILL.
I CANNOT IMAGINE HOW YOU COULD...
...FOR HIS POISON IS SO DEEP IN THE BLOOD.

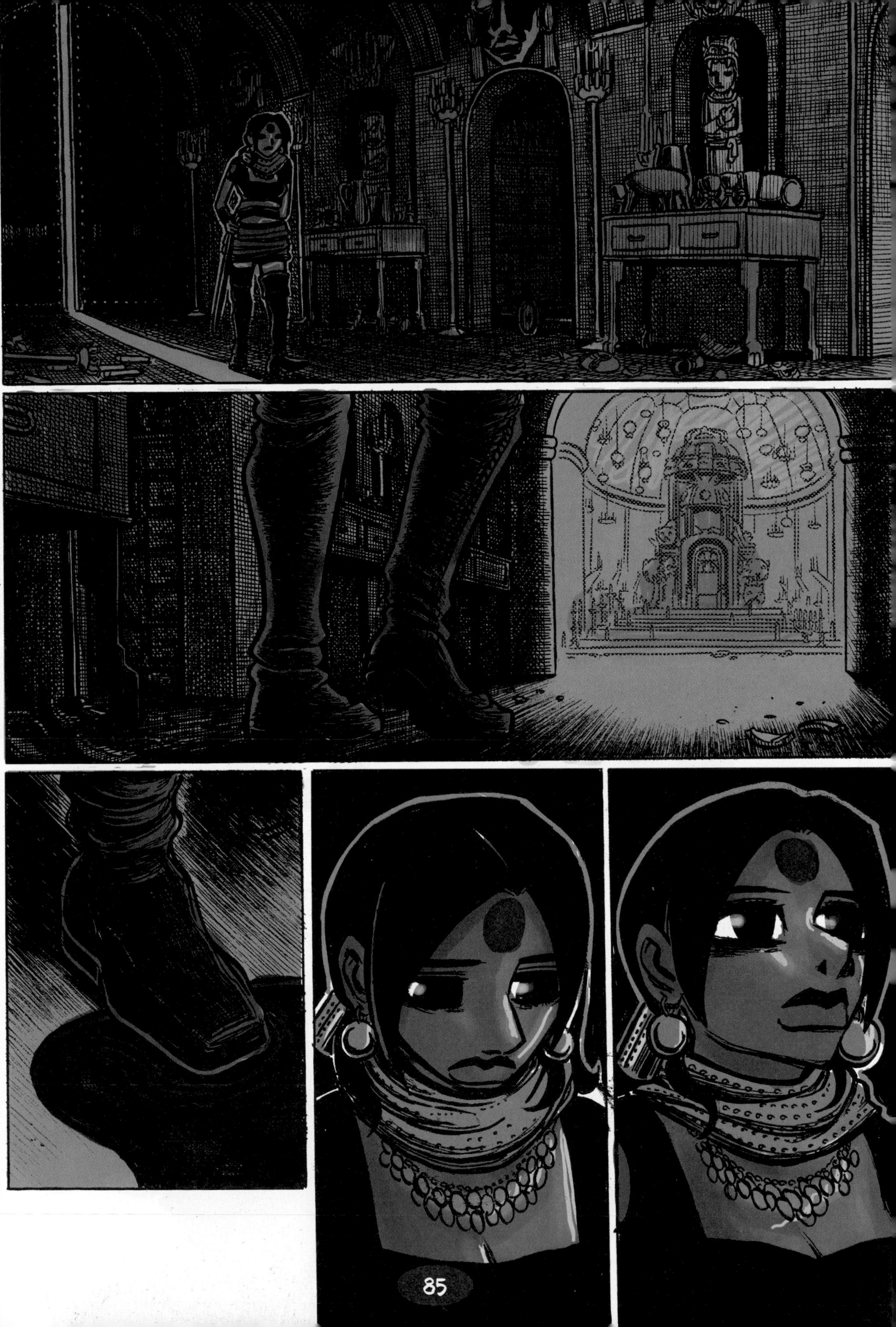

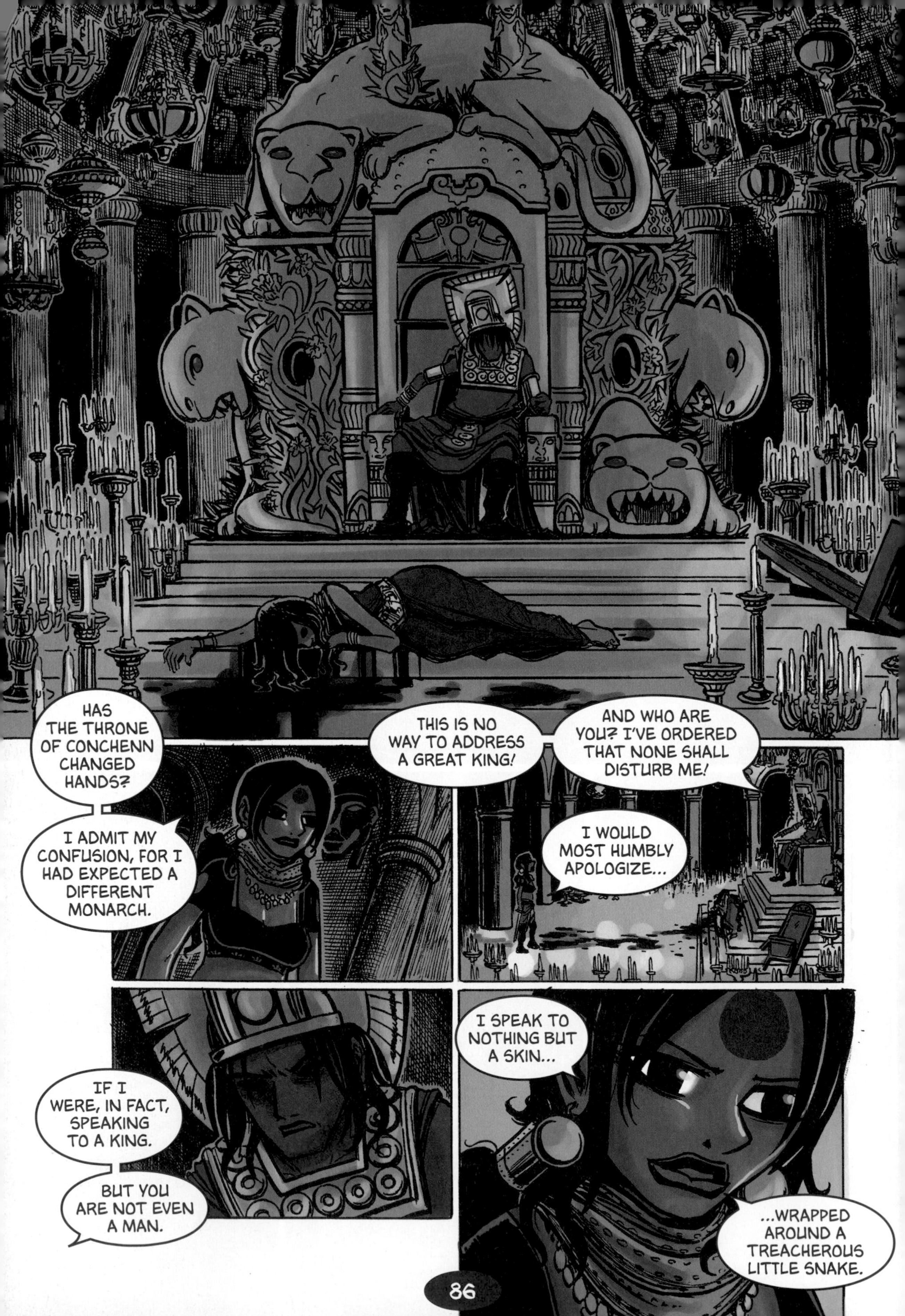
HAS THE THRONE OF CONCHENN CHANGED HANDS?
I ADMIT MY CONFUSION, FOR I HAD EXPECTED A DIFFERENT MONARCH.
THIS IS NO WAY TO ADDRESS A GREAT KING!
AND WHO ARE YOU? I'VE ORDERED THAT NONE SHALL DISTURB ME!
I WOULD MOST HUMBLY APOLOGIZE...
IF I WERE, IN FACT, SPEAKING TO A KING.
BUT YOU ARE NOT EVEN A MAN.
I SPEAK TO NOTHING BUT A SKIN...
...WRAPPED AROUND A TREACHEROUS LITTLE SNAKE.

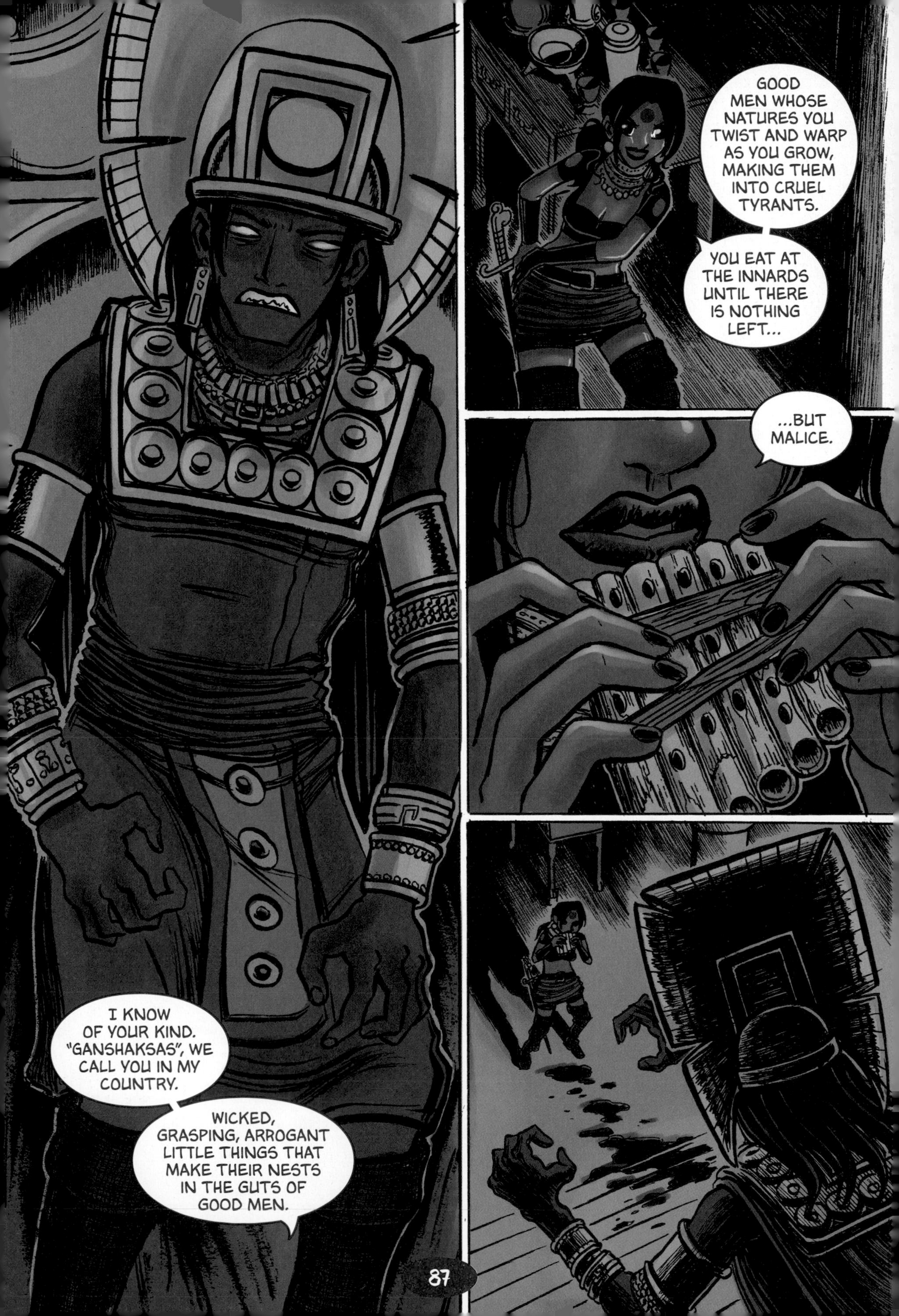
I KNOW OF YOUR KIND. "GANSHAKSAS", WE CALL YOU IN MY COUNTRY.
WICKED, GRASPING, ARROGANT LITTLE THINGS THAT MAKE THEIR NESTS IN THE GUTS OF GOOD MEN.
GOOD MEN WHOSE NATURES YOU TWIST AND WARP AS YOU GROW, MAKING THEM INTO CRUEL TYRANTS.
YOU EAT AT THE INNARDS UNTIL THERE IS NOTHING LEFT...
...BUT MALICE.

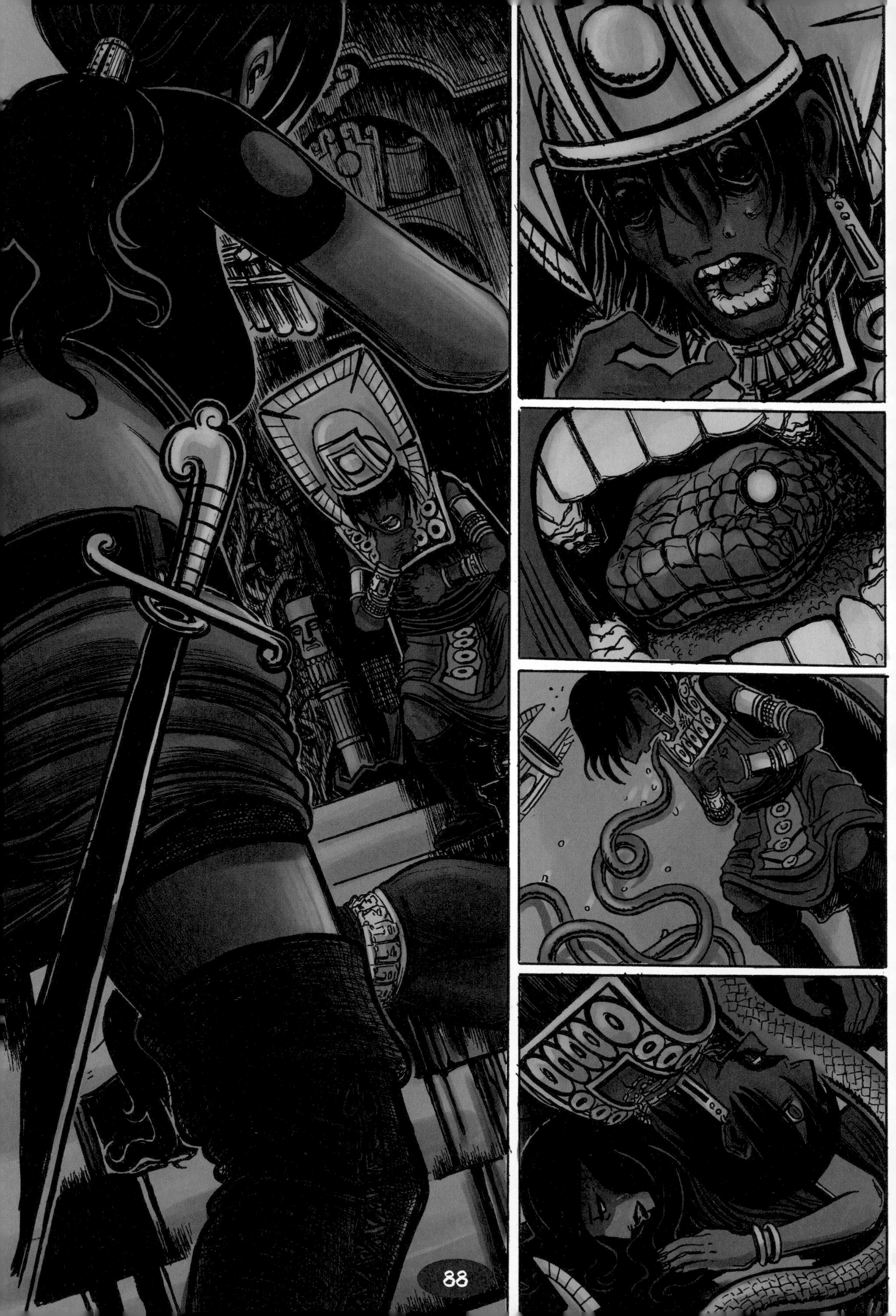

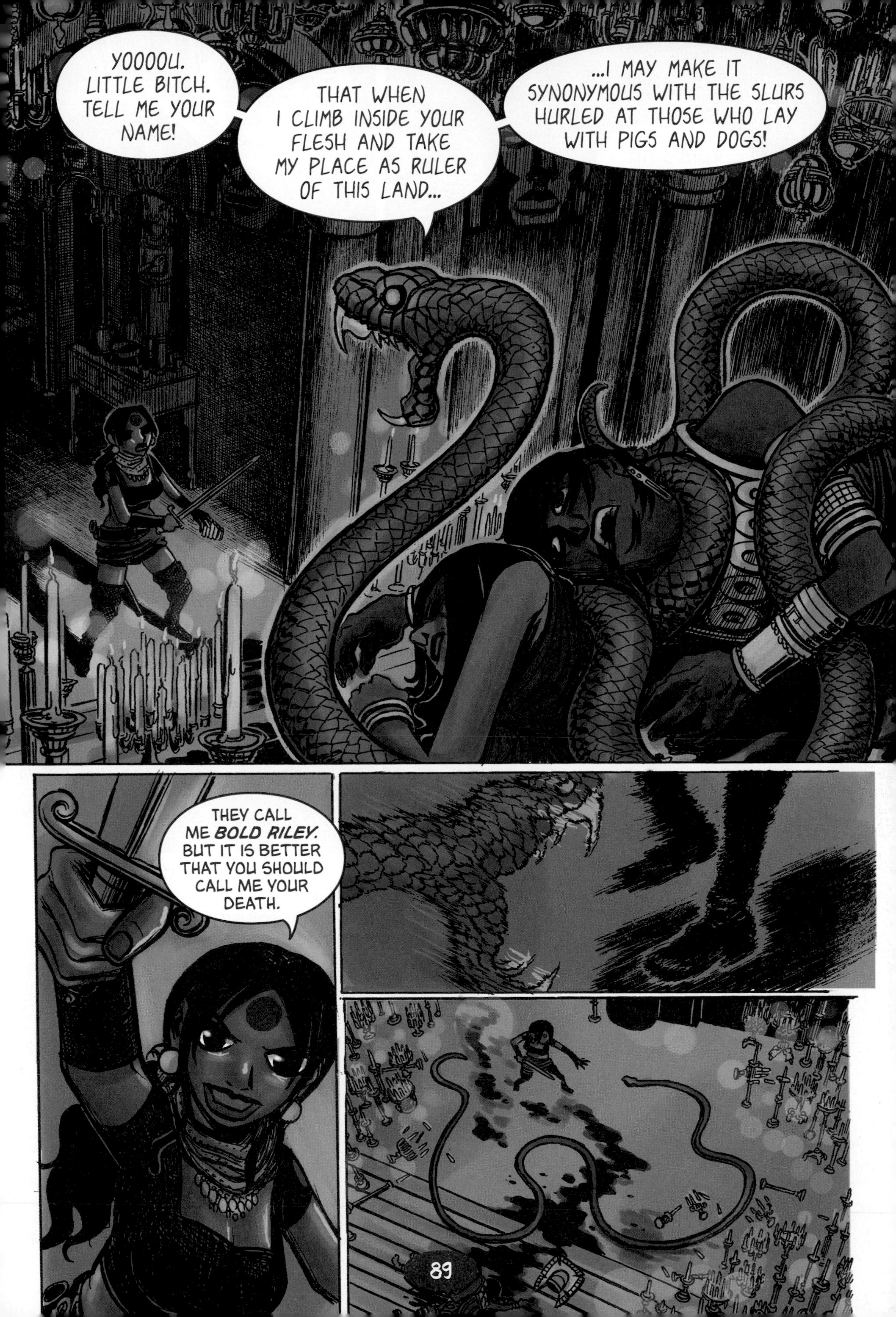
YOOOOU. LITTLE BITCH. TELL ME YOUR NAME!
THAT WHEN I CLIMB INSIDE YOUR FLESH AND TAKE MY PLACE AS RULER OF THIS LAND...
...I MAY MAKE IT SYNONYMOUS WITH THE SLURS HURLED AT THOSE WHO LAY WITH PIGS AND DOGS!
THEY CALL ME *BOLD RILEY.* BUT IT IS BETTER THAT YOU SHOULD CALL ME YOUR DEATH.

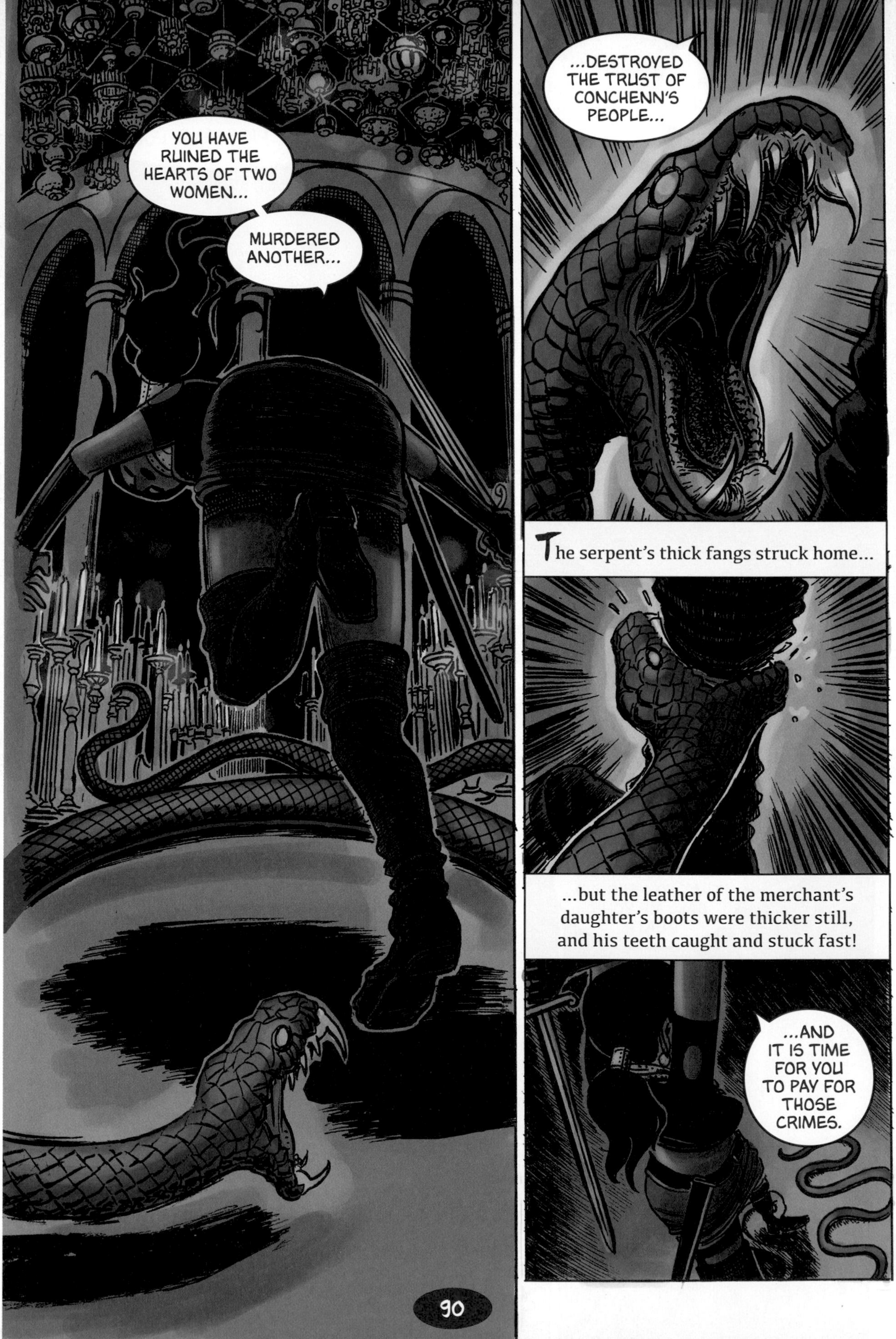
YOU HAVE RUINED THE HEARTS OF TWO WOMEN...
MURDERED ANOTHER...
...DESTROYED THE TRUST OF CONCHENN'S PEOPLE...
The serpent's thick fangs struck home...
...but the leather of the merchant's daughter's boots were thicker still, and his teeth caught and stuck fast!
...AND IT IS TIME FOR YOU TO PAY FOR THOSE CRIMES.

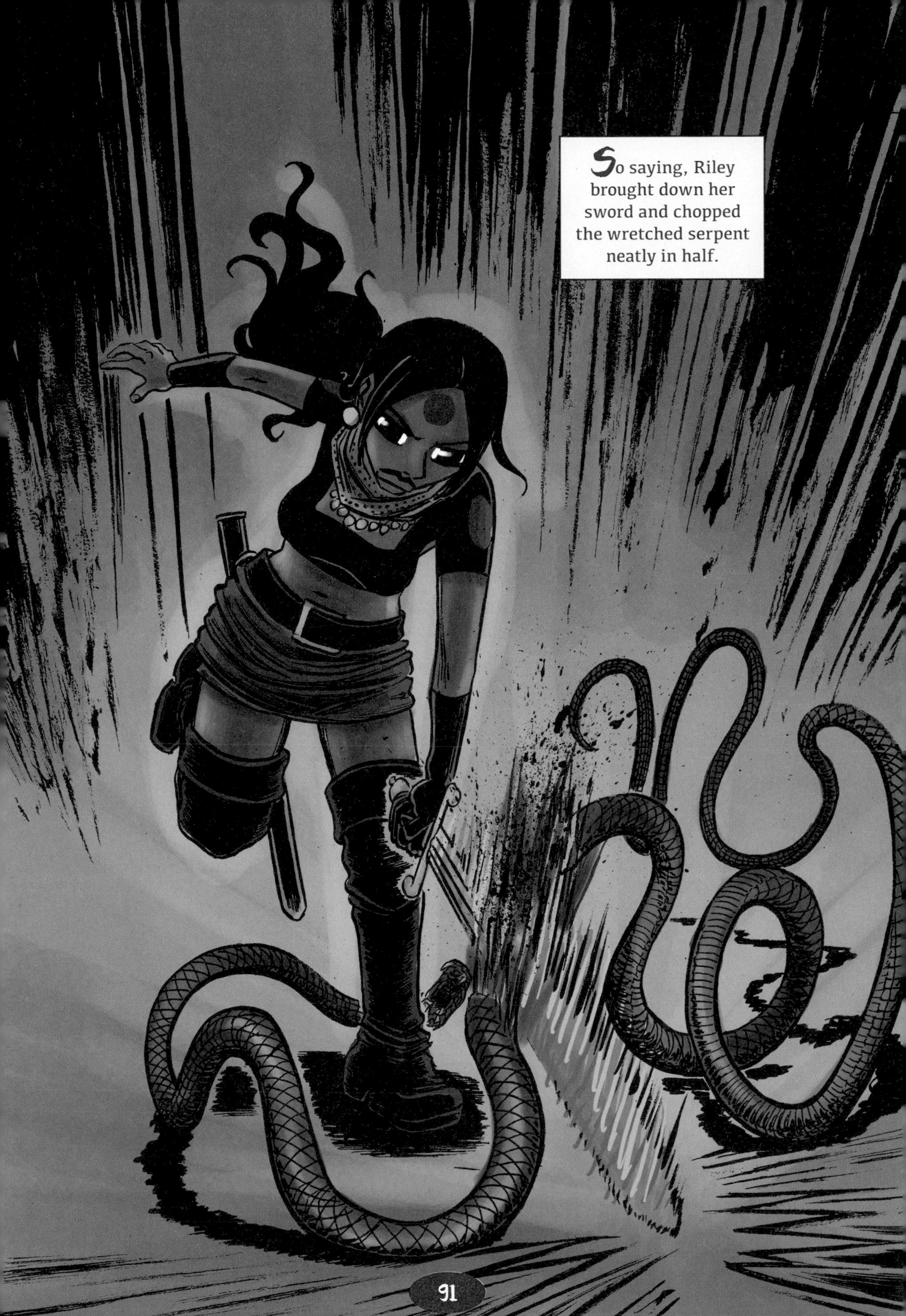
So saying, Riley brought down her sword and chopped the wretched serpent neatly in half.

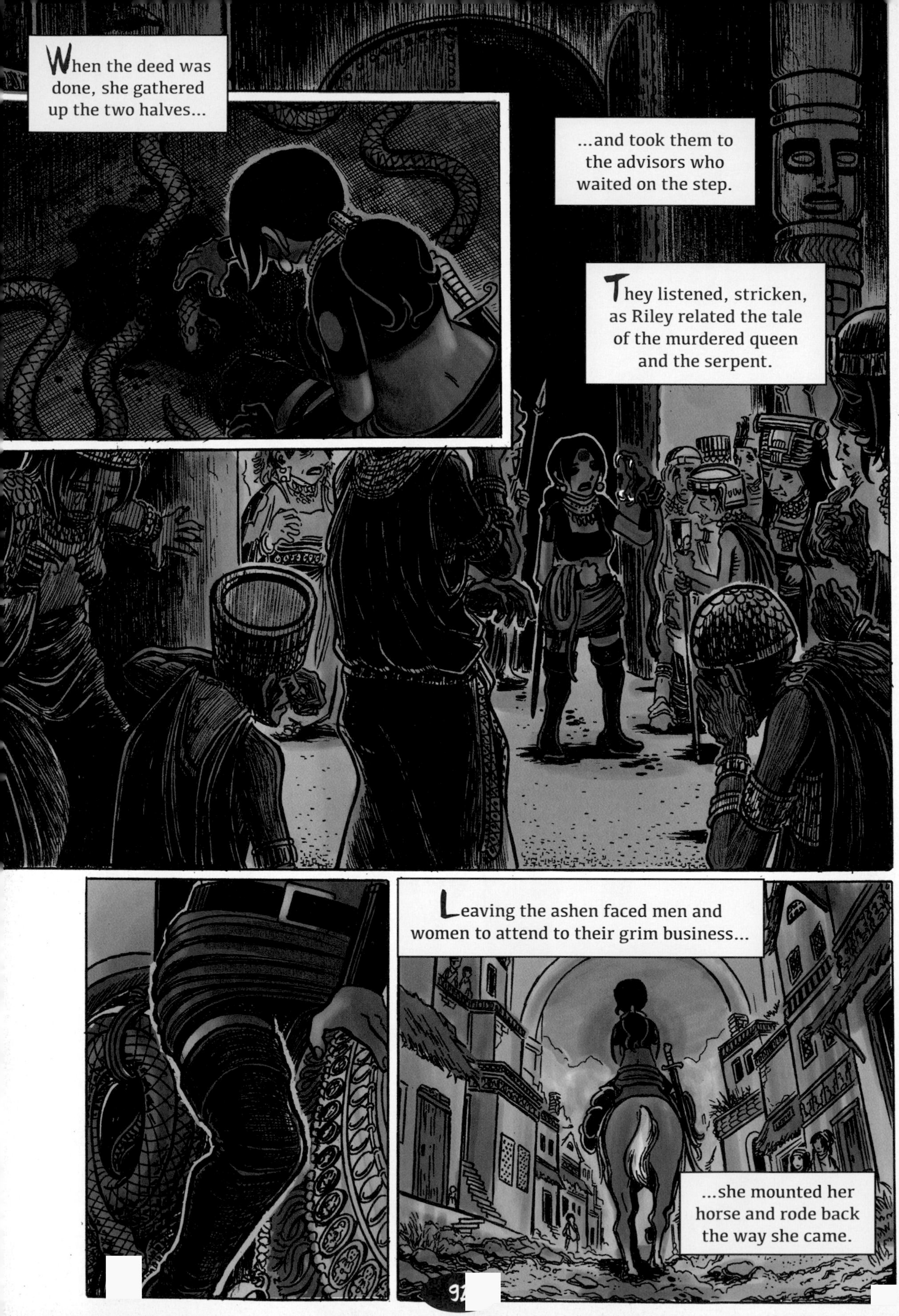
When the deed was done, she gathered up the two halves...
...and took them to the advisors who waited on the step.
They listened, stricken, as Riley related the tale of the murdered queen and the serpent.
Leaving the ashen faced men and women to attend to their grim business...
...she mounted her horse and rode back the way she came.

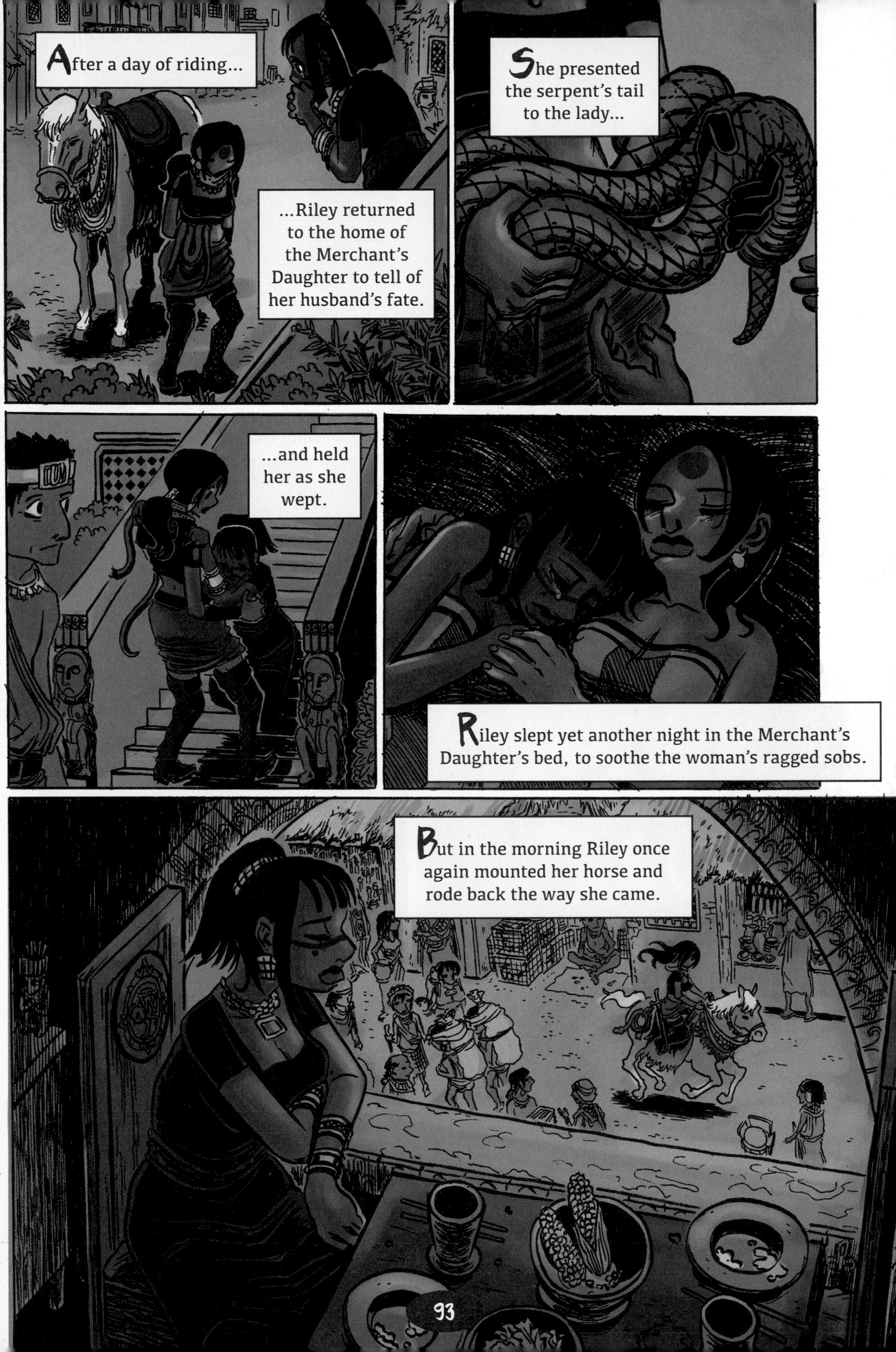
After a day of riding...
...Riley returned to the home of the Merchant's Daughter to tell of her husband's fate.
She presented the serpent's tail to the lady...
...and held her as she wept.
Riley slept yet another night in the Merchant's Daughter's bed, to soothe the woman's ragged sobs.
But in the morning Riley once again mounted her horse and rode back the way she came.

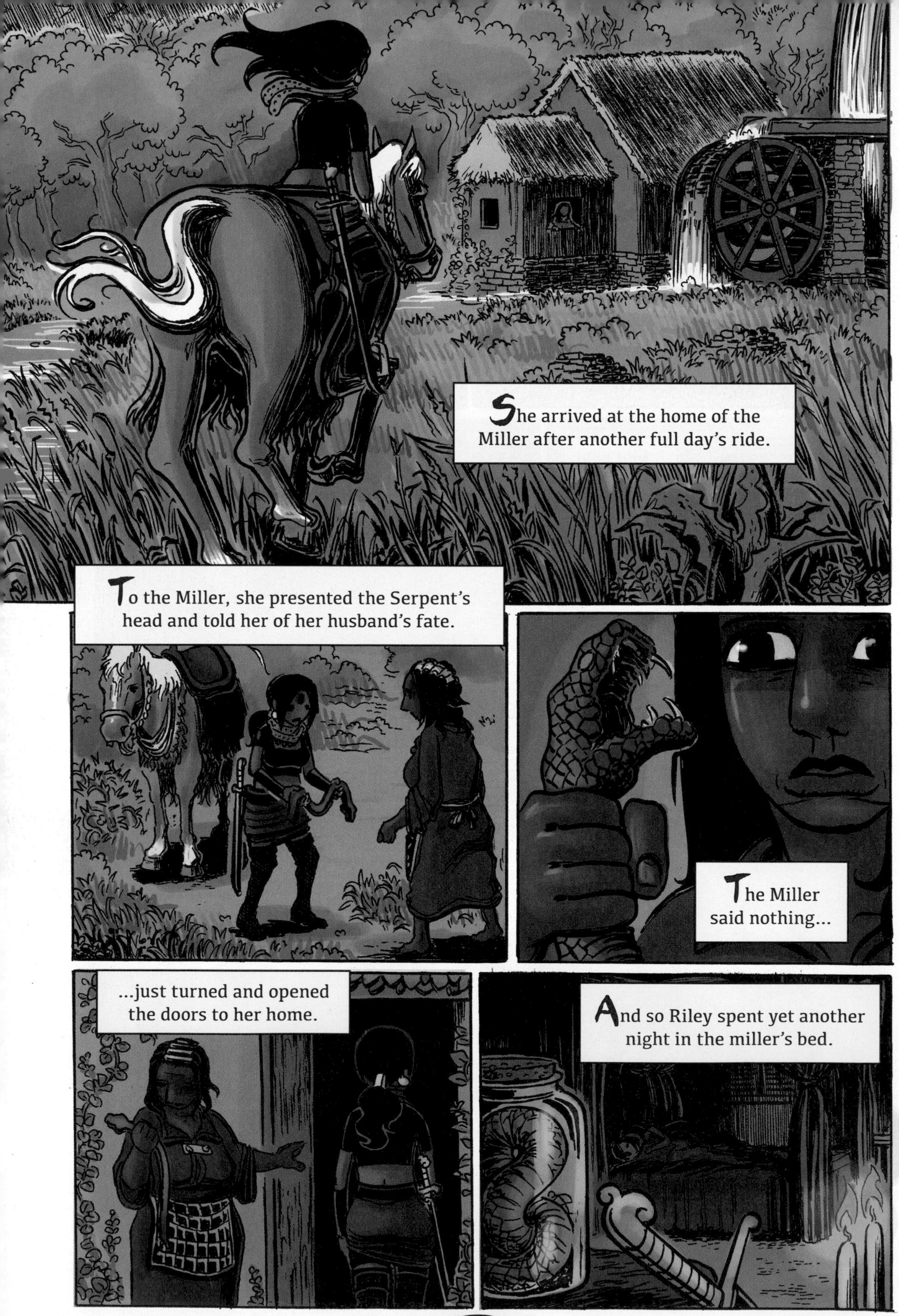
She arrived at the home of the Miller after another full day's ride.
To the Miller, she presented the Serpent's head and told her of her husband's fate.
The Miller said nothing...
...just turned and opened the doors to her home.
And so Riley spent yet another night in the miller's bed.

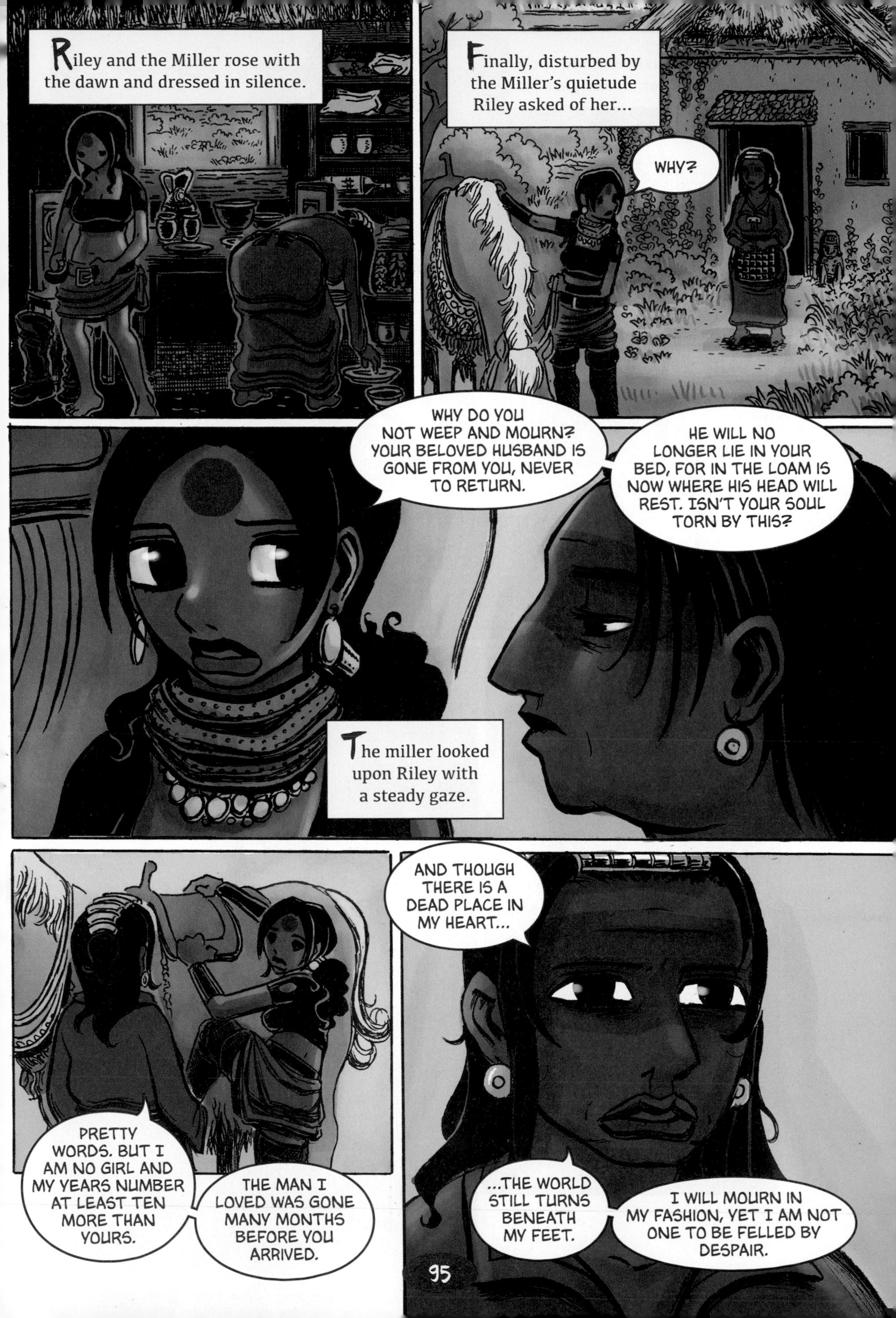
Riley and the Miller rose with the dawn and dressed in silence.
Finally, disturbed by the Miller's quietude Riley asked of her...
WHY?
WHY DO YOU NOT WEEP AND MOURN? YOUR BELOVED HUSBAND IS GONE FROM YOU, NEVER TO RETURN.
HE WILL NO LONGER LIE IN YOUR BED, FOR IN THE LOAM IS NOW WHERE HIS HEAD WILL REST. ISN'T YOUR SOUL TORN BY THIS?
The miller looked upon Riley with a steady gaze.
PRETTY WORDS. BUT I AM NO GIRL AND MY YEARS NUMBER AT LEAST TEN MORE THAN YOURS.
THE MAN I LOVED WAS GONE MANY MONTHS BEFORE YOU ARRIVED.
AND THOUGH THERE IS A DEAD PLACE IN MY HEART...
...THE WORLD STILL TURNS BENEATH MY FEET.
I WILL MOURN IN MY FASHION, YET I AM NOT ONE TO BE FELLED BY DESPAIR.

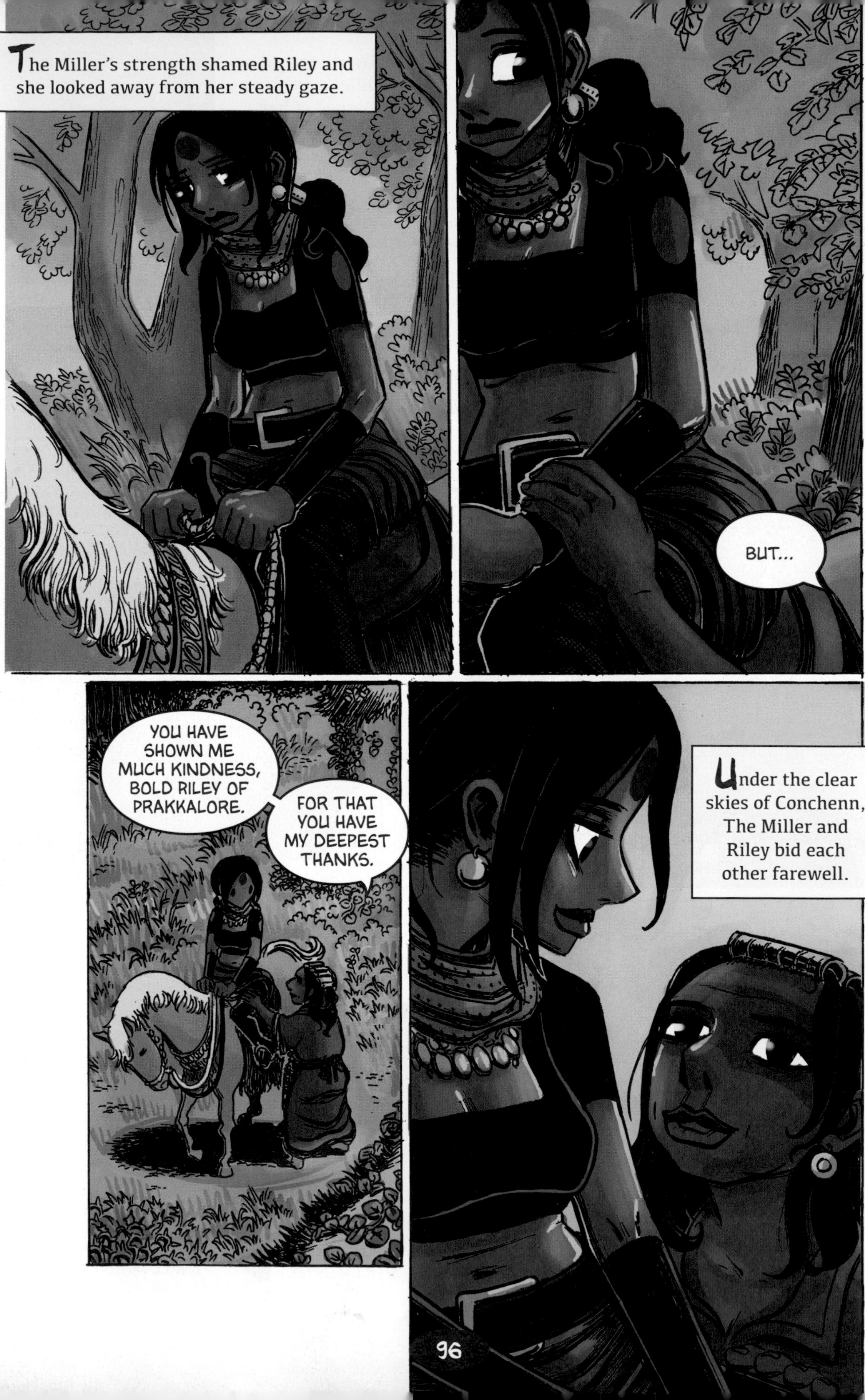
The Miller's strength shamed Riley and she looked away from her steady gaze.
BUT...
YOU HAVE SHOWN ME MUCH KINDNESS, BOLD RILEY OF PRAKKALORE.
FOR THAT YOU HAVE MY DEEPEST THANKS.
Under the clear skies of Conchenn, The Miller and Riley bid each other farewell.

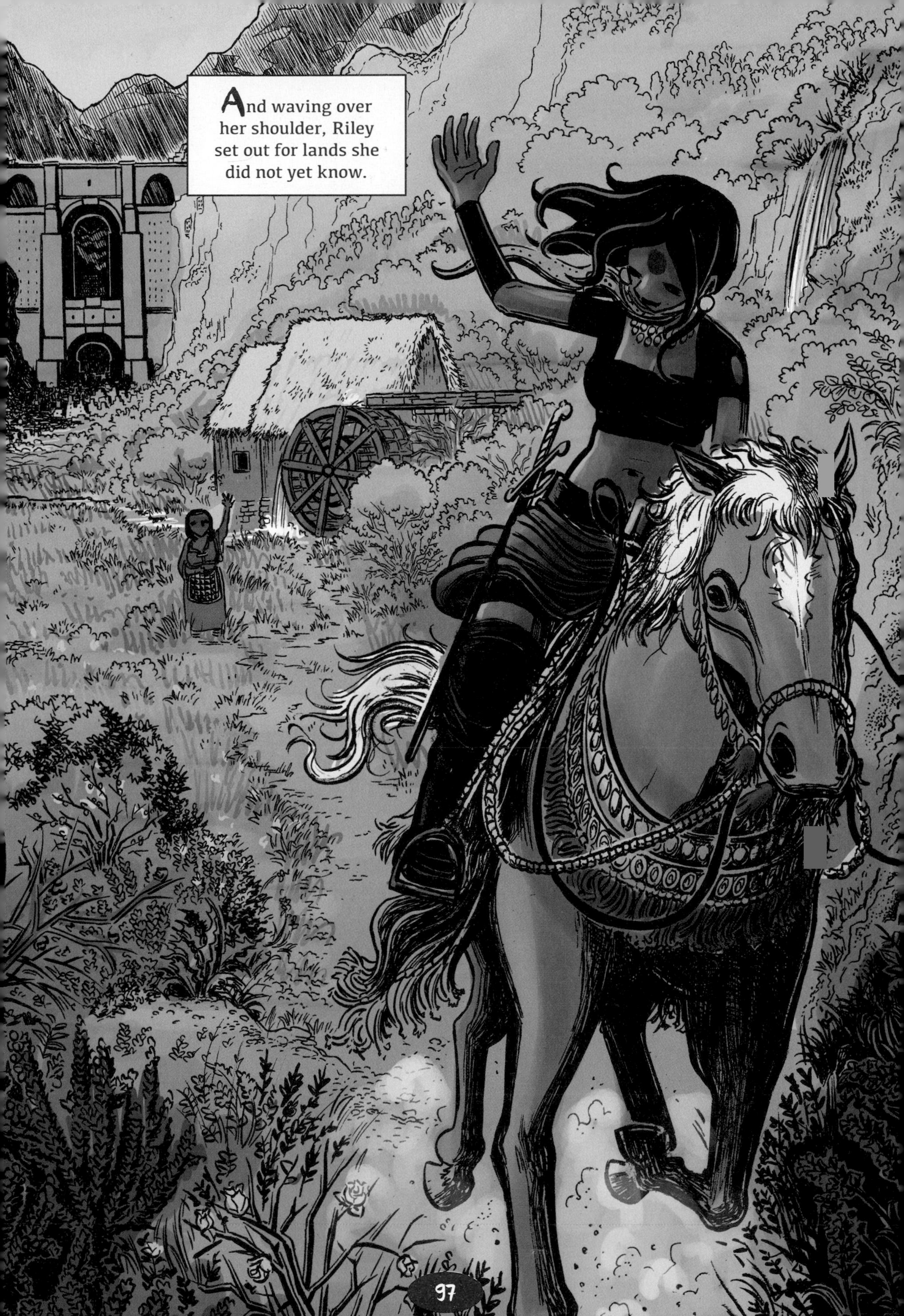
And waving over her shoulder, Riley set out for lands she did not yet know.

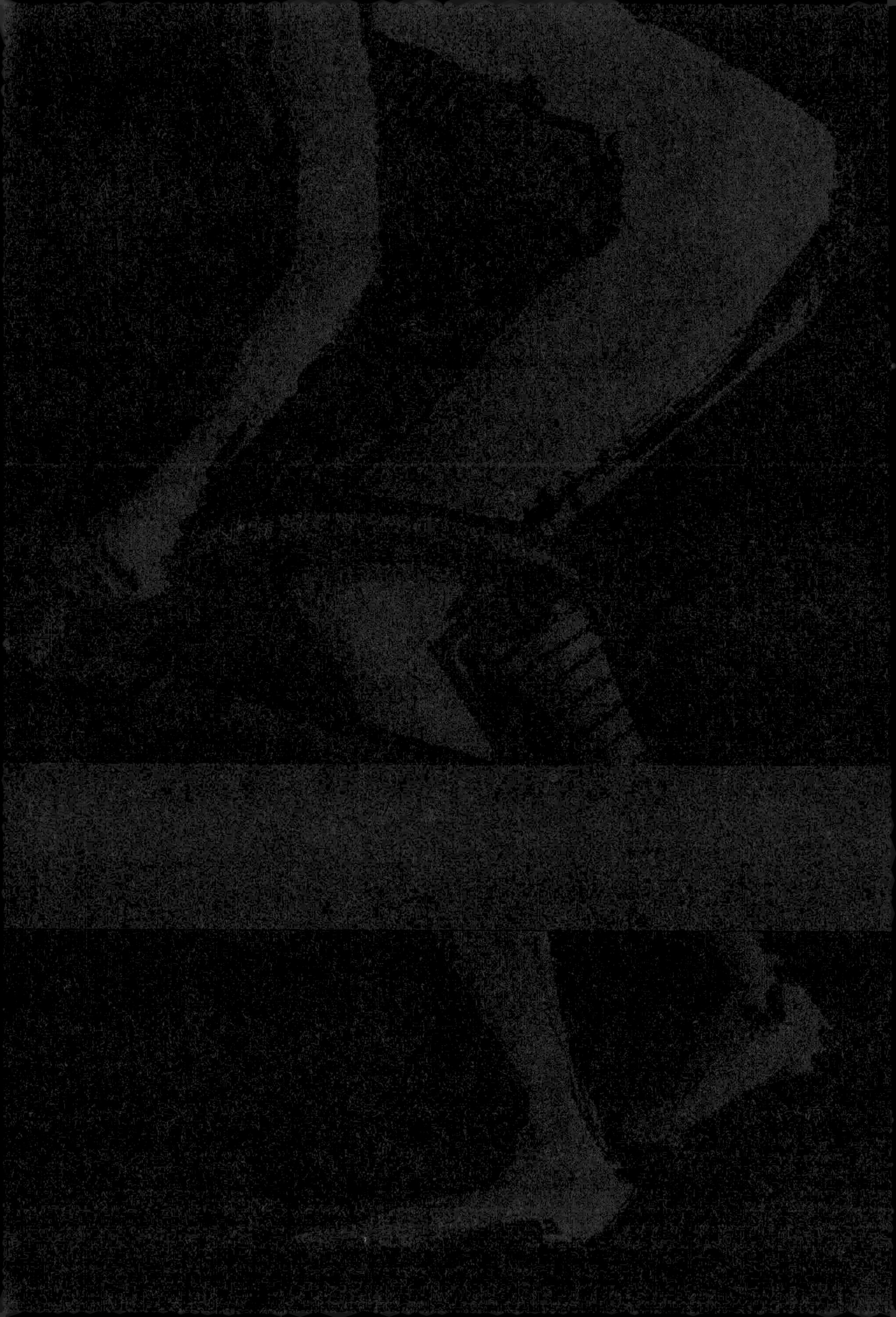

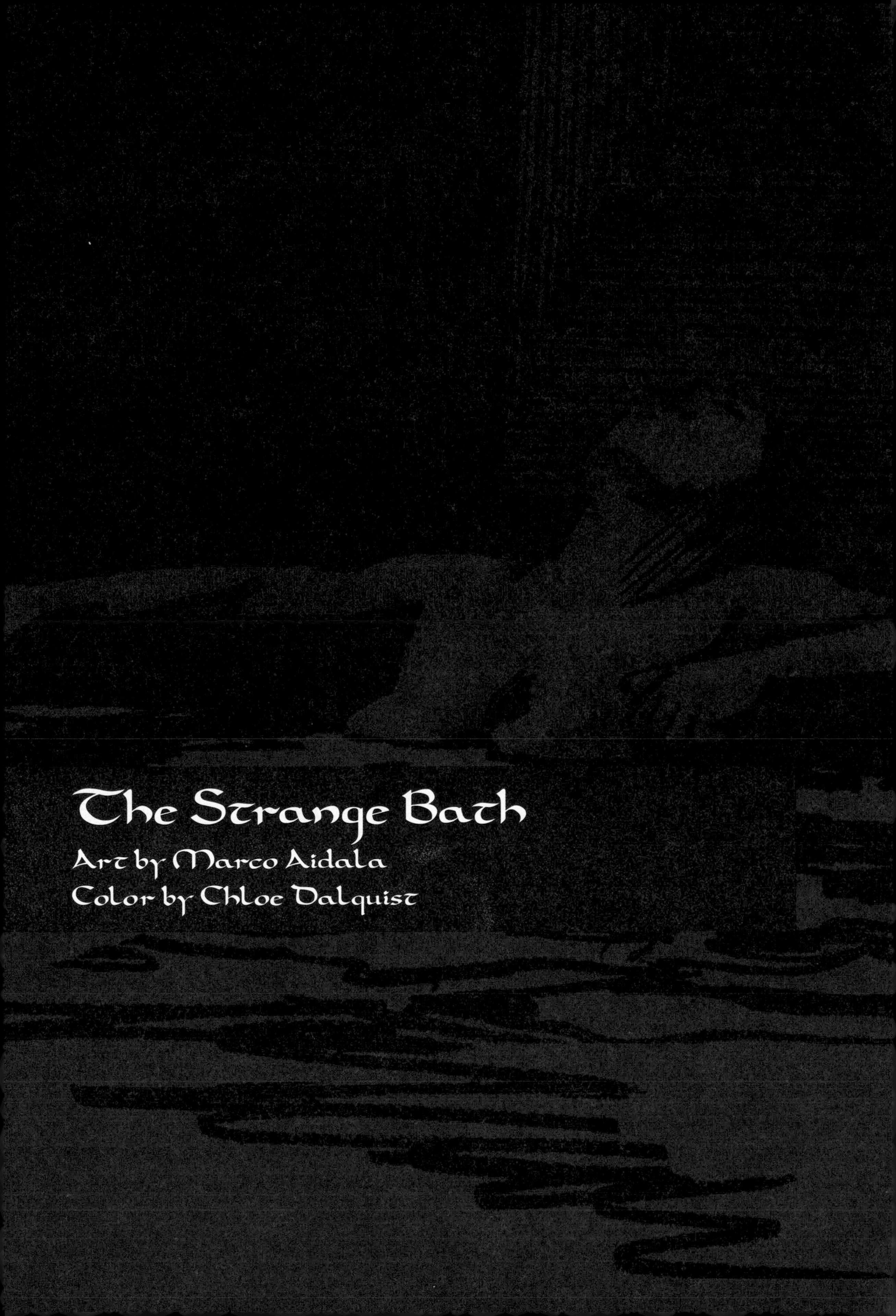

The Strange Bath

Art by Marco Aidala
Color by Chloe Dalquist

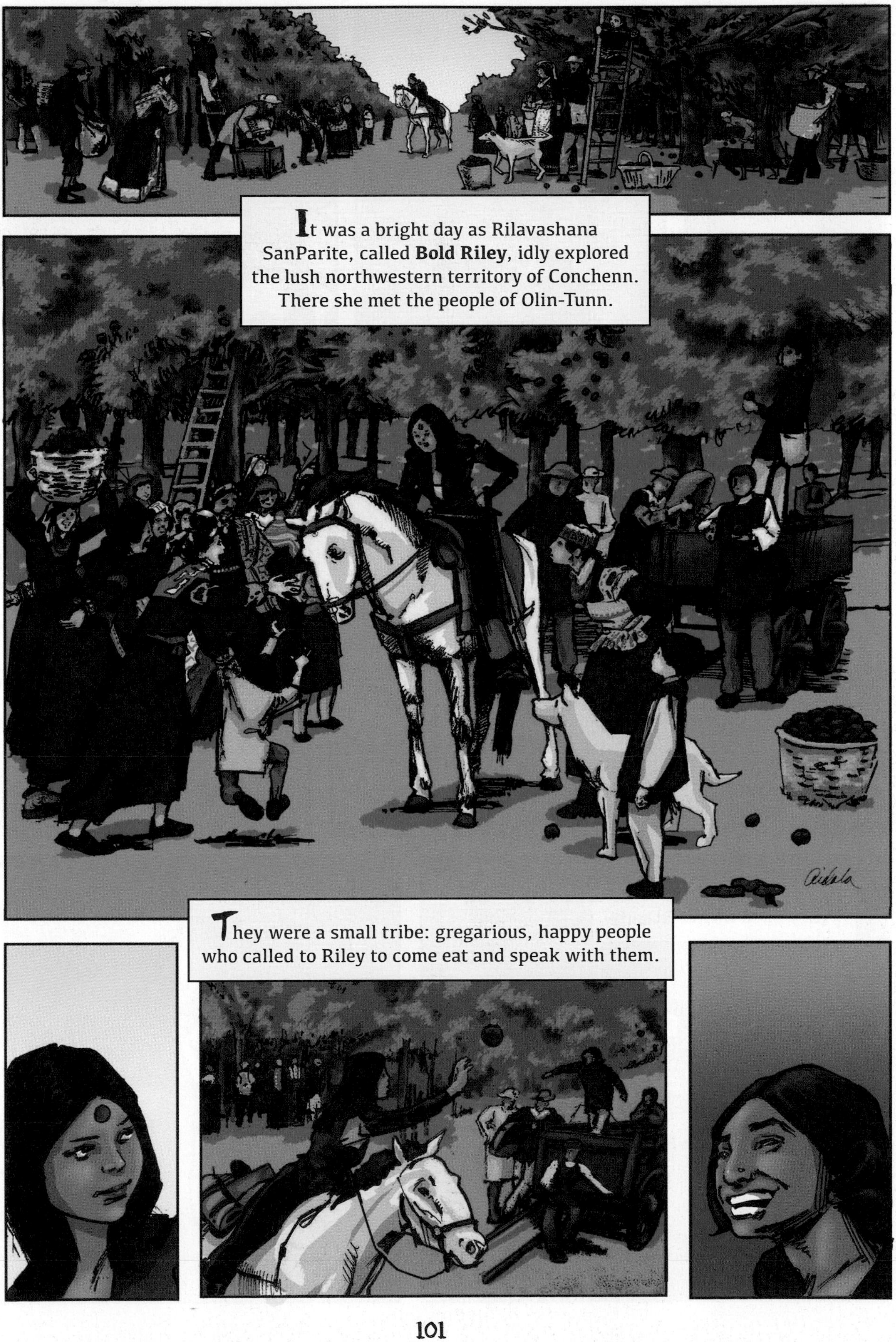
It was a bright day as Rilavashana SanParite, called **Bold Riley**, idly explored the lush northwestern territory of Conchenn. There she met the people of Olin-Tunn.
They were a small tribe: gregarious, happy people who called to Riley to come eat and speak with them.

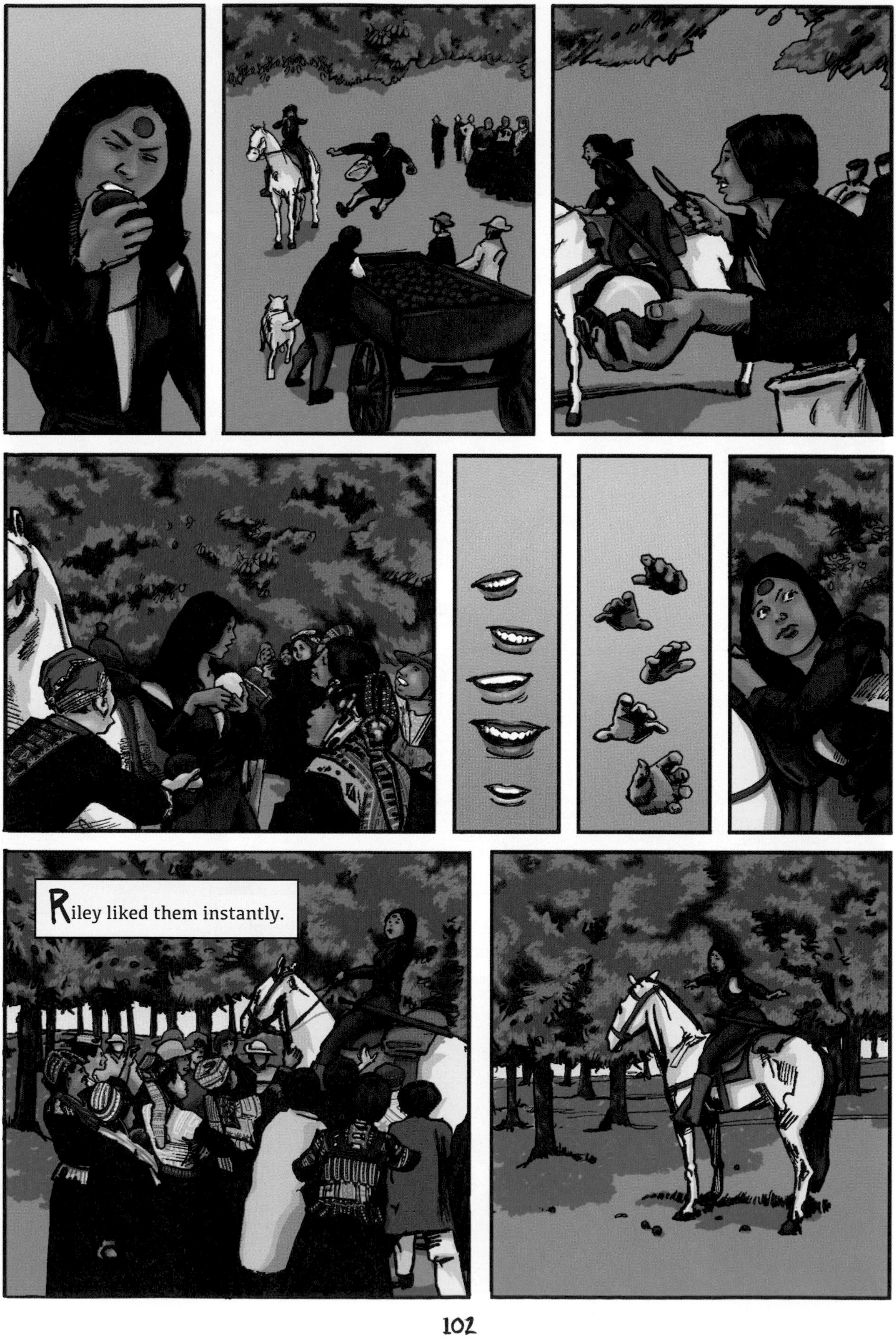
Riley liked them instantly.

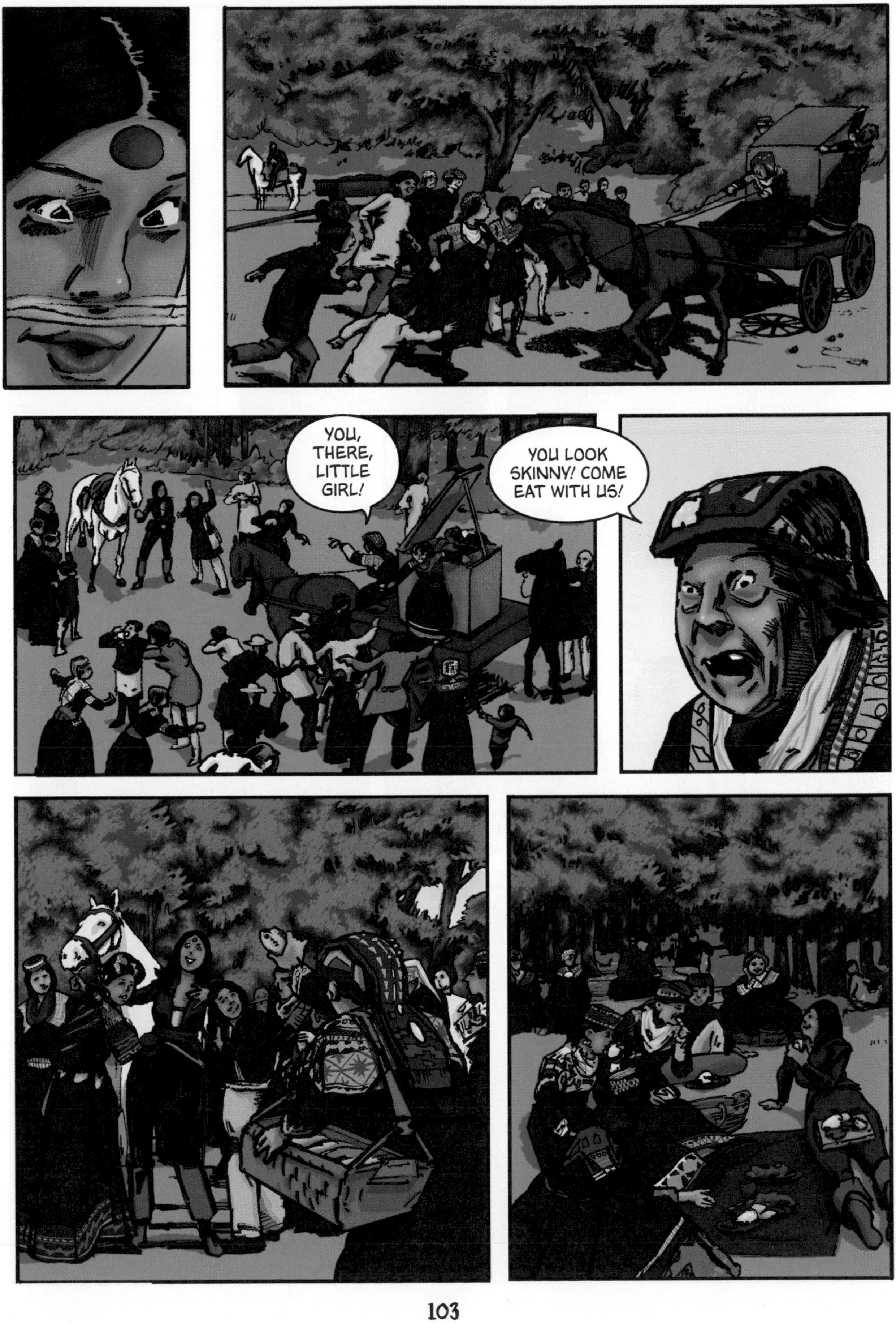
YOU, THERE, LITTLE GIRL!
YOU LOOK SKINNY! COME EAT WITH US!

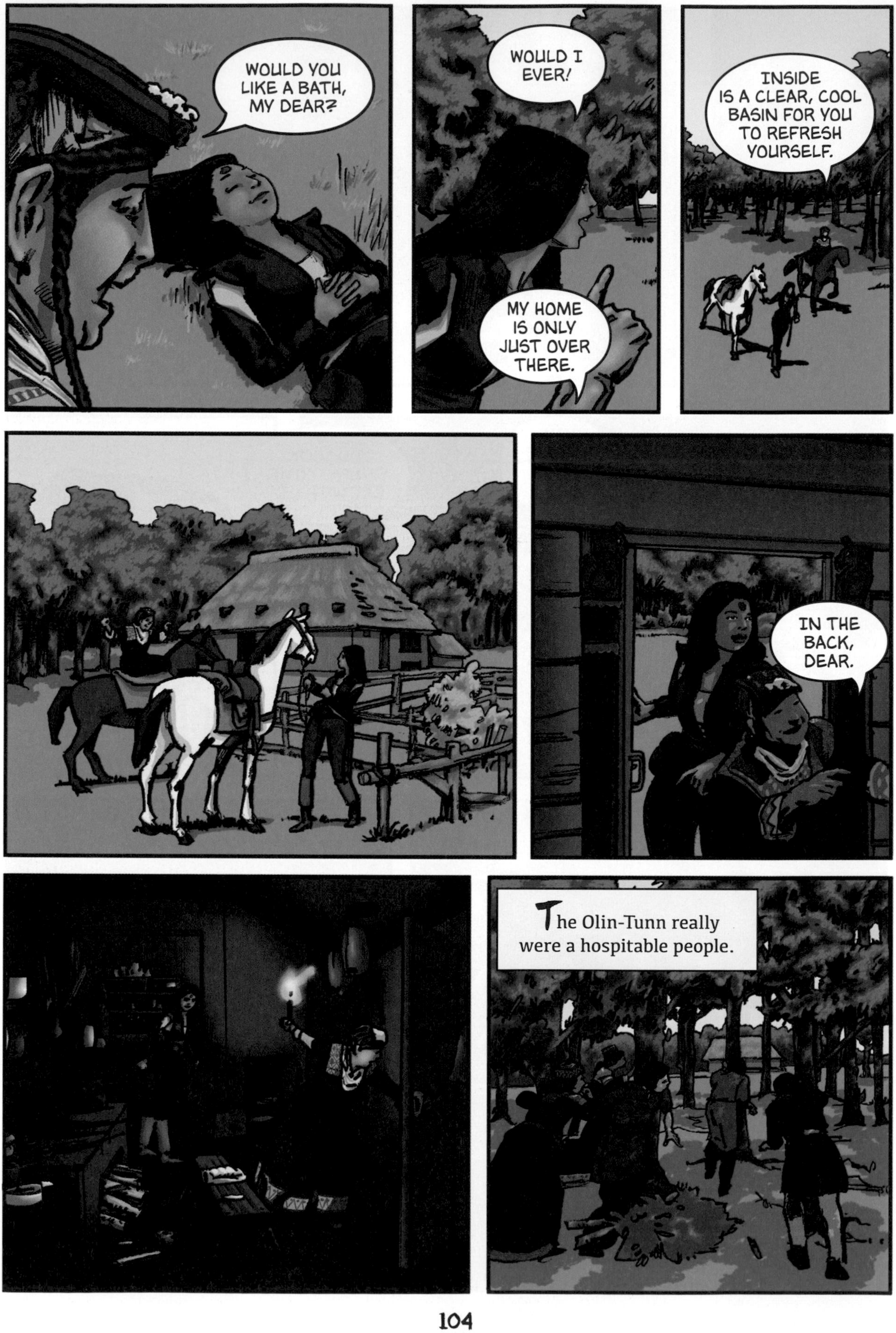
WOULD YOU LIKE A BATH, MY DEAR?
WOULD I EVER!
MY HOME IS ONLY JUST OVER THERE.
INSIDE IS A CLEAR, COOL BASIN FOR YOU TO REFRESH YOURSELF.
IN THE BACK, DEAR.
The Olin-Tunn really were a hospitable people.

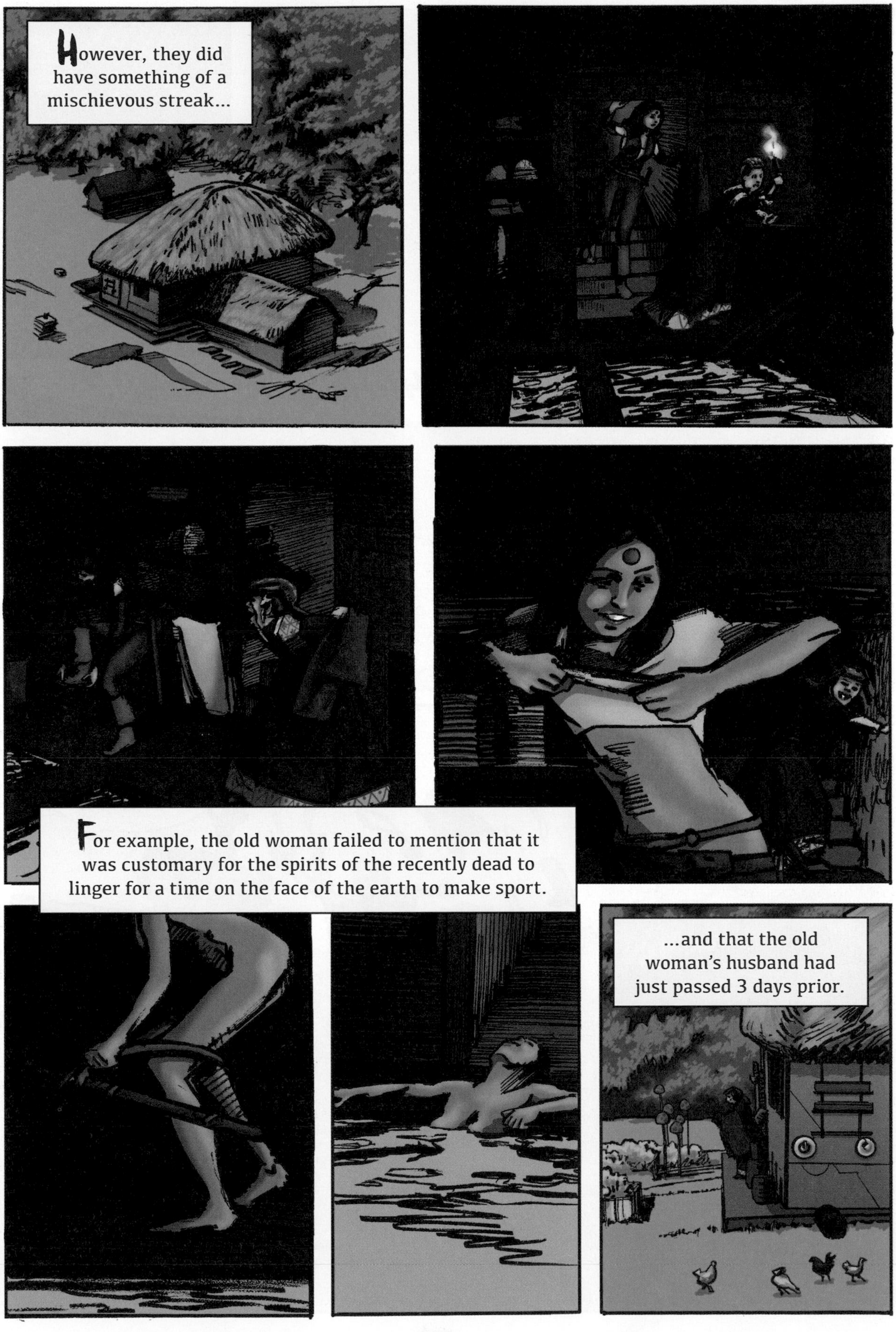
However, they did have something of a mischievous streak...
For example, the old woman failed to mention that it was customary for the spirits of the recently dead to linger for a time on the face of the earth to make sport.
...and that the old woman's husband had just passed 3 days prior.

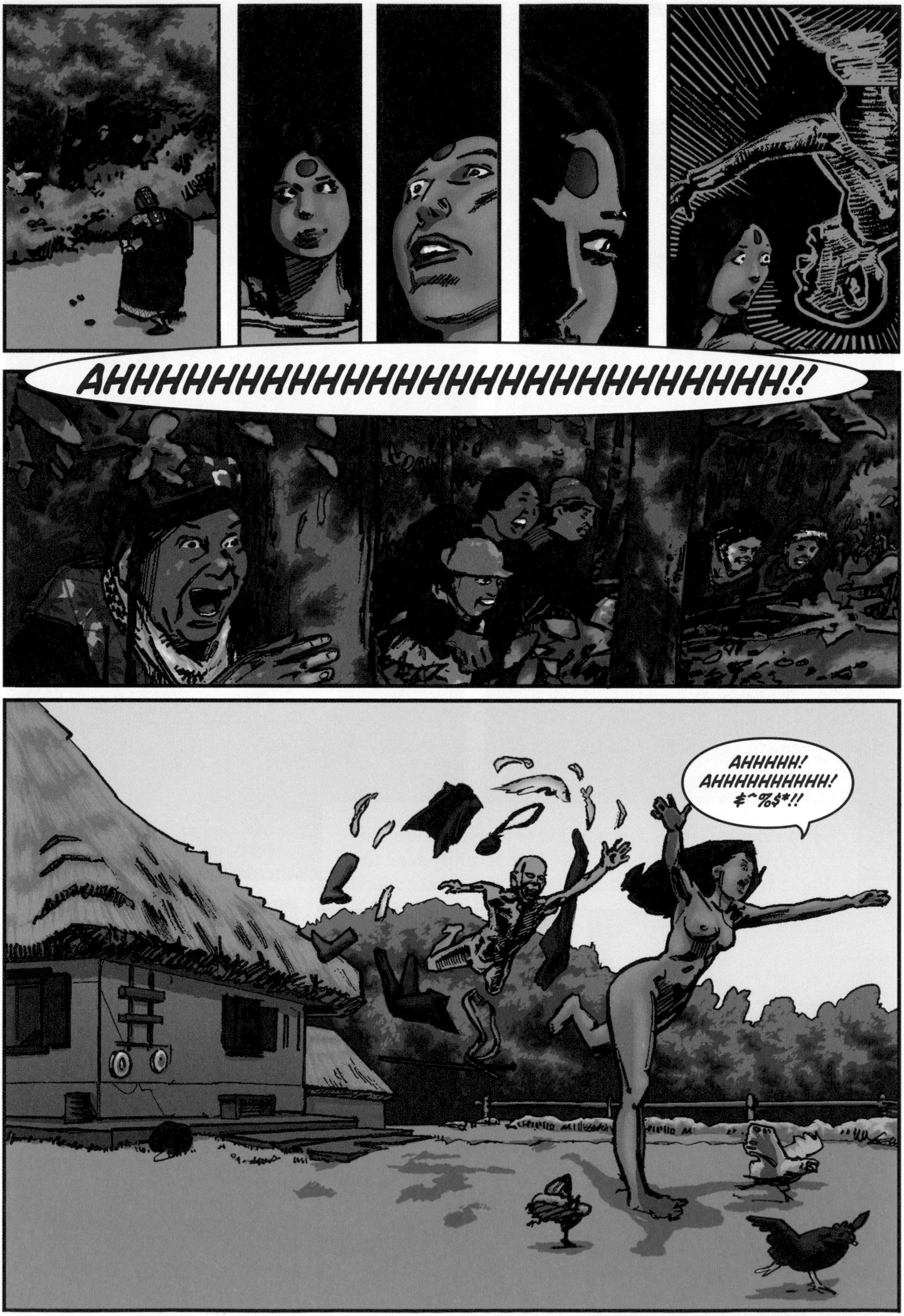
AHHHHHHHHHHHHHHHHHHHHHHHHHHHHH!!
AHHHHH!
AHHHHHHHHHHH!
≨^%$*!!

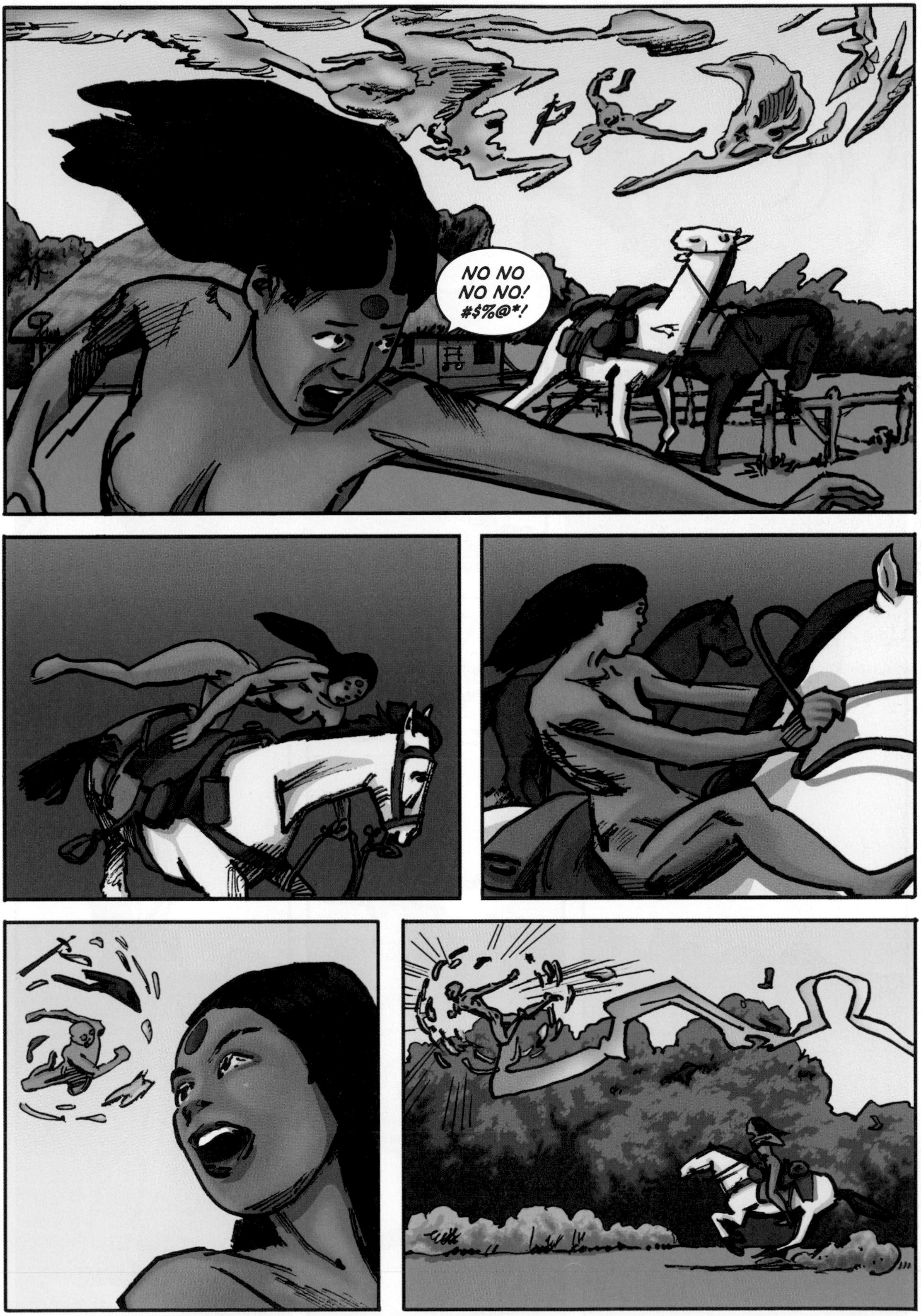
NO NO
NO NO!
#$%@*!

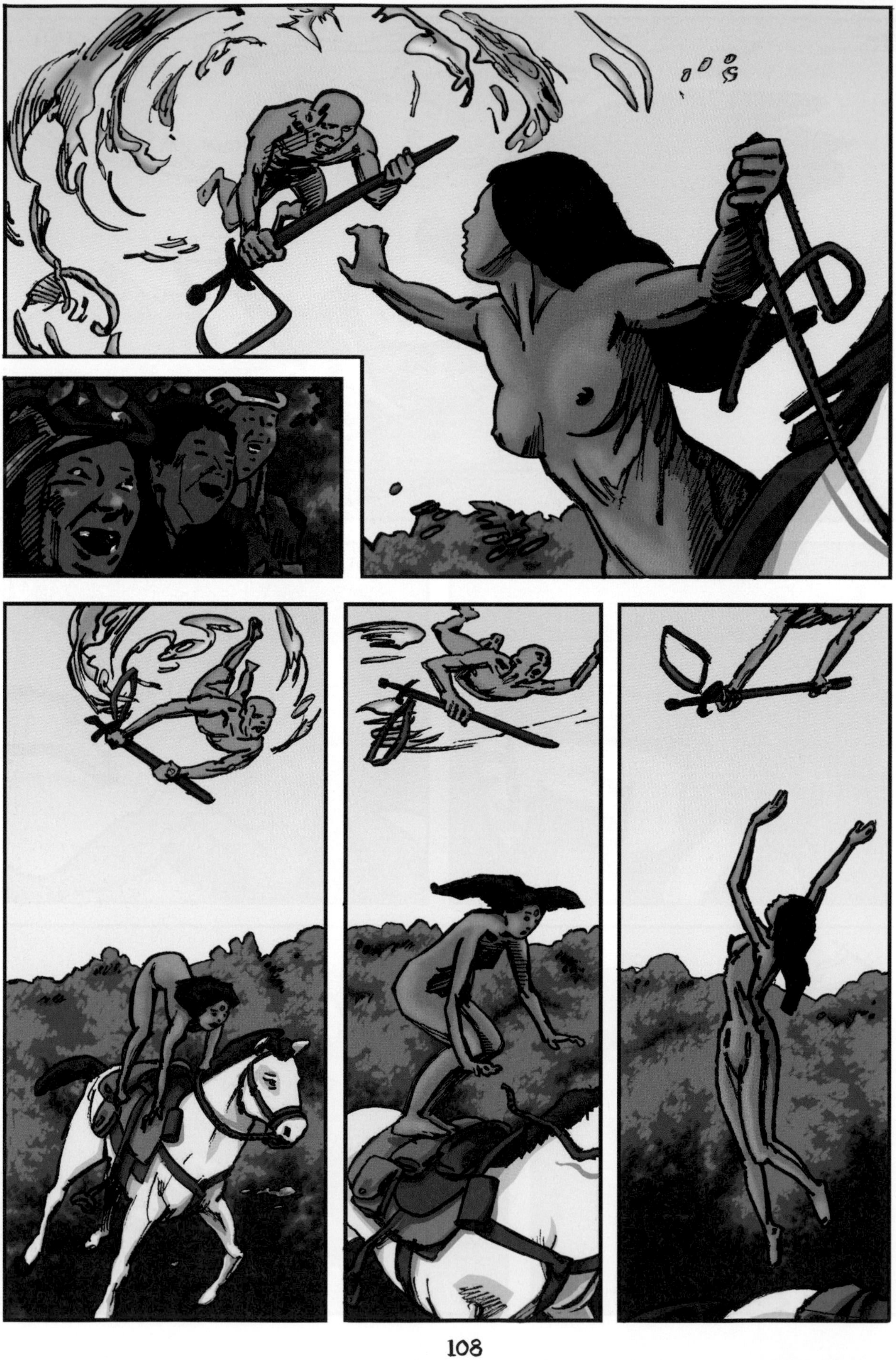

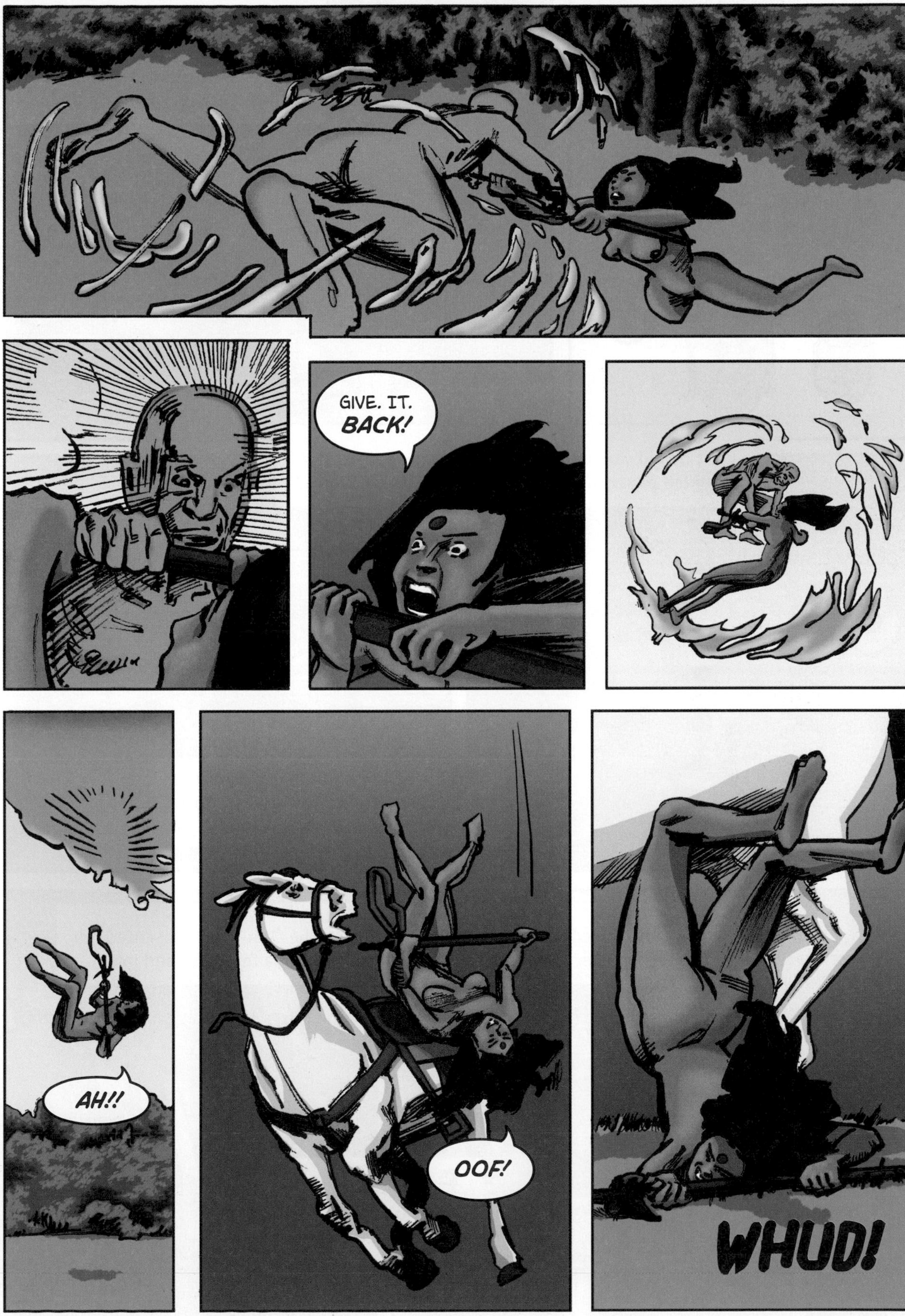
GIVE. IT. BACK!
AH!!
OOF!
WHUD!

At the very least, the Olin-Tunn were mildly apologetic when they explained this to Bold Riley through their laughter.

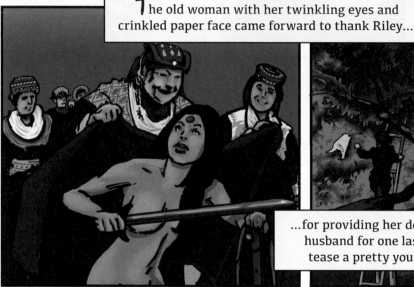

The old woman with her twinkling eyes and crinkled paper face came forward to thank Riley...

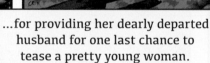

...for providing her dearly departed husband for one last chance to tease a pretty young woman.

She kissed her hands and called her "Daughter".

The Olin-Tunn presented her with a few gifts and joked.

Faced with this, it was difficult for Riley to pass from slight indignation to true anger.

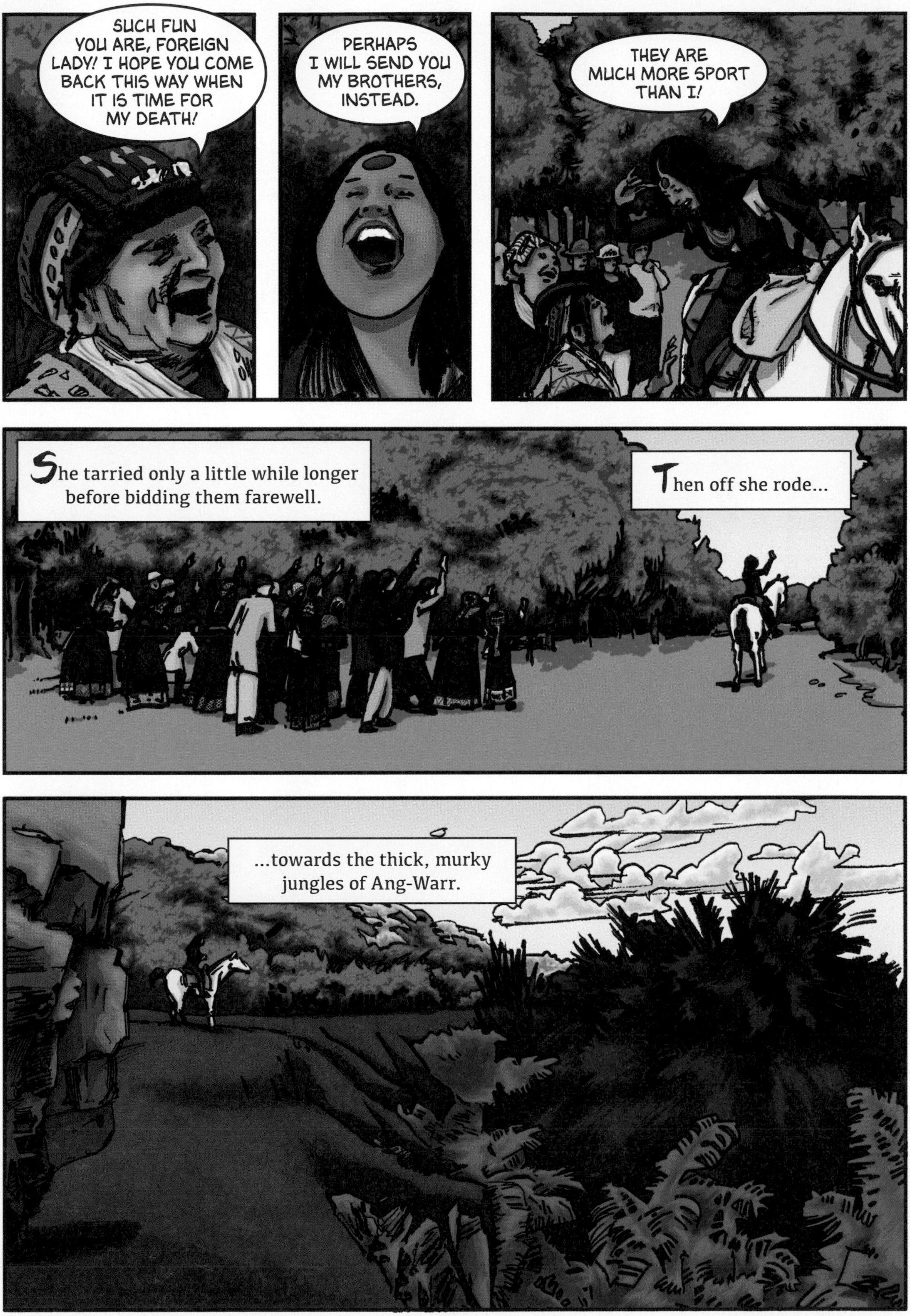
SUCH FUN YOU ARE, FOREIGN LADY! I HOPE YOU COME BACK THIS WAY WHEN IT IS TIME FOR MY DEATH!
PERHAPS I WILL SEND YOU MY BROTHERS, INSTEAD.
THEY ARE MUCH MORE SPORT THAN I!
She tarried only a little while longer before bidding them farewell.
Then off she rode...
...towards the thick, murky jungles of Ang-Warr.

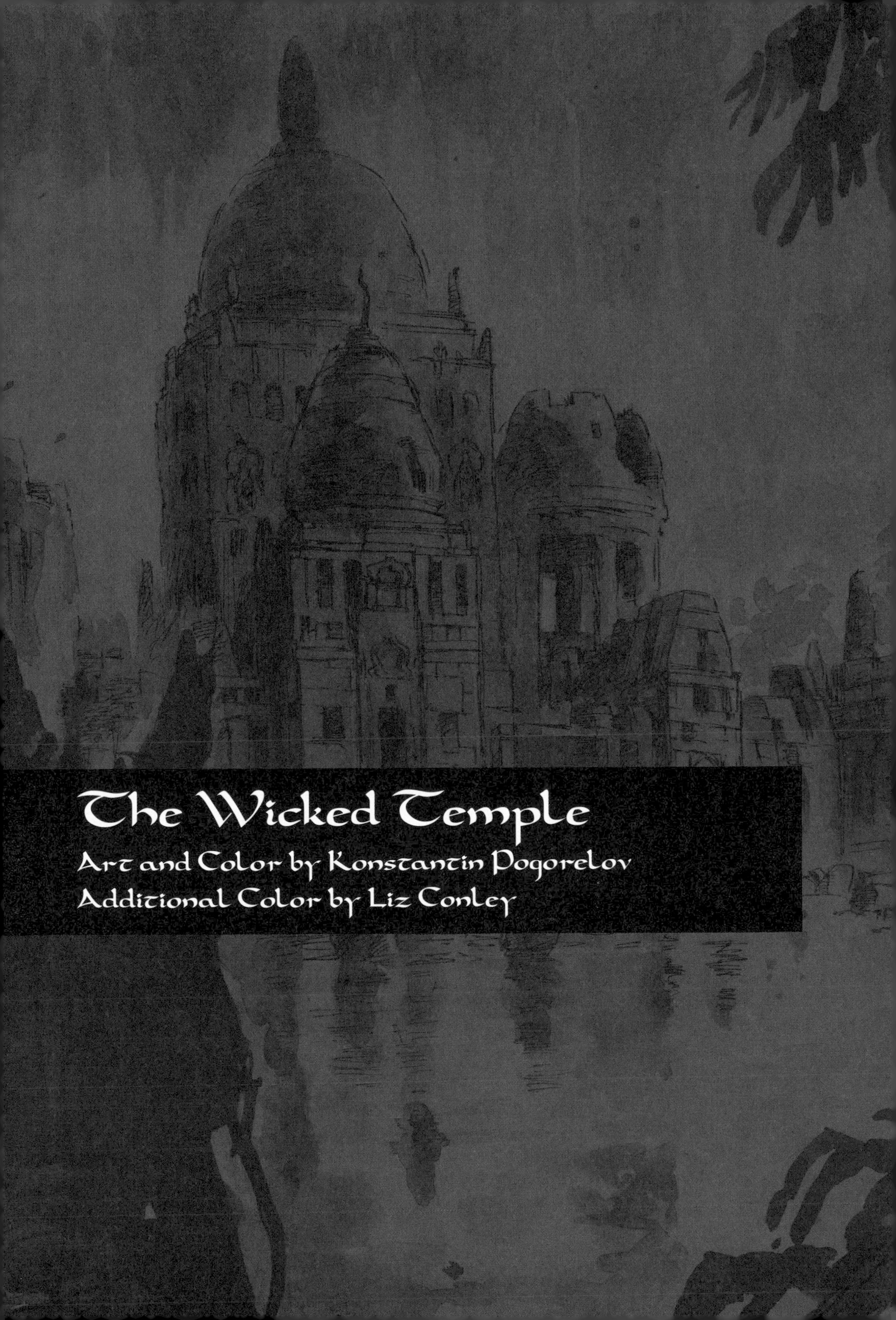

The Wicked Temple

Art and Color by Konstantin Pogorelov

Additional Color by Liz Conley

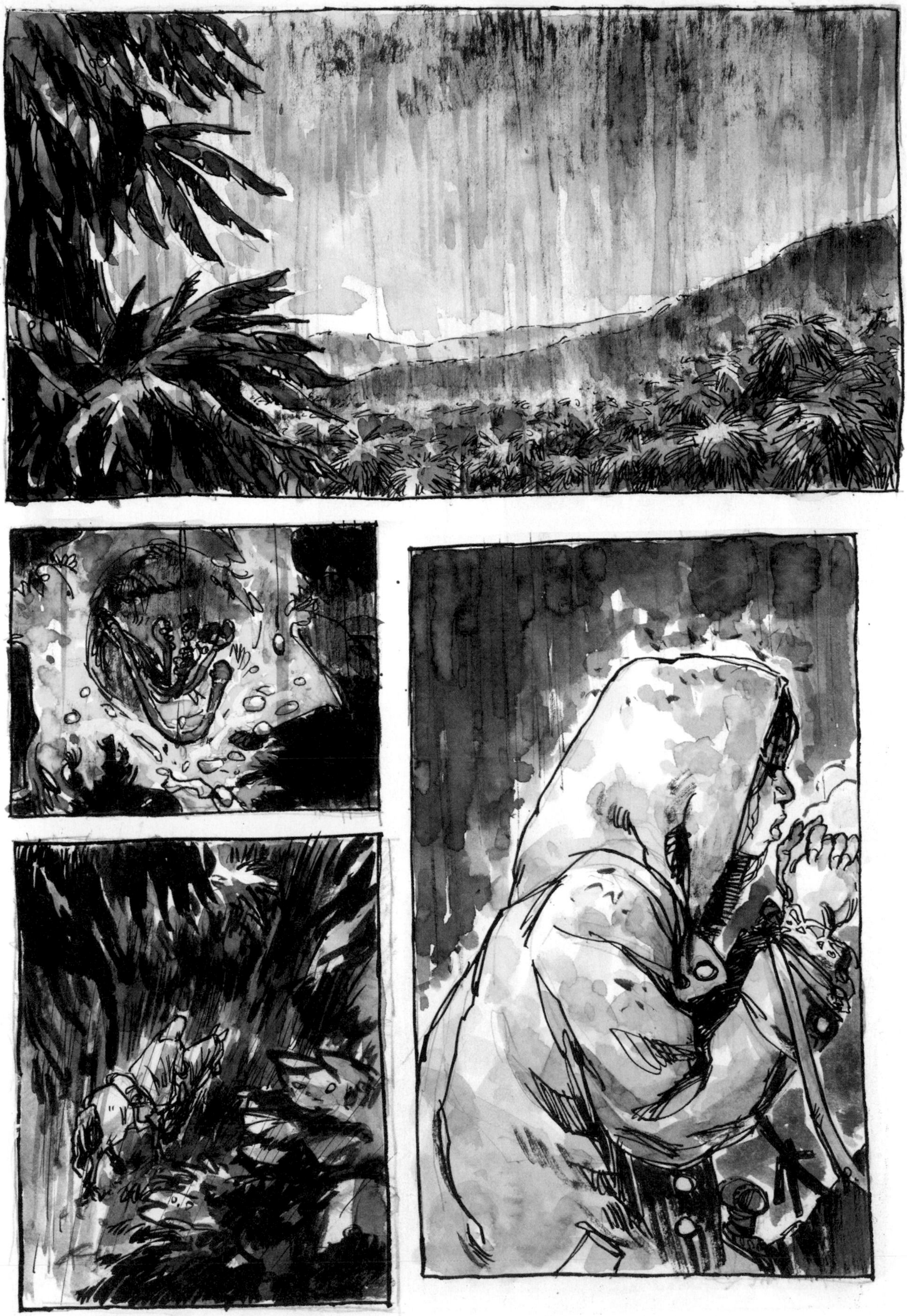

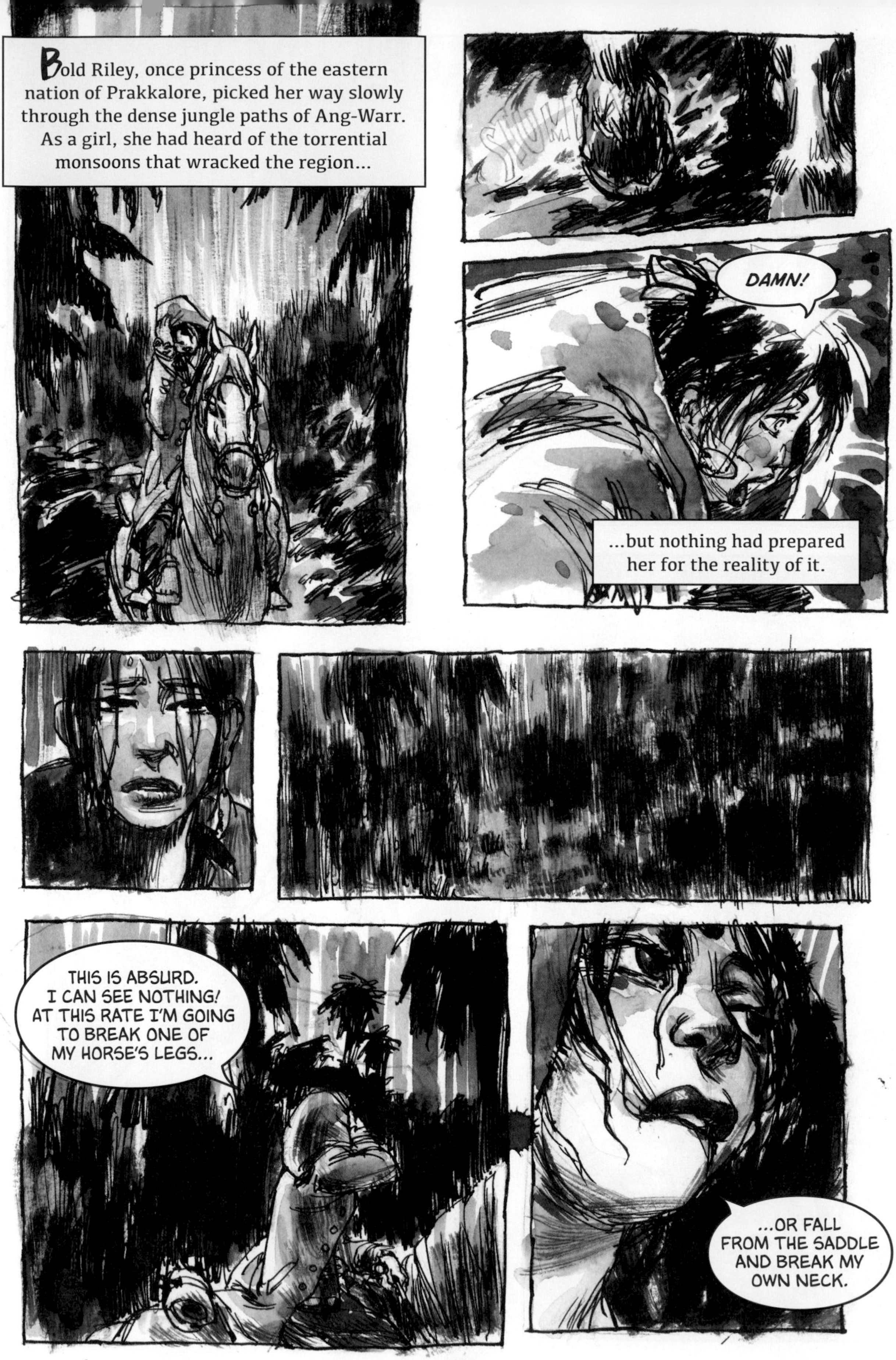
Bold Riley, once princess of the eastern nation of Prakkalore, picked her way slowly through the dense jungle paths of Ang-Warr. As a girl, she had heard of the torrential monsoons that wracked the region...
DAMN!
...but nothing had prepared her for the reality of it.
THIS IS ABSURD. I CAN SEE NOTHING! AT THIS RATE I'M GOING TO BREAK ONE OF MY HORSE'S LEGS...
...OR FALL FROM THE SADDLE AND BREAK MY OWN NECK.

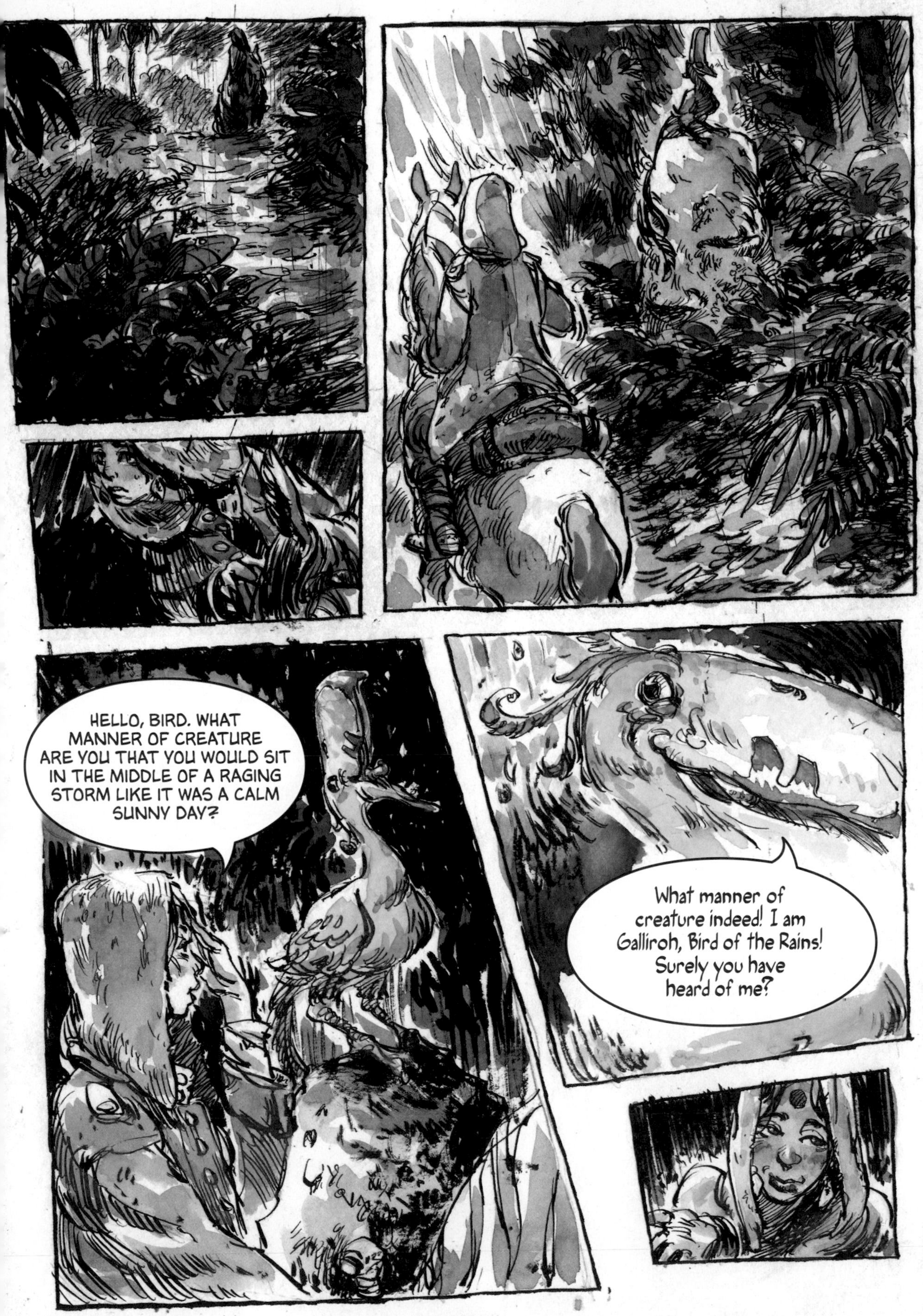
HELLO, BIRD. WHAT MANNER OF CREATURE ARE YOU THAT YOU WOULD SIT IN THE MIDDLE OF A RAGING STORM LIKE IT WAS A CALM SUNNY DAY?
What manner of creature indeed! I am Galliroh, Bird of the Rains! Surely you have heard of me?

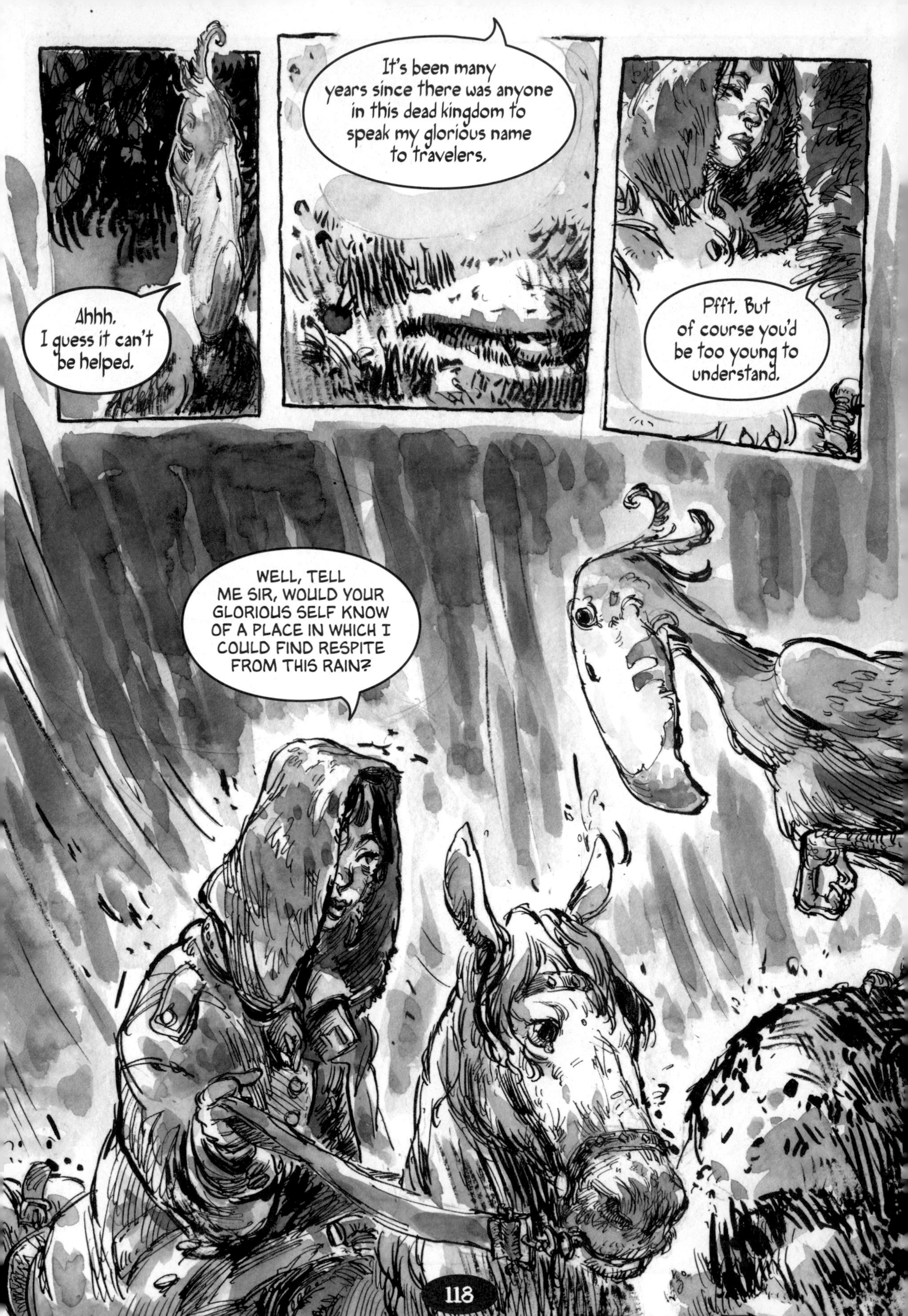
Ahhh.
I guess it can't be helped.
It's been many years since there was anyone in this dead kingdom to speak my glorious name to travelers.
Pfft. But of course you'd be too young to understand.
WELL, TELL ME SIR, WOULD YOUR GLORIOUS SELF KNOW OF A PLACE IN WHICH I COULD FIND RESPITE FROM THIS RAIN?

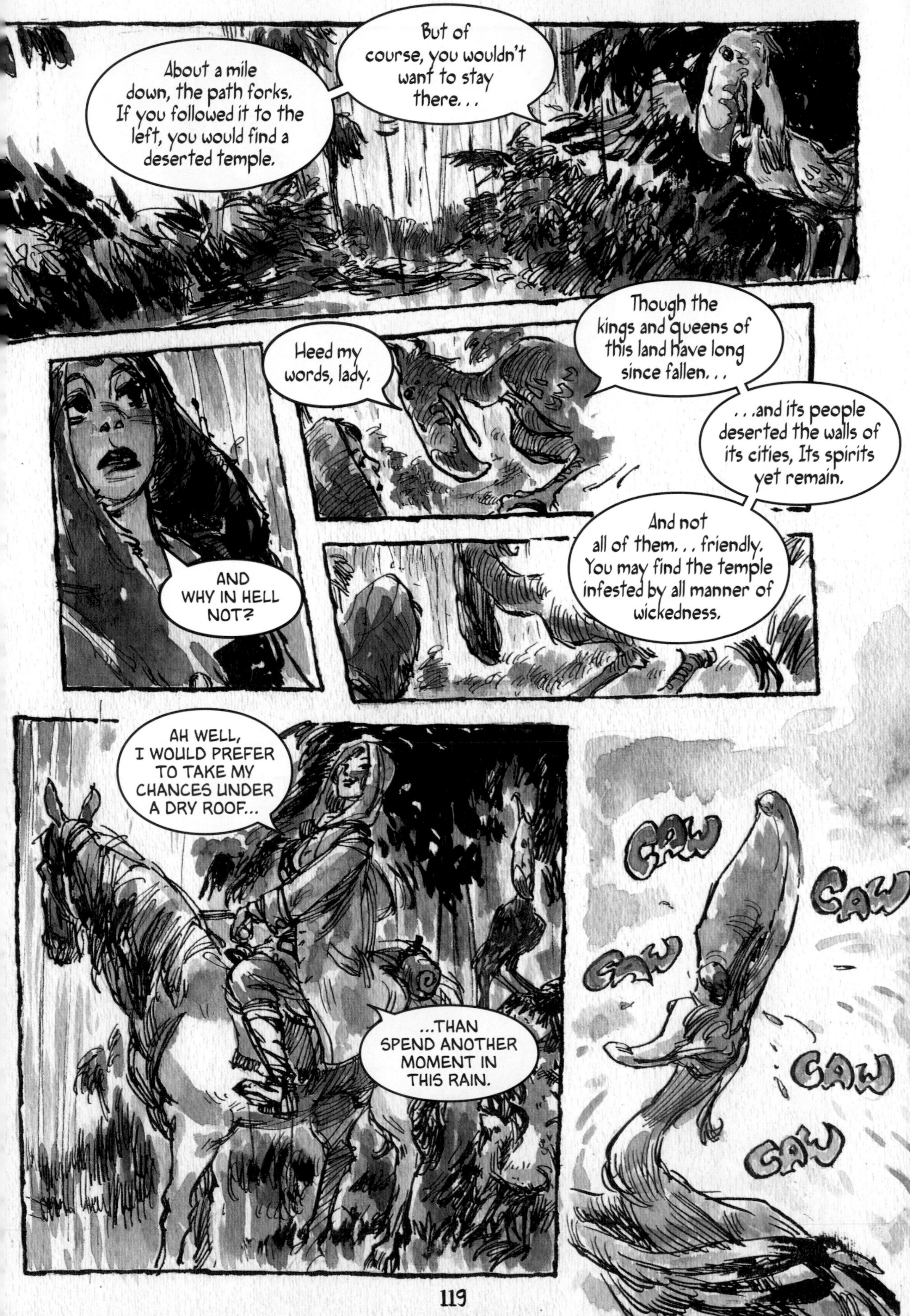
About a mile down, the path forks. If you followed it to the left, you would find a deserted temple.
But of course, you wouldn't want to stay there. . .
Heed my words, lady.
Though the kings and queens of this land have long since fallen. . .
. . .and its people deserted the walls of its cities, Its spirits yet remain.
And not all of them. . . friendly. You may find the temple infested by all manner of wickedness.
AND WHY IN HELL NOT?
AH WELL, I WOULD PREFER TO TAKE MY CHANCES UNDER A DRY ROOF...
...THAN SPEND ANOTHER MOMENT IN THIS RAIN.
CAW
CAW
CAW
CAW
CAW

What folly! What spirit!

What is your name, girl?

I AM RILAVASHANA SANPARITE, CALLED BOLD RILEY. DAUGHTER OF SHYRAMRANA AND PENCHABII SANPARITE.

Of Prakkalore?

YES.

Girl, I saw your great great grandfather's procession to the king's palace in the capital many years ago! He was a fine man indeed.

In fact, I had the pleasure of eating fruit from his hand and chatting with him for a brief moment before his audience with the king of Ang-Warr.

"I must say, despite his being a human, I quite enjoyed his company."

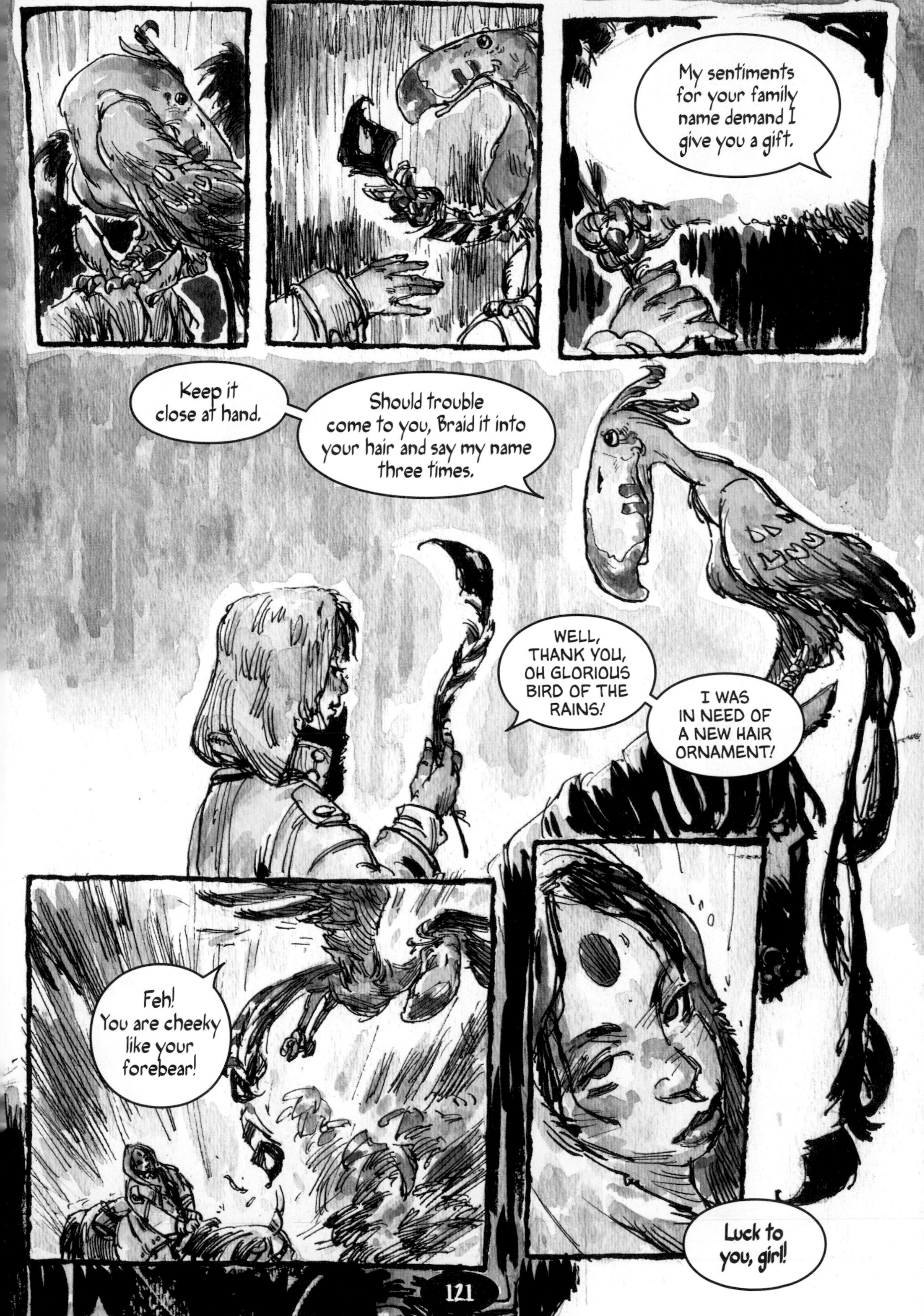
My sentiments for your family name demand I give you a gift.
Keep it close at hand.
Should trouble come to you, Braid it into your hair and say my name three times.
WELL, THANK YOU, OH GLORIOUS BIRD OF THE RAINS!
I WAS IN NEED OF A NEW HAIR ORNAMENT!
Feh! You are cheeky like your forebear!
Luck to you, girl!

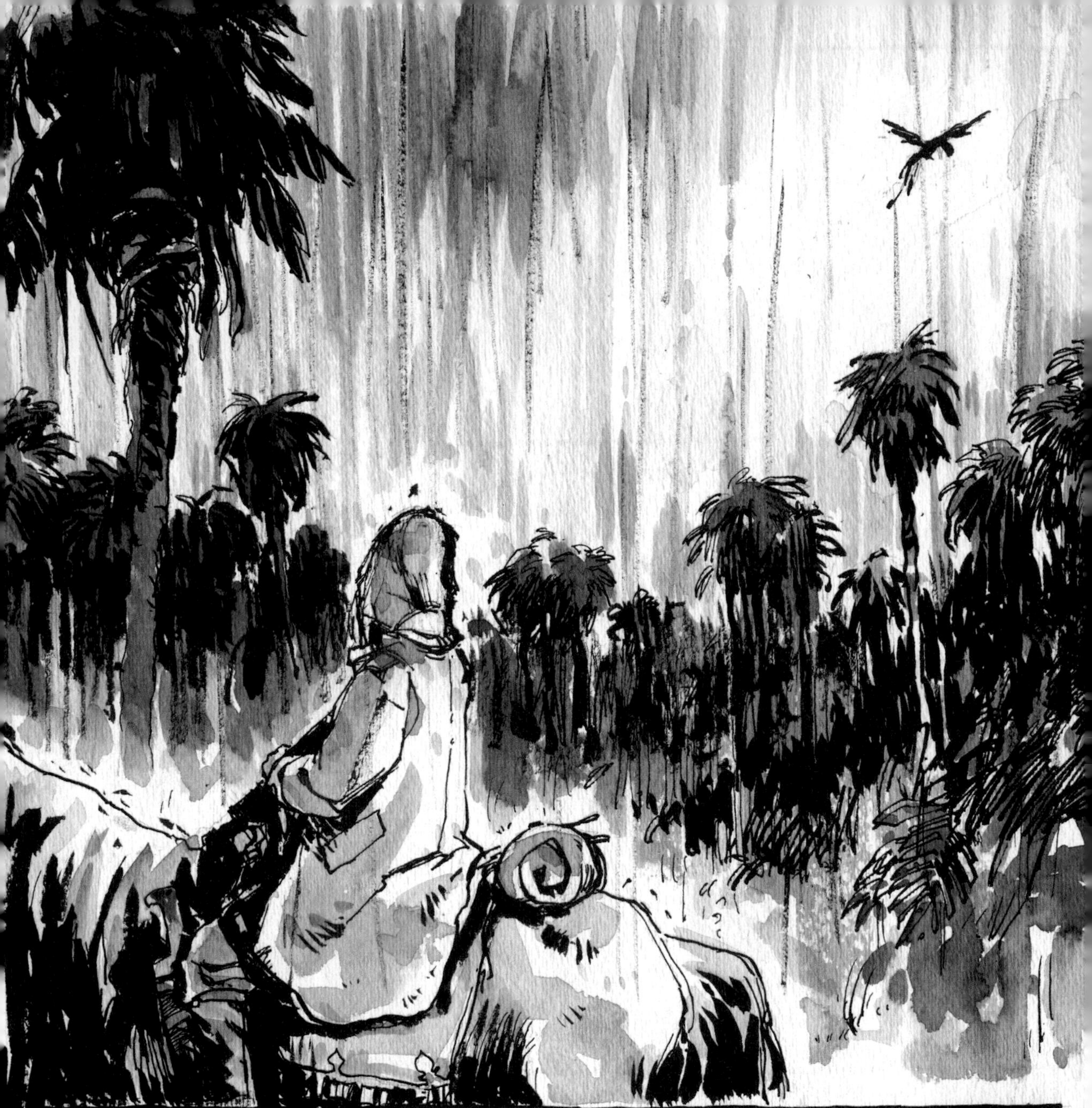

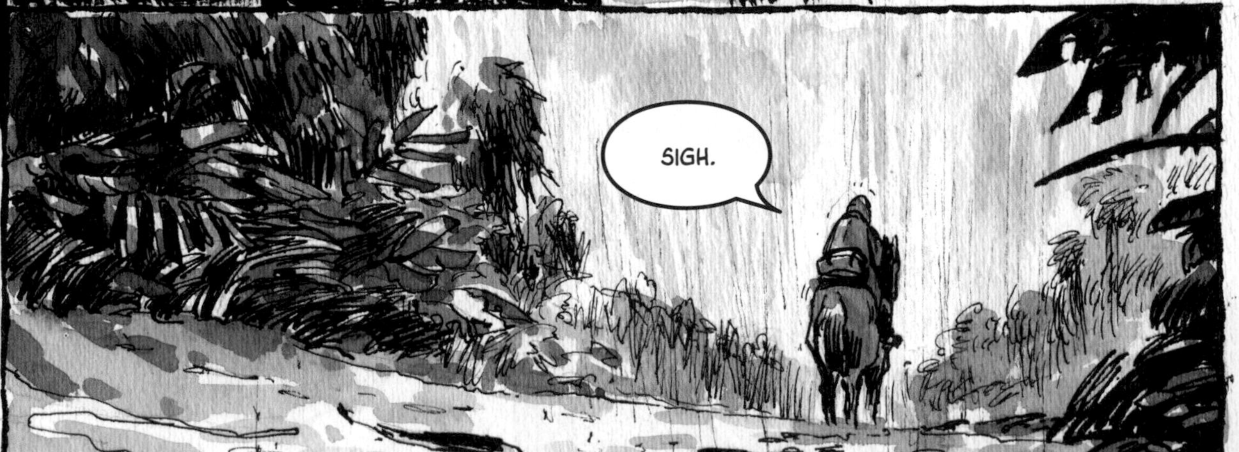
SIGH.

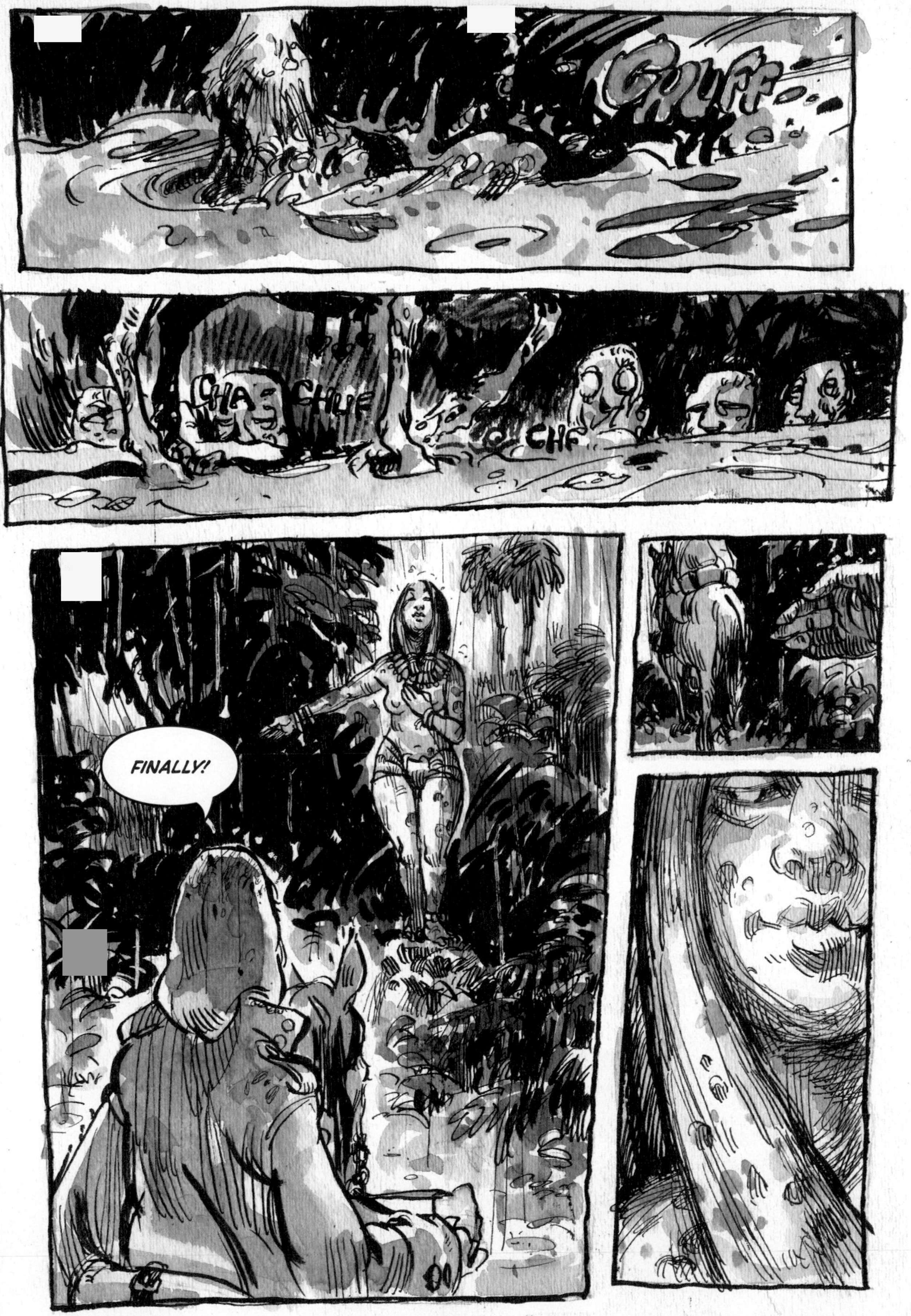
CHUFF
CHA
CHUF
CHF
FINALLY!

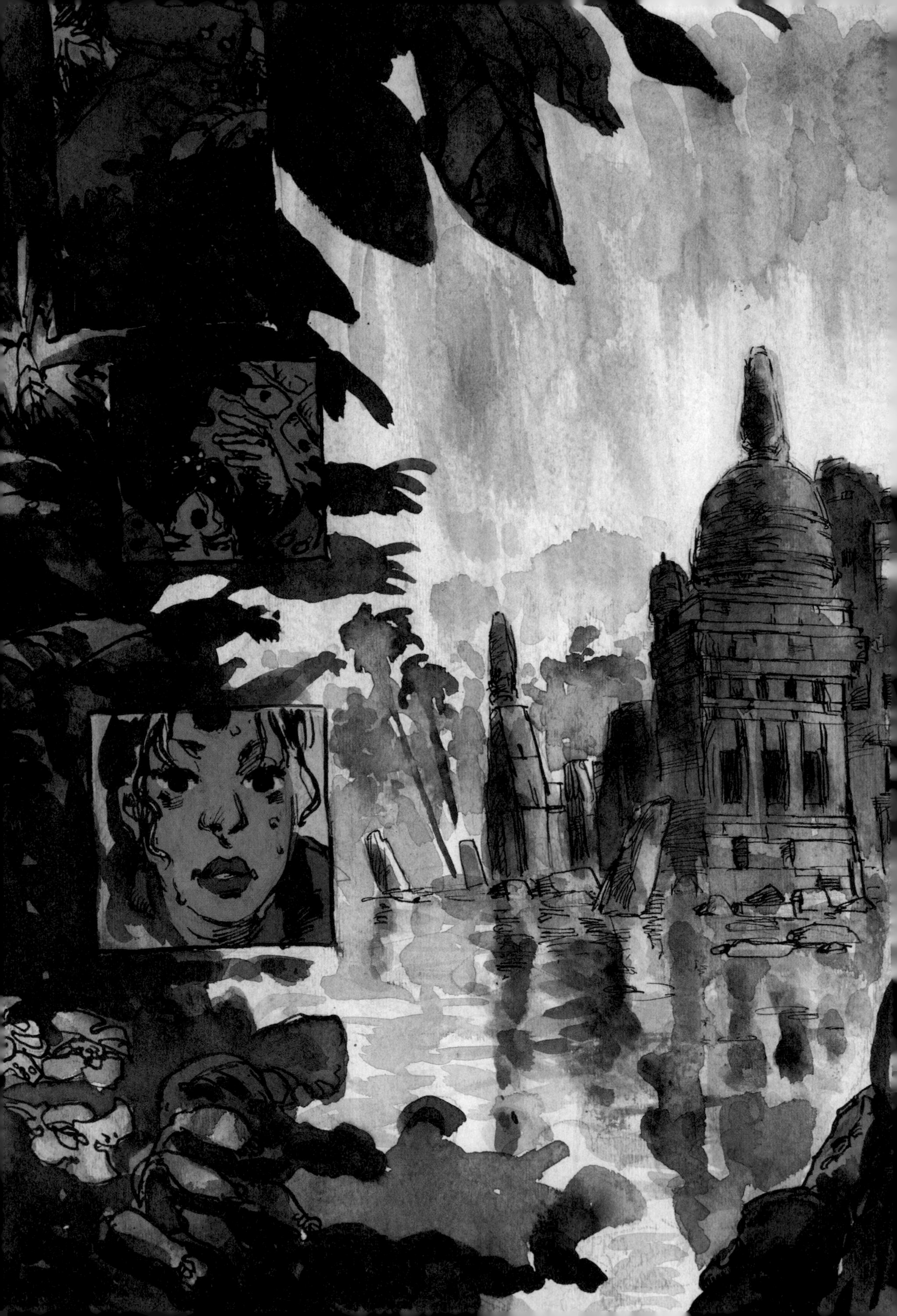

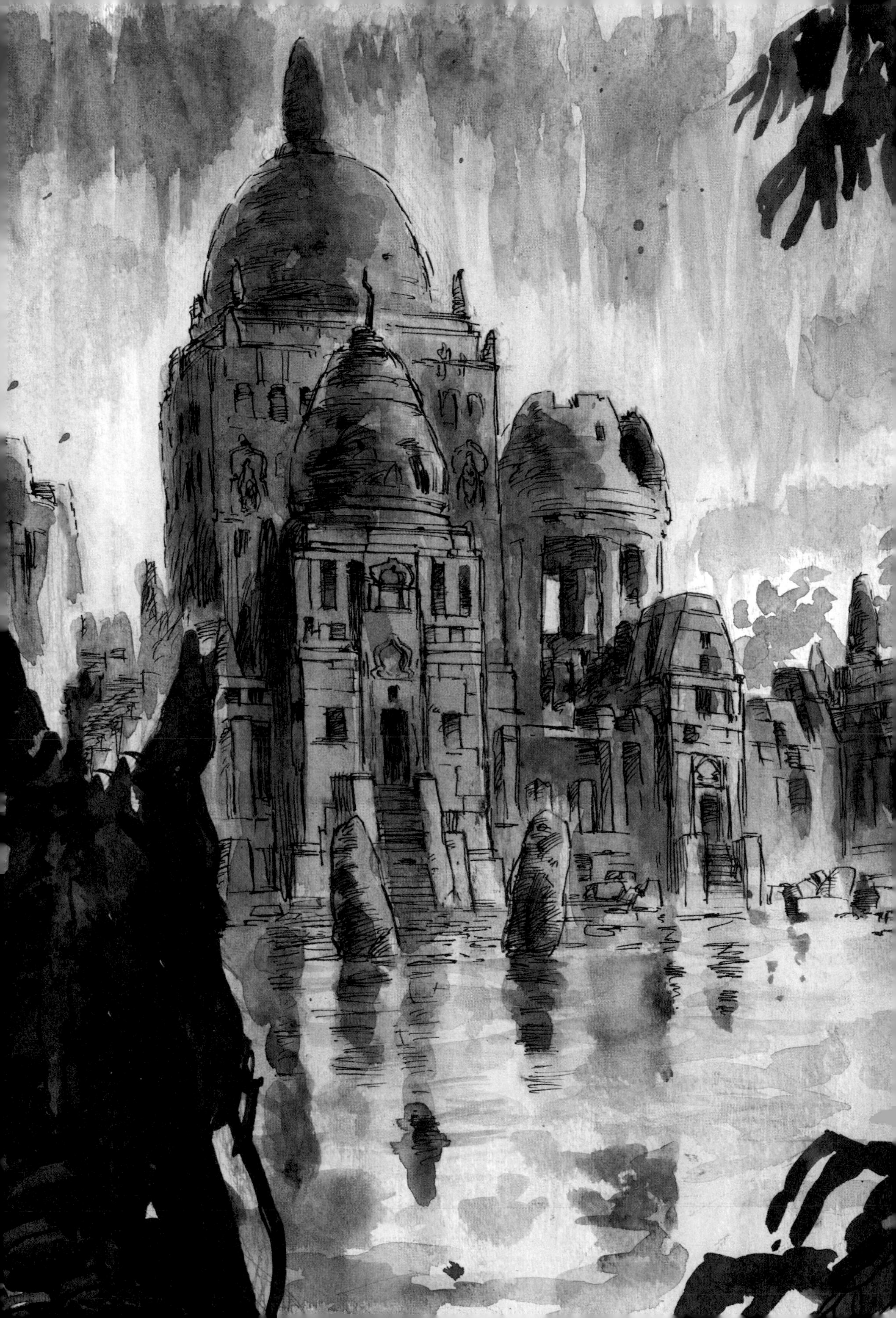

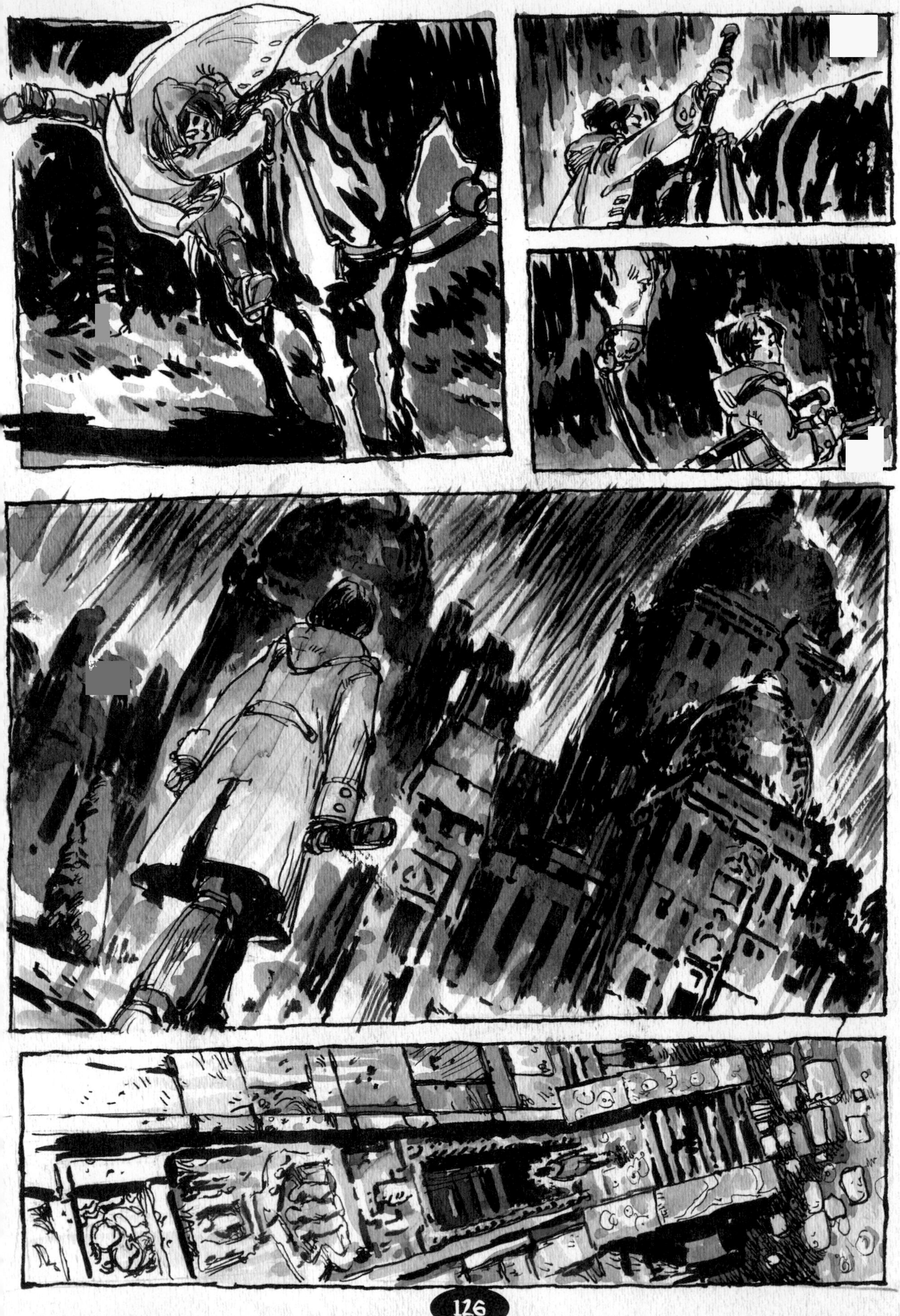

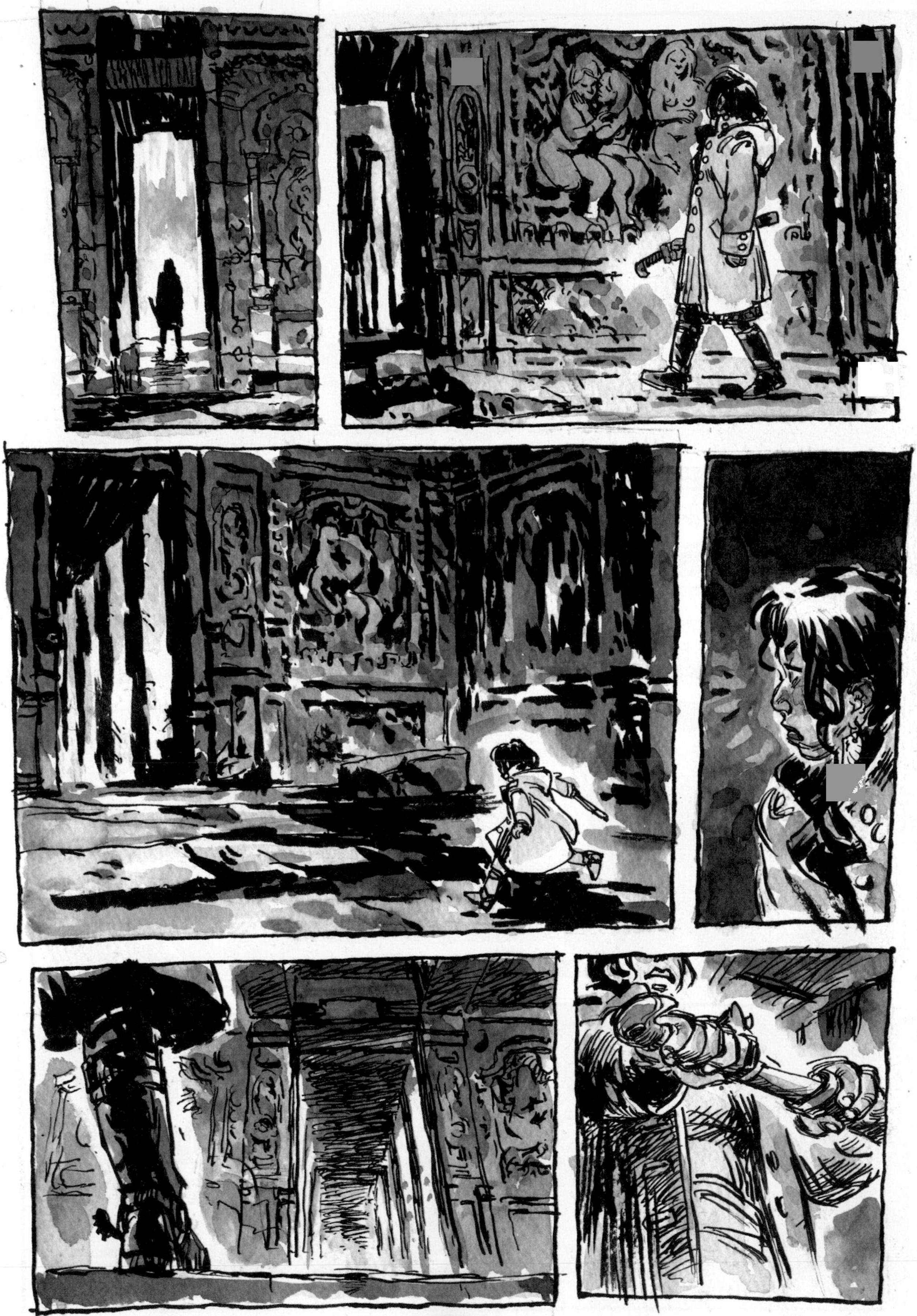

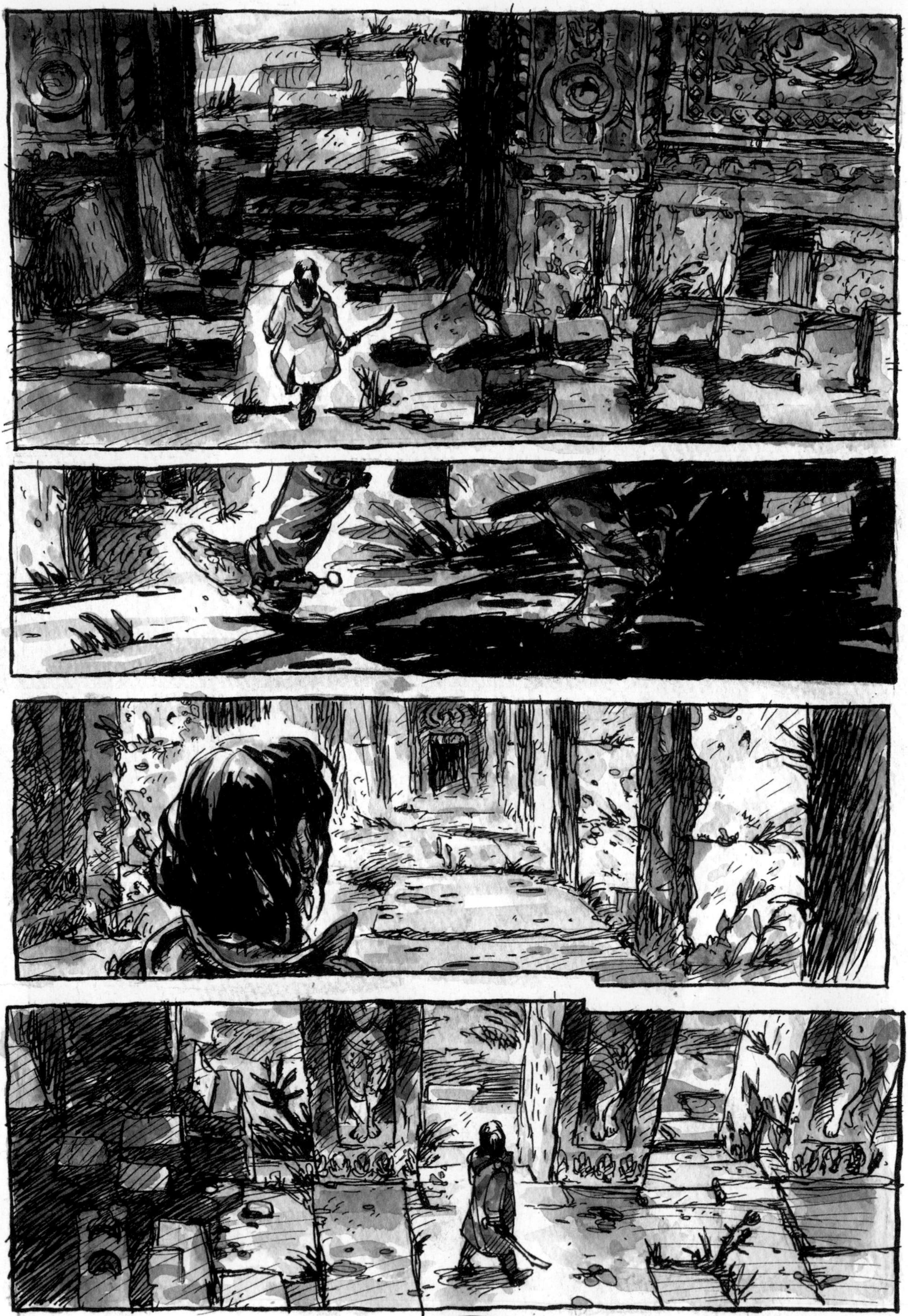

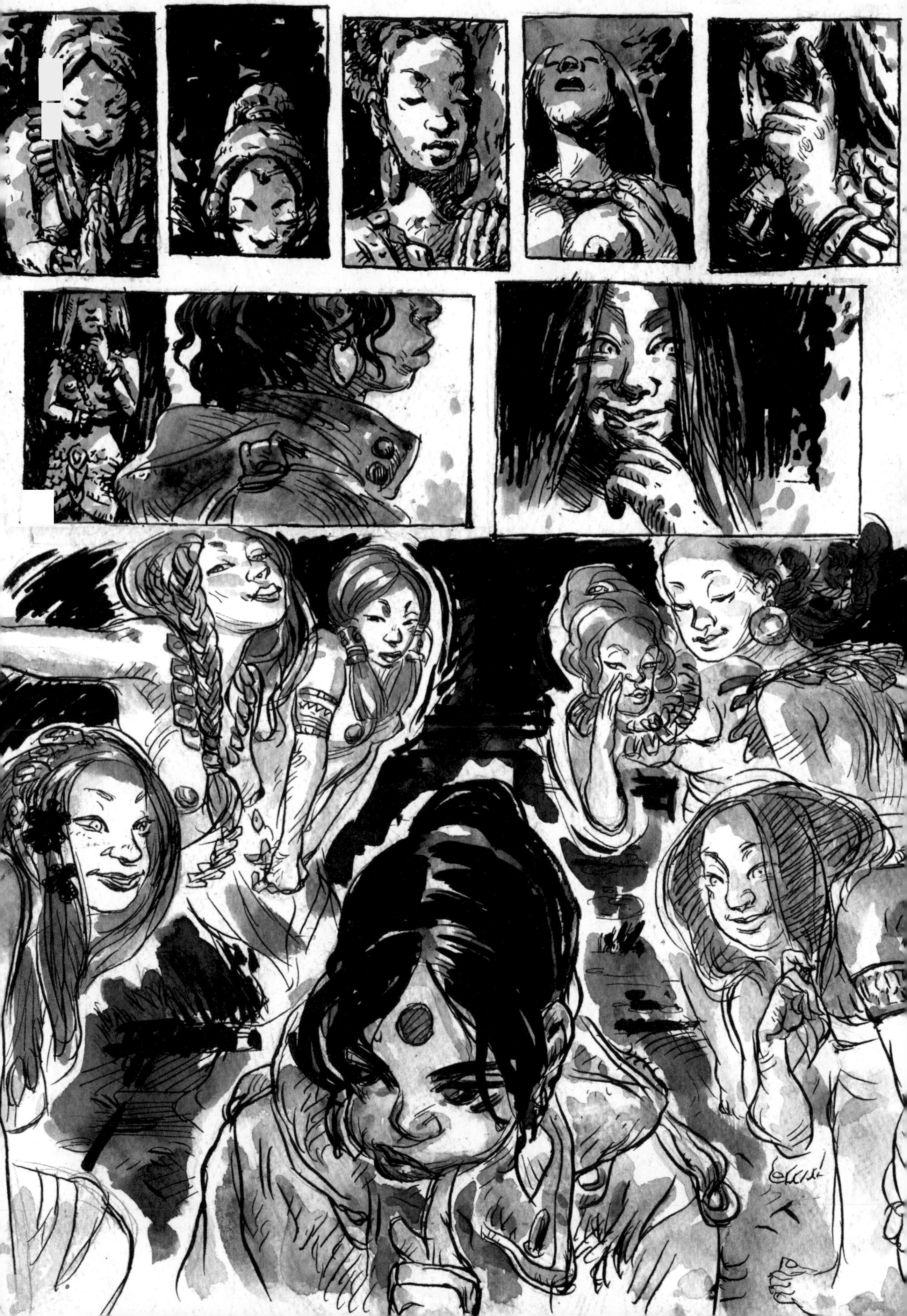

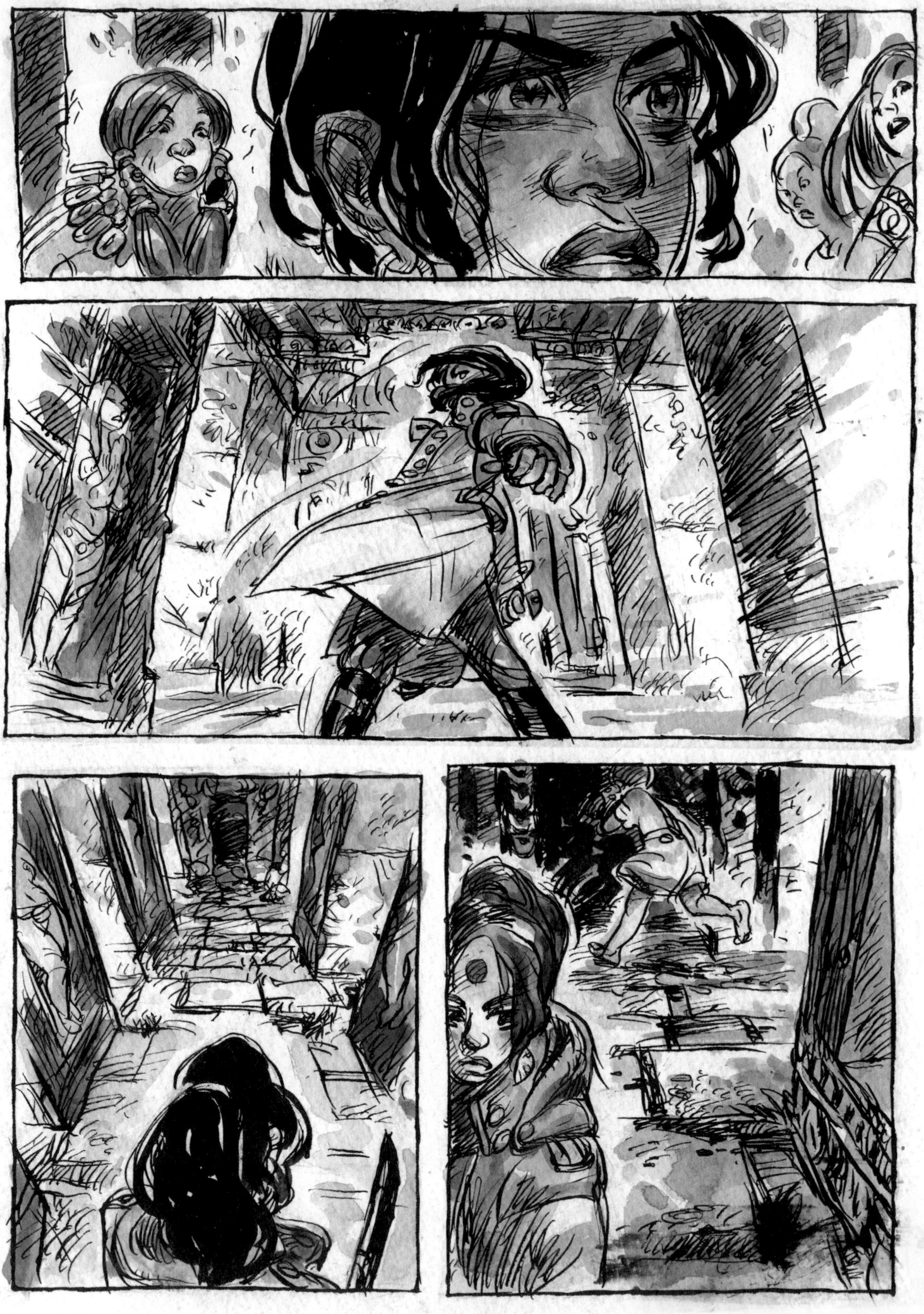

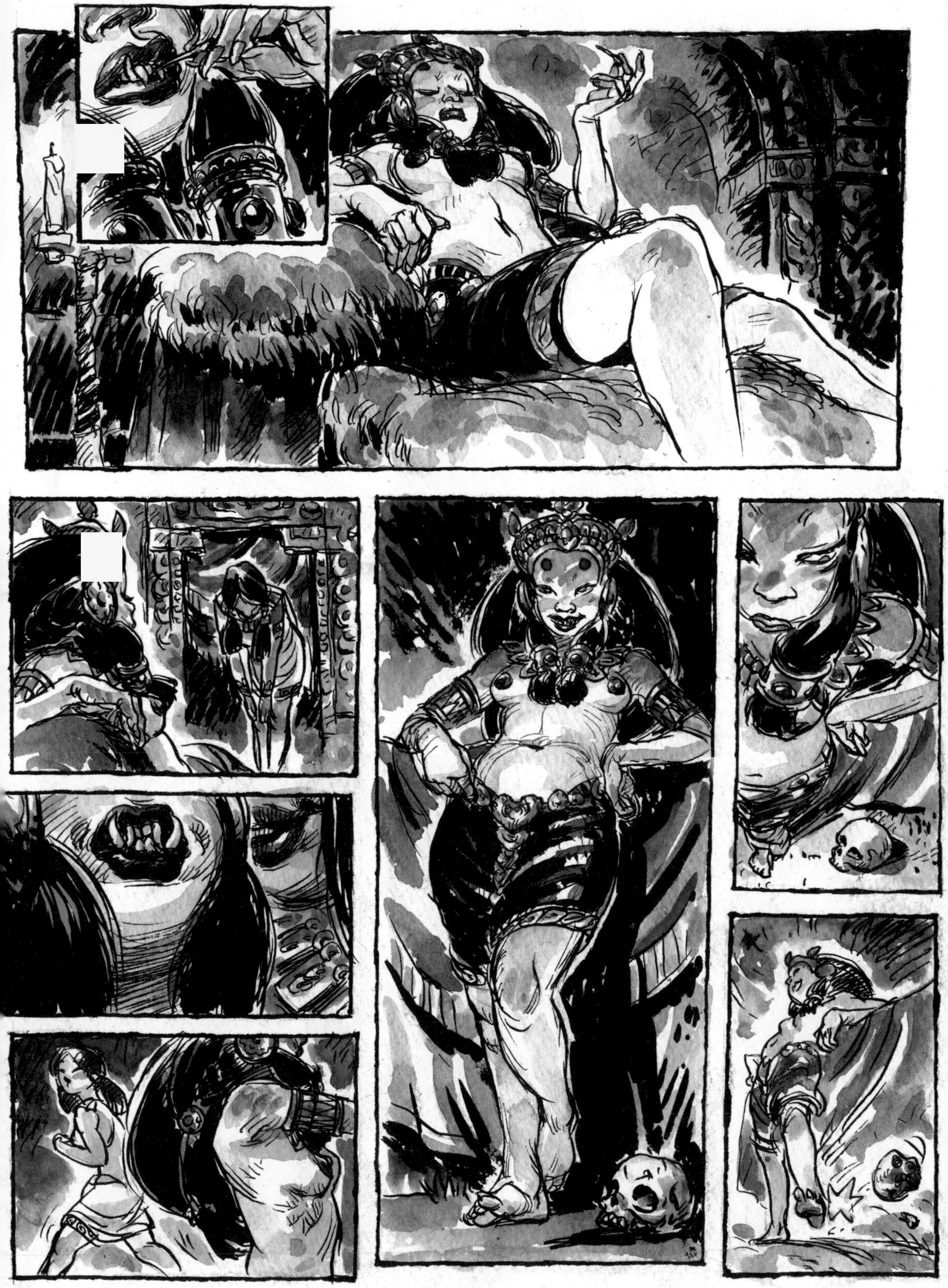

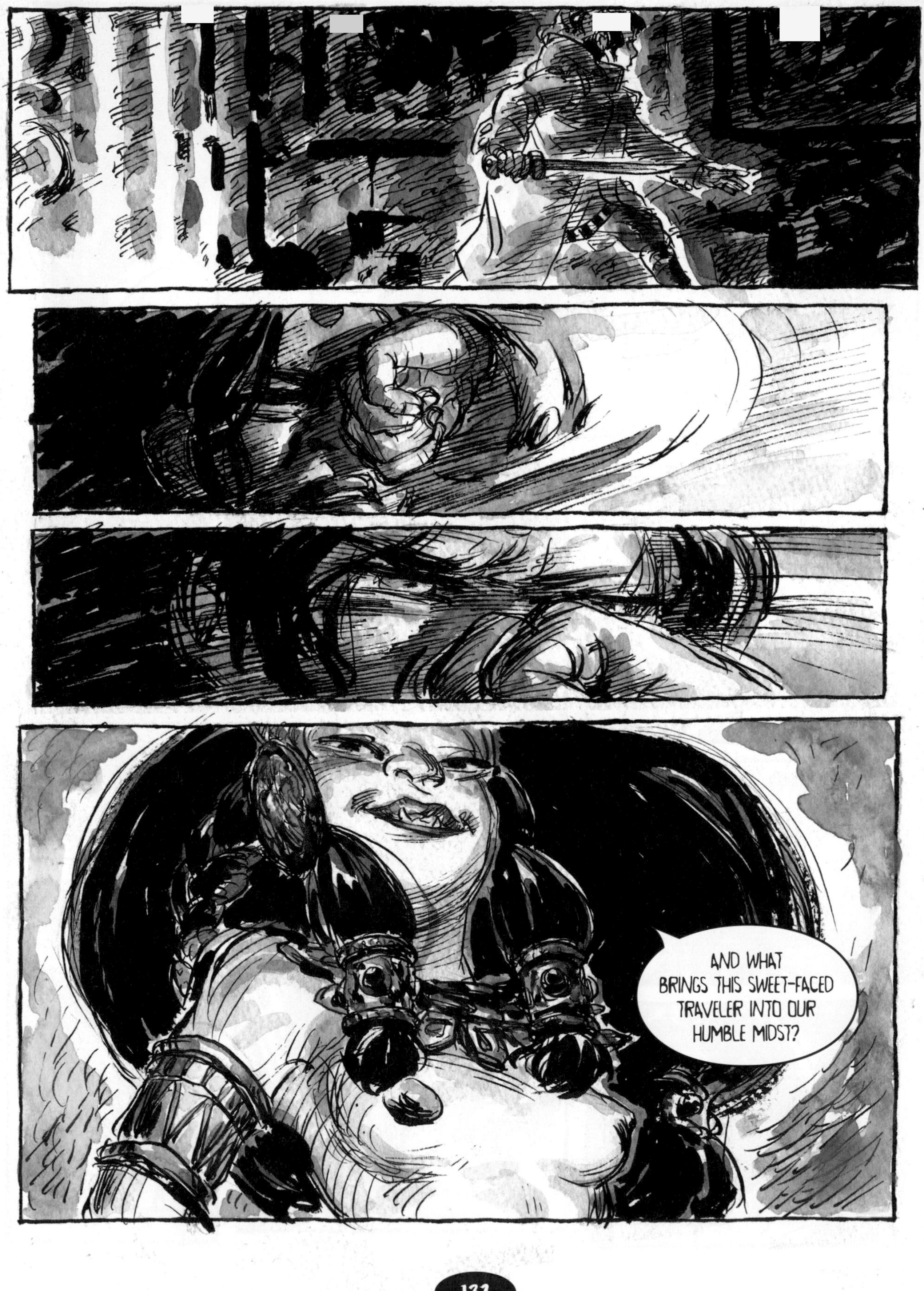
AND WHAT BRINGS THIS SWEET-FACED TRAVELER INTO OUR HUMBLE MIDST?

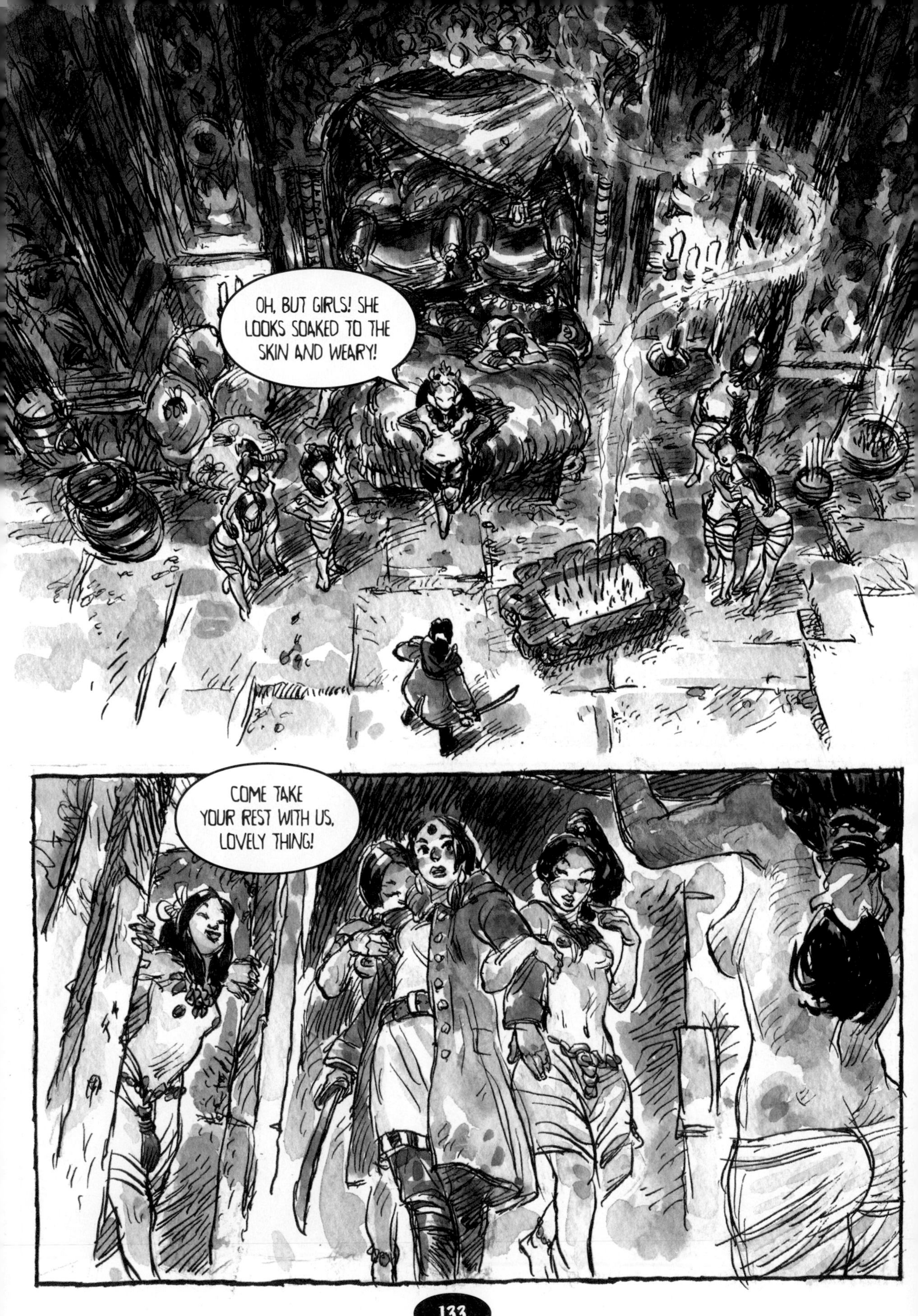

OH, BUT GIRLS! SHE LOOKS SOAKED TO THE SKIN AND WEARY!
COME TAKE YOUR REST WITH US, LOVELY THING!

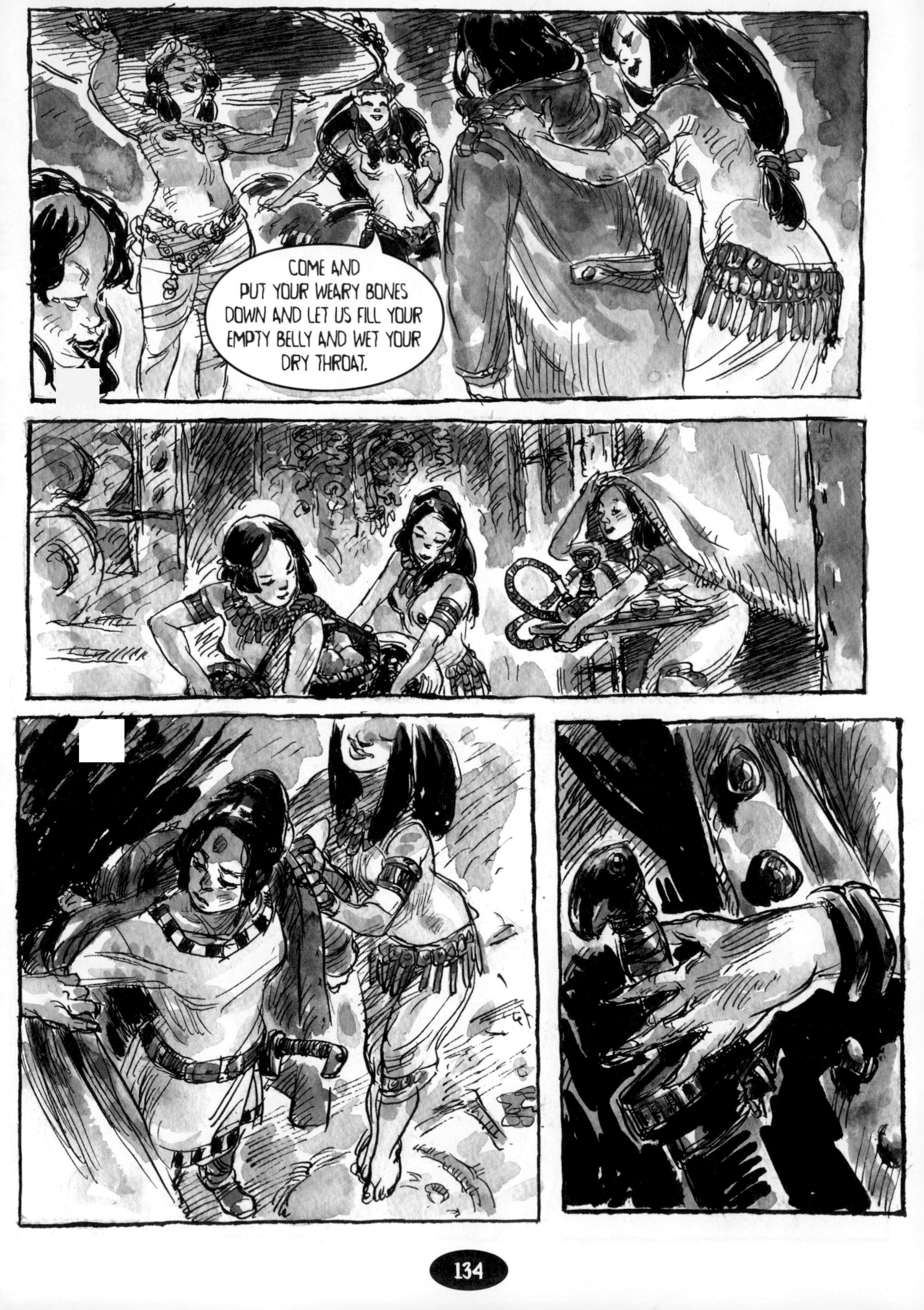
COME AND PUT YOUR WEARY BONES DOWN AND LET US FILL YOUR EMPTY BELLY AND WET YOUR DRY THROAT.

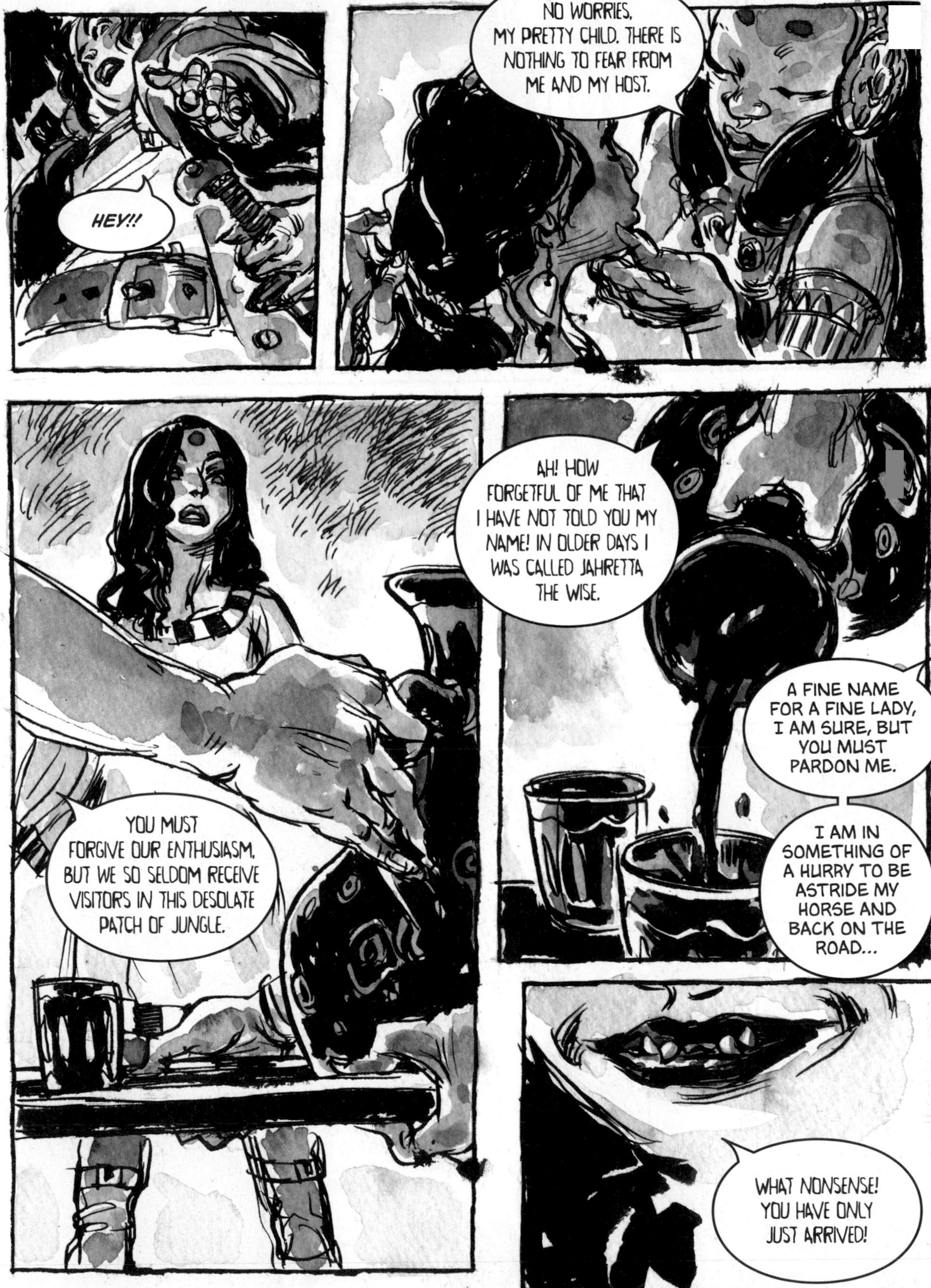
HEY!!
NO WORRIES, MY PRETTY CHILD. THERE IS NOTHING TO FEAR FROM ME AND MY HOST.
YOU MUST FORGIVE OUR ENTHUSIASM, BUT WE SO SELDOM RECEIVE VISITORS IN THIS DESOLATE PATCH OF JUNGLE.
AH! HOW FORGETFUL OF ME THAT I HAVE NOT TOLD YOU MY NAME! IN OLDER DAYS I WAS CALLED JAHRETTA THE WISE.
A FINE NAME FOR A FINE LADY, I AM SURE, BUT YOU MUST PARDON ME.
I AM IN SOMETHING OF A HURRY TO BE ASTRIDE MY HORSE AND BACK ON THE ROAD...
WHAT NONSENSE! YOU HAVE ONLY JUST ARRIVED!

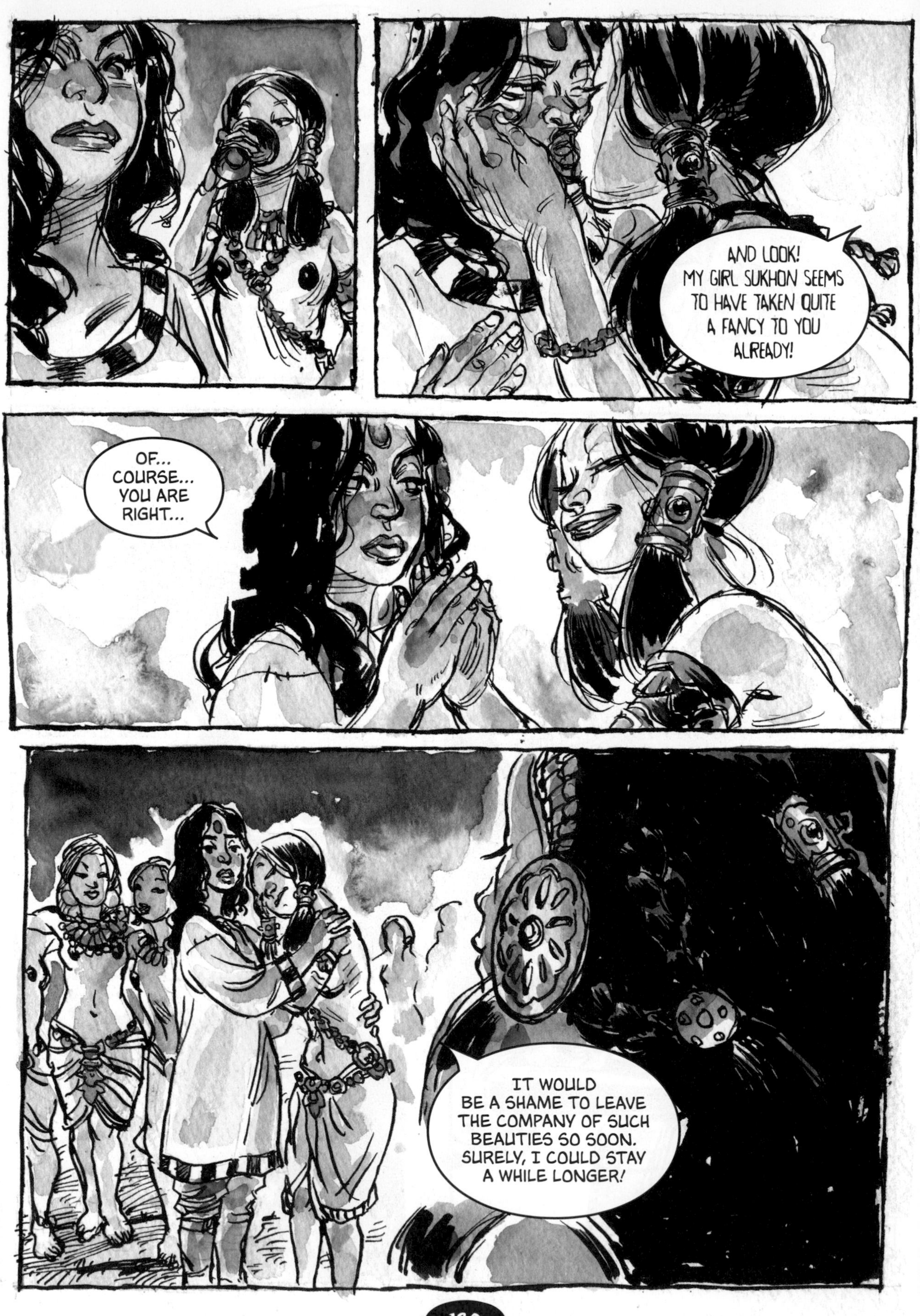
AND LOOK! MY GIRL SUKHON SEEMS TO HAVE TAKEN QUITE A FANCY TO YOU ALREADY!
OF... COURSE... YOU ARE RIGHT...
IT WOULD BE A SHAME TO LEAVE THE COMPANY OF SUCH BEAUTIES SO SOON. SURELY, I COULD STAY A WHILE LONGER!

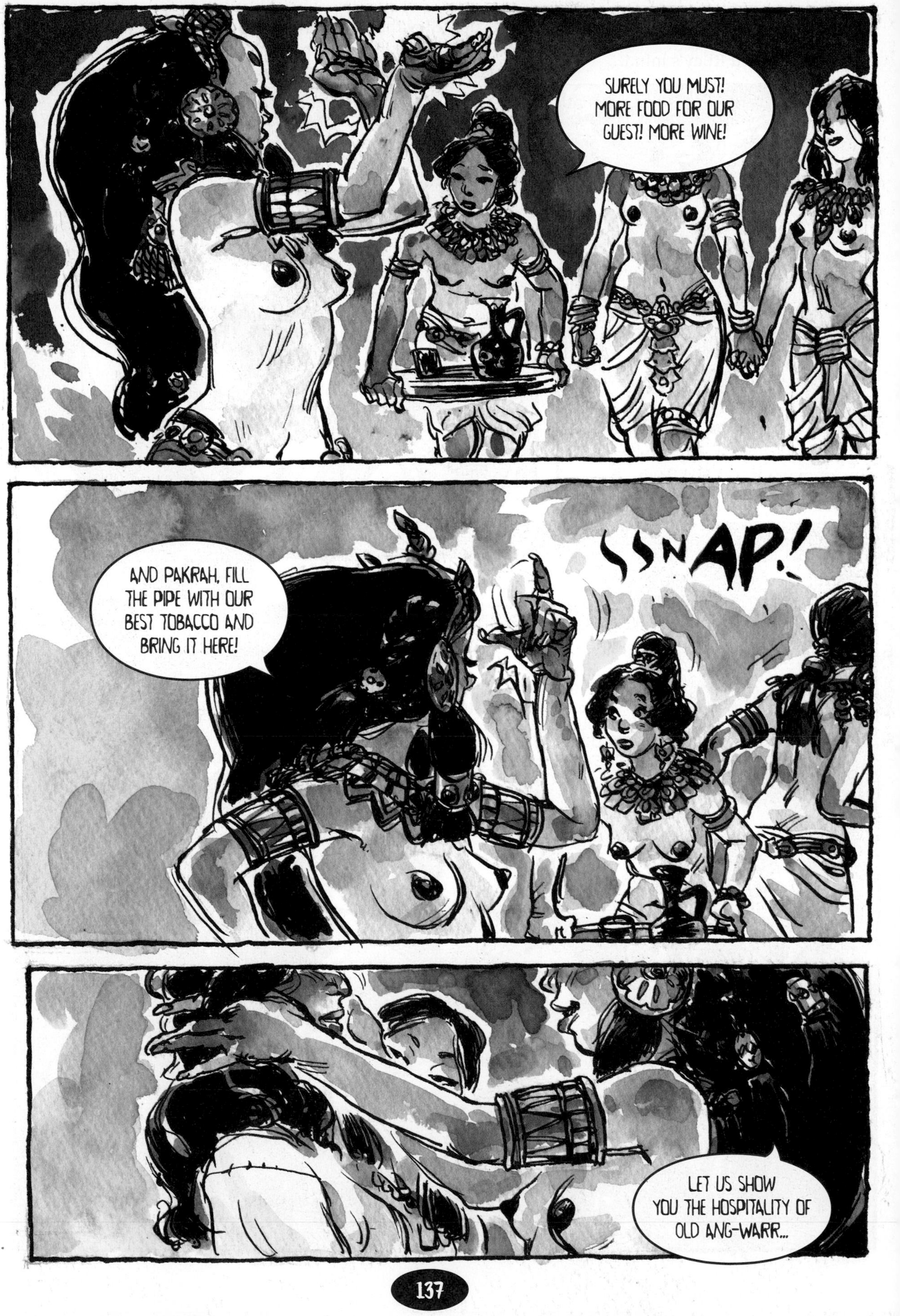
SURELY YOU MUST! MORE FOOD FOR OUR GUEST! MORE WINE!
AND PAKRAH, FILL THE PIPE WITH OUR BEST TOBACCO AND BRING IT HERE!
SSNAP!
LET US SHOW YOU THE HOSPITALITY OF OLD ANG-WARR...

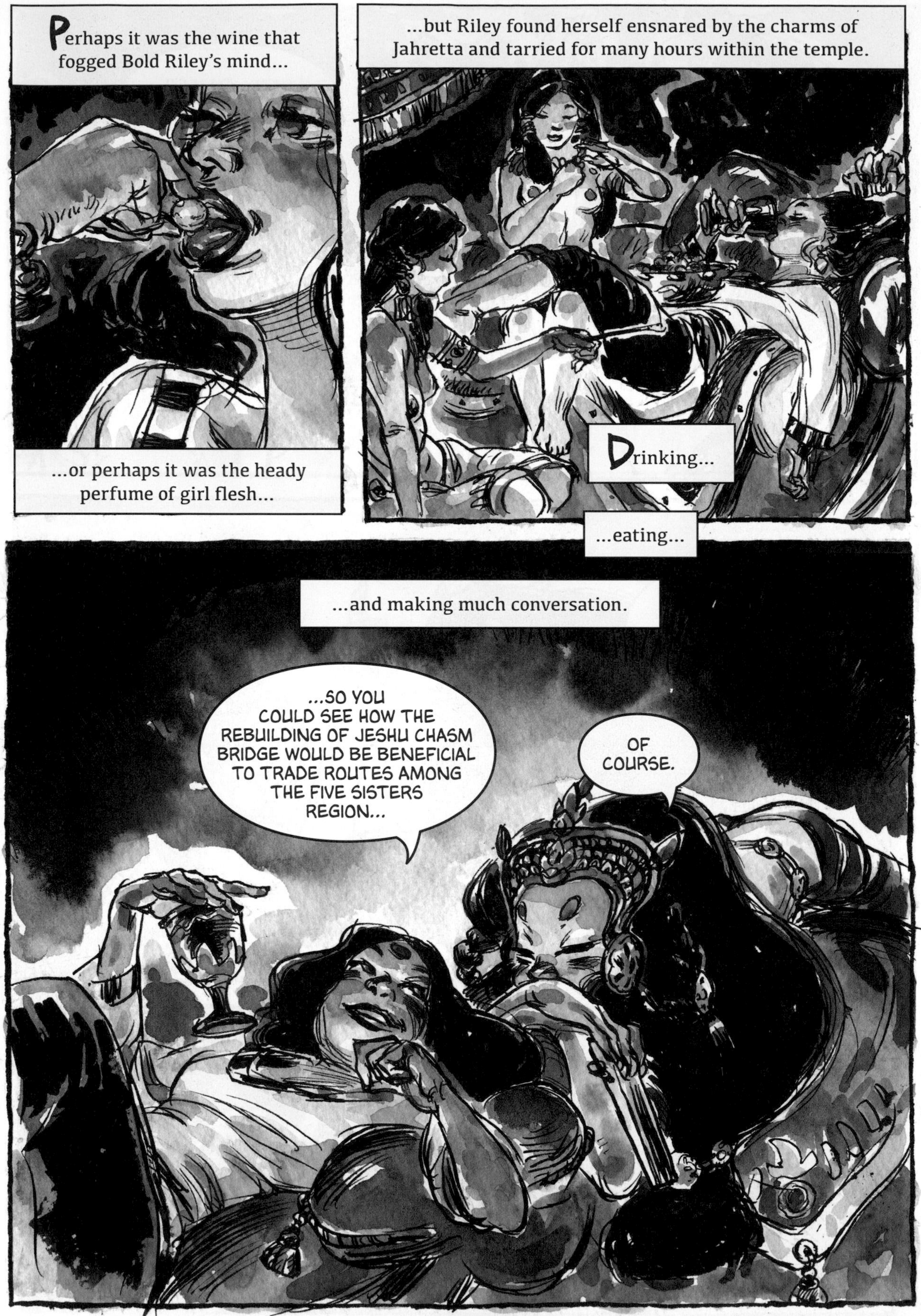
Perhaps it was the wine that fogged Bold Riley's mind...
...or perhaps it was the heady perfume of girl flesh...
...but Riley found herself ensnared by the charms of Jahretta and tarried for many hours within the temple.
Drinking...
...eating...
...and making much conversation.
...SO YOU COULD SEE HOW THE REBUILDING OF JESHU CHASM BRIDGE WOULD BE BENEFICIAL TO TRADE ROUTES AMONG THE FIVE SISTERS REGION...
OF COURSE.

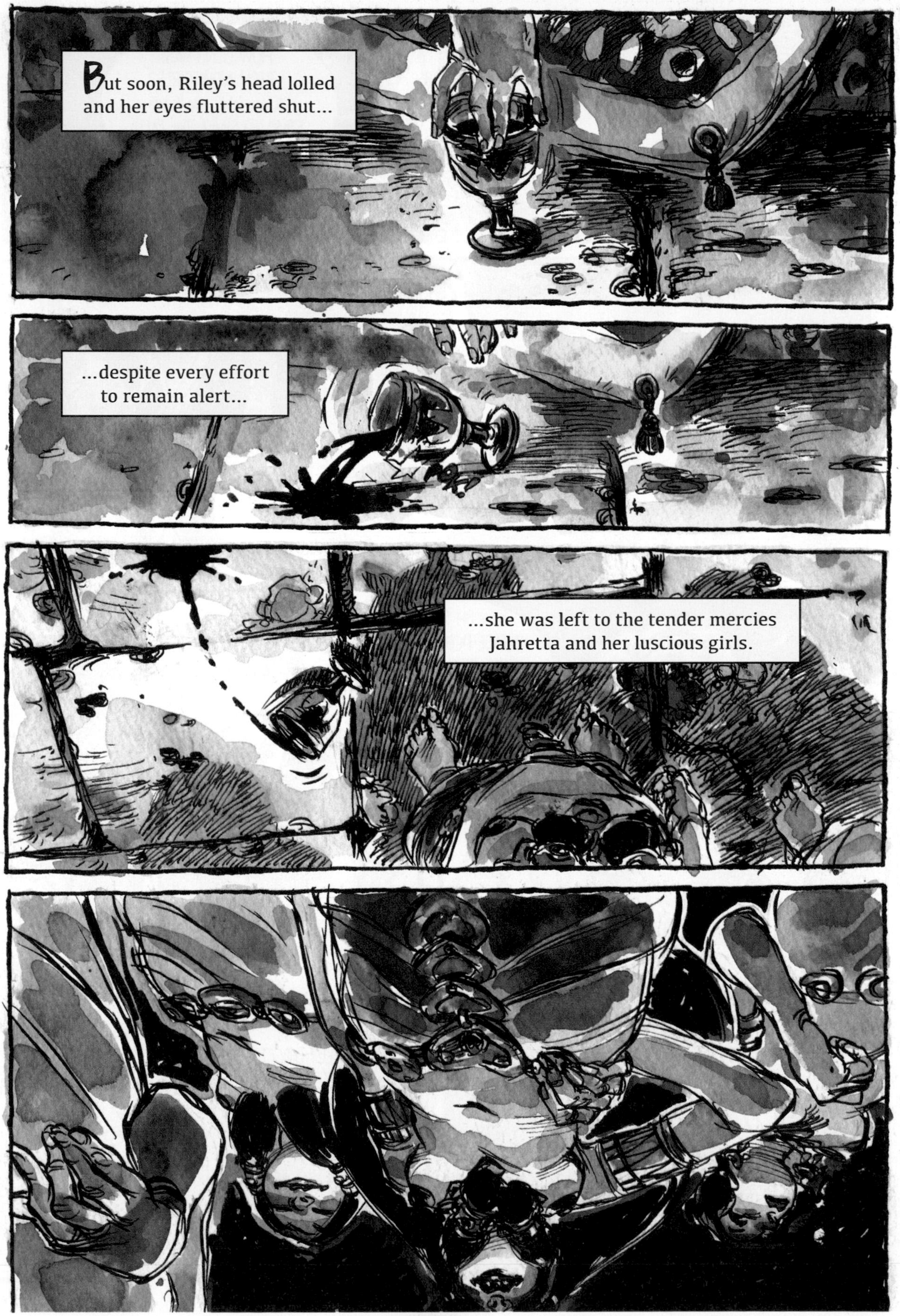
But soon, Riley's head lolled and her eyes fluttered shut...
...despite every effort to remain alert...
...she was left to the tender mercies Jahretta and her luscious girls.

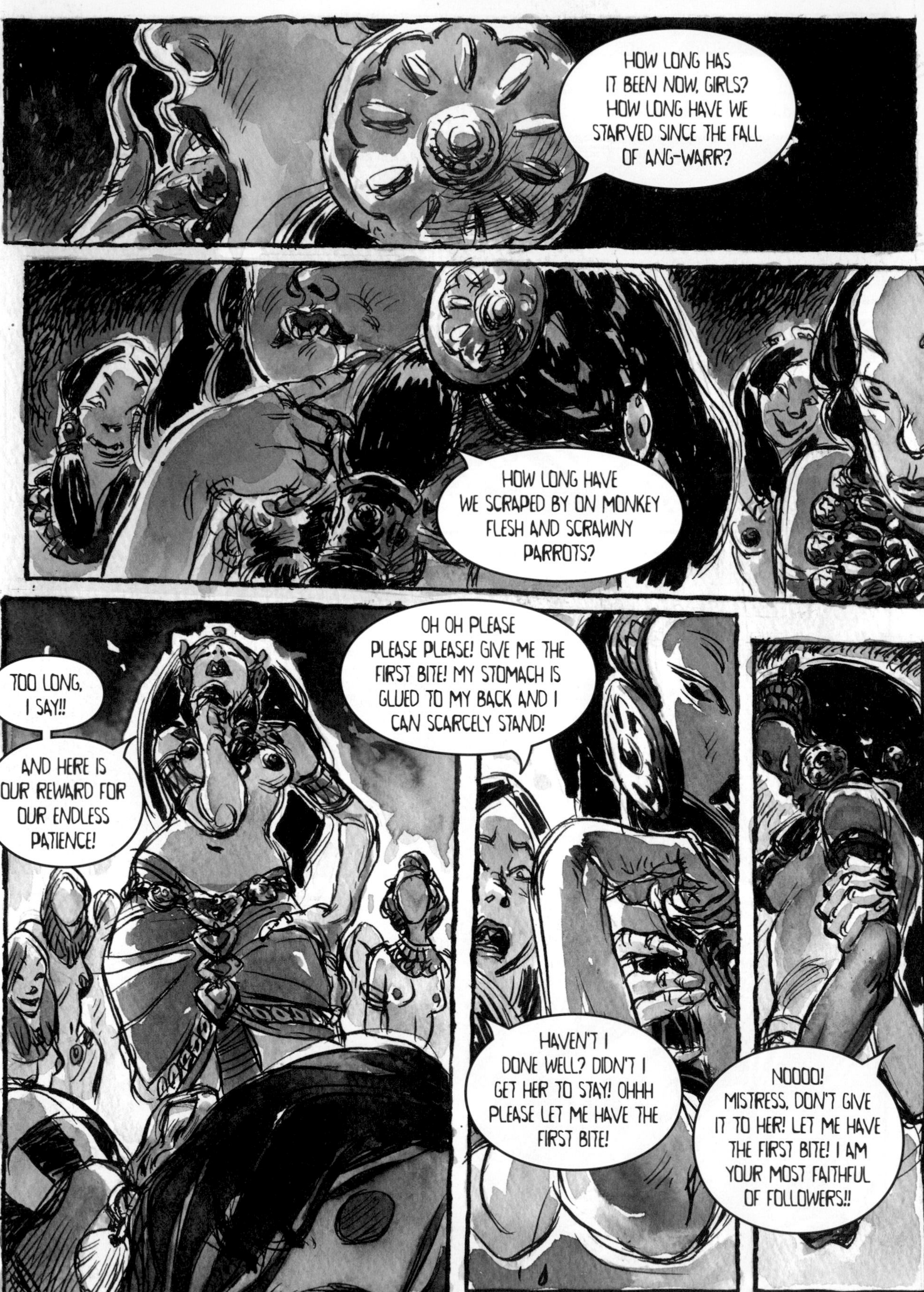
HOW LONG HAS IT BEEN NOW, GIRLS? HOW LONG HAVE WE STARVED SINCE THE FALL OF ANG-WARR?
HOW LONG HAVE WE SCRAPED BY ON MONKEY FLESH AND SCRAWNY PARROTS?
TOO LONG, I SAY!!
AND HERE IS OUR REWARD FOR OUR ENDLESS PATIENCE!
OH OH PLEASE PLEASE PLEASE! GIVE ME THE FIRST BITE! MY STOMACH IS GLUED TO MY BACK AND I CAN SCARCELY STAND!
HAVEN'T I DONE WELL? DIDN'T I GET HER TO STAY! OHHH PLEASE LET ME HAVE THE FIRST BITE!
NOOOO! MISTRESS, DON'T GIVE IT TO HER! LET ME HAVE THE FIRST BITE! I AM YOUR MOST FAITHFUL OF FOLLOWERS!!

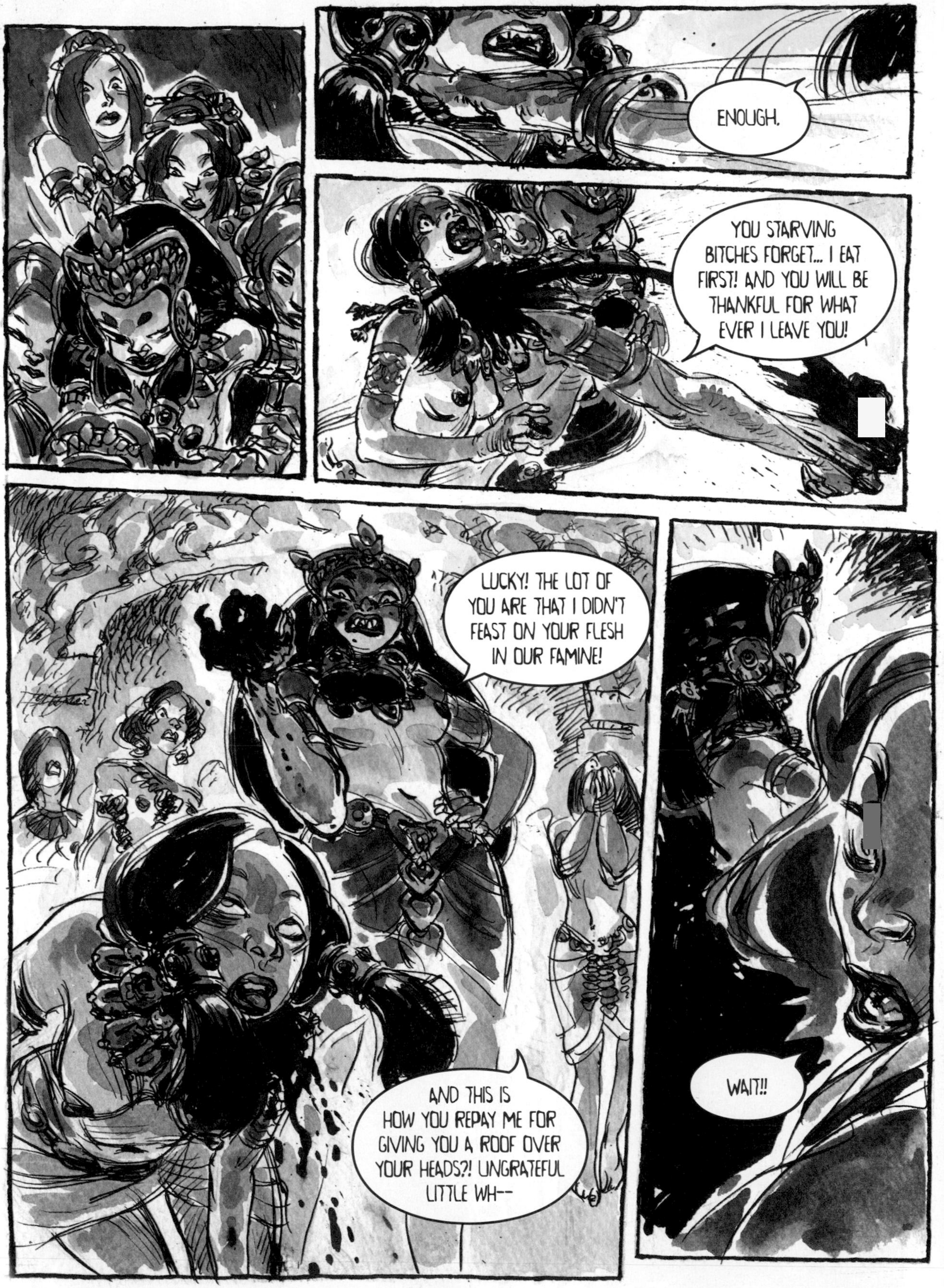
ENOUGH.
YOU STARVING BITCHES FORGET... I EAT FIRST! AND YOU WILL BE THANKFUL FOR WHAT EVER I LEAVE YOU!
LUCKY! THE LOT OF YOU ARE THAT I DIDN'T FEAST ON YOUR FLESH IN OUR FAMINE!
AND THIS IS HOW YOU REPAY ME FOR GIVING YOU A ROOF OVER YOUR HEADS?! UNGRATEFUL LITTLE WH--
WAIT!!

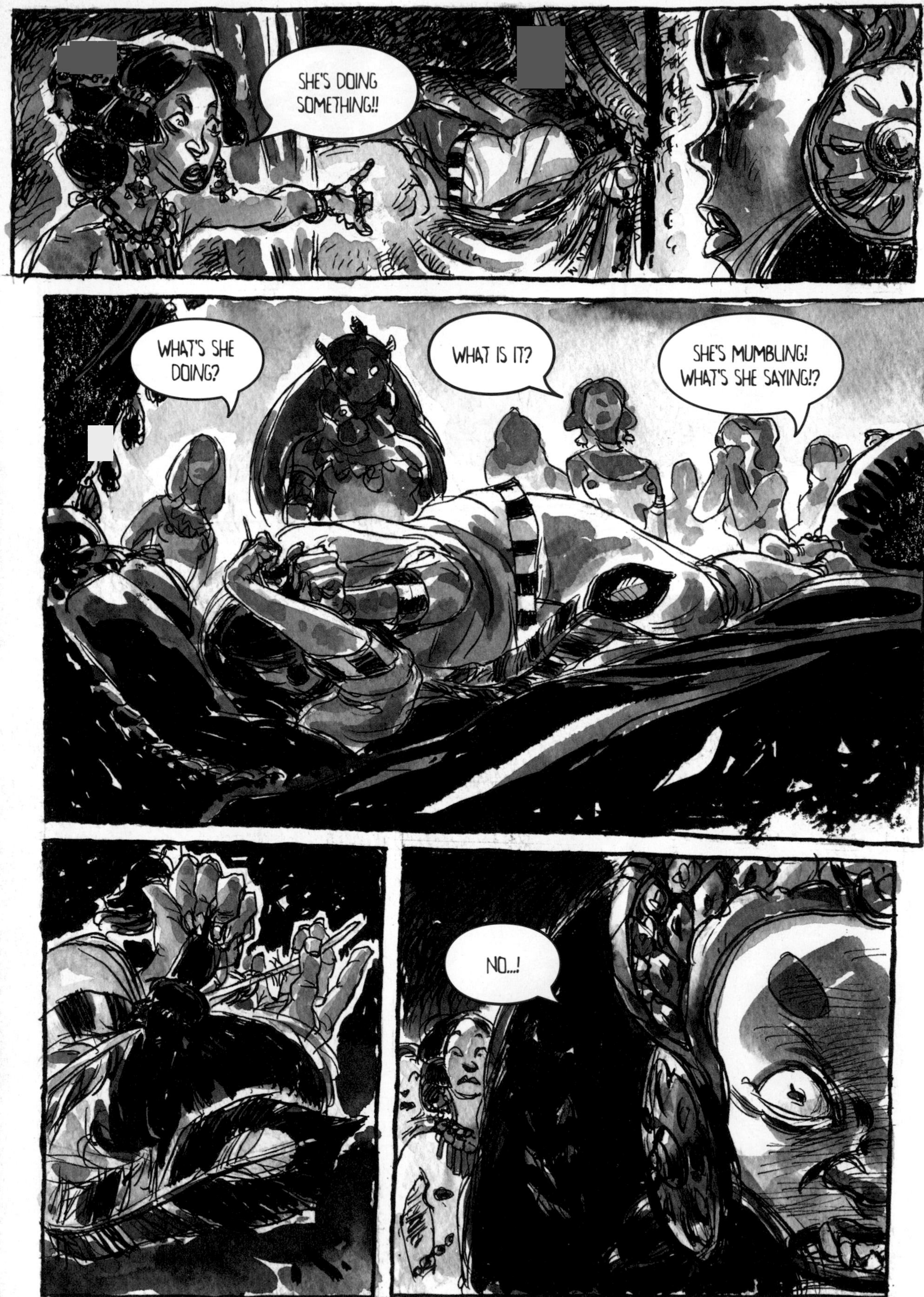
SHE'S DOING SOMETHING!!
WHAT'S SHE DOING?
WHAT IS IT?
SHE'S MUMBLING! WHAT'S SHE SAYING!?
NO...!

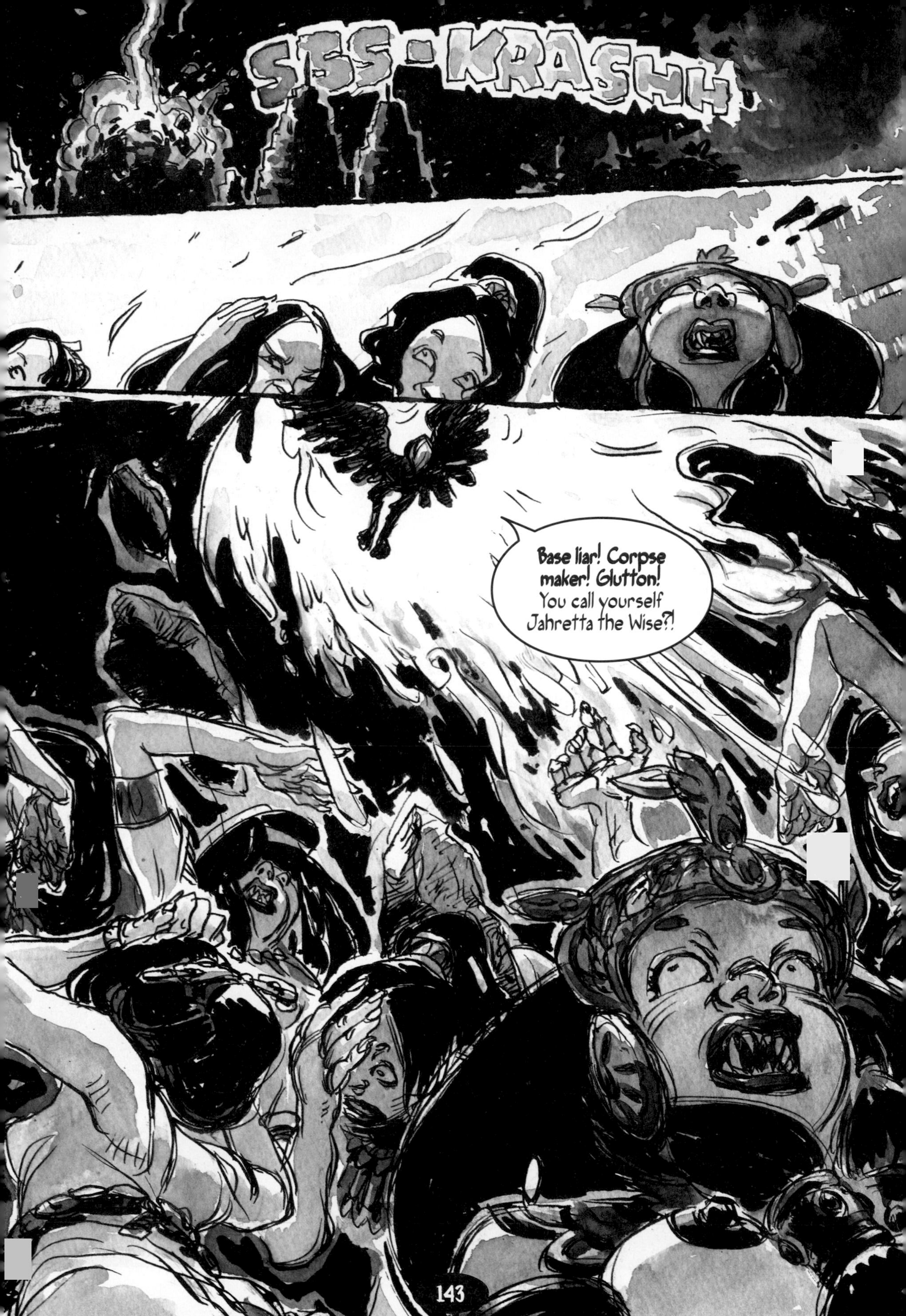
SSS-KRASHH
Base liar! Corpse maker! Glutton! You call yourself Jahretta the Wise?!

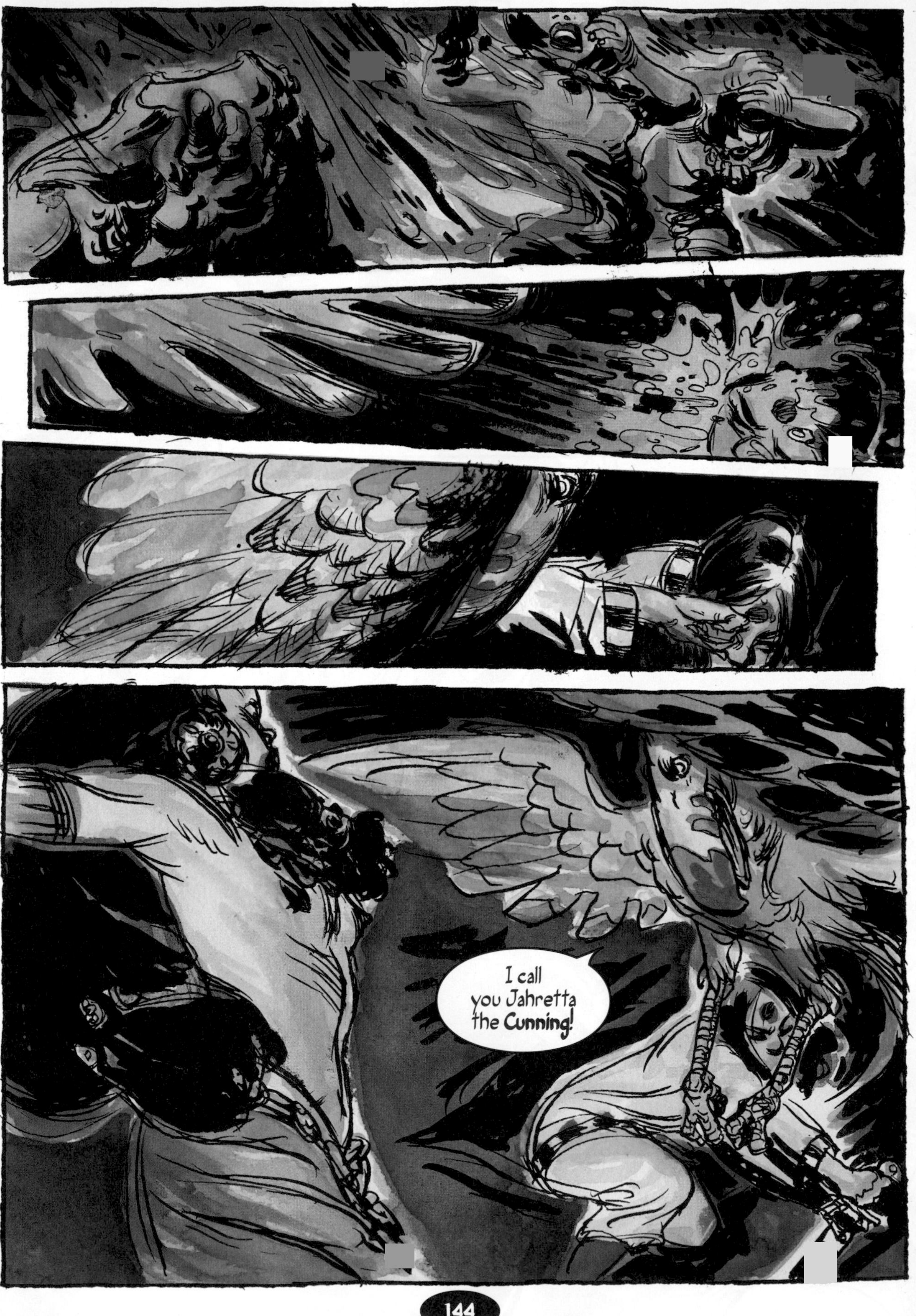
I call you Jahretta the **Cunning**!

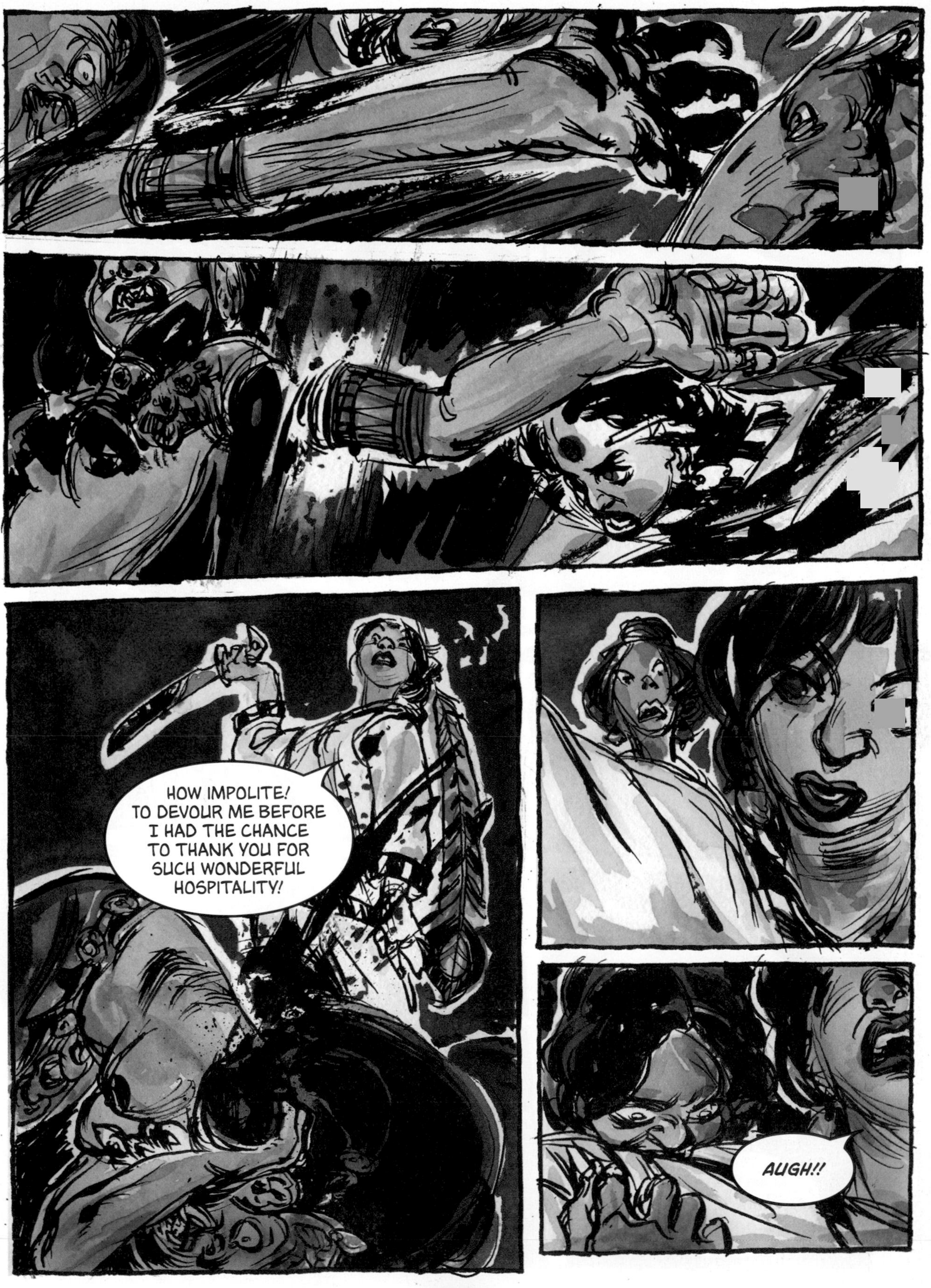
HOW IMPOLITE! TO DEVOUR ME BEFORE I HAD THE CHANCE TO THANK YOU FOR SUCH WONDERFUL HOSPITALITY!
AUGH!!

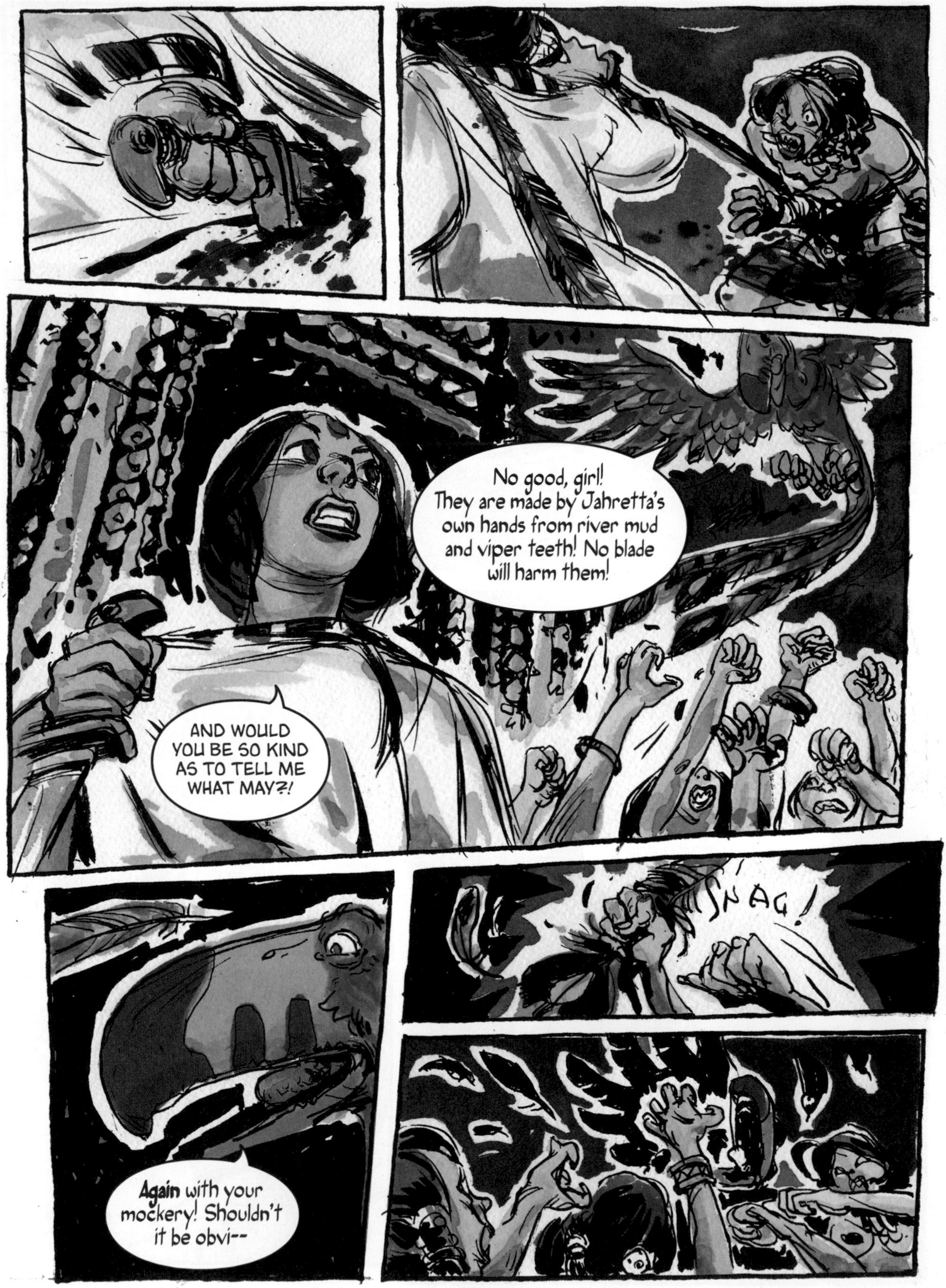
No good, girl! They are made by Jahretta's own hands from river mud and viper teeth! No blade will harm them!
AND WOULD YOU BE SO KIND AS TO TELL ME WHAT MAY?!
SNAG!
Again with your mockery! Shouldn't it be obvi--

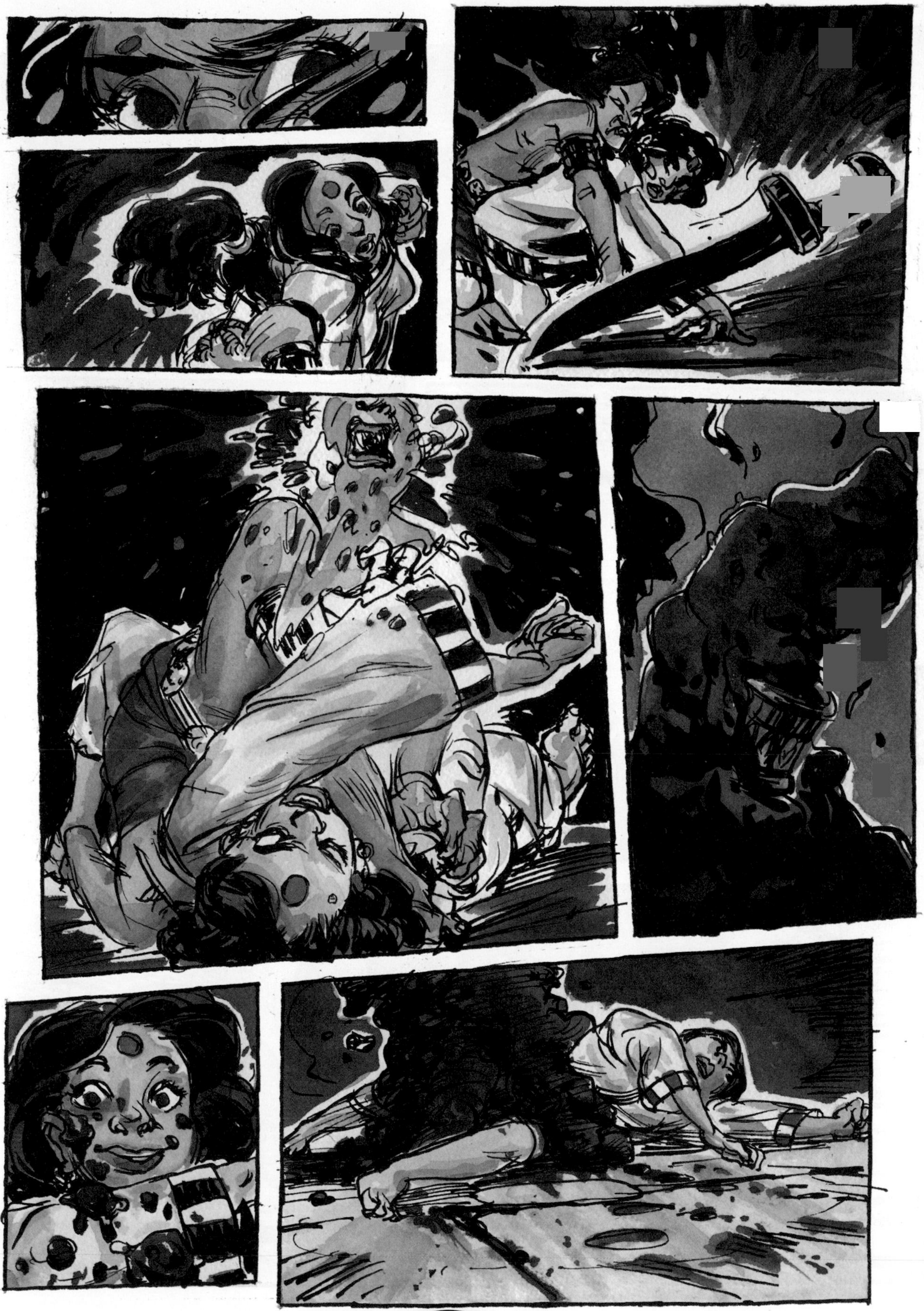

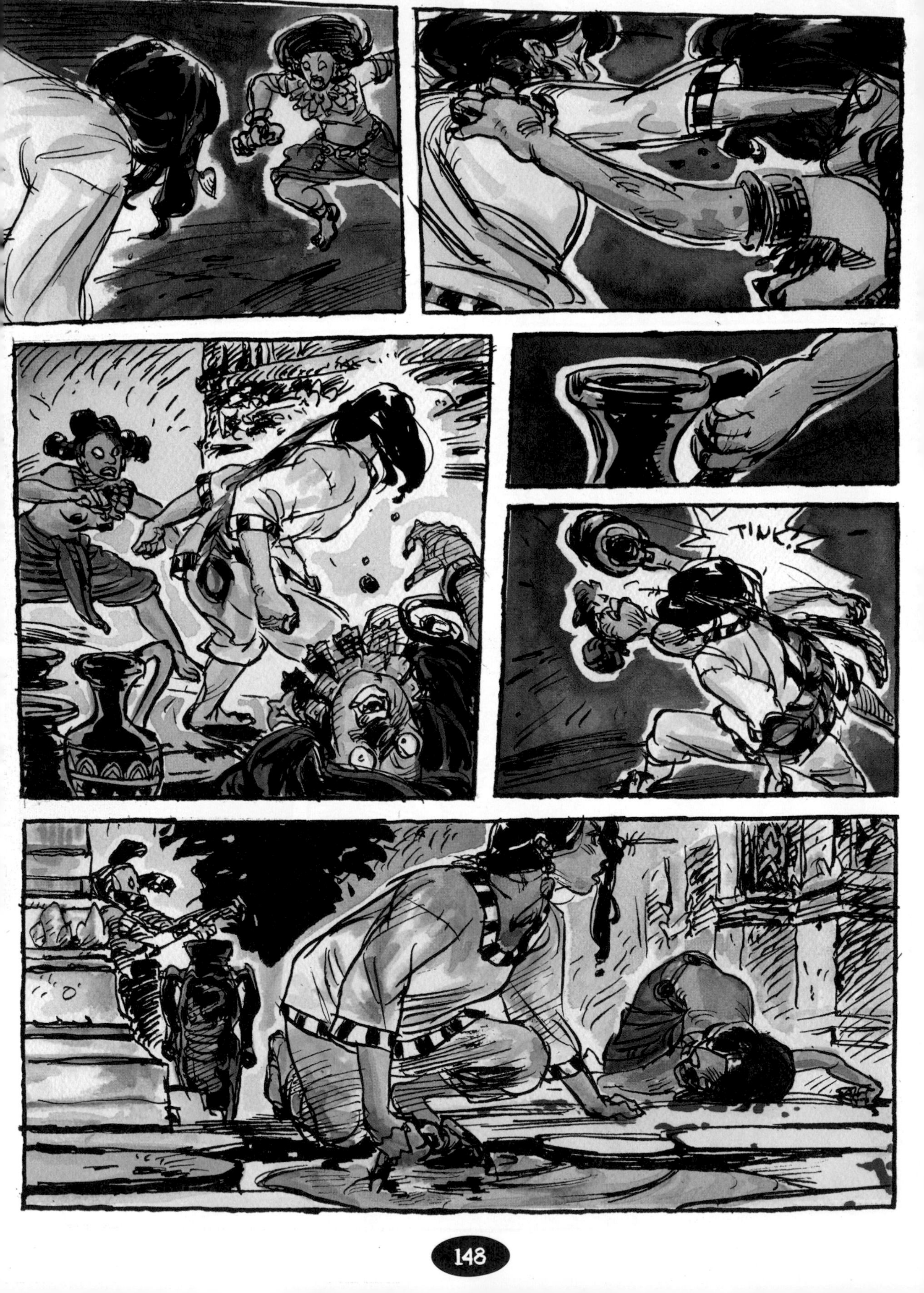
TINK!

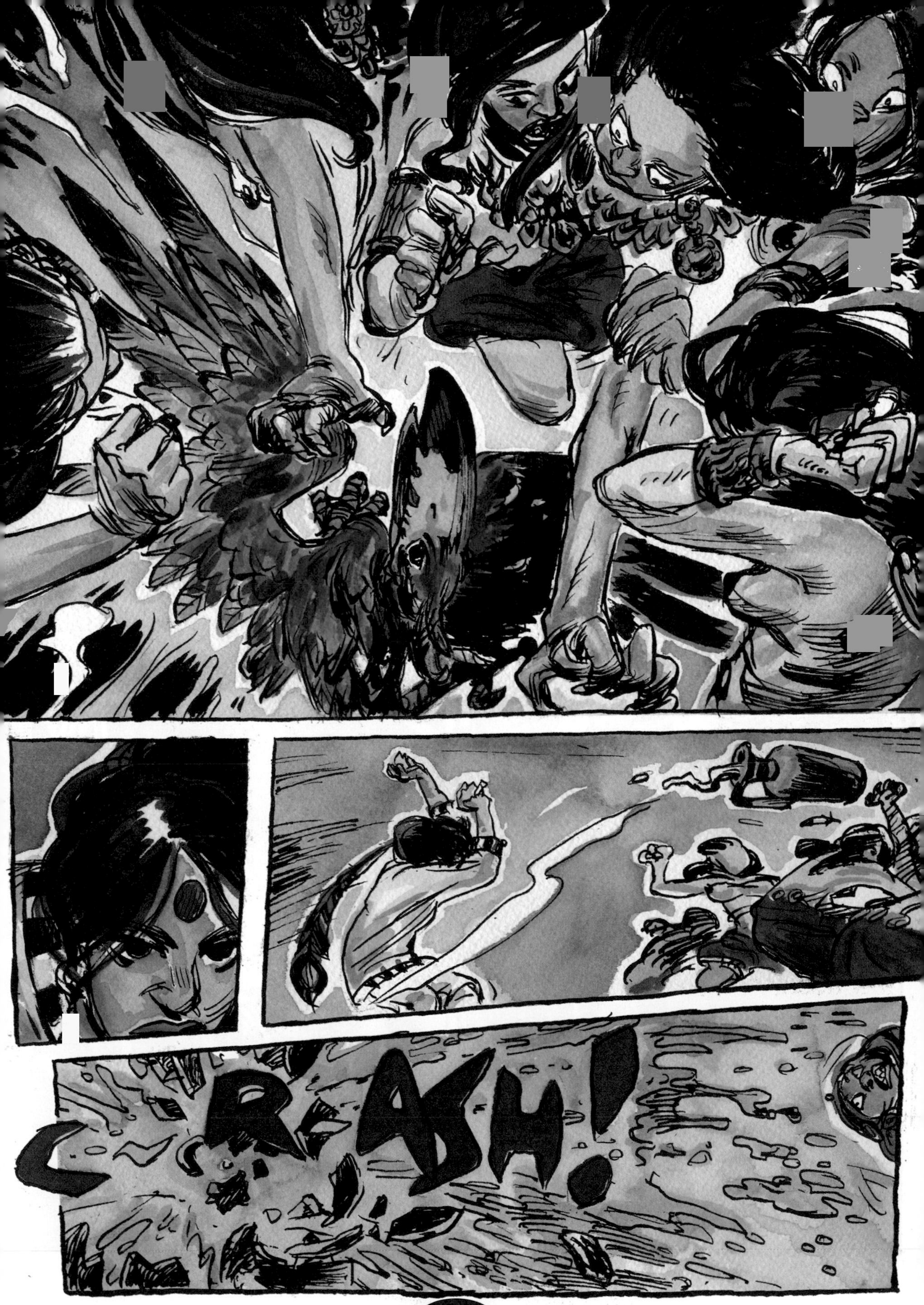
CRASH!

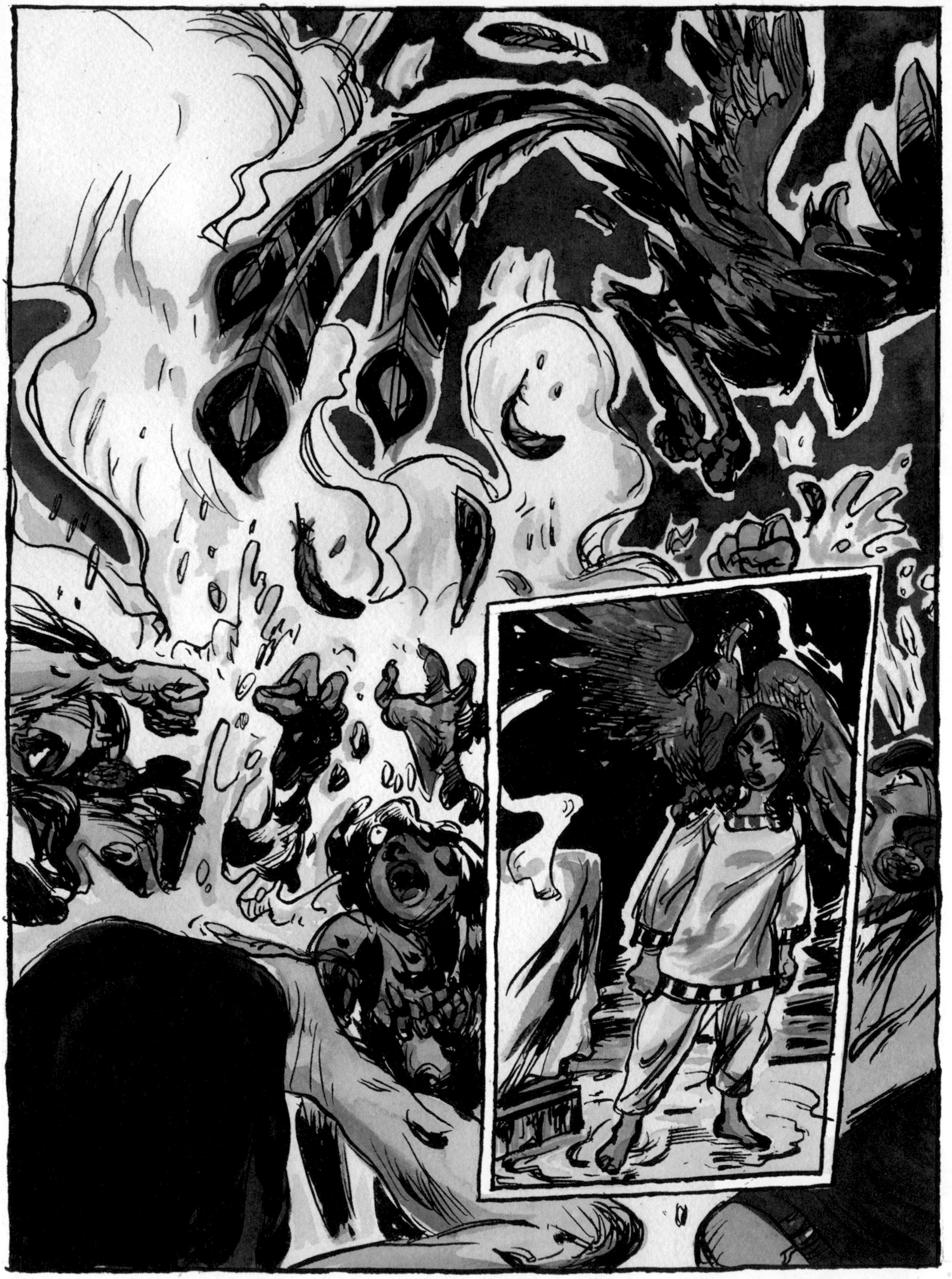

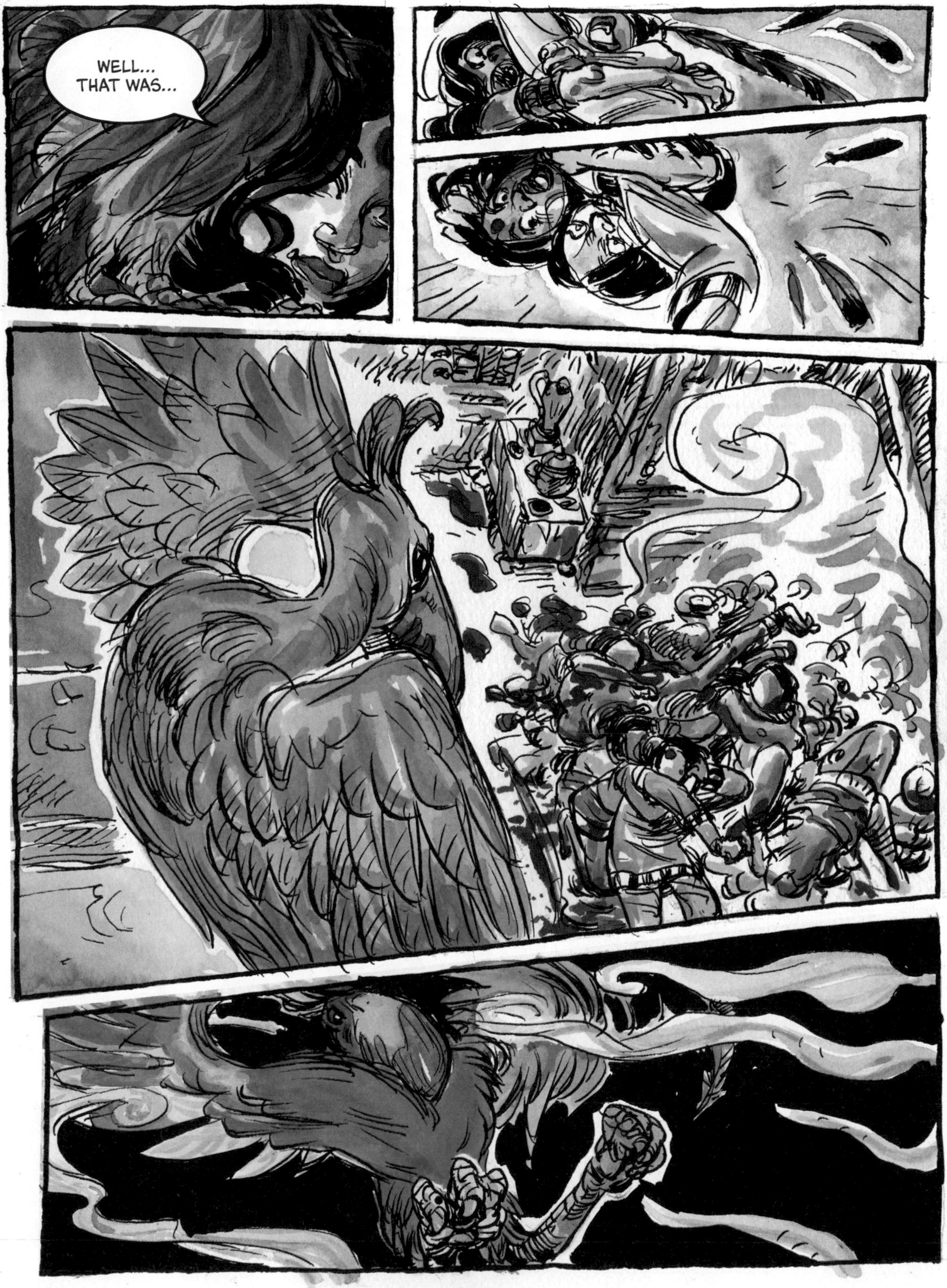
WELL... THAT WAS...

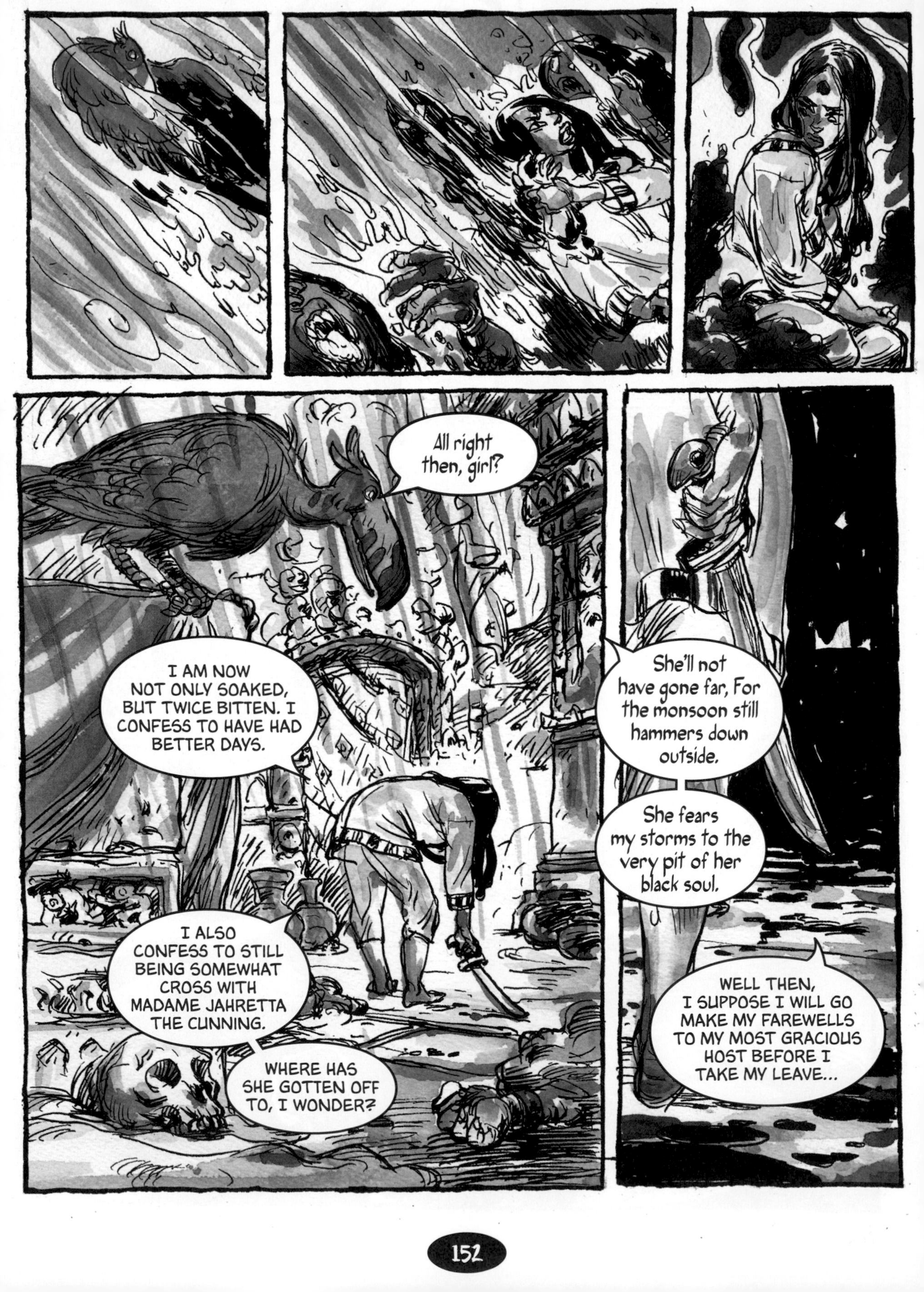
All right then, girl?
I AM NOW NOT ONLY SOAKED, BUT TWICE BITTEN. I CONFESS TO HAVE HAD BETTER DAYS.
I ALSO CONFESS TO STILL BEING SOMEWHAT CROSS WITH MADAME JAHRETTA THE CUNNING.
WHERE HAS SHE GOTTEN OFF TO, I WONDER?
She'll not have gone far, For the monsoon still hammers down outside.
She fears my storms to the very pit of her black soul.
WELL THEN, I SUPPOSE I WILL GO MAKE MY FAREWELLS TO MY MOST GRACIOUS HOST BEFORE I TAKE MY LEAVE...

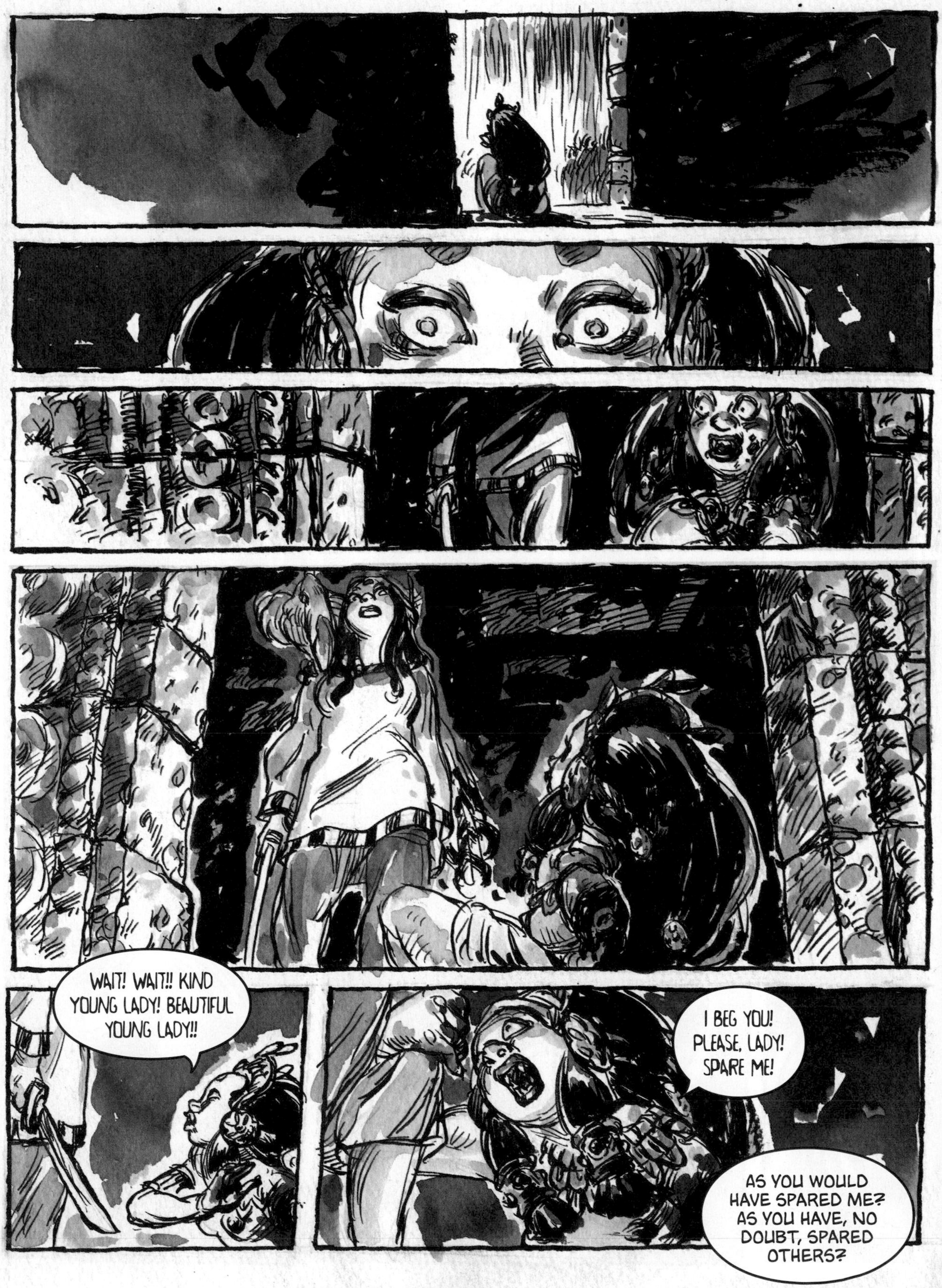
WAIT! WAIT!! KIND YOUNG LADY! BEAUTIFUL YOUNG LADY!!
I BEG YOU! PLEASE, LADY! SPARE ME!
AS YOU WOULD HAVE SPARED ME? AS YOU HAVE, NO DOUBT, SPARED OTHERS?

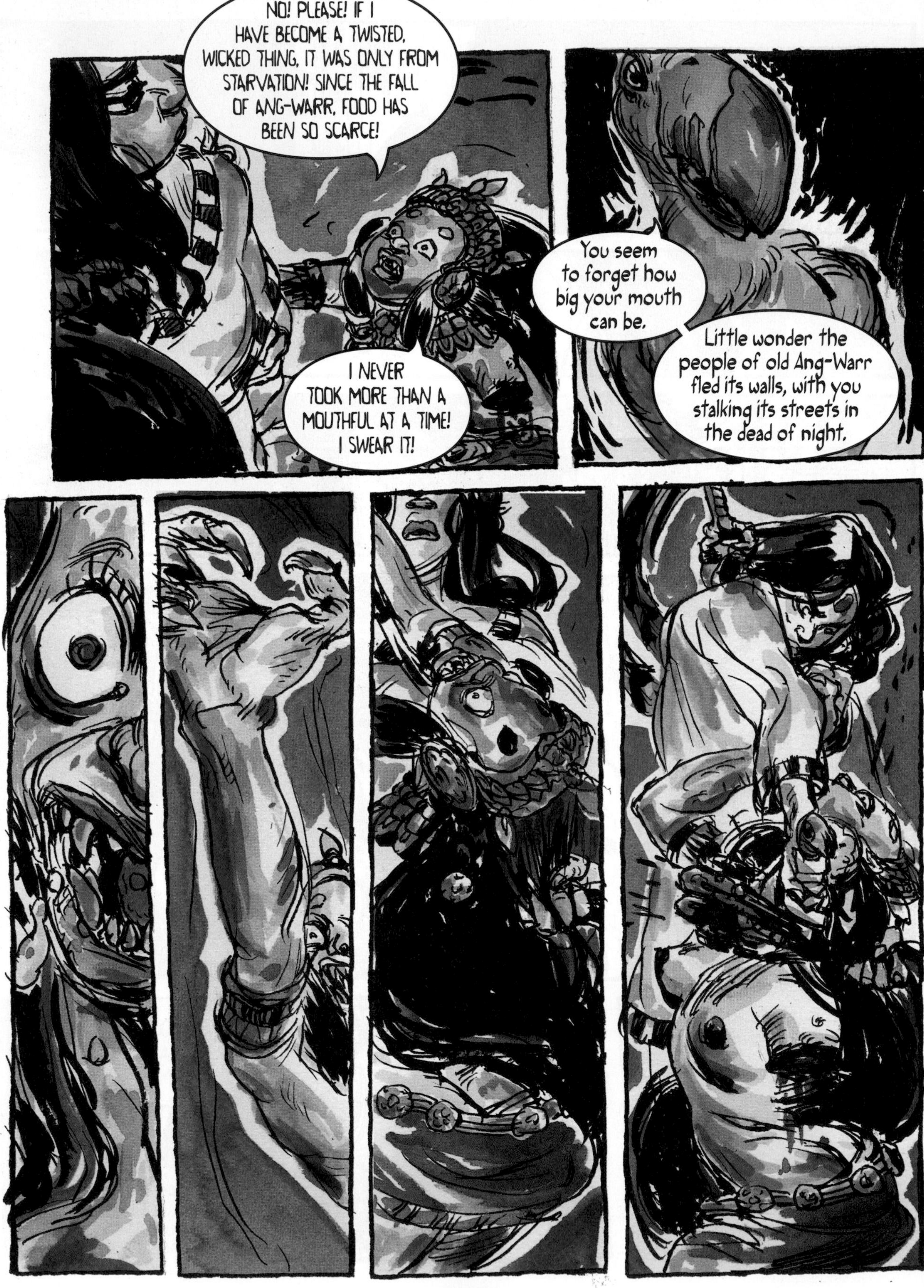
NO! PLEASE! IF I HAVE BECOME A TWISTED, WICKED THING, IT WAS ONLY FROM STARVATION! SINCE THE FALL OF ANG-WARR, FOOD HAS BEEN SO SCARCE!
I NEVER TOOK MORE THAN A MOUTHFUL AT A TIME! I SWEAR IT!
You seem to forget how big your mouth can be.
Little wonder the people of old Ang-Warr fled its walls, with you stalking its streets in the dead of night.

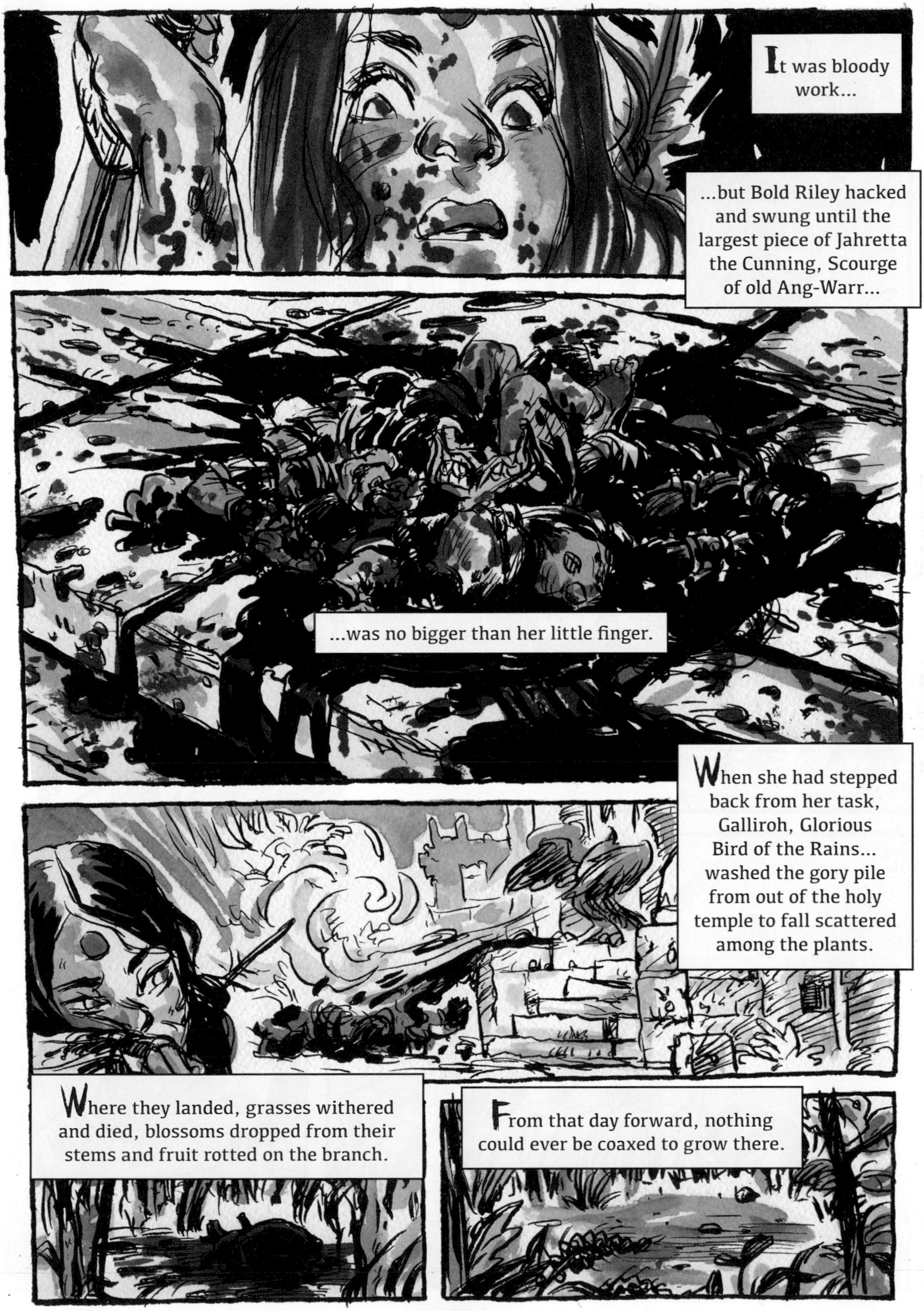
It was bloody work...
...but Bold Riley hacked and swung until the largest piece of Jahretta the Cunning, Scourge of old Ang-Warr...
...was no bigger than her little finger.
When she had stepped back from her task, Galliroh, Glorious Bird of the Rains... washed the gory pile from out of the holy temple to fall scattered among the plants.
Where they landed, grasses withered and died, blossoms dropped from their stems and fruit rotted on the branch.
From that day forward, nothing could ever be coaxed to grow there.

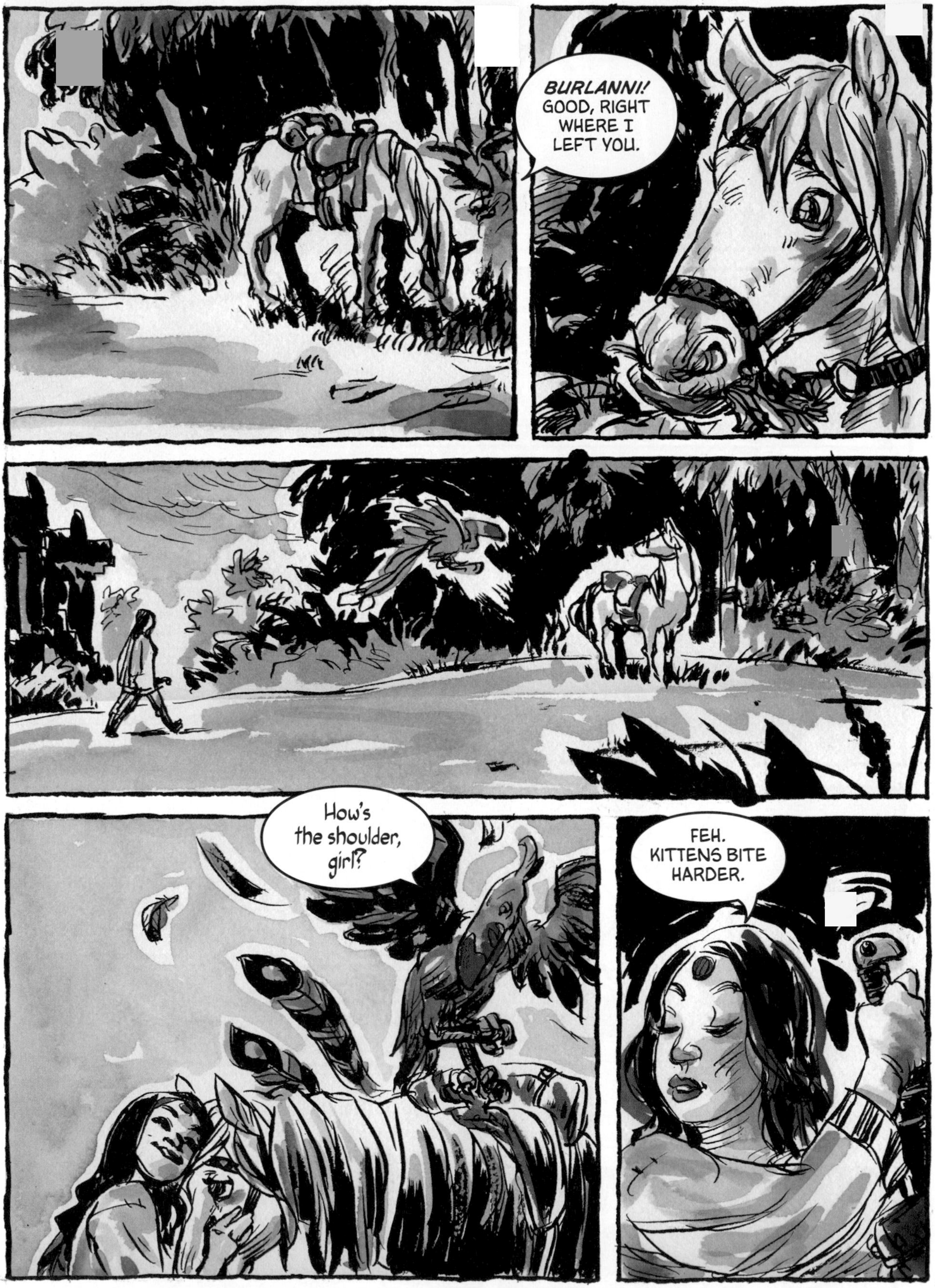
BURLANNI! GOOD, RIGHT WHERE I LEFT YOU.
How's the shoulder, girl?
FEH. KITTENS BITE HARDER.

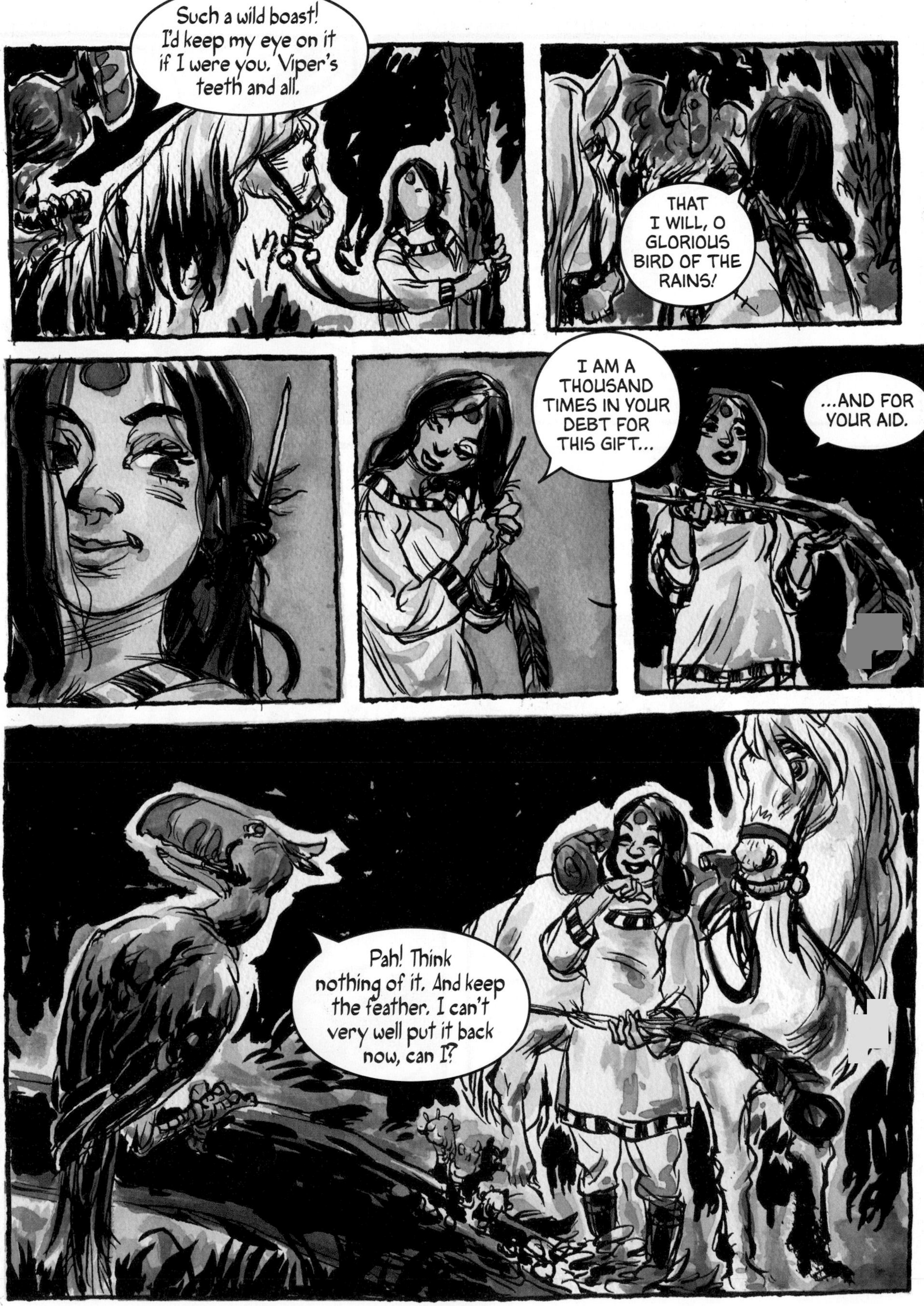
Such a wild boast! I'd keep my eye on it if I were you. Viper's teeth and all.
THAT I WILL, O GLORIOUS BIRD OF THE RAINS!
I AM A THOUSAND TIMES IN YOUR DEBT FOR THIS GIFT...
...AND FOR YOUR AID.
Pah! Think nothing of it. And keep the feather. I can't very well put it back now, can I?

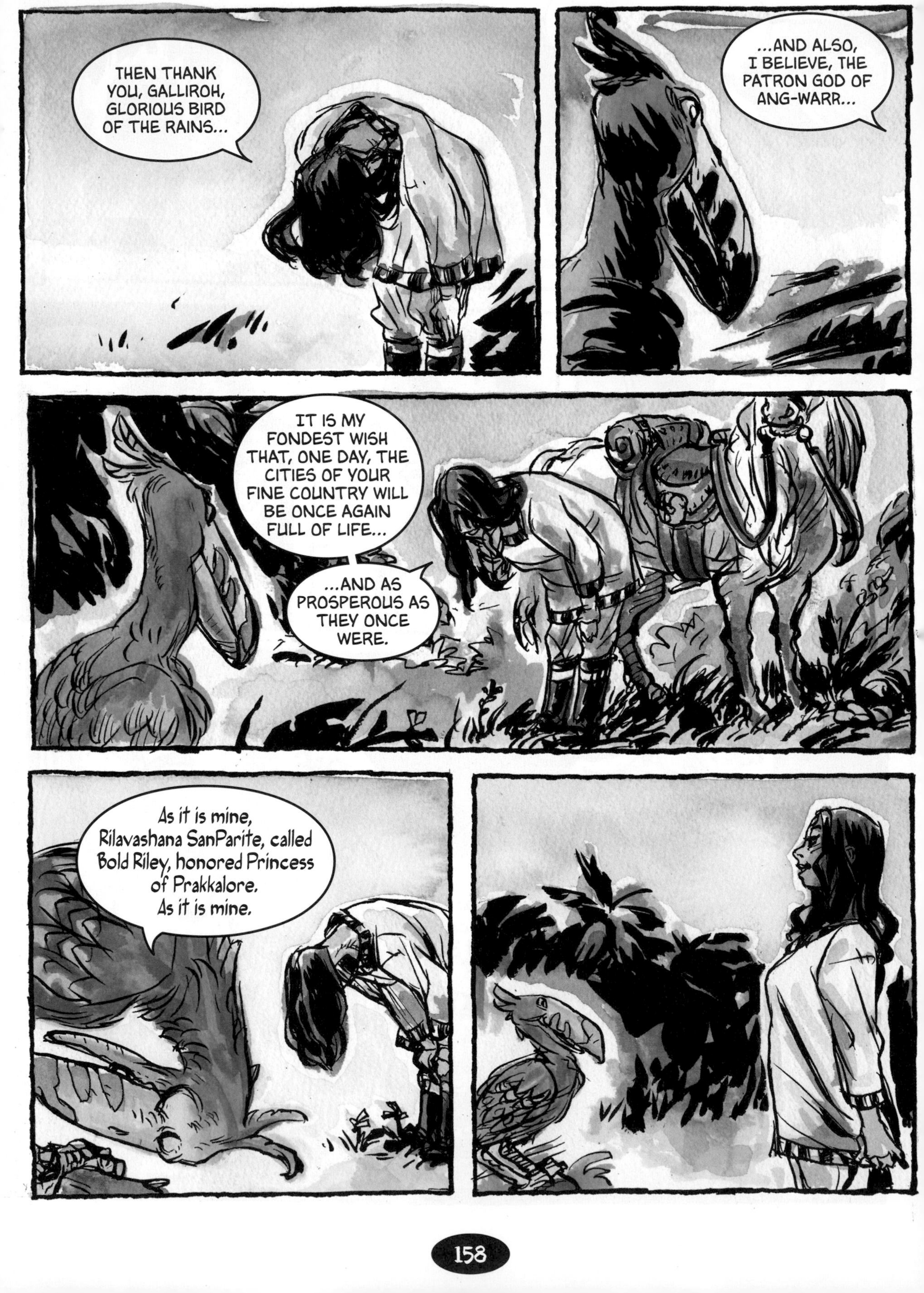
THEN THANK YOU, GALLIROH, GLORIOUS BIRD OF THE RAINS...
...AND ALSO, I BELIEVE, THE PATRON GOD OF ANG-WARR...
IT IS MY FONDEST WISH THAT, ONE DAY, THE CITIES OF YOUR FINE COUNTRY WILL BE ONCE AGAIN FULL OF LIFE...
...AND AS PROSPEROUS AS THEY ONCE WERE.
As it is mine, Rilavashana SanParite, called Bold Riley, honored Princess of Prakkalore. As it is mine.

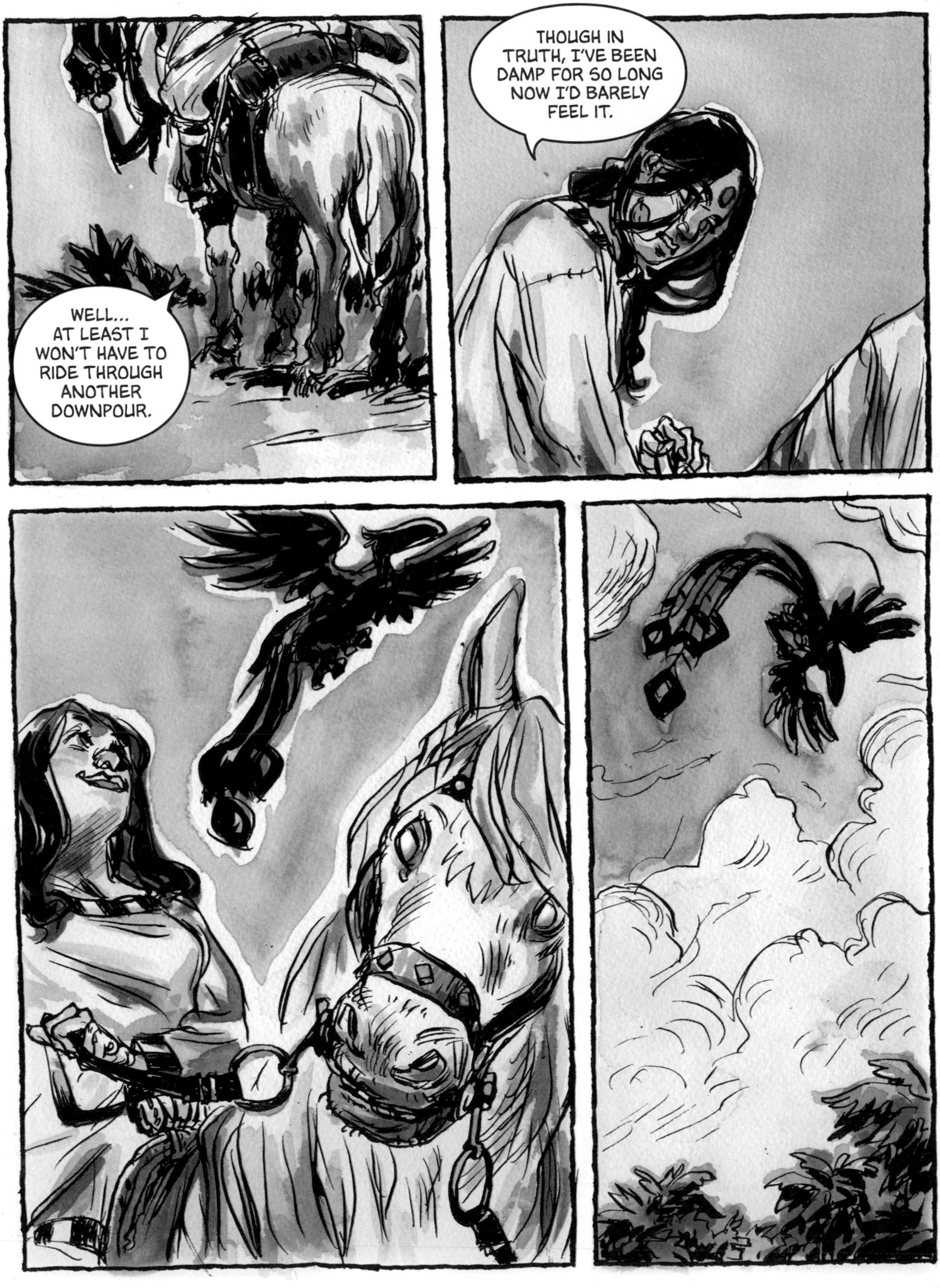
WELL...
AT LEAST I
WON'T HAVE TO
RIDE THROUGH
ANOTHER
DOWNPOUR.
THOUGH IN
TRUTH, I'VE BEEN
DAMP FOR SO LONG
NOW I'D BARELY
FEEL IT.

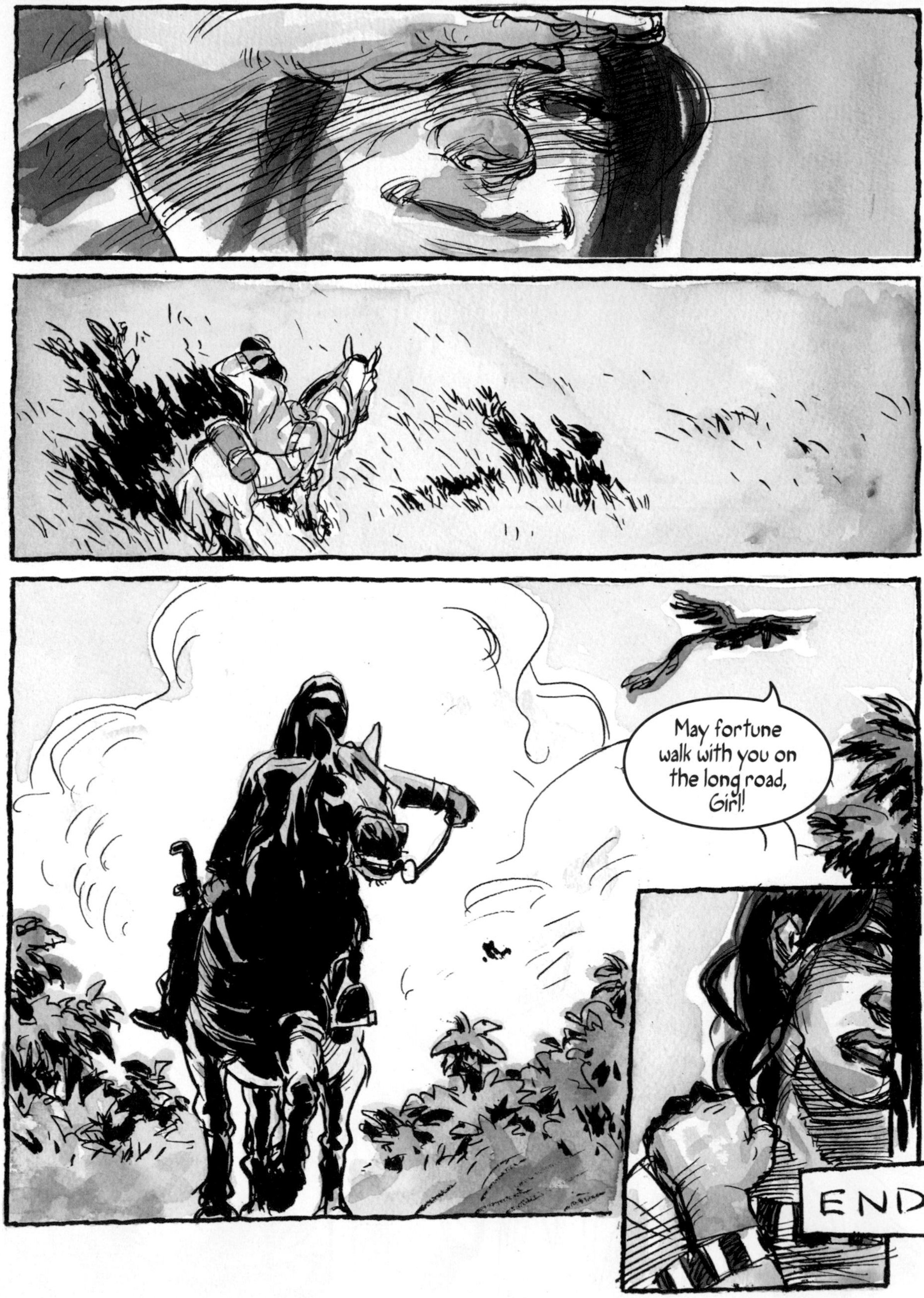
May fortune walk with you on the long road, Girl!
END.

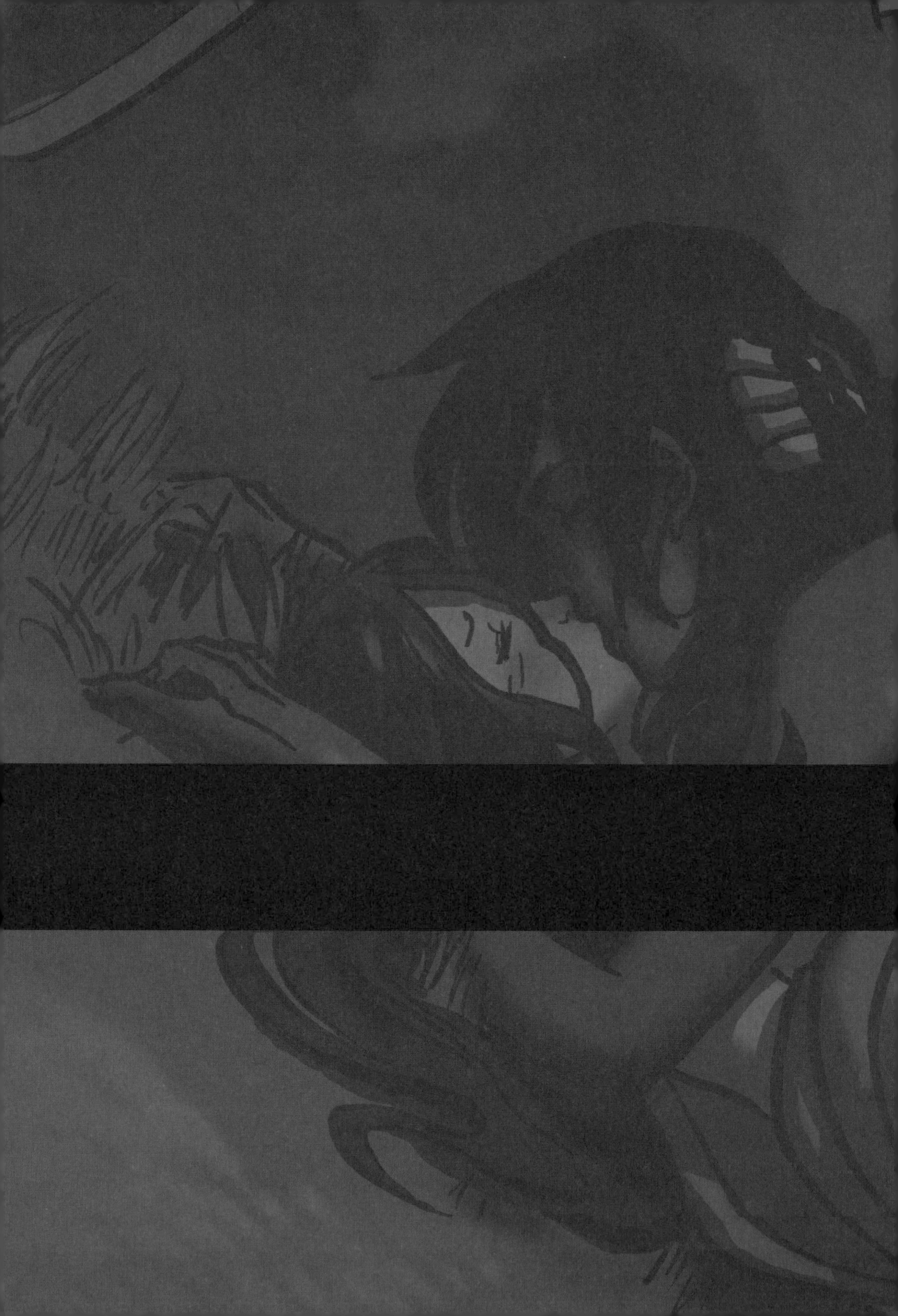

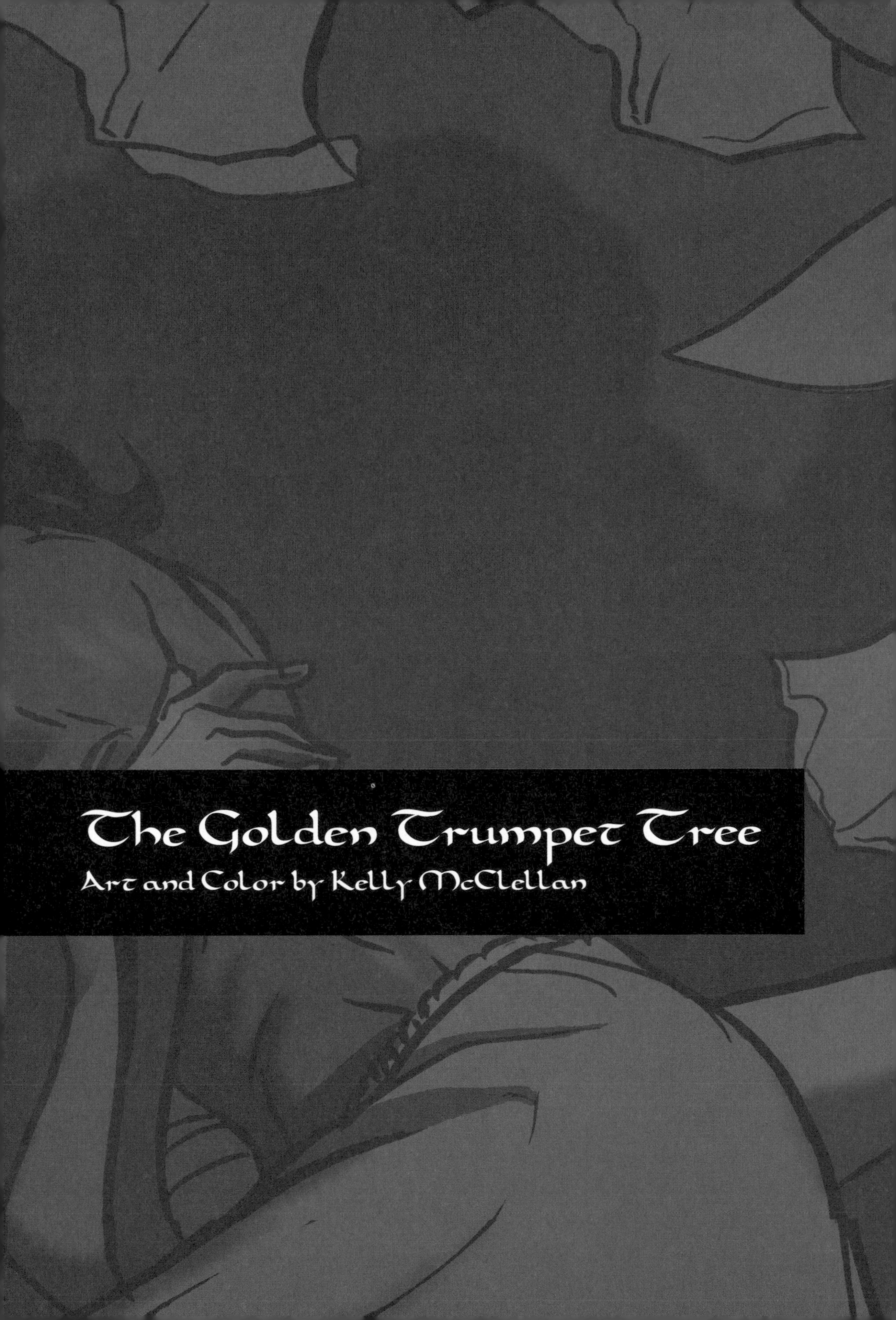

The Golden Trumpet Tree

Art and Color by Kelly McClellan

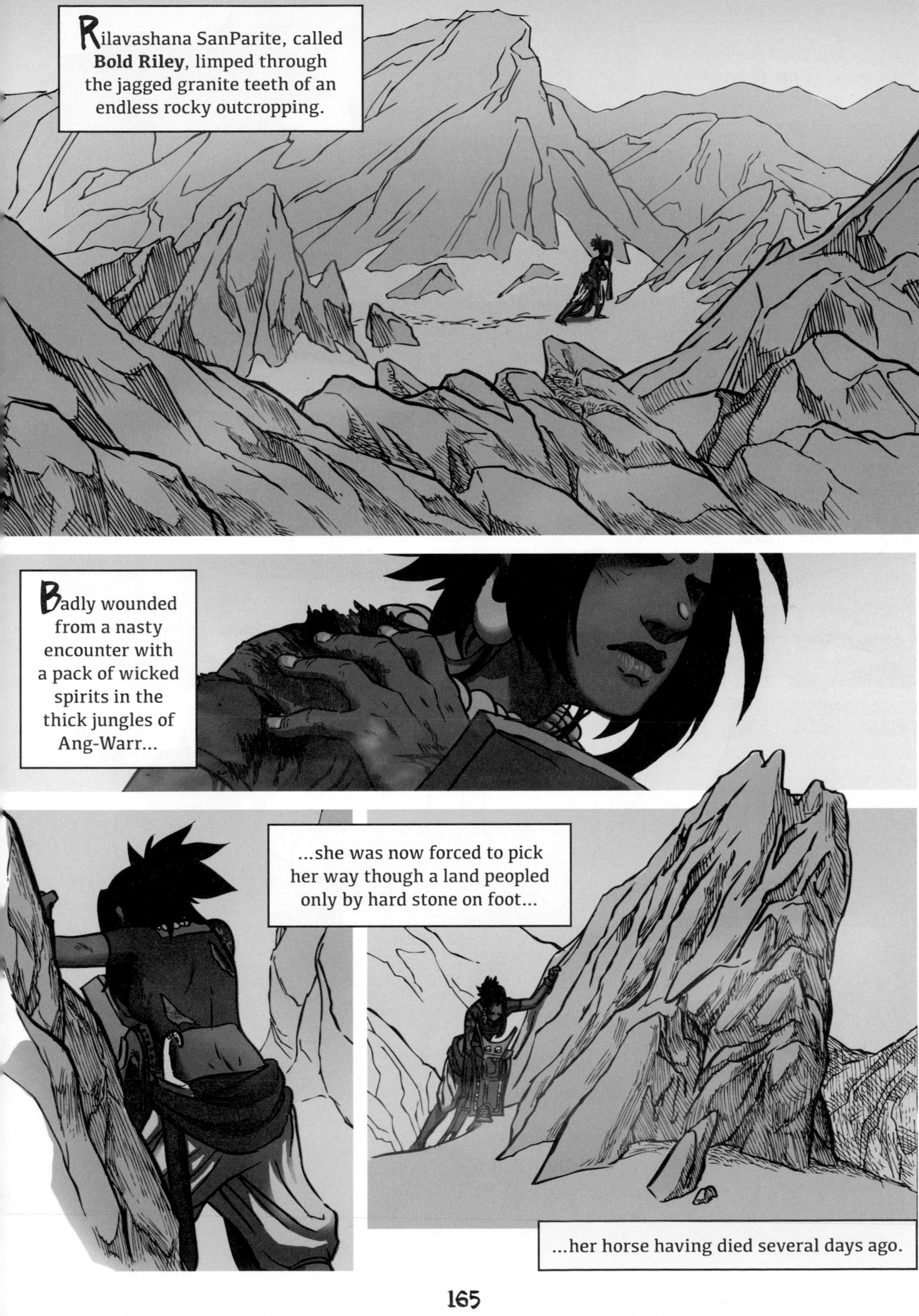
Rilavashana SanParite, called **Bold Riley**, limped through the jagged granite teeth of an endless rocky outcropping.
Badly wounded from a nasty encounter with a pack of wicked spirits in the thick jungles of Ang-Warr...
...she was now forced to pick her way though a land peopled only by hard stone on foot...
...her horse having died several days ago.

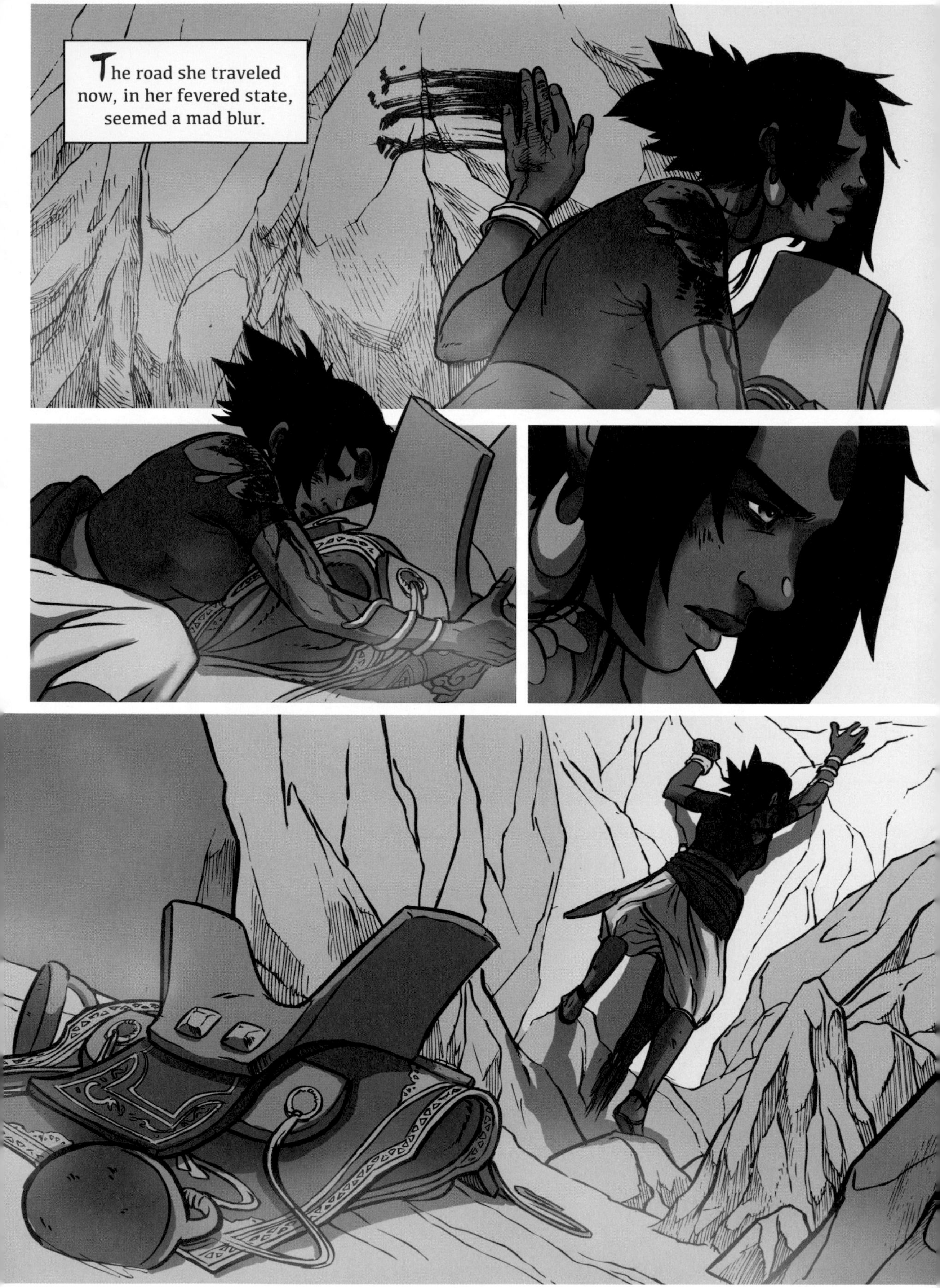
The road she traveled now, in her fevered state, seemed a mad blur.

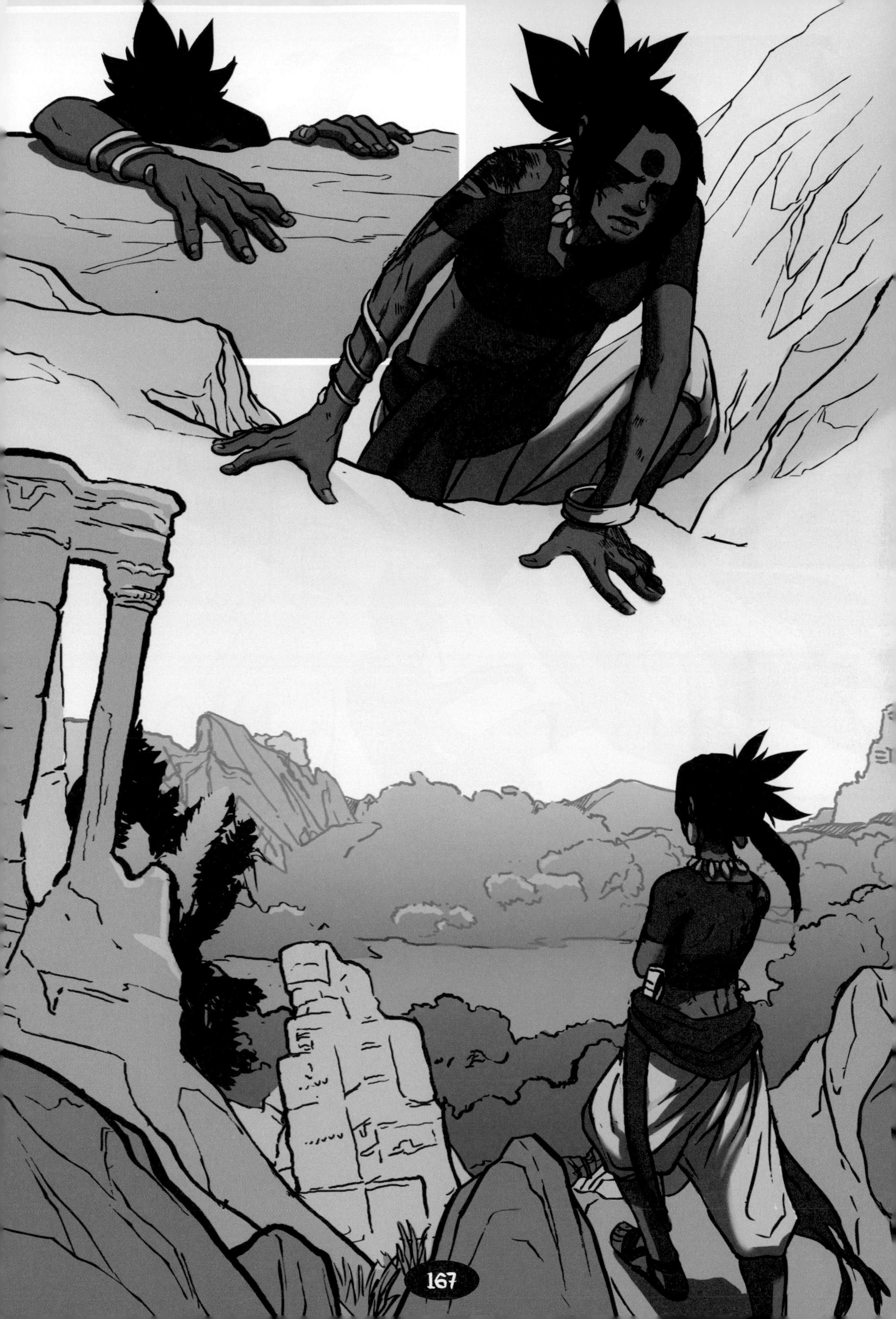

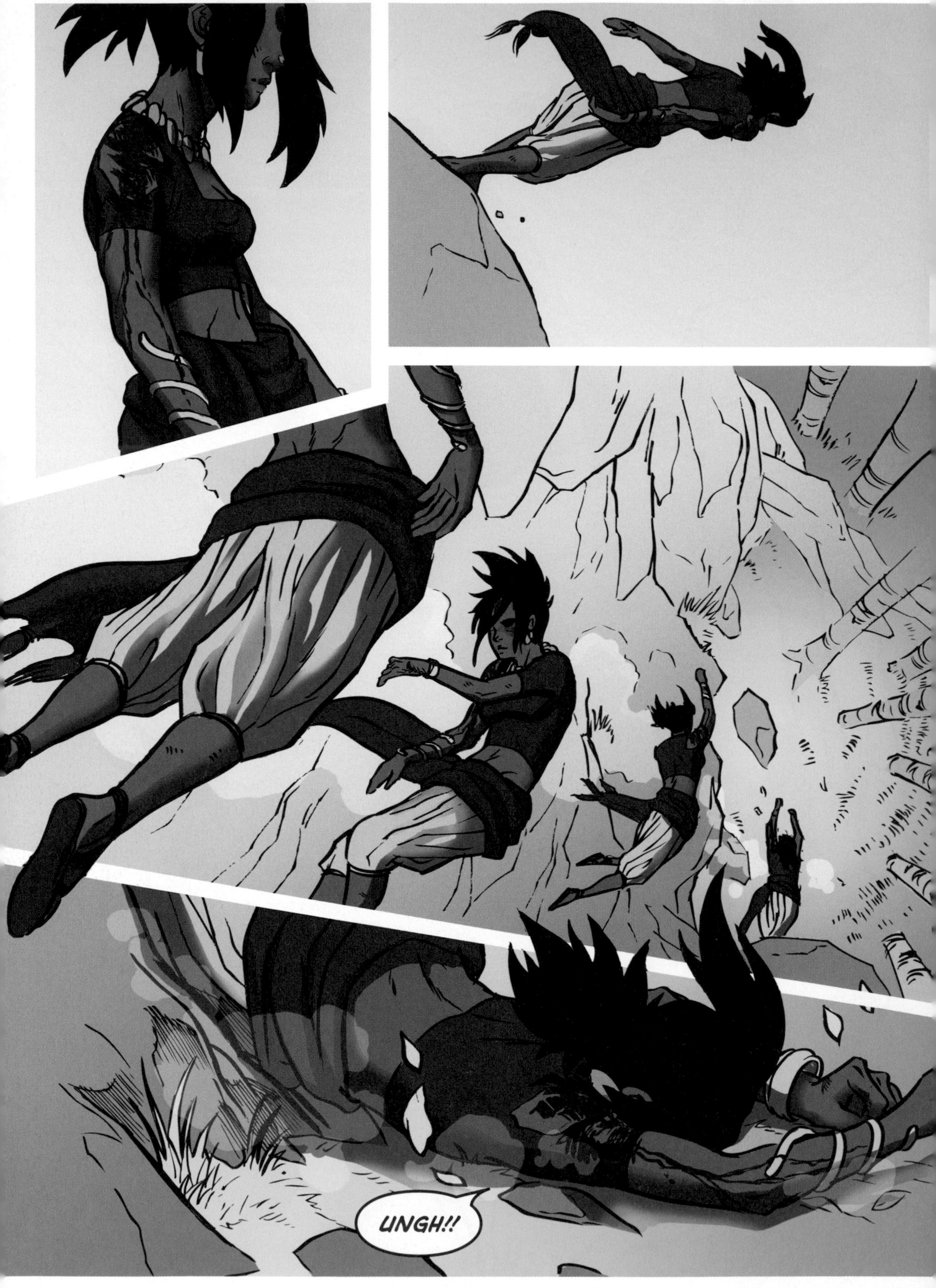
UNGH!!

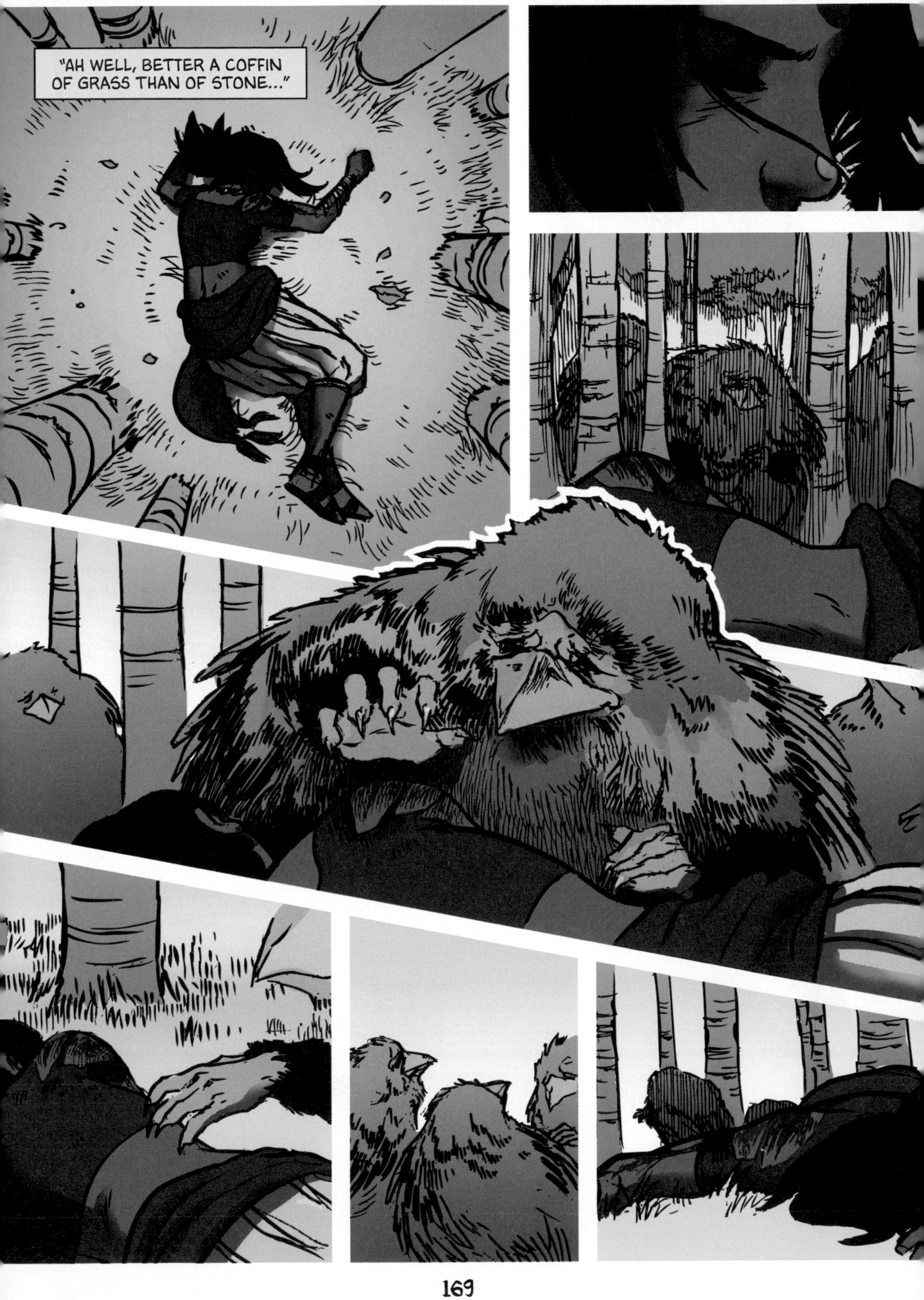
"AH WELL, BETTER A COFFIN OF GRASS THAN OF STONE..."

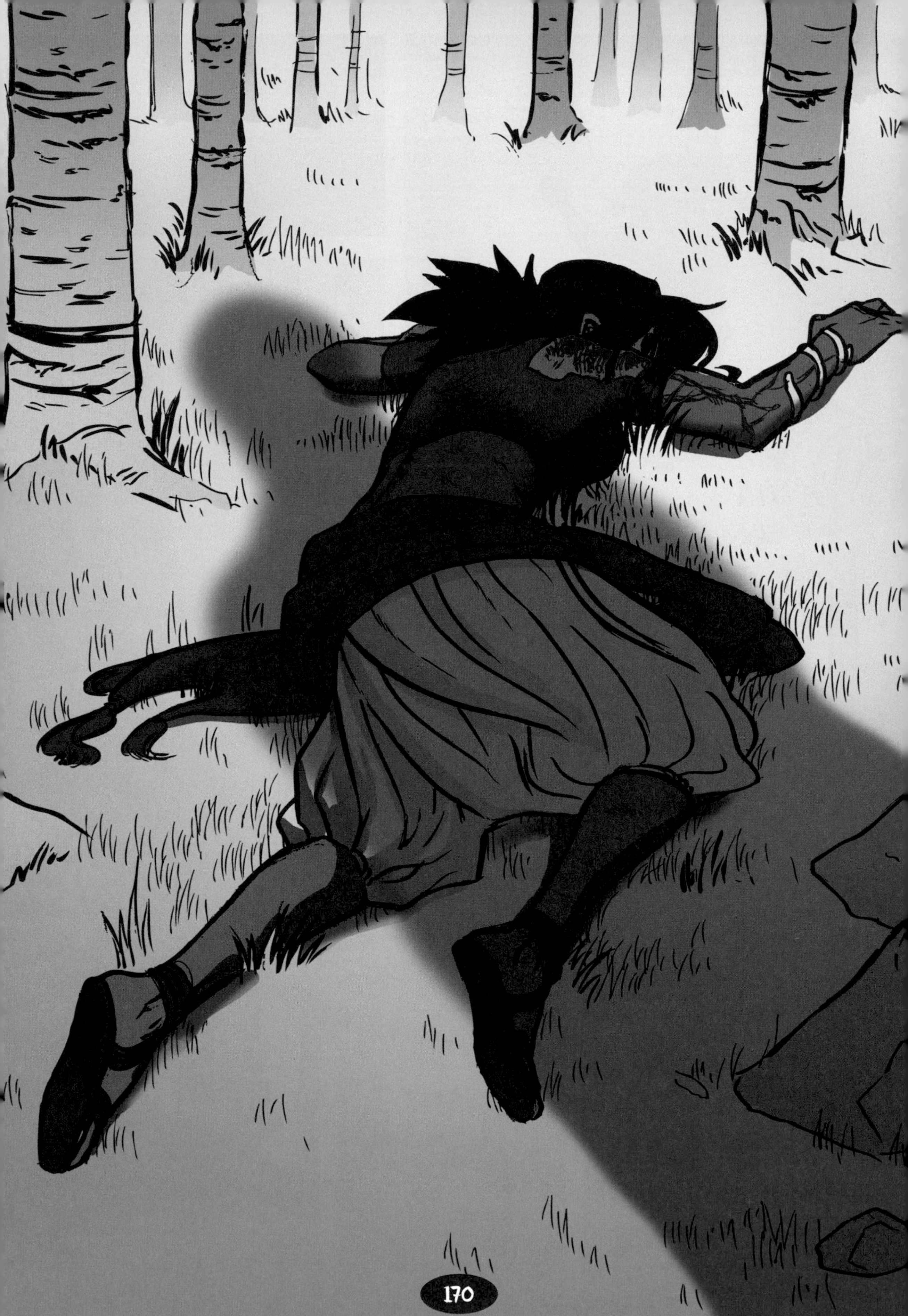

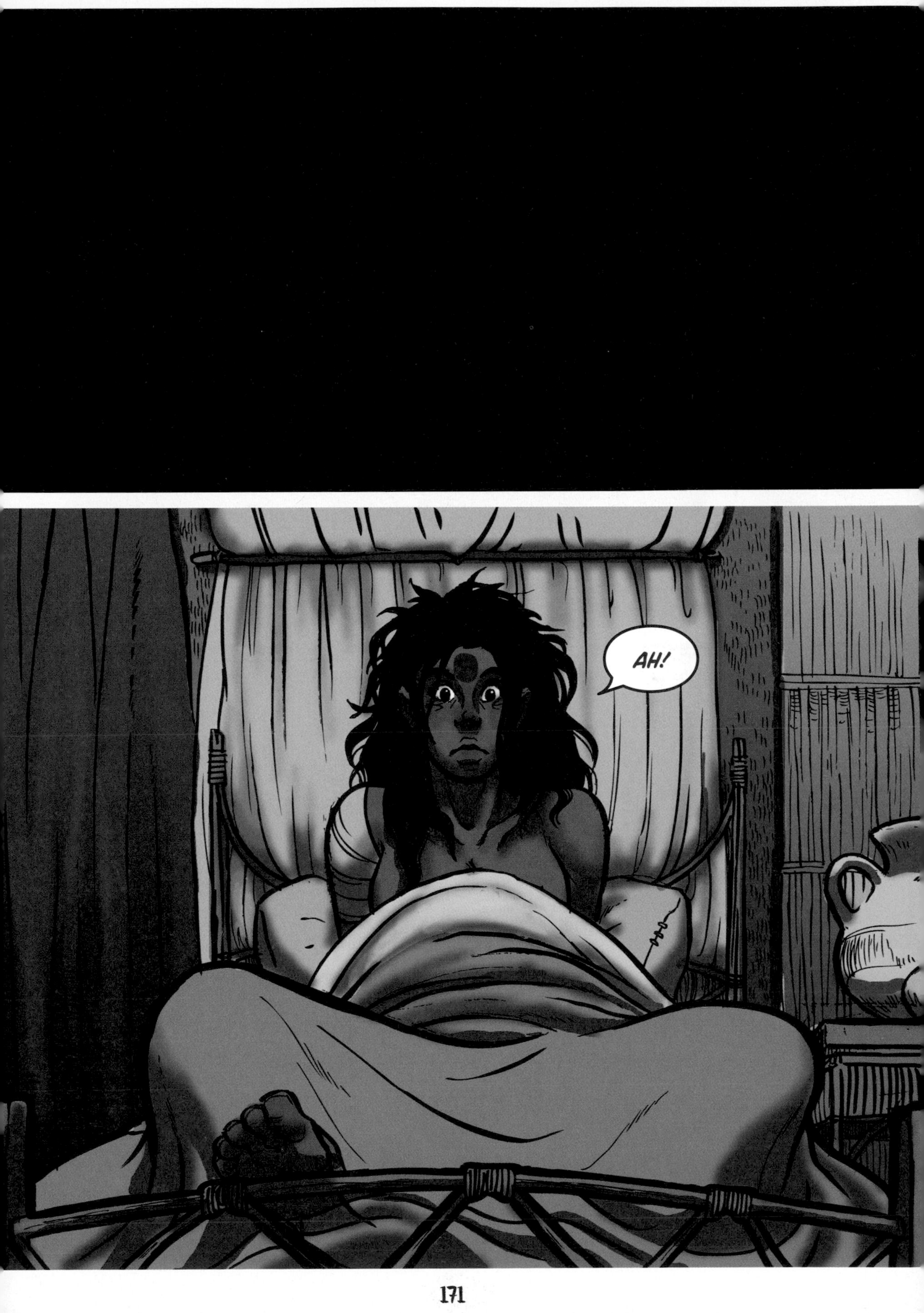
AH!

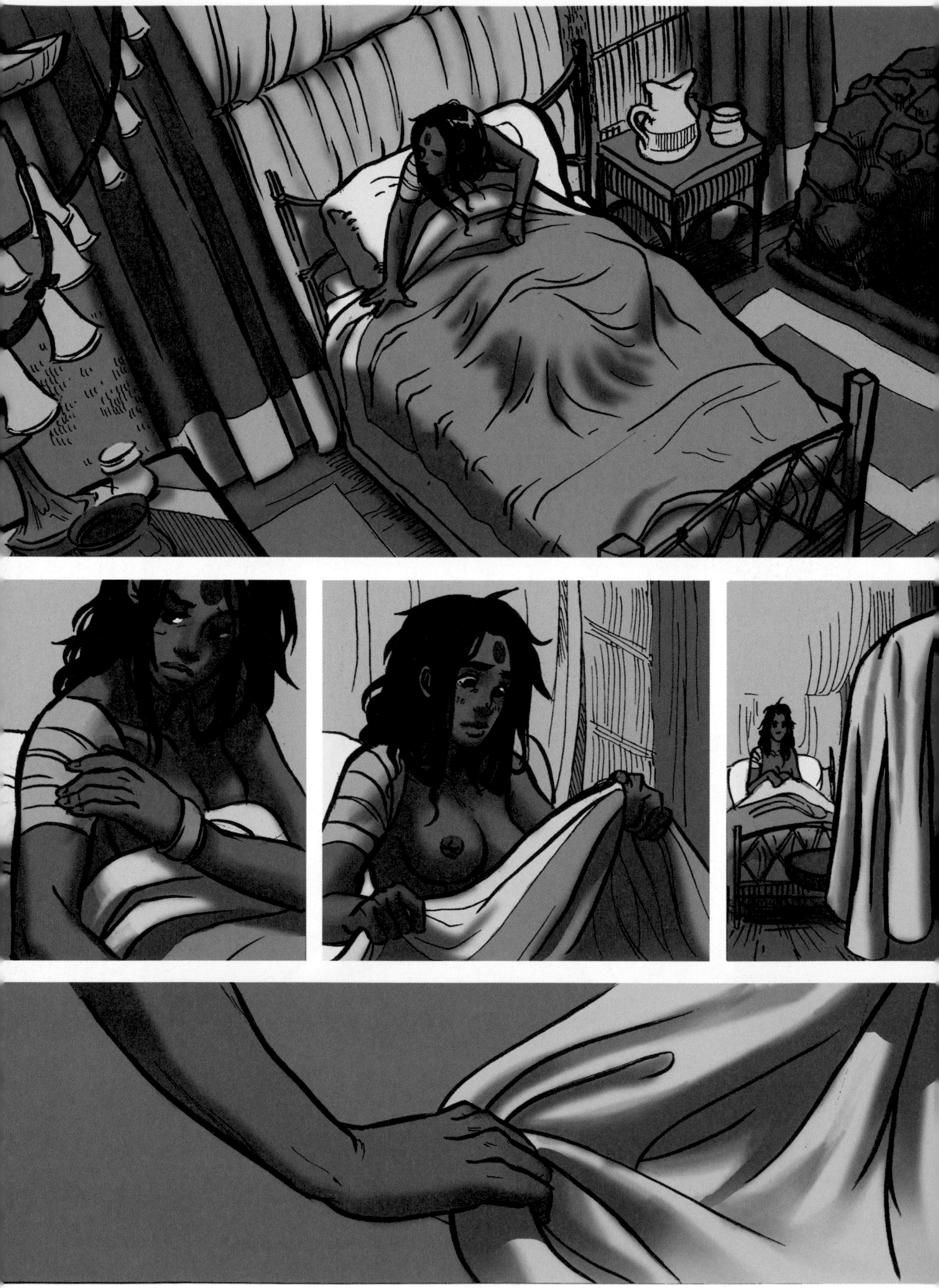

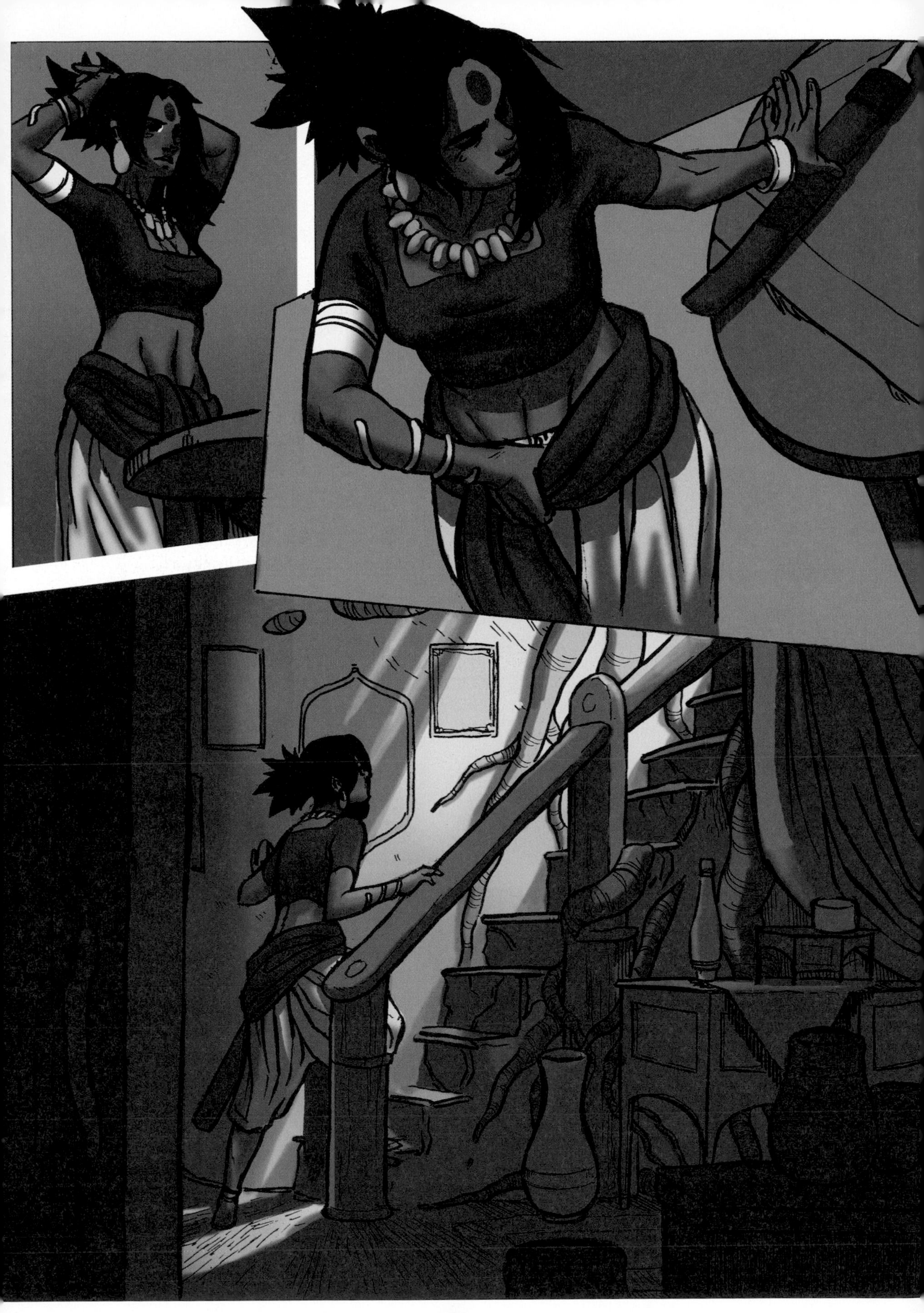

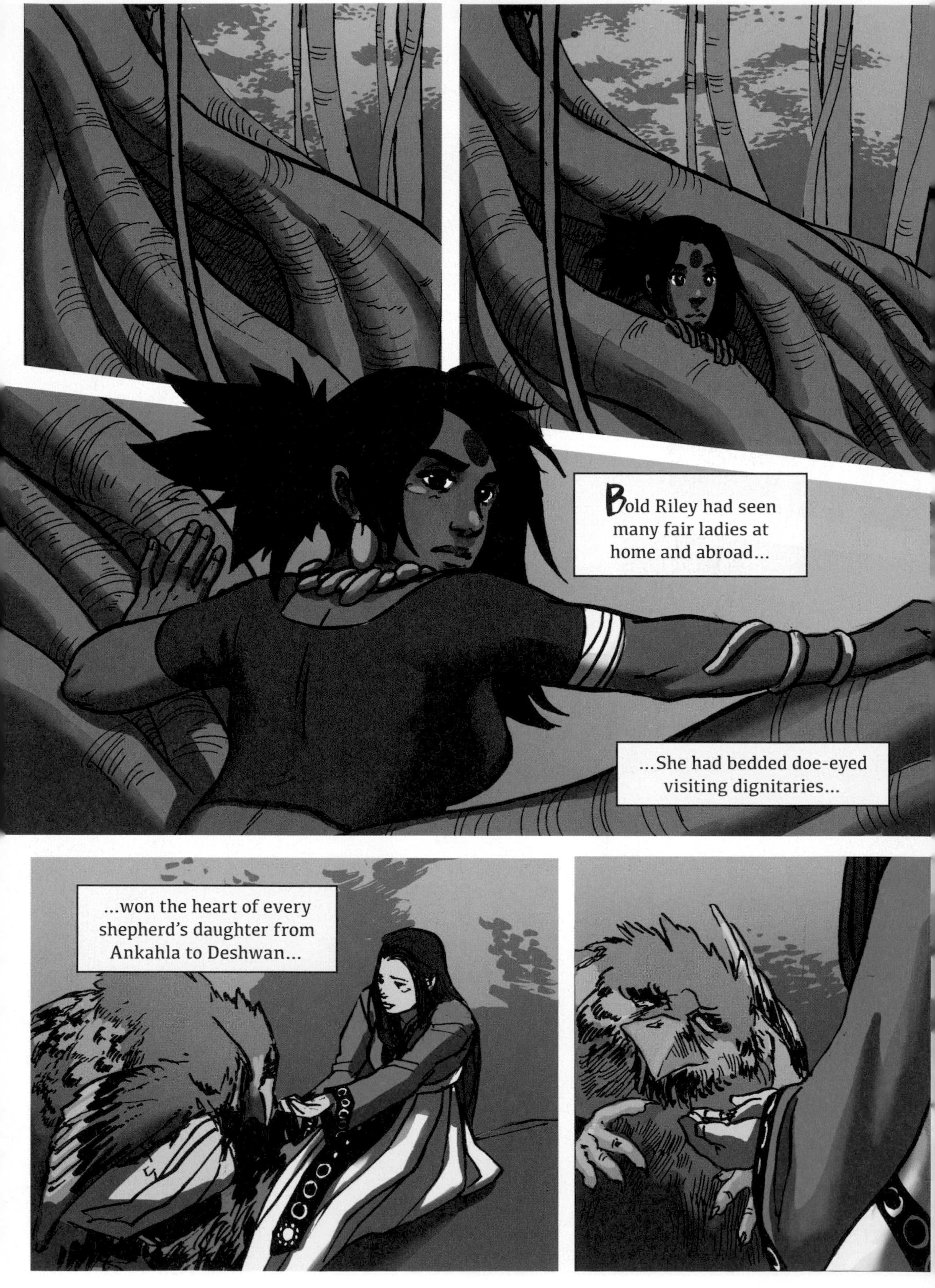
Bold Riley had seen many fair ladies at home and abroad...
...She had bedded doe-eyed visiting dignitaries...
...won the heart of every shepherd's daughter from Ankahla to Deshwan...

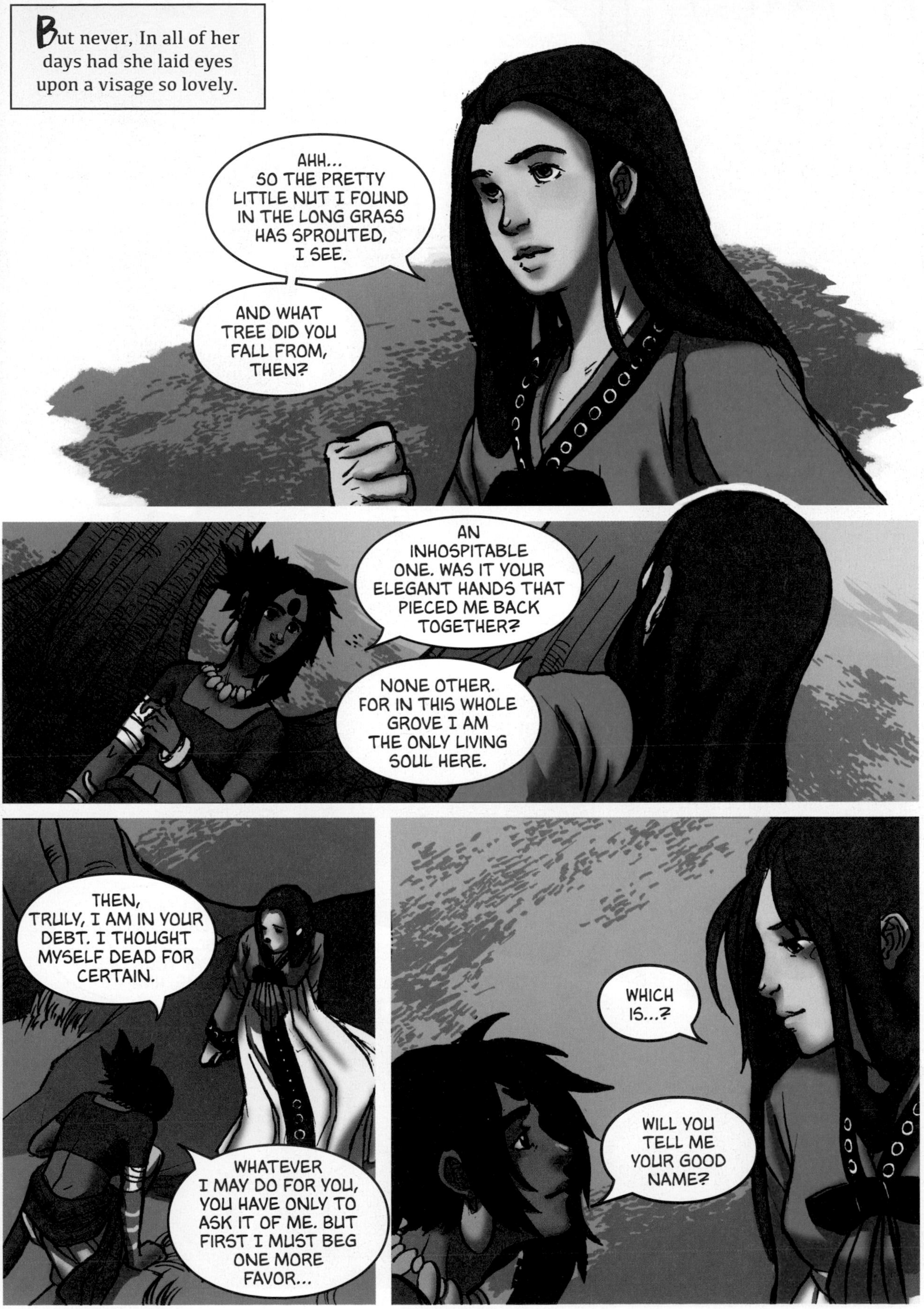
But never, In all of her days had she laid eyes upon a visage so lovely.
AHH... SO THE PRETTY LITTLE NUT I FOUND IN THE LONG GRASS HAS SPROUTED, I SEE.
AND WHAT TREE DID YOU FALL FROM, THEN?
AN INHOSPITABLE ONE. WAS IT YOUR ELEGANT HANDS THAT PIECED ME BACK TOGETHER?
NONE OTHER. FOR IN THIS WHOLE GROVE I AM THE ONLY LIVING SOUL HERE.
THEN, TRULY, I AM IN YOUR DEBT. I THOUGHT MYSELF DEAD FOR CERTAIN.
WHATEVER I MAY DO FOR YOU, YOU HAVE ONLY TO ASK IT OF ME. BUT FIRST I MUST BEG ONE MORE FAVOR...
WHICH IS...?
WILL YOU TELL ME YOUR GOOD NAME?

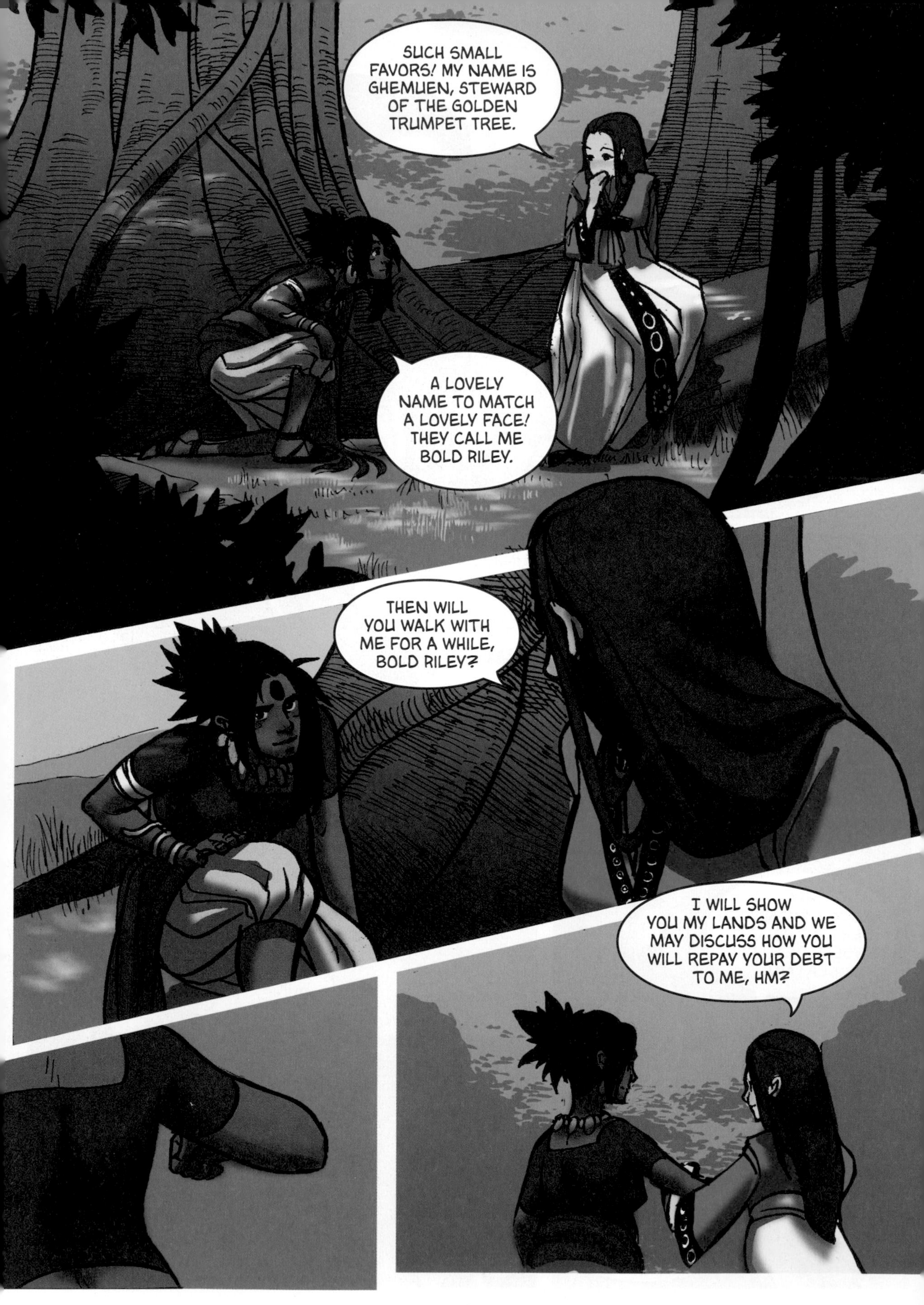

SUCH SMALL FAVORS! MY NAME IS GHEMUEN, STEWARD OF THE GOLDEN TRUMPET TREE.
A LOVELY NAME TO MATCH A LOVELY FACE! THEY CALL ME BOLD RILEY.
THEN WILL YOU WALK WITH ME FOR A WHILE, BOLD RILEY?
I WILL SHOW YOU MY LANDS AND WE MAY DISCUSS HOW YOU WILL REPAY YOUR DEBT TO ME, HM?

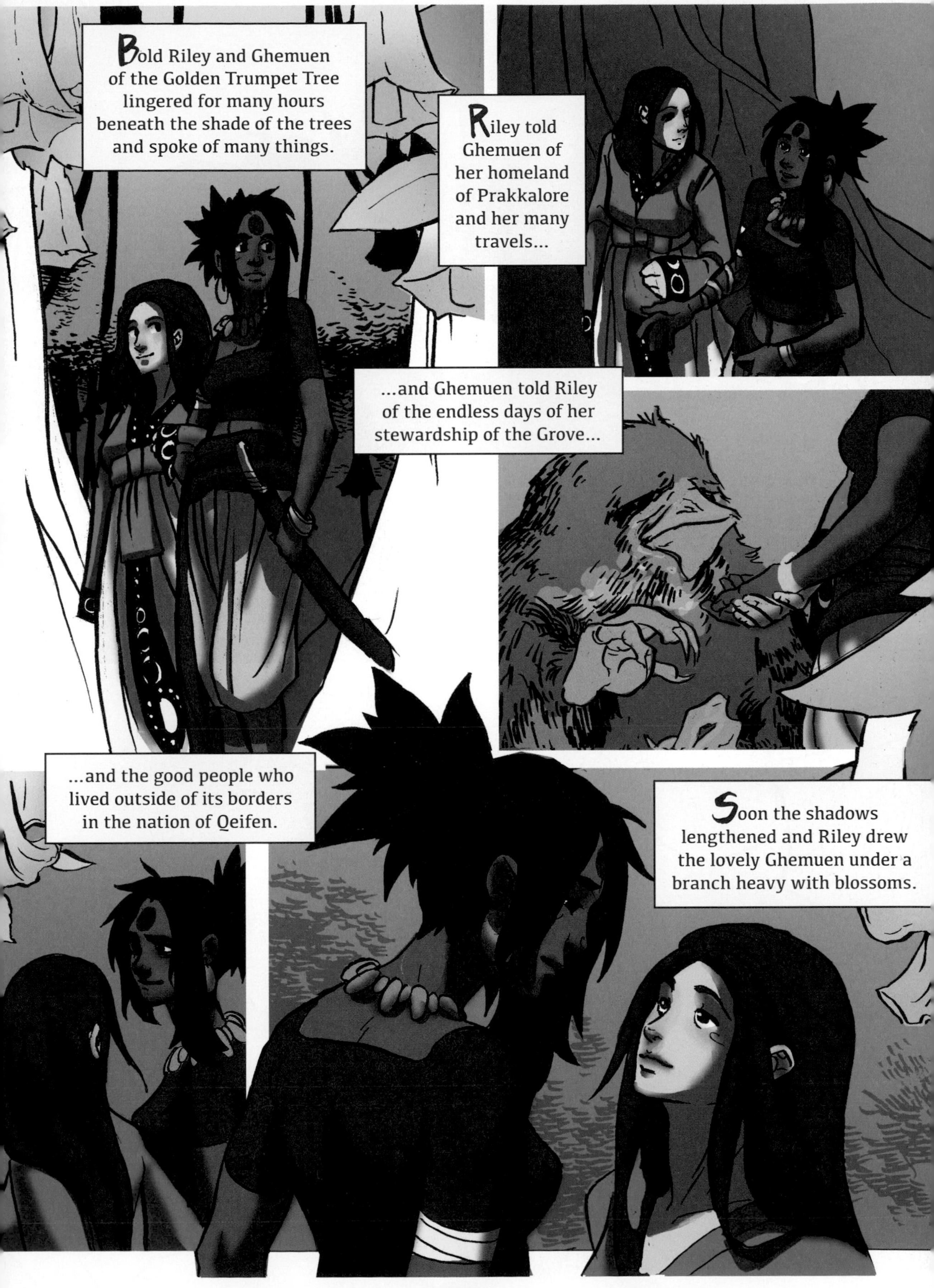
Bold Riley and Ghemuen of the Golden Trumpet Tree lingered for many hours beneath the shade of the trees and spoke of many things.
Riley told Ghemuen of her homeland of Prakkalore and her many travels...
...and Ghemuen told Riley of the endless days of her stewardship of the Grove...
...and the good people who lived outside of its borders in the nation of Qeifen.
Soon the shadows lengthened and Riley drew the lovely Ghemuen under a branch heavy with blossoms.

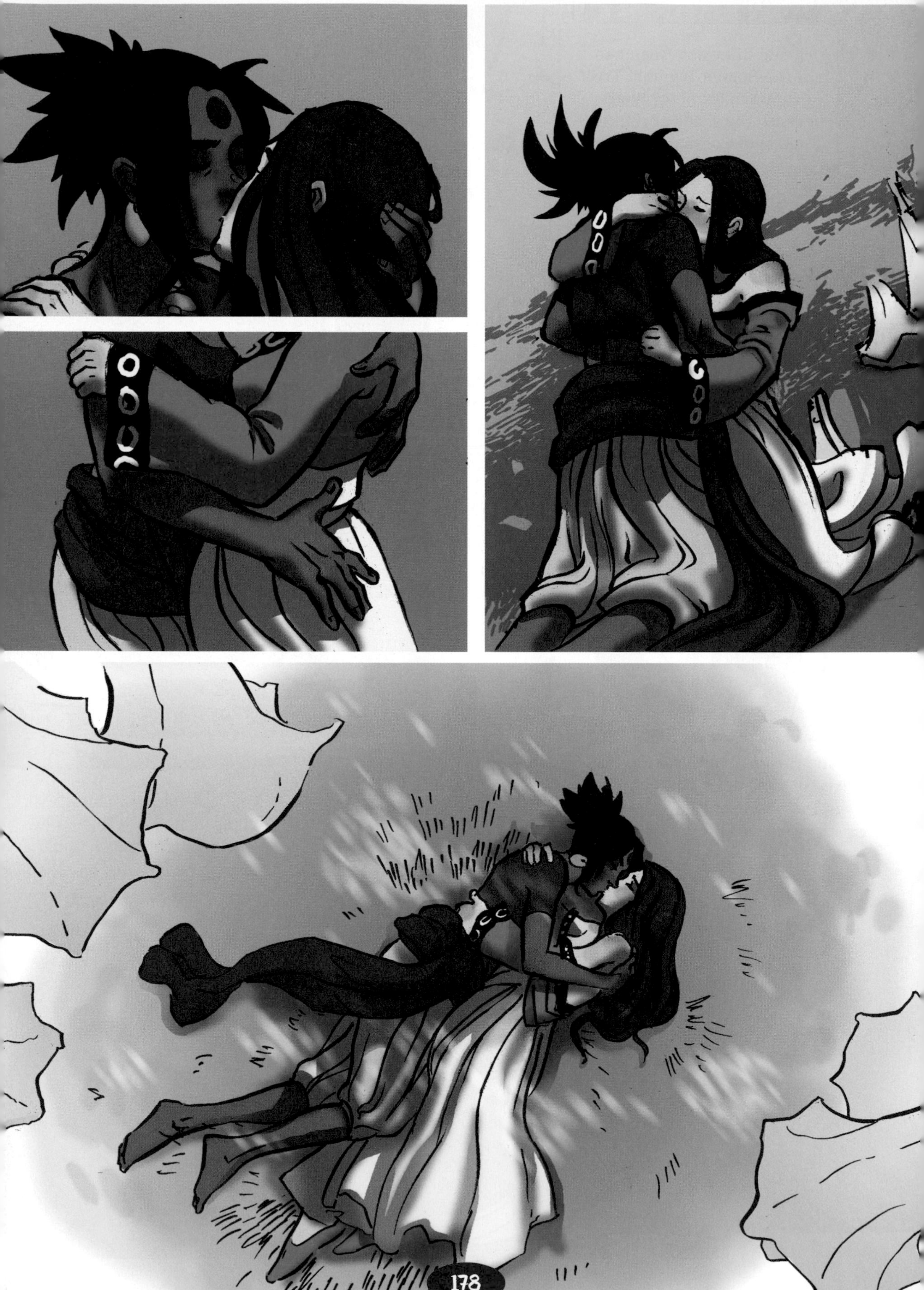

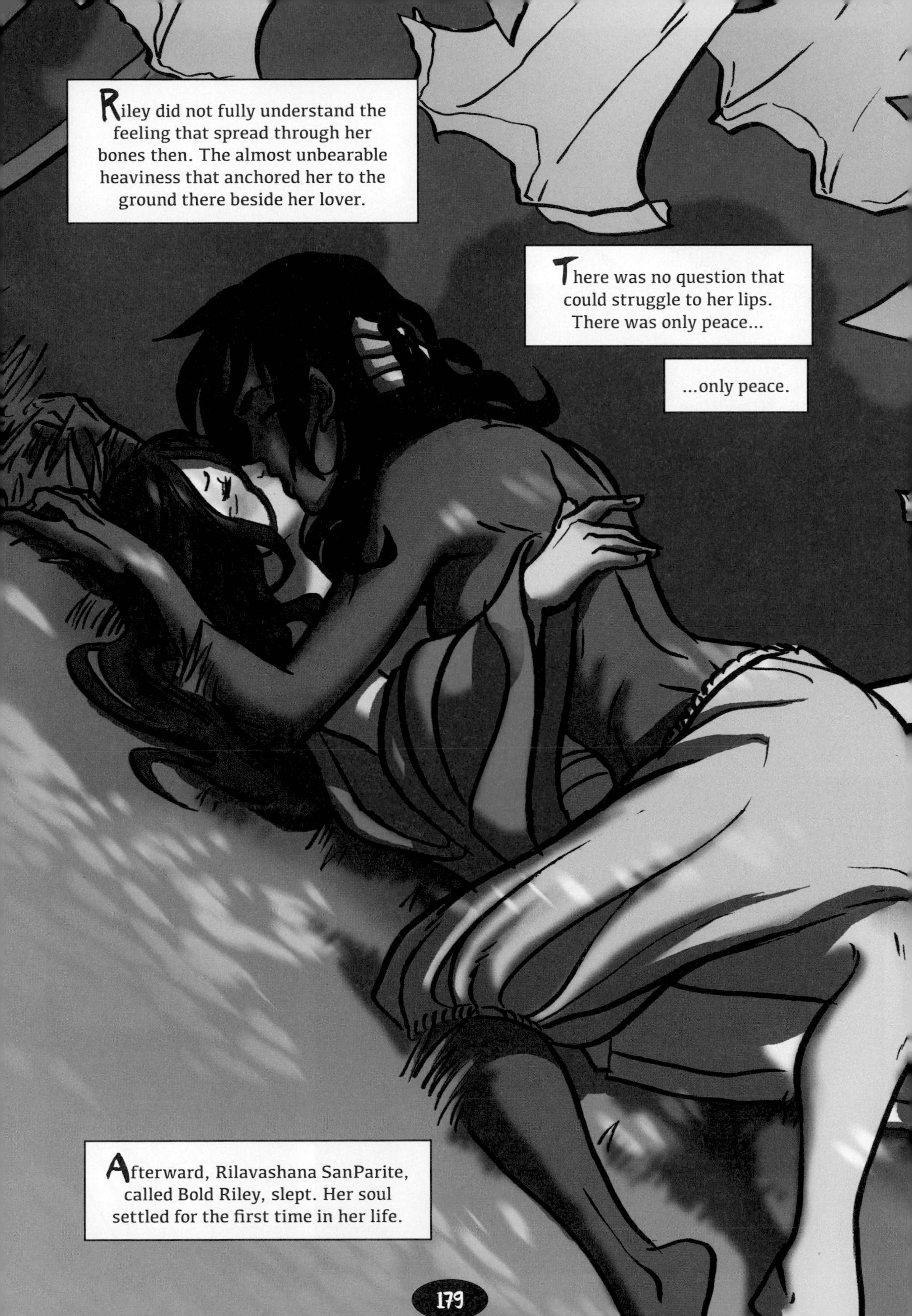
Riley did not fully understand the feeling that spread through her bones then. The almost unbearable heaviness that anchored her to the ground there beside her lover.
There was no question that could struggle to her lips. There was only peace...
...only peace.
Afterward, Rilavashana SanParite, called Bold Riley, slept. Her soul settled for the first time in her life.

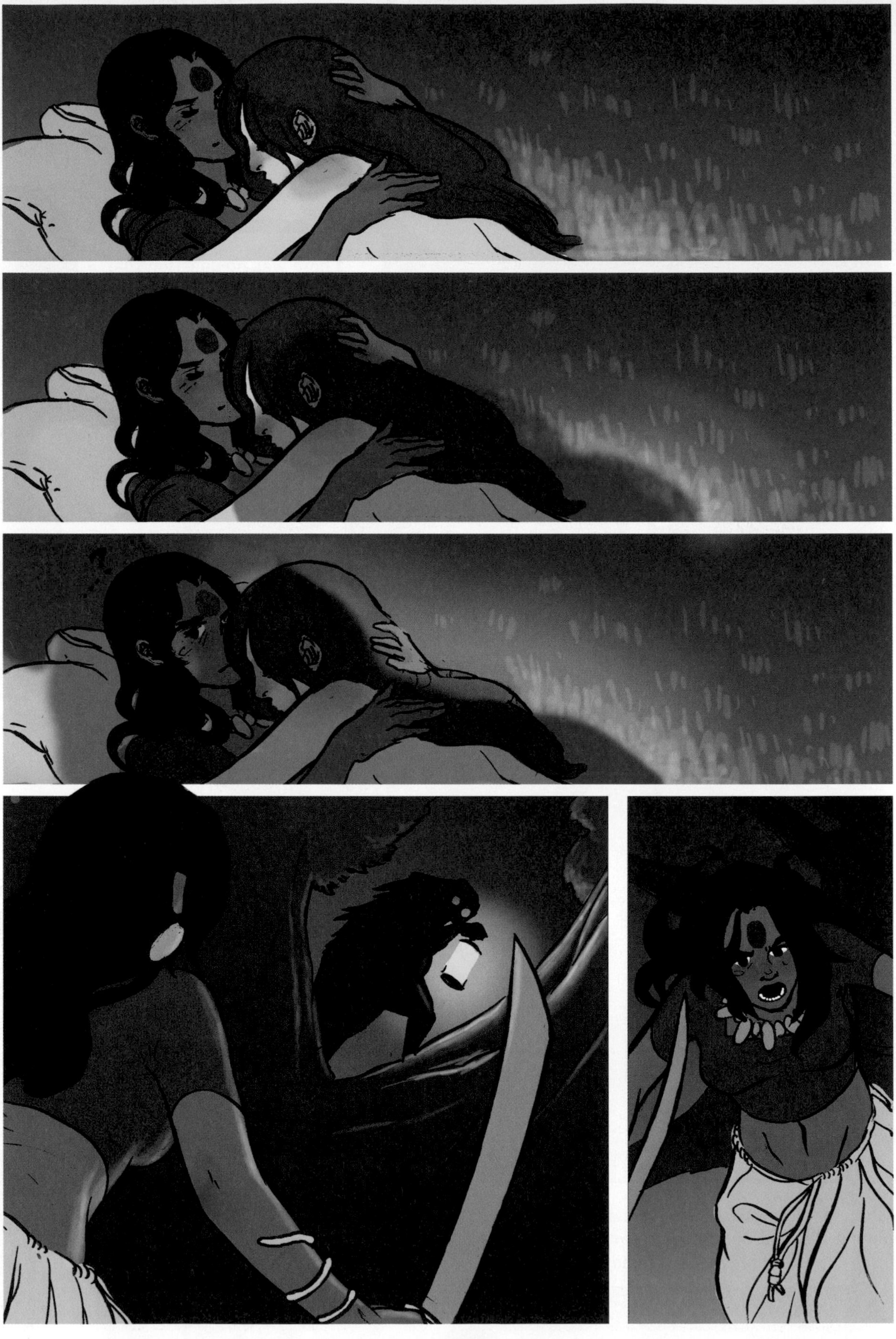

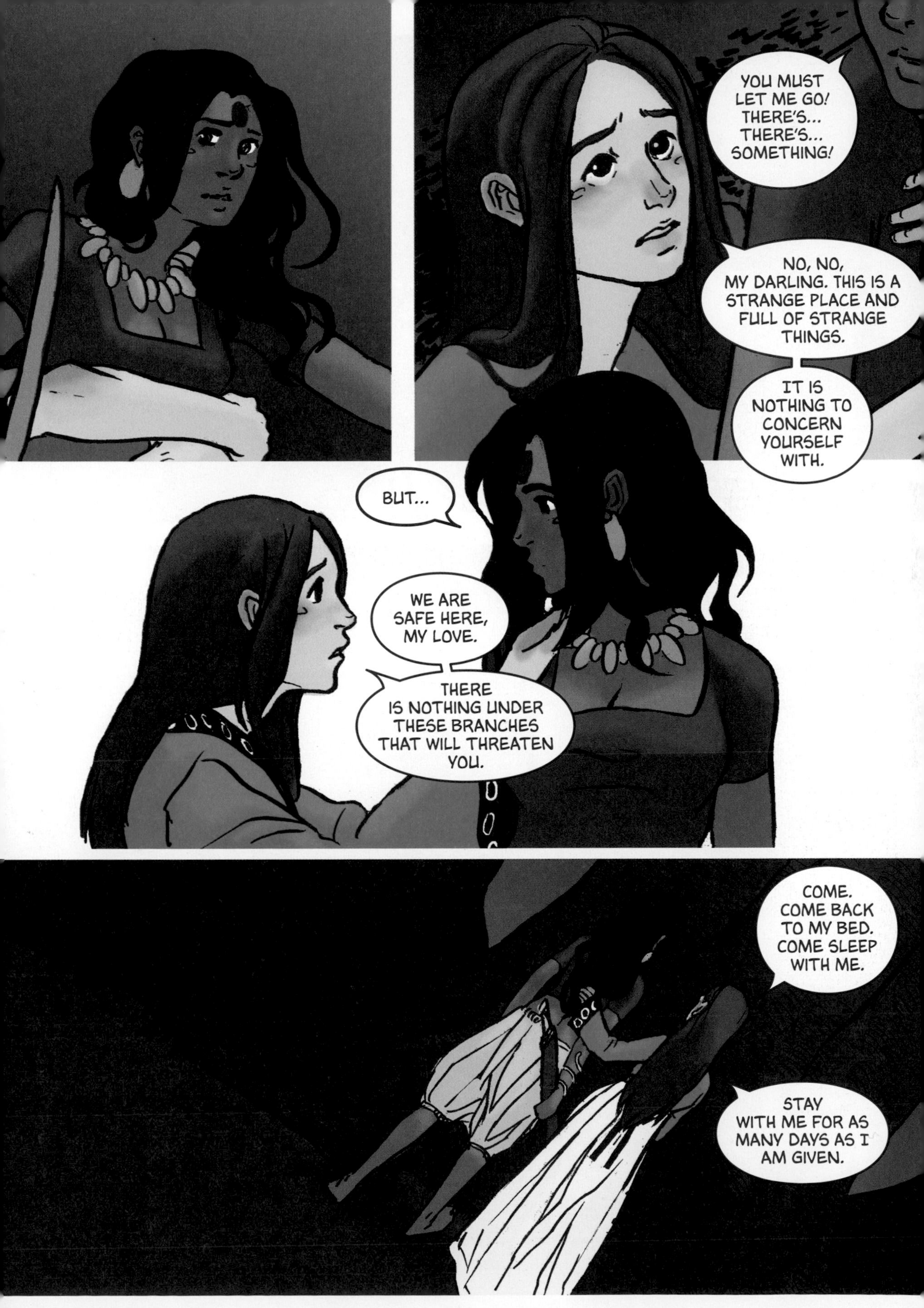
YOU MUST LET ME GO! THERE'S... THERE'S... SOMETHING!
NO, NO, MY DARLING. THIS IS A STRANGE PLACE AND FULL OF STRANGE THINGS.
IT IS NOTHING TO CONCERN YOURSELF WITH.
BUT...
WE ARE SAFE HERE, MY LOVE.
THERE IS NOTHING UNDER THESE BRANCHES THAT WILL THREATEN YOU.
COME. COME BACK TO MY BED. COME SLEEP WITH ME.
STAY WITH ME FOR AS MANY DAYS AS I AM GIVEN.

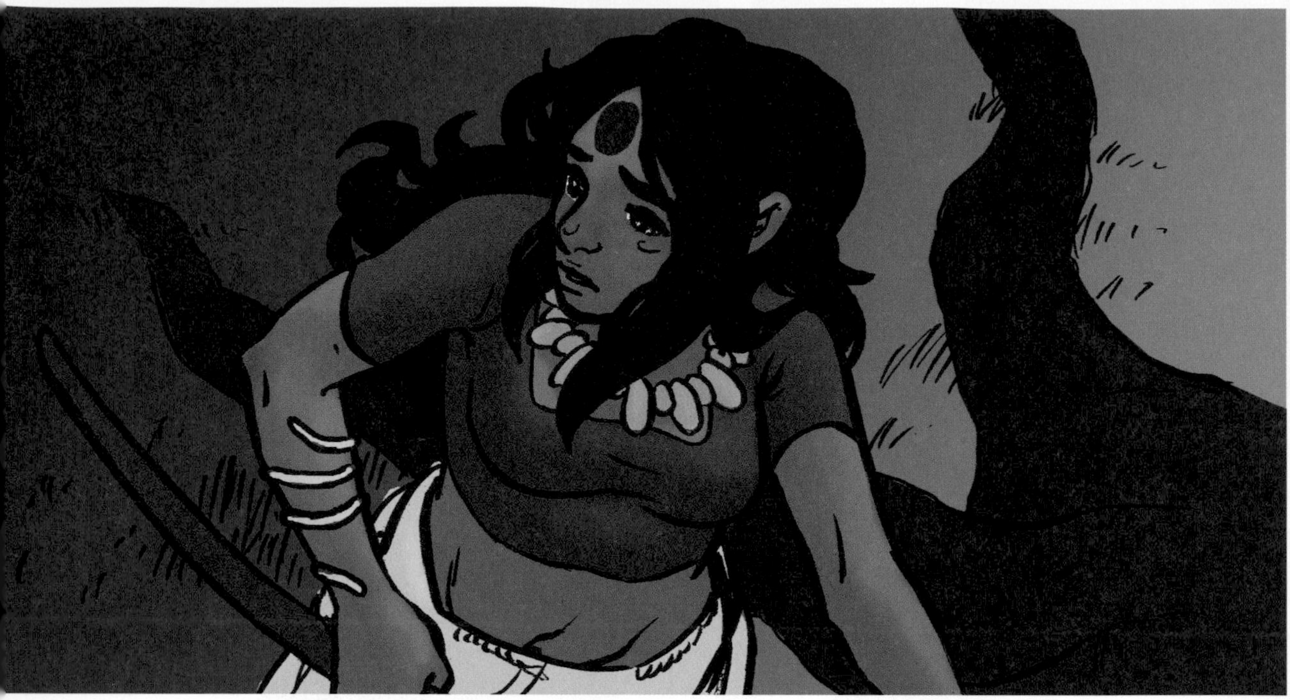

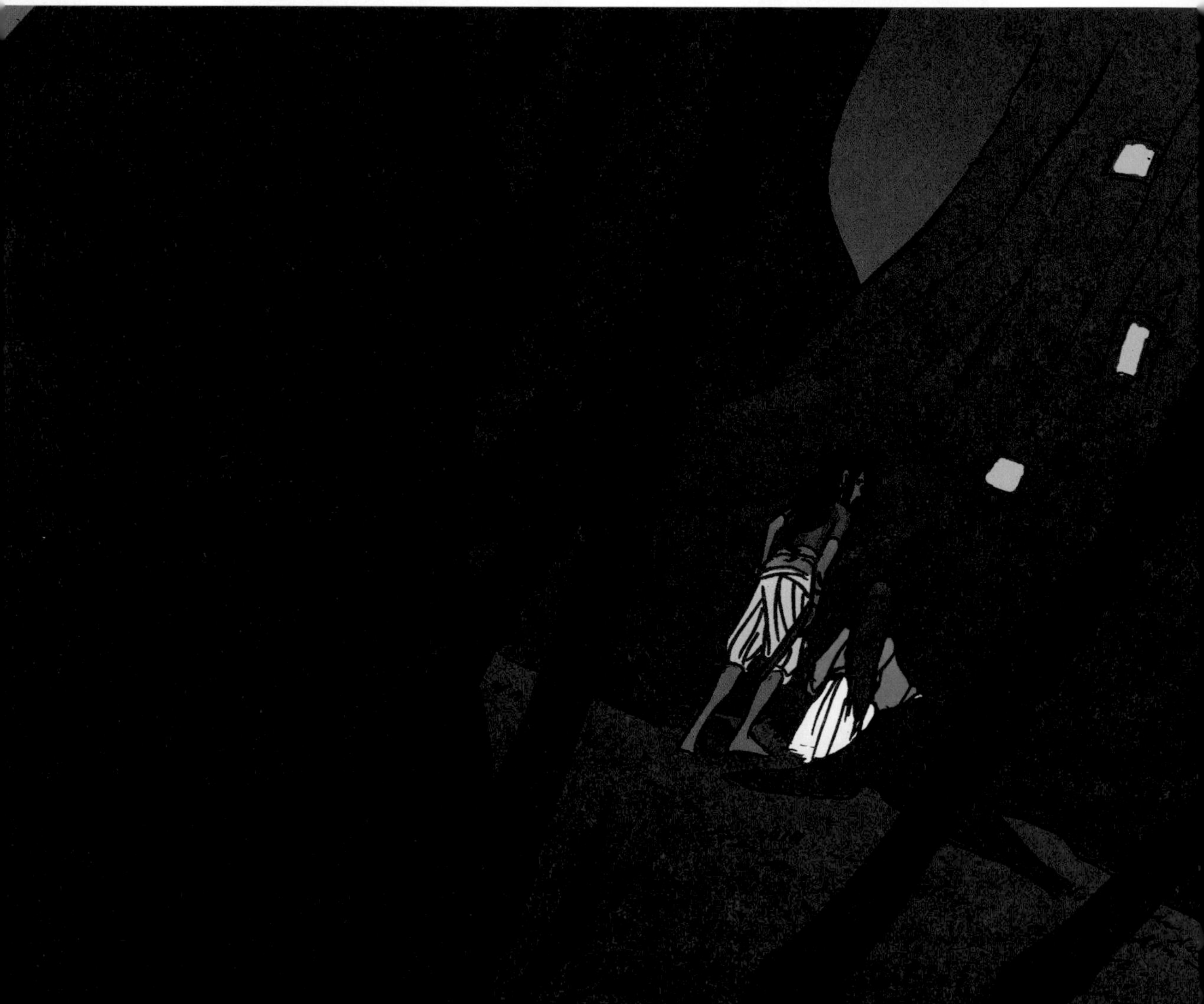

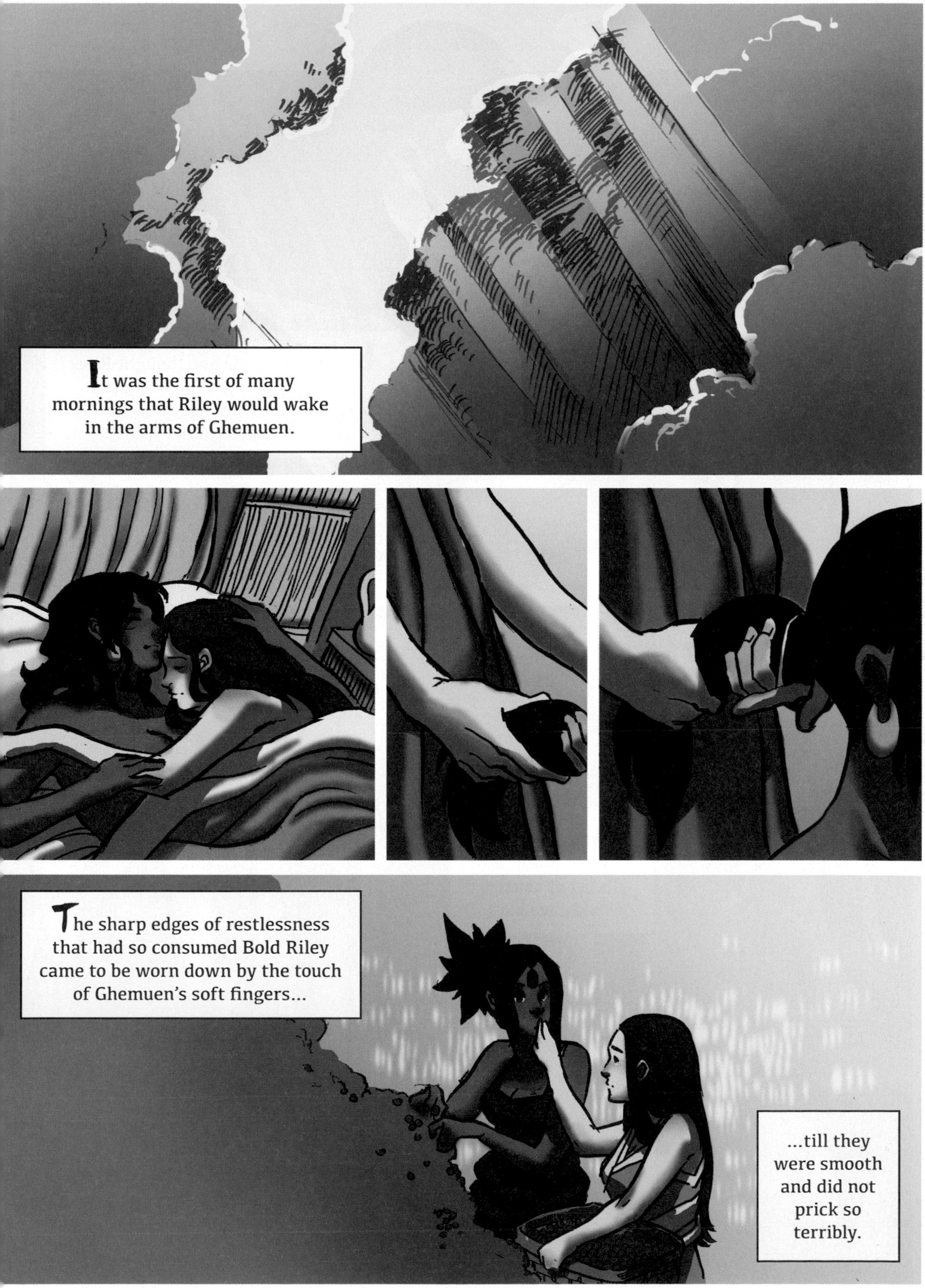
It was the first of many mornings that Riley would wake in the arms of Ghemuen.
The sharp edges of restlessness that had so consumed Bold Riley came to be worn down by the touch of Ghemuen's soft fingers...
...till they were smooth and did not prick so terribly.

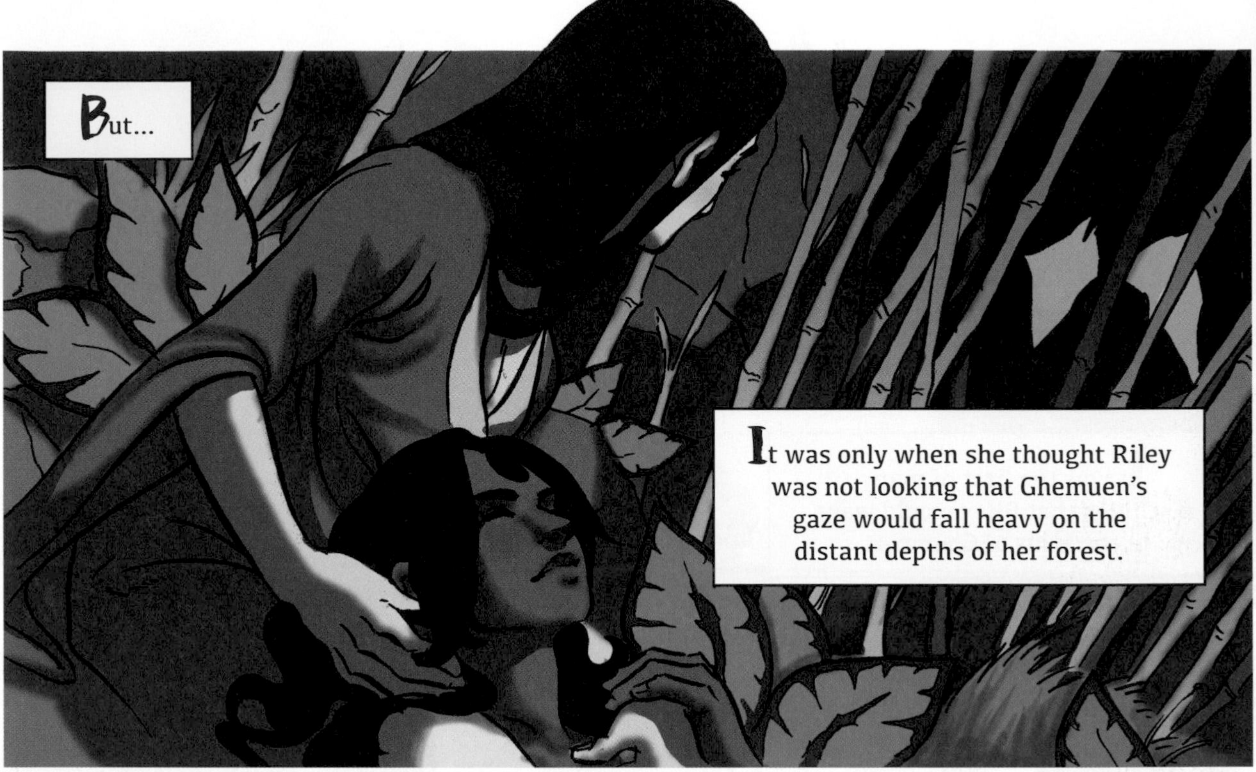
But...
It was only when she thought Riley was not looking that Ghemuen's gaze would fall heavy on the distant depths of her forest.

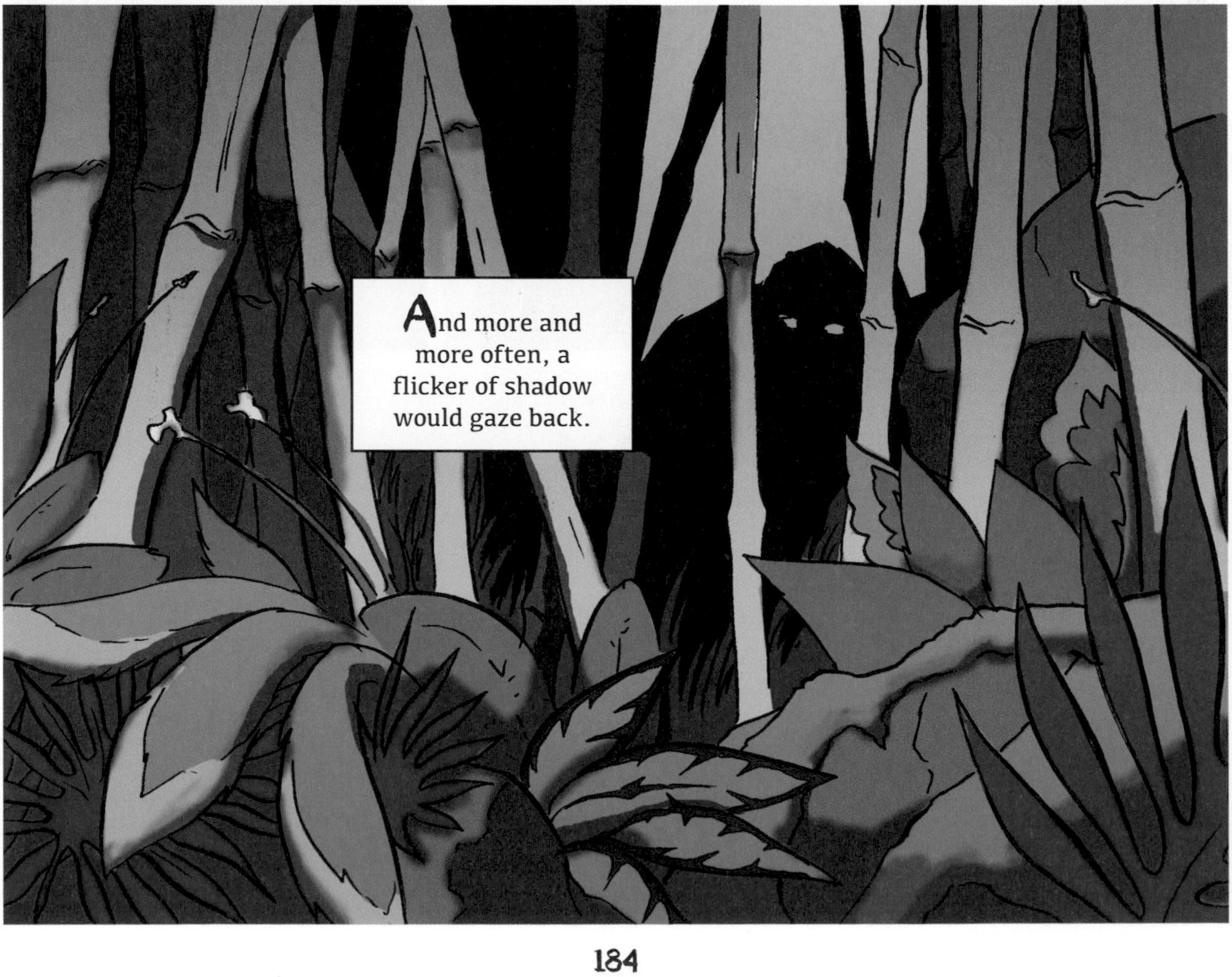
And more and more often, a flicker of shadow would gaze back.

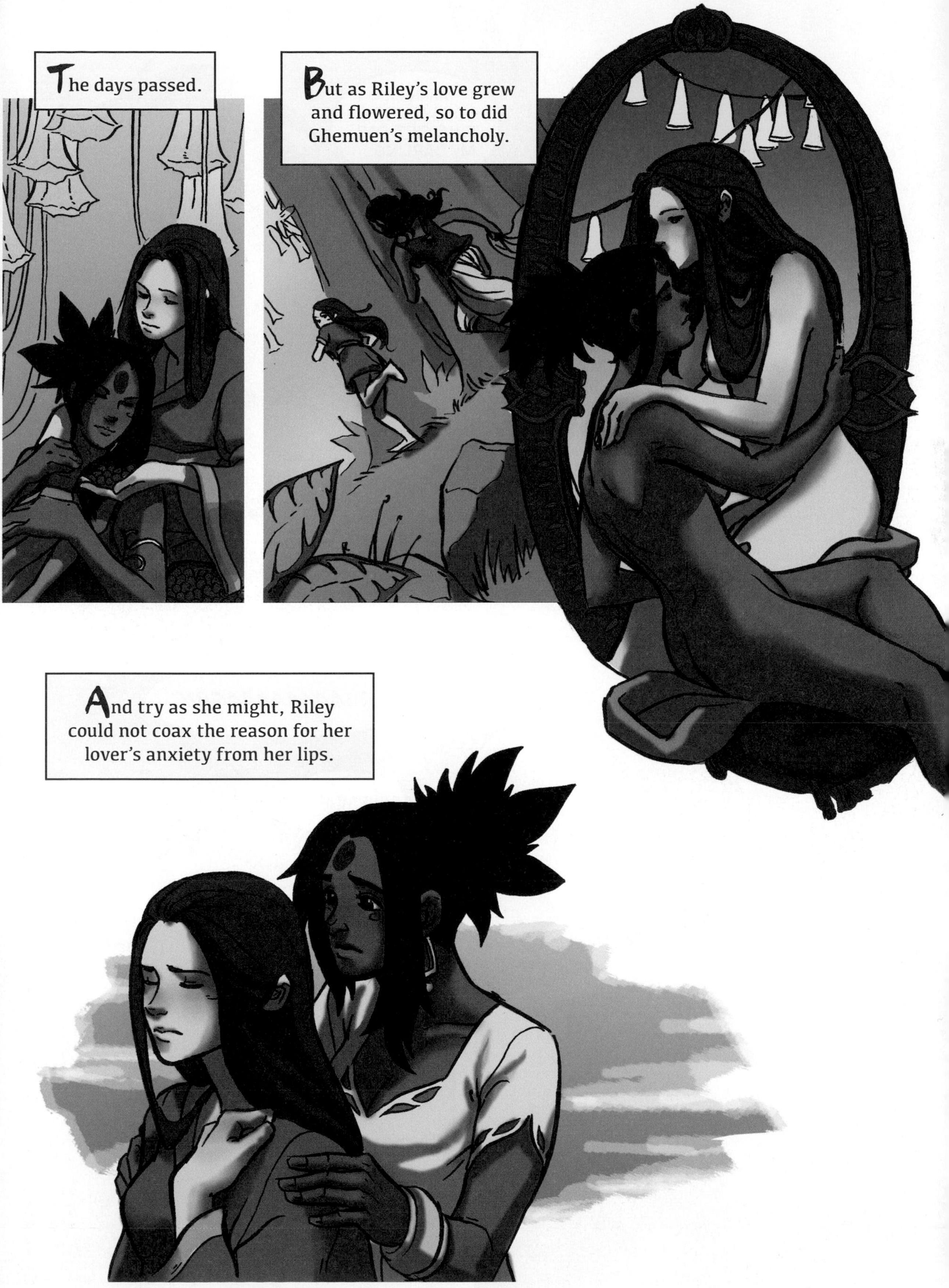
The days passed.
But as Riley's love grew and flowered, so to did Ghemuen's melancholy.
And try as she might, Riley could not coax the reason for her lover's anxiety from her lips.

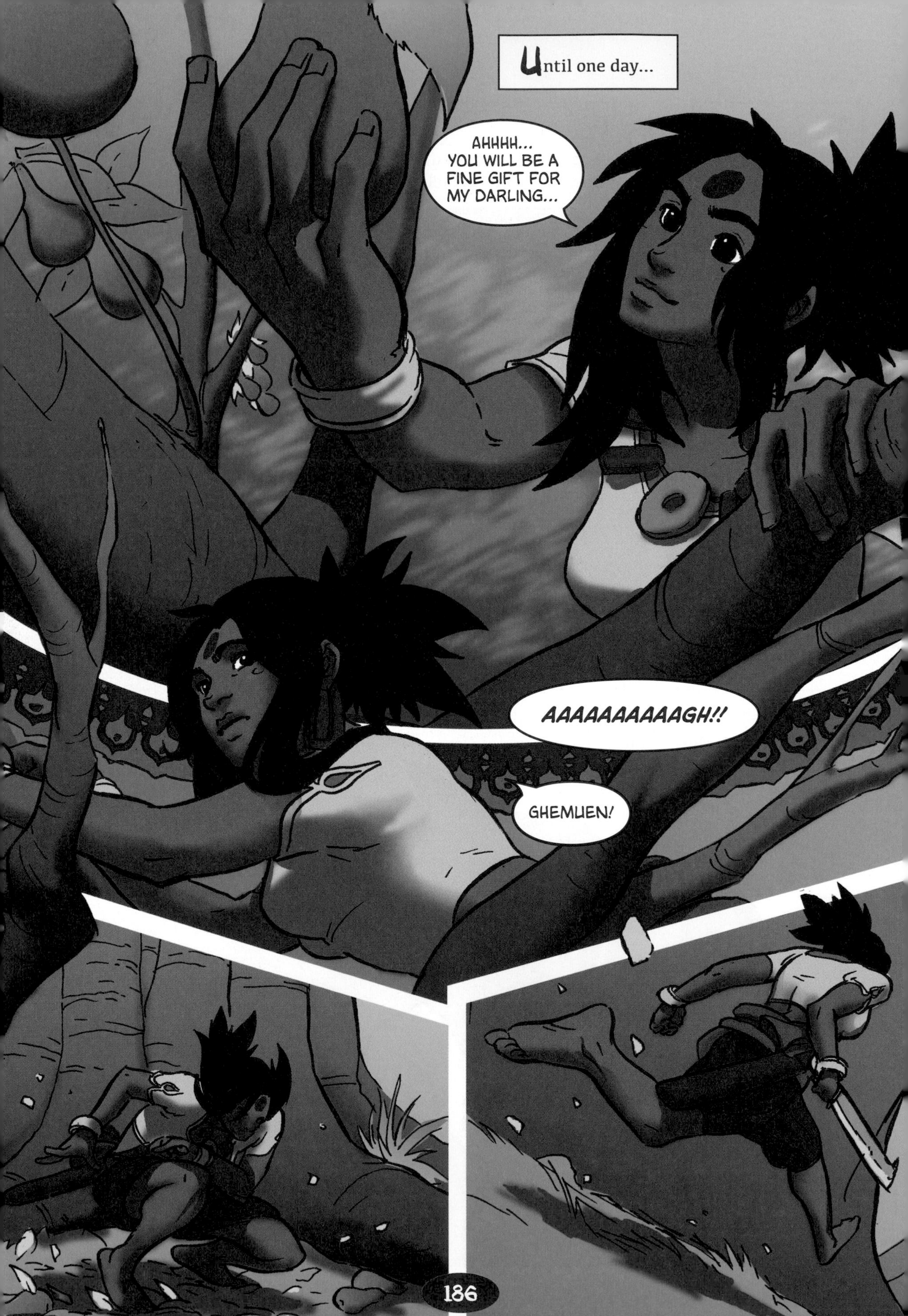
Until one day...
AHHHH... YOU WILL BE A FINE GIFT FOR MY DARLING...
AAAAAAAAAAGH!!
GHEMUEN!

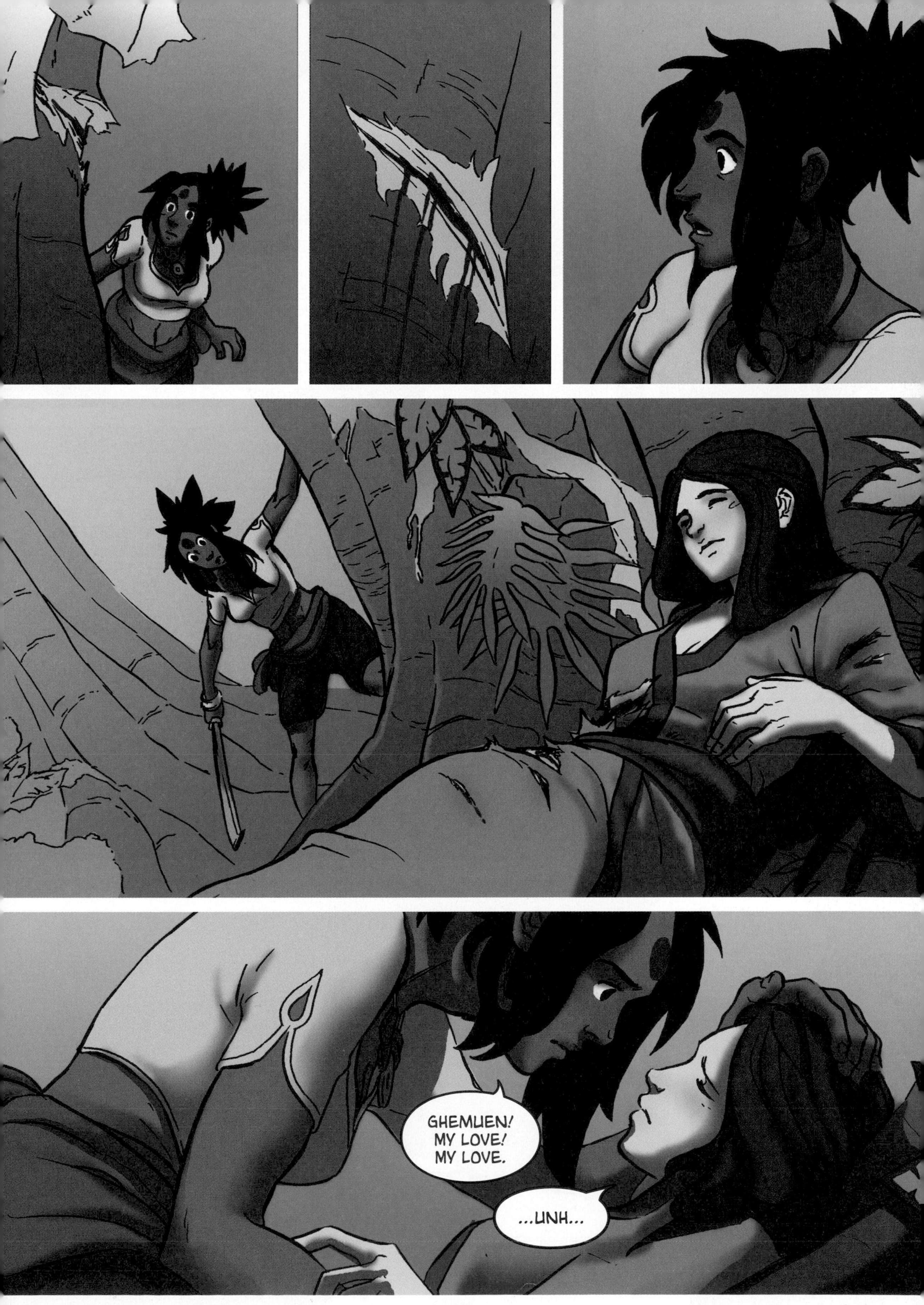
GHEMUEN! MY LOVE! MY LOVE.
...UNH...

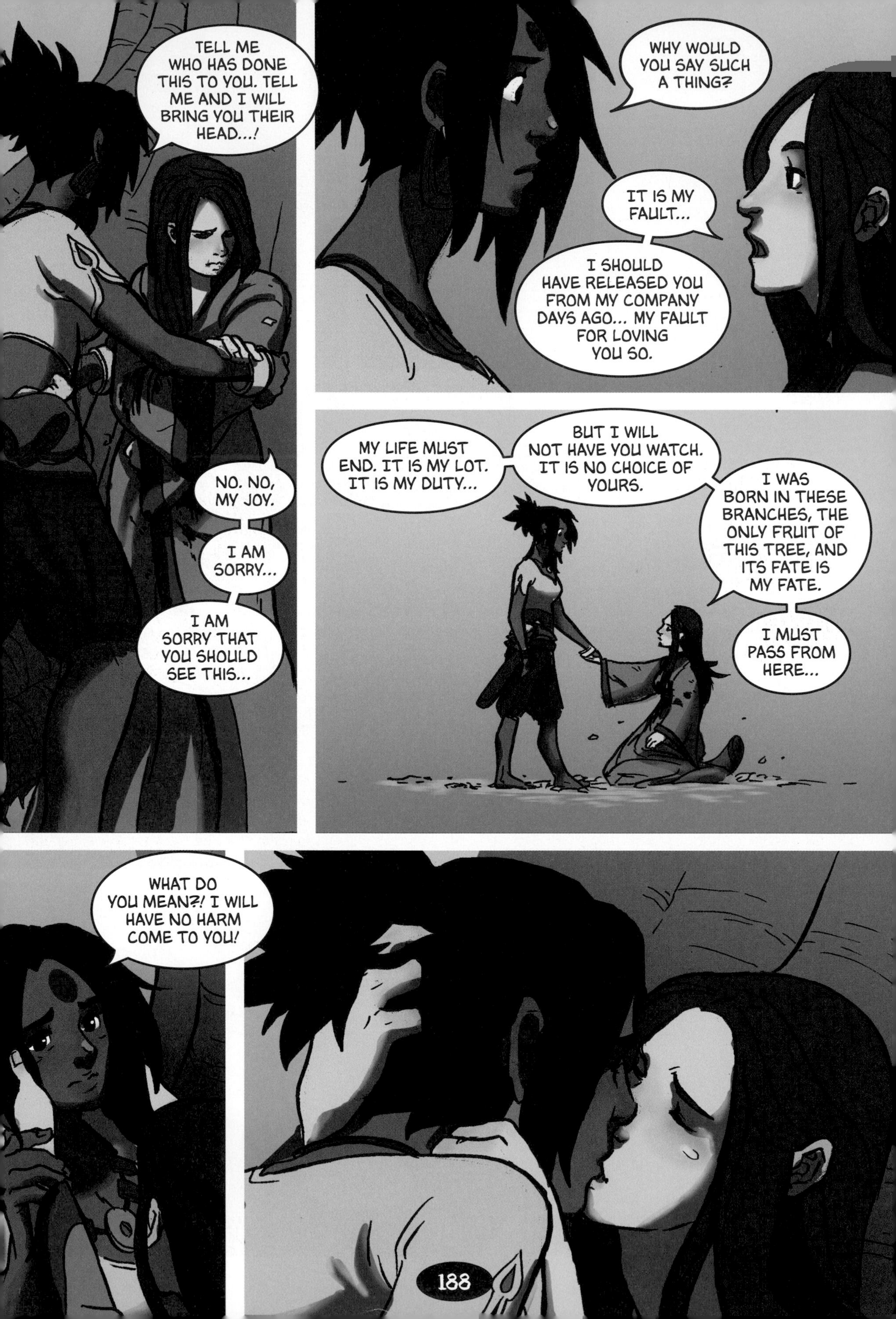
TELL ME WHO HAS DONE THIS TO YOU. TELL ME AND I WILL BRING YOU THEIR HEAD...!
NO. NO, MY JOY.
I AM SORRY...
I AM SORRY THAT YOU SHOULD SEE THIS...
WHY WOULD YOU SAY SUCH A THING?
IT IS MY FAULT...
I SHOULD HAVE RELEASED YOU FROM MY COMPANY DAYS AGO... MY FAULT FOR LOVING YOU SO.
MY LIFE MUST END. IT IS MY LOT. IT IS MY DUTY...
BUT I WILL NOT HAVE YOU WATCH. IT IS NO CHOICE OF YOURS.
I WAS BORN IN THESE BRANCHES, THE ONLY FRUIT OF THIS TREE, AND ITS FATE IS MY FATE.
I MUST PASS FROM HERE...
WHAT DO YOU MEAN?! I WILL HAVE NO HARM COME TO YOU!

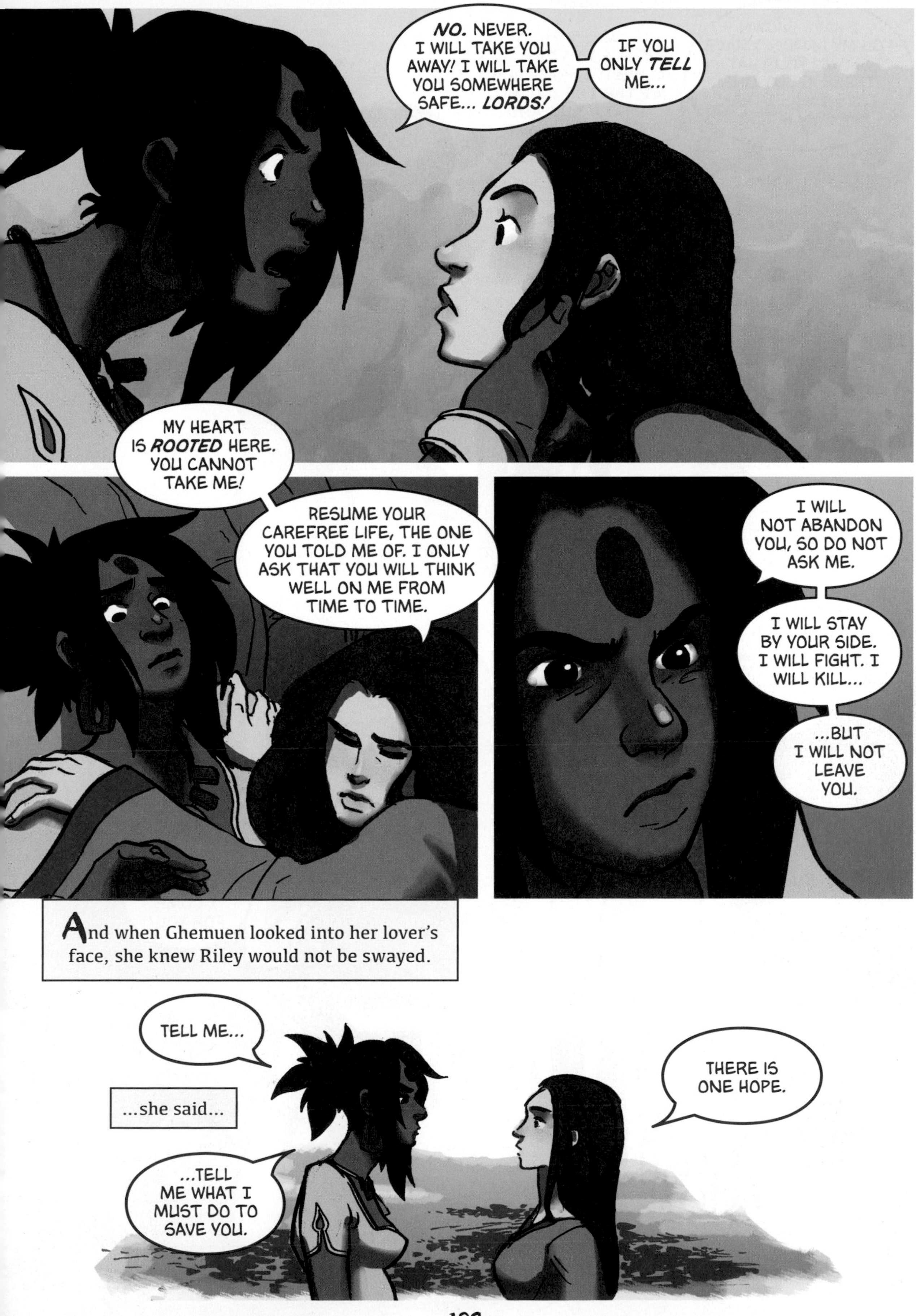
NO. NEVER. I WILL TAKE YOU AWAY! I WILL TAKE YOU SOMEWHERE SAFE... LORDS!
IF YOU ONLY TELL ME...
MY HEART IS ROOTED HERE. YOU CANNOT TAKE ME!
RESUME YOUR CAREFREE LIFE, THE ONE YOU TOLD ME OF. I ONLY ASK THAT YOU WILL THINK WELL ON ME FROM TIME TO TIME.
I WILL NOT ABANDON YOU, SO DO NOT ASK ME.
I WILL STAY BY YOUR SIDE. I WILL FIGHT. I WILL KILL...
...BUT I WILL NOT LEAVE YOU.
And when Ghemuen looked into her lover's face, she knew Riley would not be swayed.
TELL ME...
...she said...
...TELL ME WHAT I MUST DO TO SAVE YOU.
THERE IS ONE HOPE.

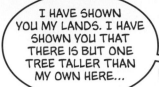

I HAVE SHOWN YOU MY LANDS. I HAVE SHOWN YOU THAT THERE IS BUT ONE TREE TALLER THAN MY OWN HERE...

GO TO IT. CLIMB ITS BRANCHES. AT THE TOP YOU WILL FIND A NUT, AND A COCKEREL WHO SHARPENS HIS BEAK UPON IT.

BRING ME THIS NUT. FOR THERE IS SOME HOPE THAT IT MAY SAVE ME.

BUT HOW...

MY LOVE, DO NOT ASK ME! ONLY GO, FOR TIME IS SO SHORT!

GO INTO THE HOUSE. BOLT THE DOOR.

DO NOT LEAVE UNTIL I COME FOR YOU!

GOOD BYE, MY HEART. AT THE VERY LEAST YOU WILL NOT BE HERE TO SEE...

190

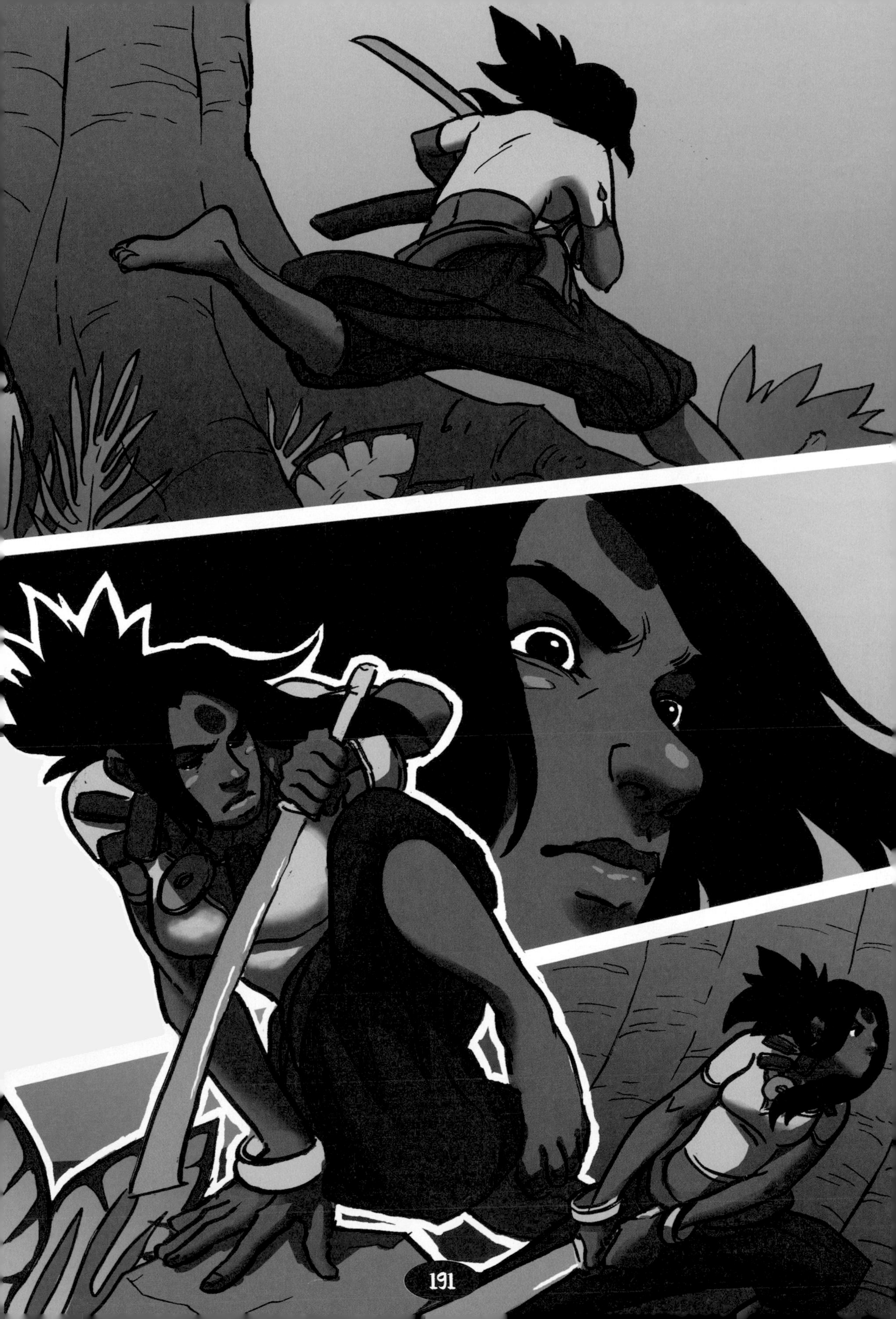

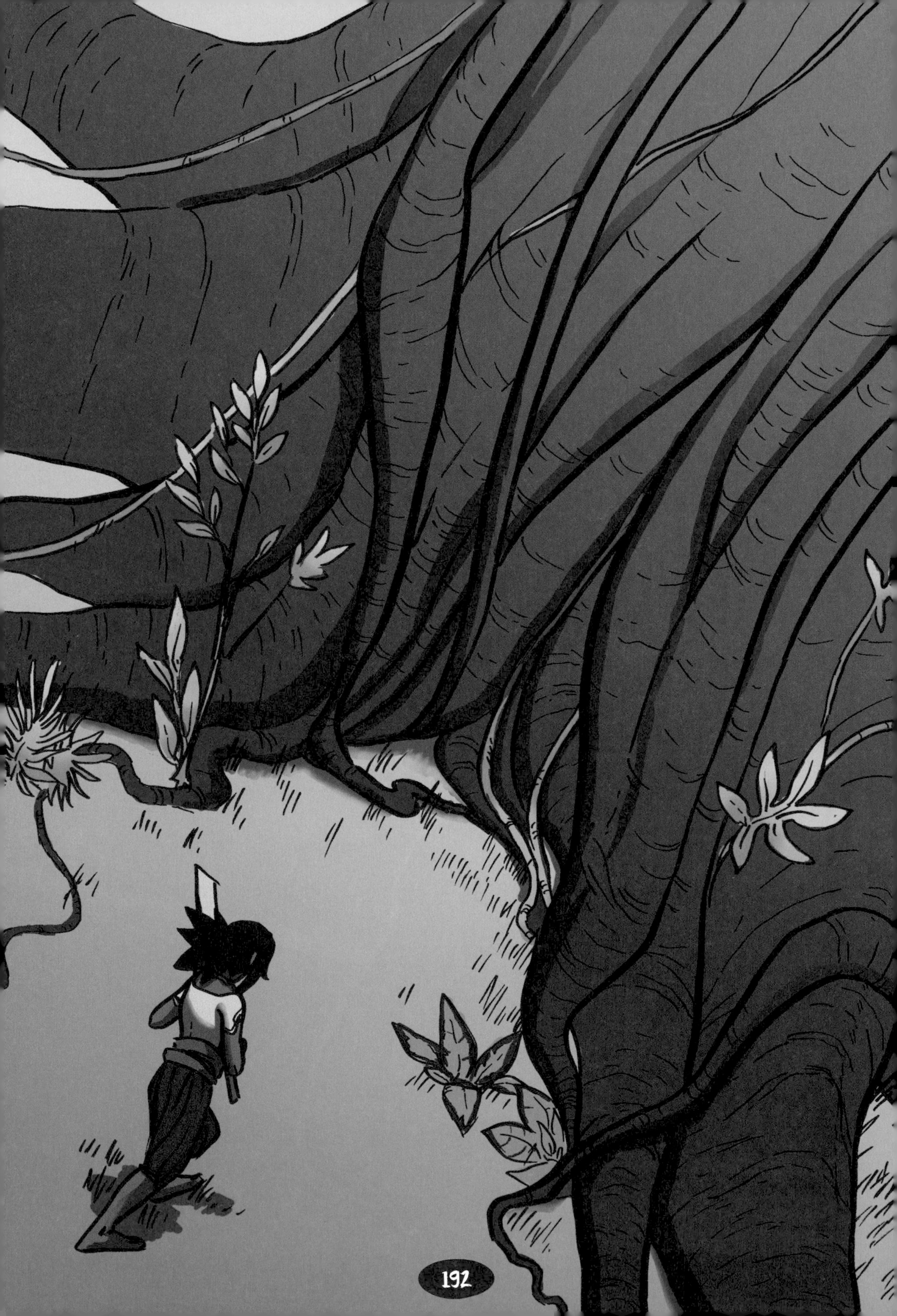

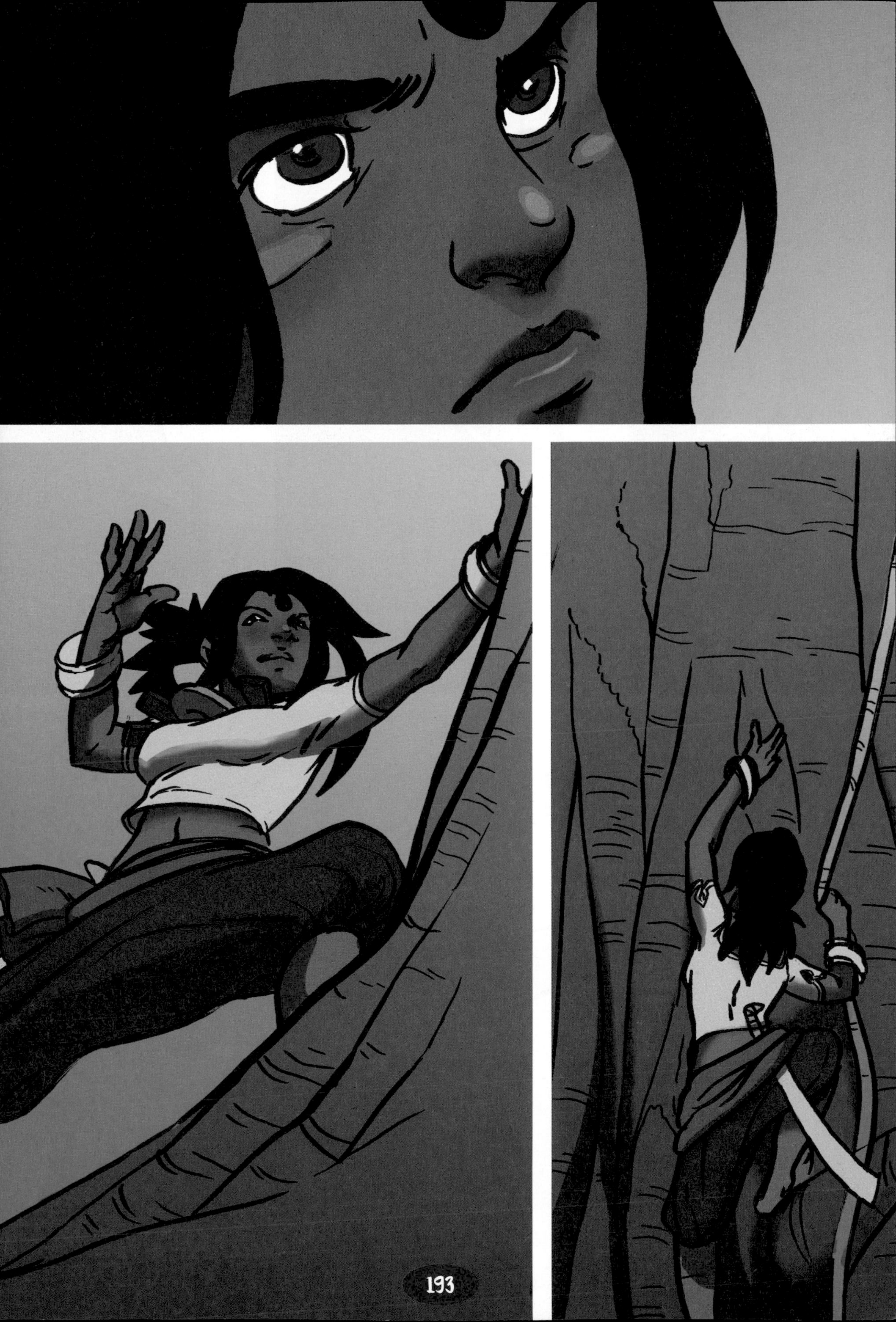

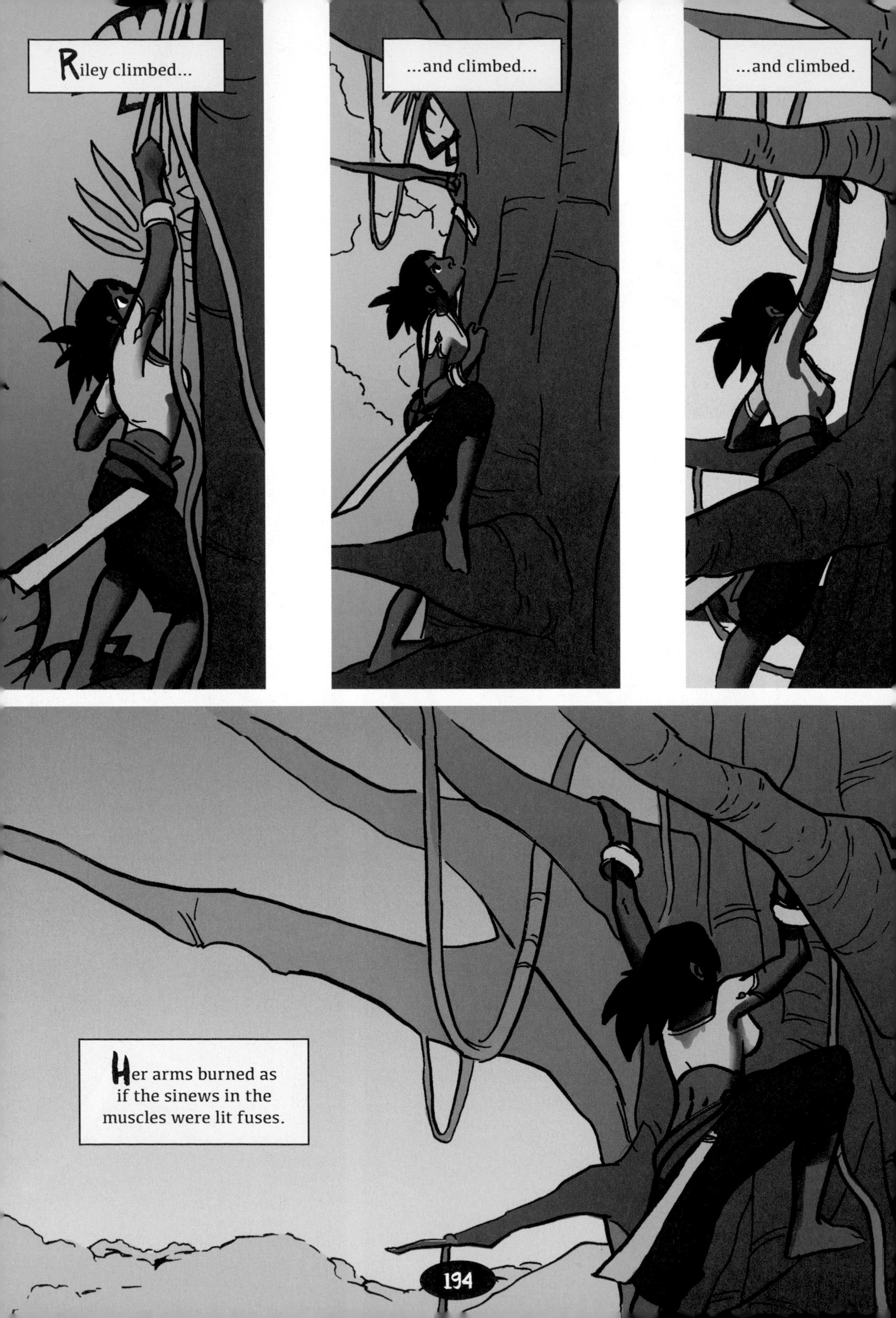
Riley climbed...
...and climbed...
...and climbed.
Her arms burned as if the sinews in the muscles were lit fuses.

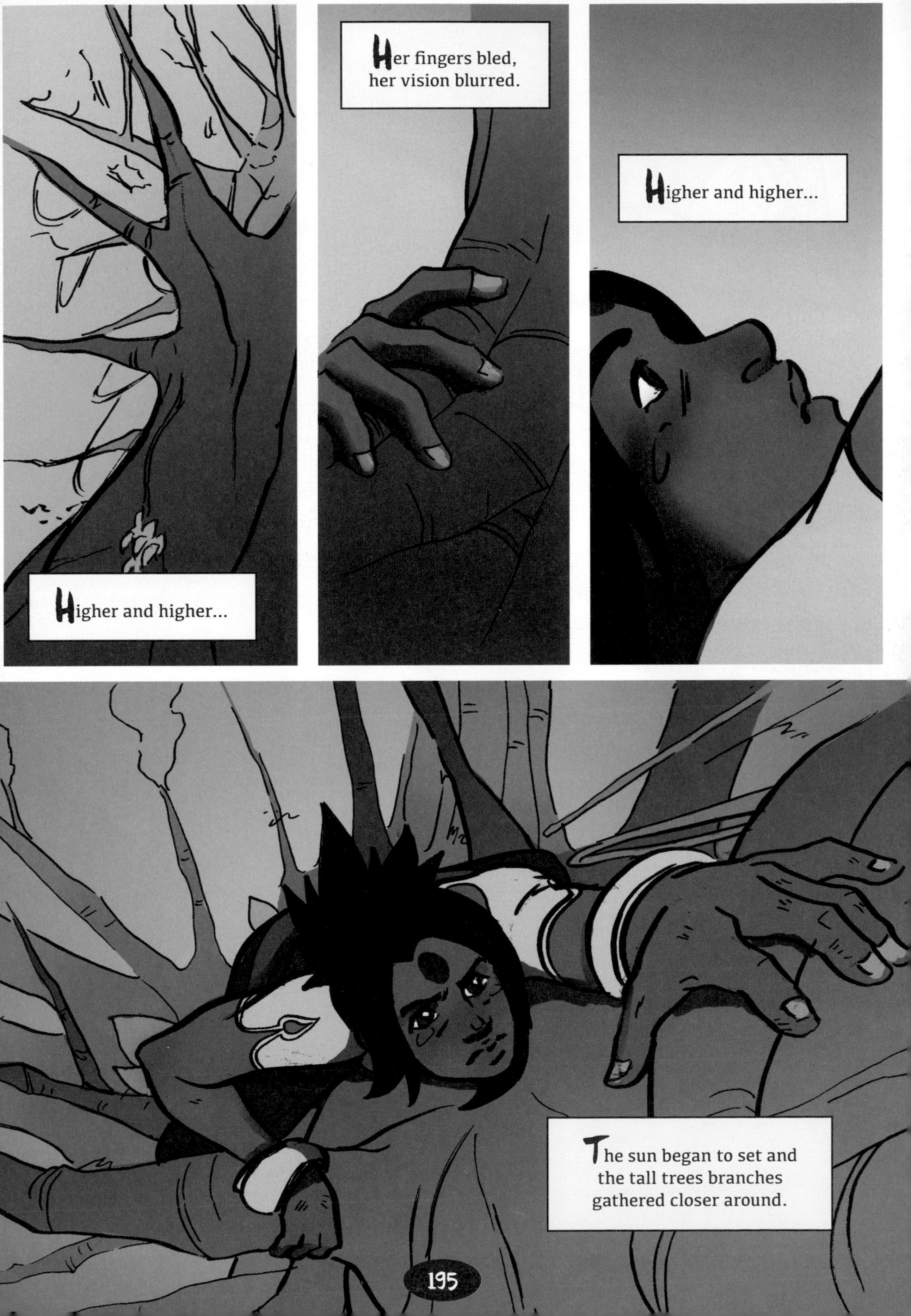
Higher and higher...
Her fingers bled, her vision blurred.
Higher and higher...
The sun began to set and the tall trees branches gathered closer around.

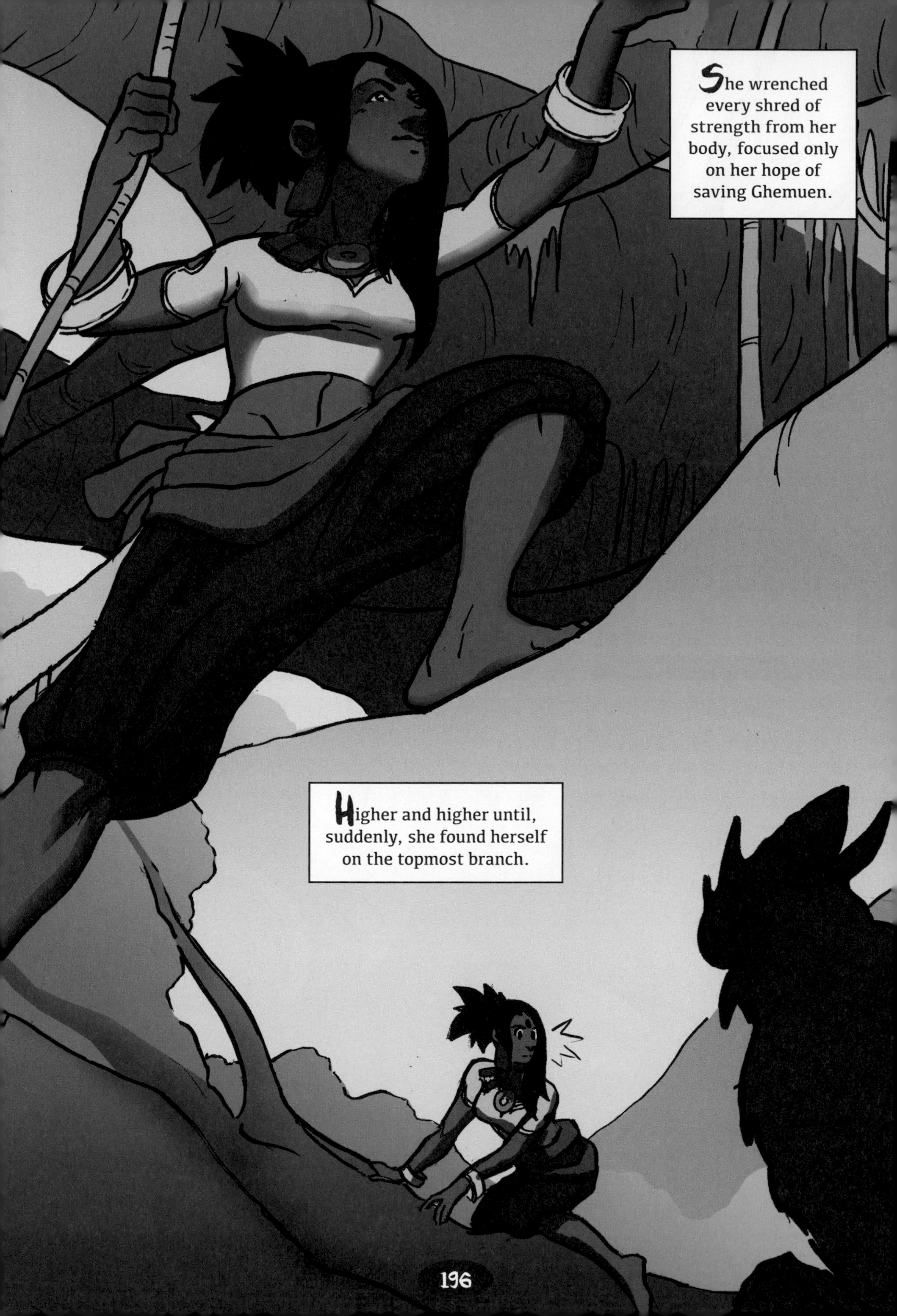
She wrenched every shred of strength from her body, focused only on her hope of saving Ghemuen.
Higher and higher until, suddenly, she found herself on the topmost branch.

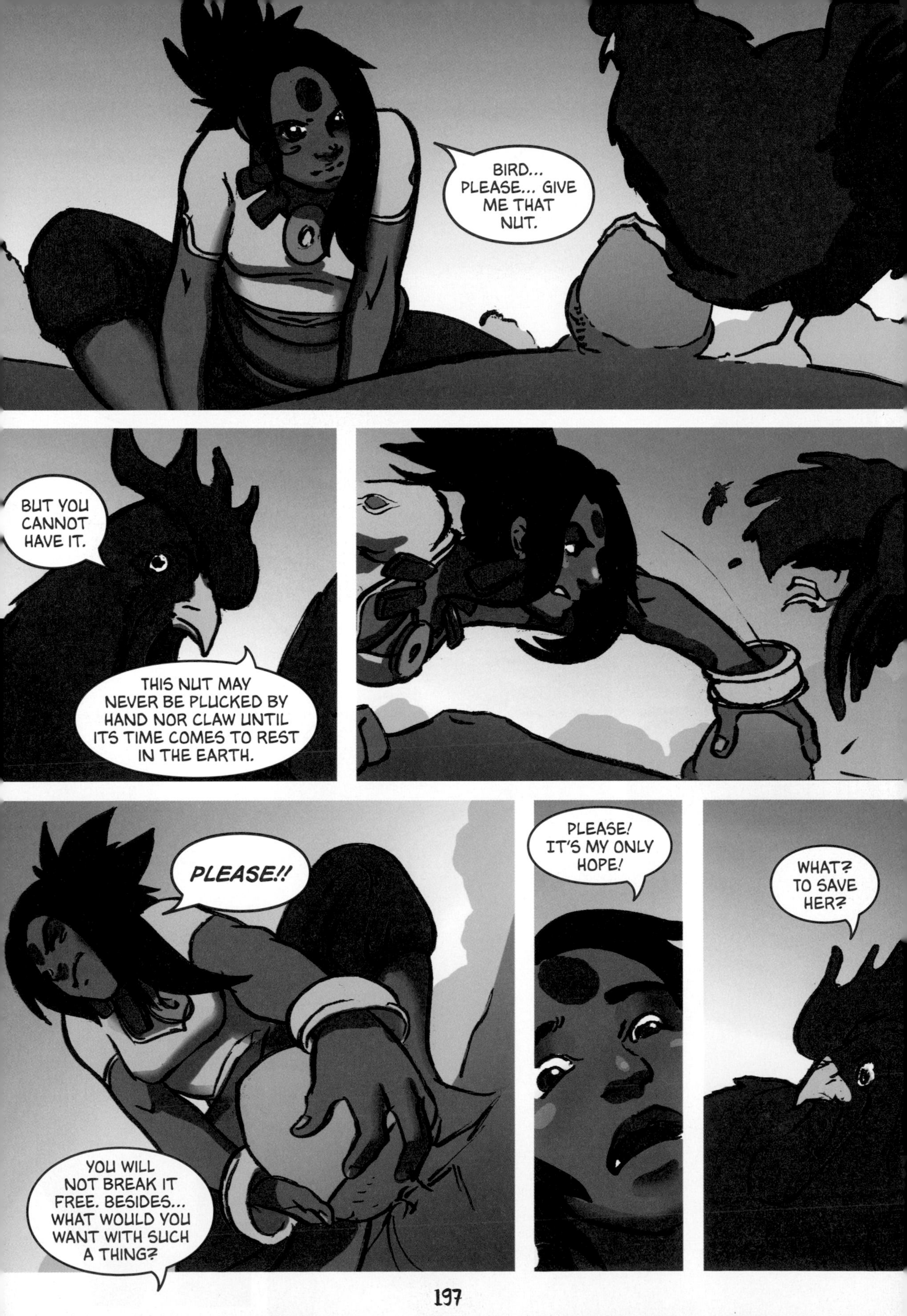
BIRD... PLEASE... GIVE ME THAT NUT.
BUT YOU CANNOT HAVE IT.
THIS NUT MAY NEVER BE PLUCKED BY HAND NOR CLAW UNTIL ITS TIME COMES TO REST IN THE EARTH.
PLEASE!!
YOU WILL NOT BREAK IT FREE. BESIDES... WHAT WOULD YOU WANT WITH SUCH A THING?
PLEASE! IT'S MY ONLY HOPE!
WHAT? TO SAVE HER?

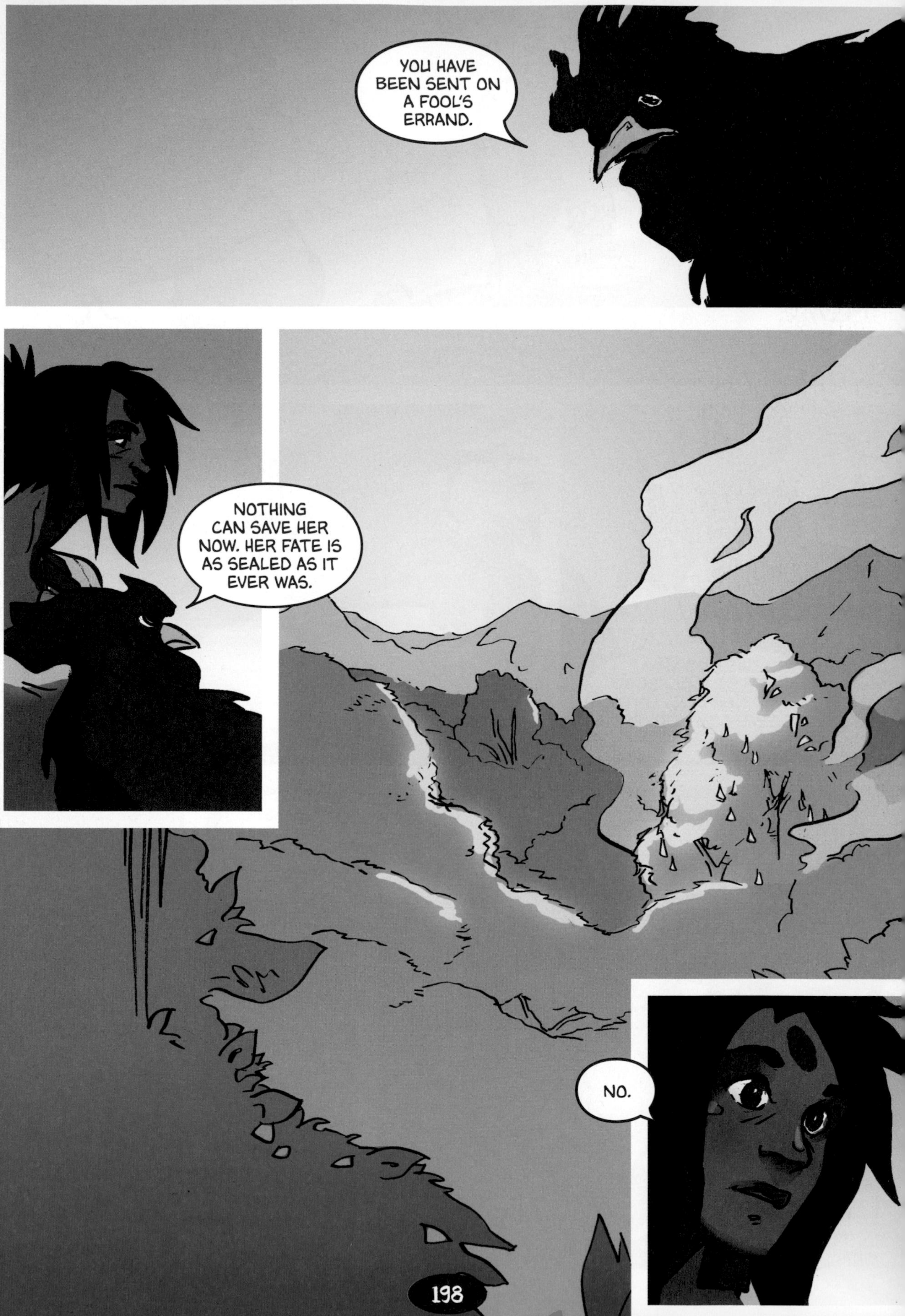
YOU HAVE BEEN SENT ON A FOOL'S ERRAND.
NOTHING CAN SAVE HER NOW. HER FATE IS AS SEALED AS IT EVER WAS.
NO.

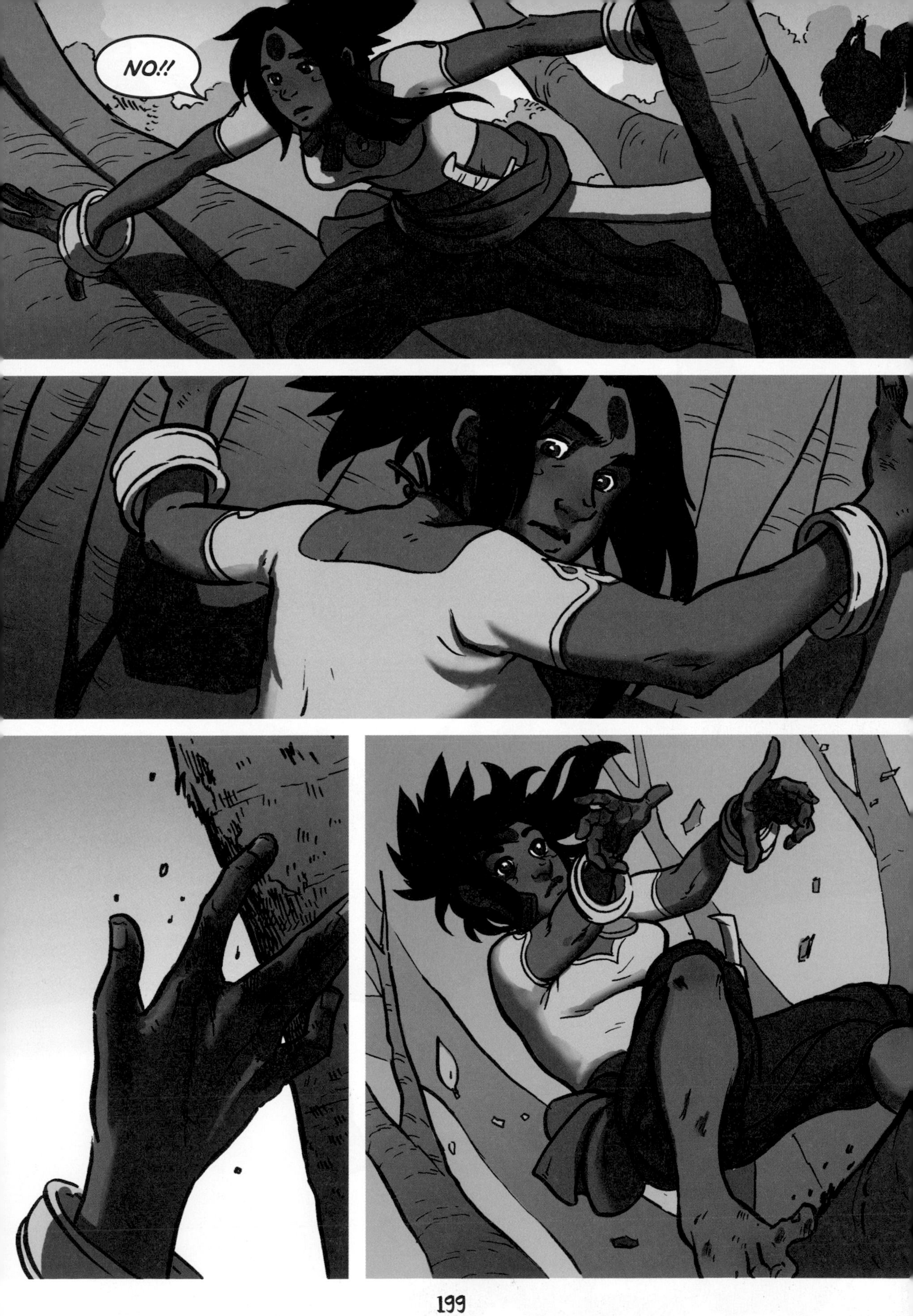
NO!!

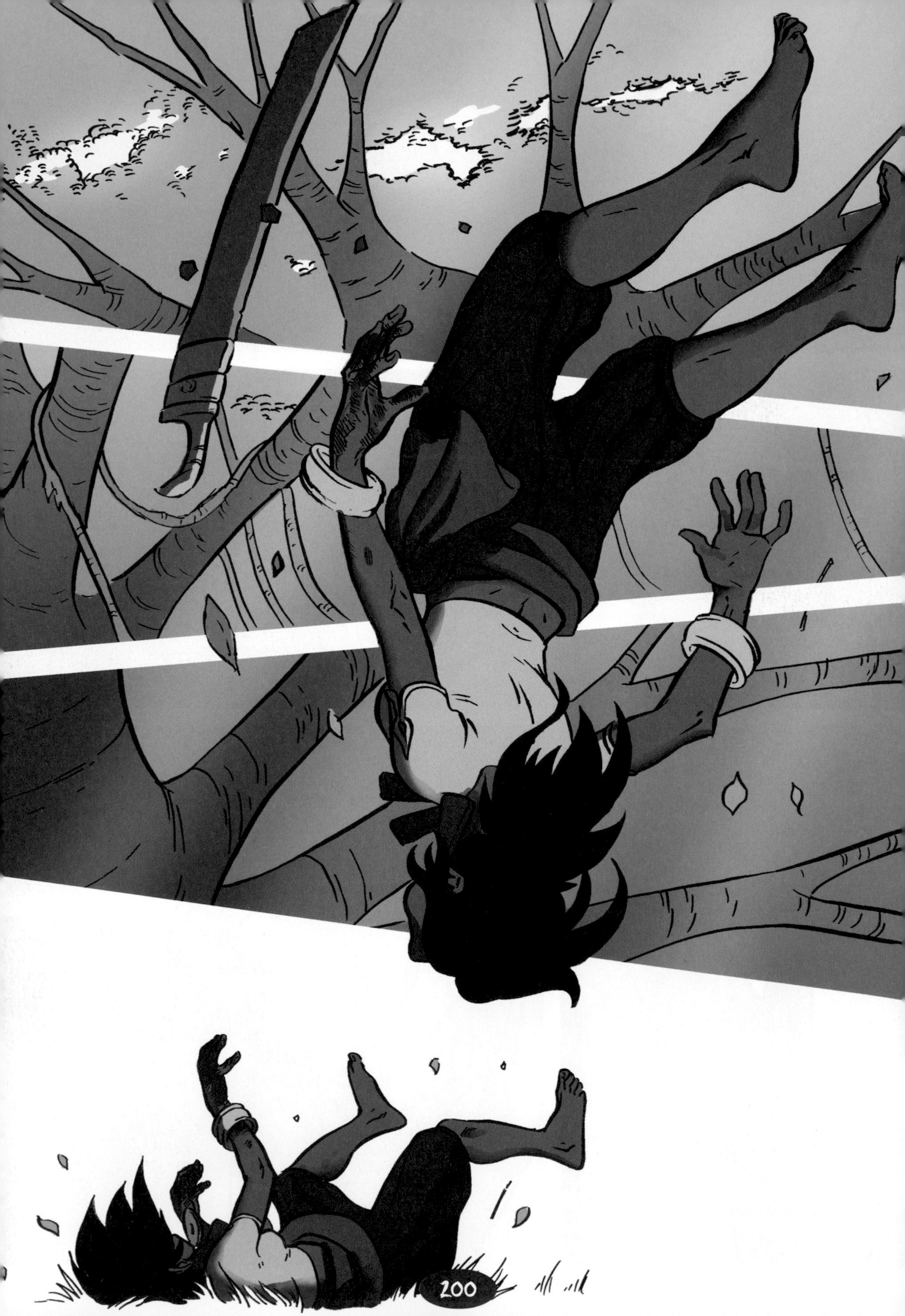

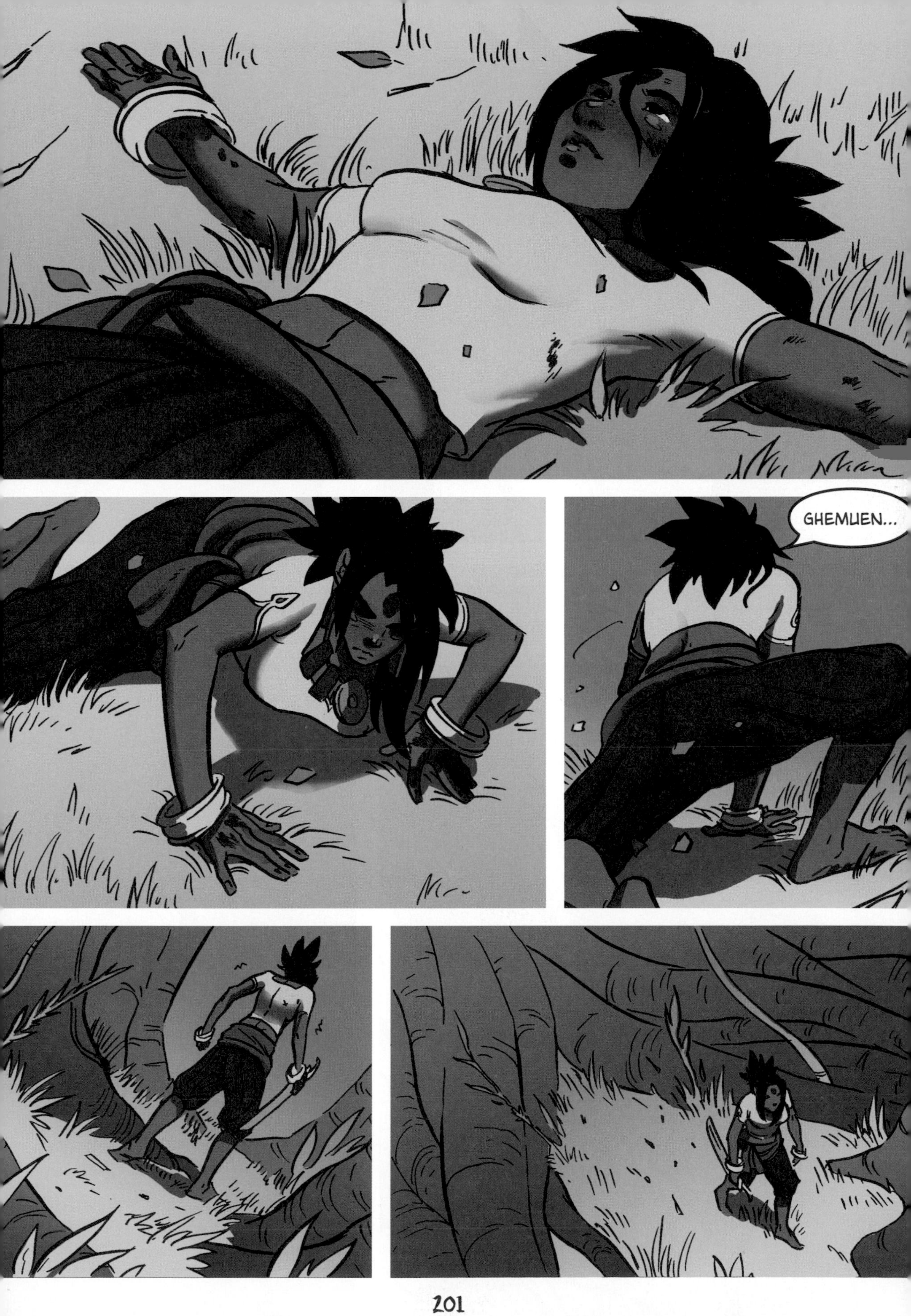
GHEMUEN...

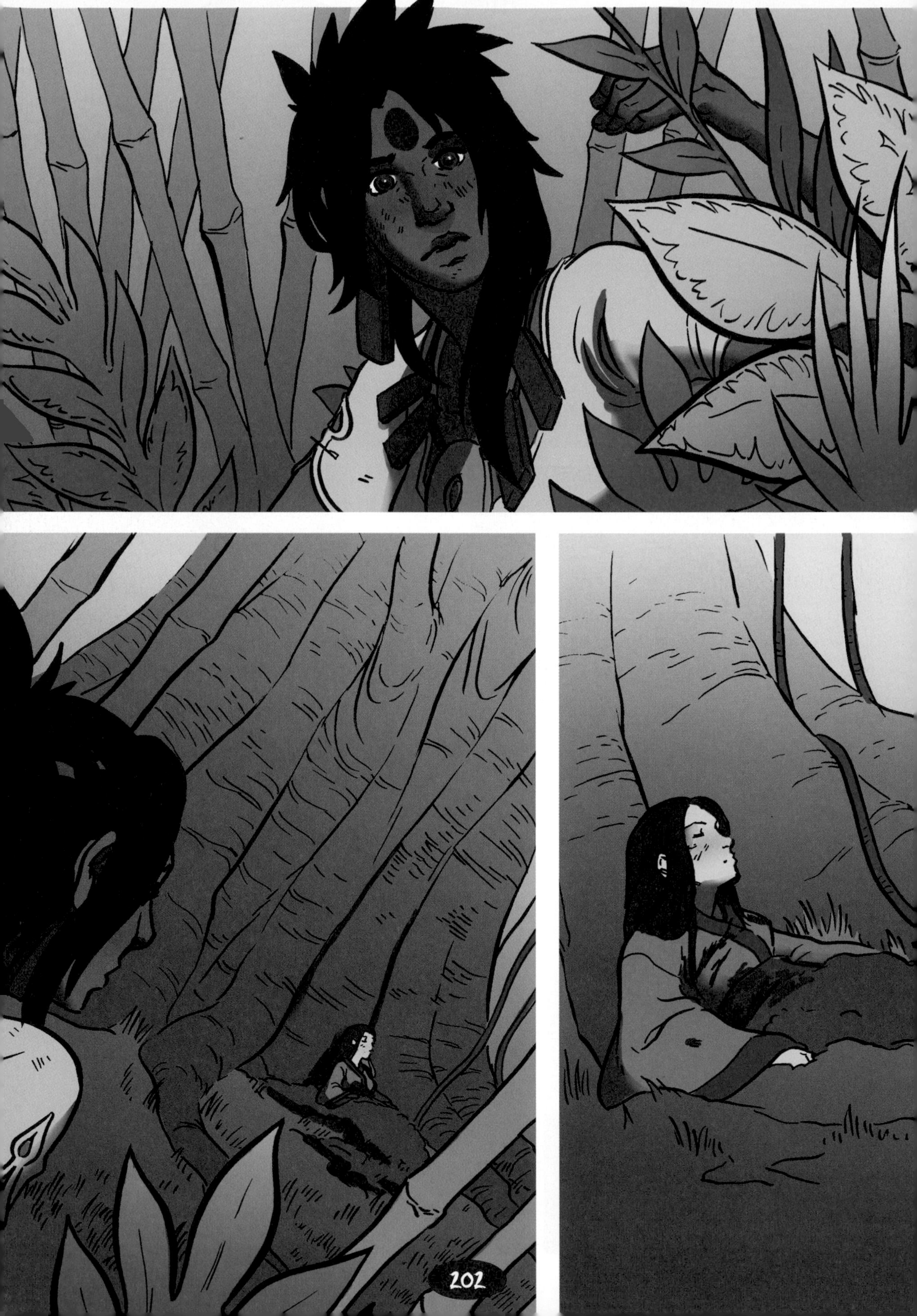

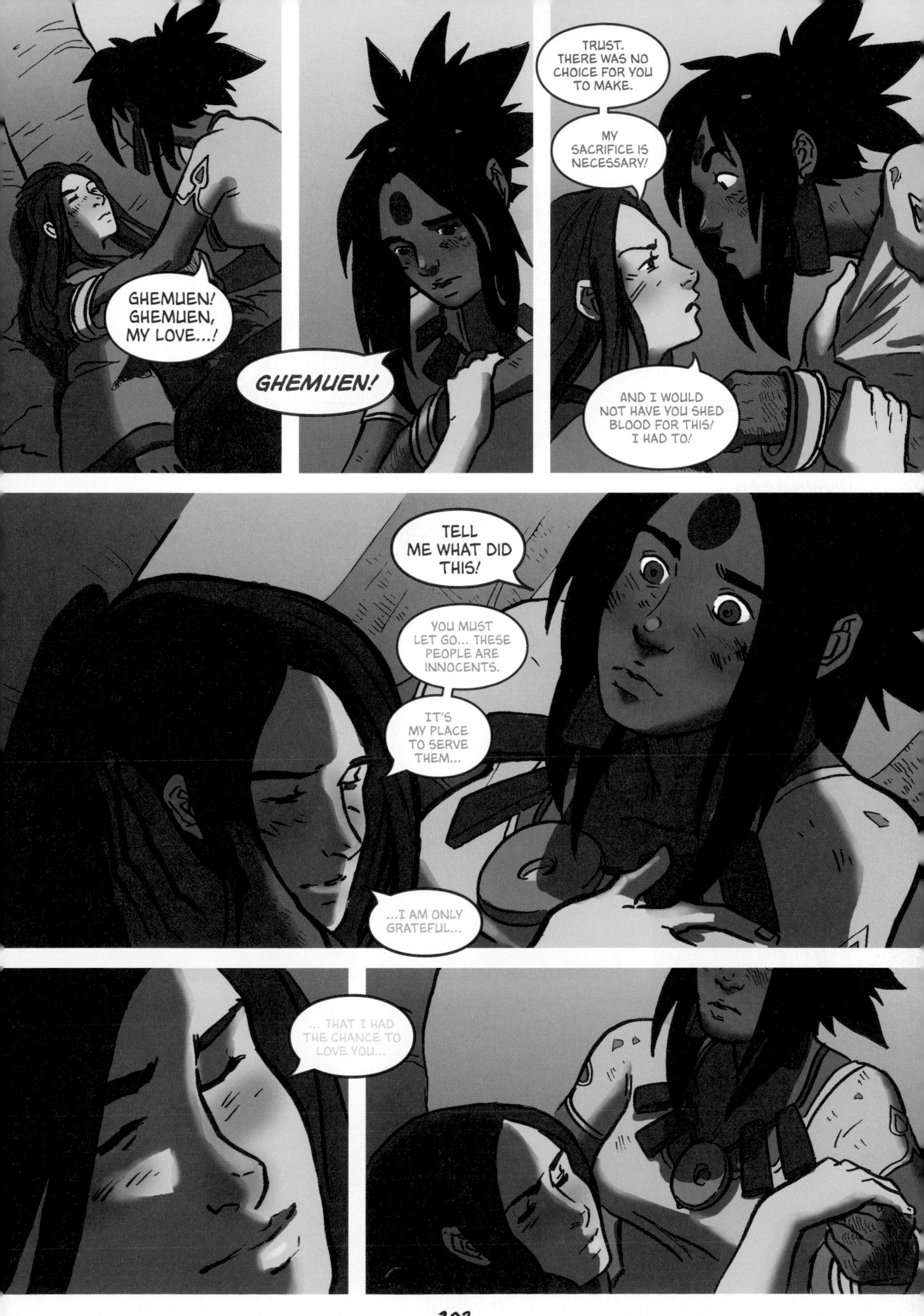
GHEMUEN! GHEMUEN, MY LOVE...!
GHEMUEN!
TRUST. THERE WAS NO CHOICE FOR YOU TO MAKE.
MY SACRIFICE IS NECESSARY!
AND I WOULD NOT HAVE YOU SHED BLOOD FOR THIS! I HAD TO!
TELL ME WHAT DID THIS!
YOU MUST LET GO... THESE PEOPLE ARE INNOCENTS.
IT'S MY PLACE TO SERVE THEM...
...I AM ONLY GRATEFUL...
... THAT I HAD THE CHANCE TO LOVE YOU...

NNNGAAAA
AAAAHHH!!!

AAAAAUGH...

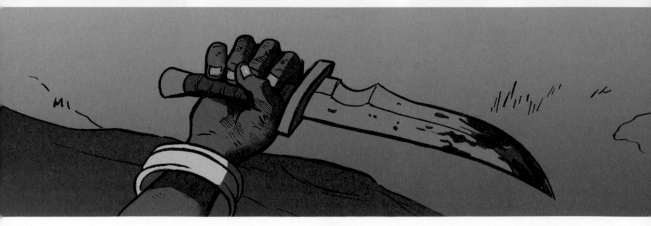

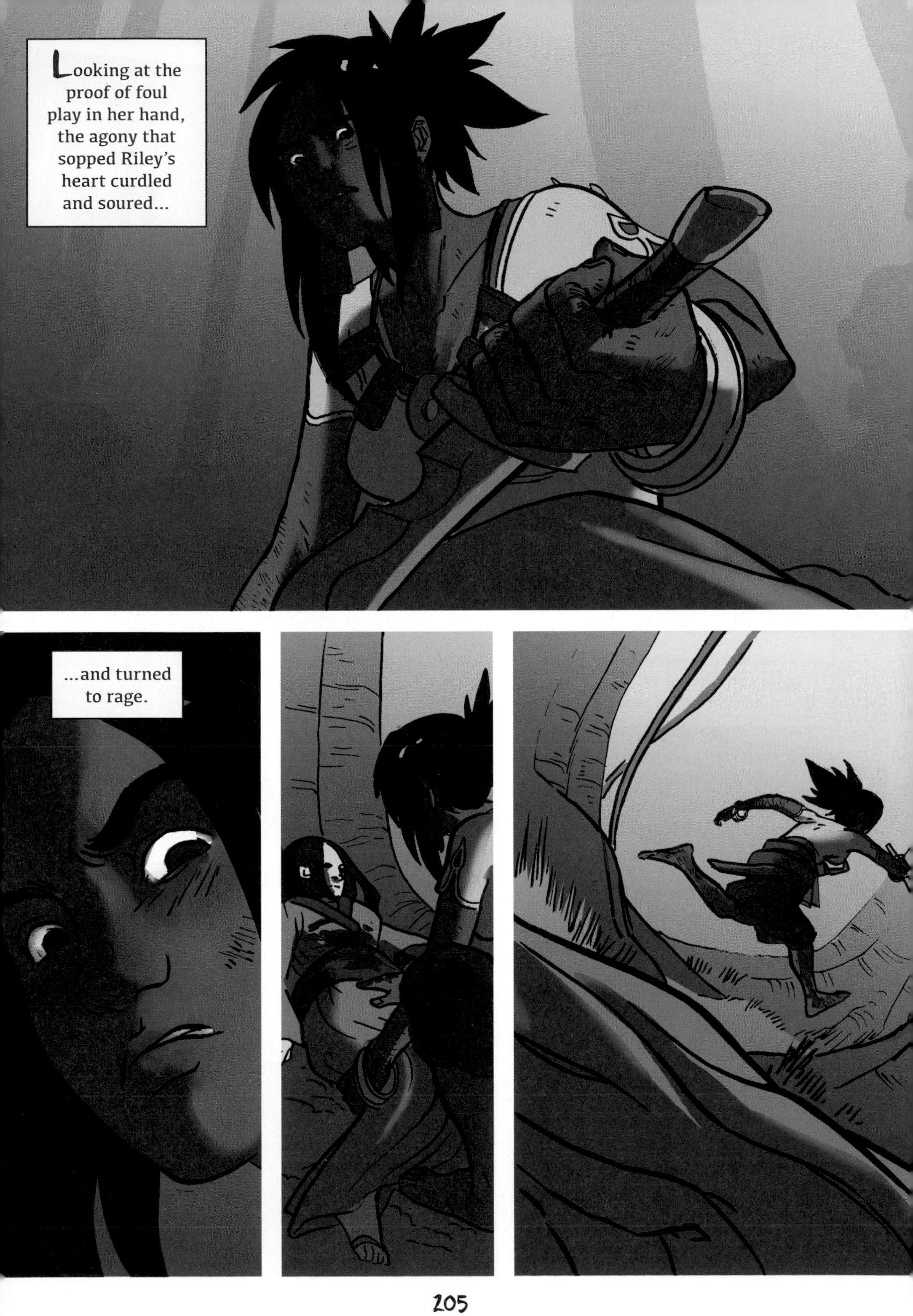
Looking at the proof of foul play in her hand, the agony that sopped Riley's heart curdled and soured...
...and turned to rage.

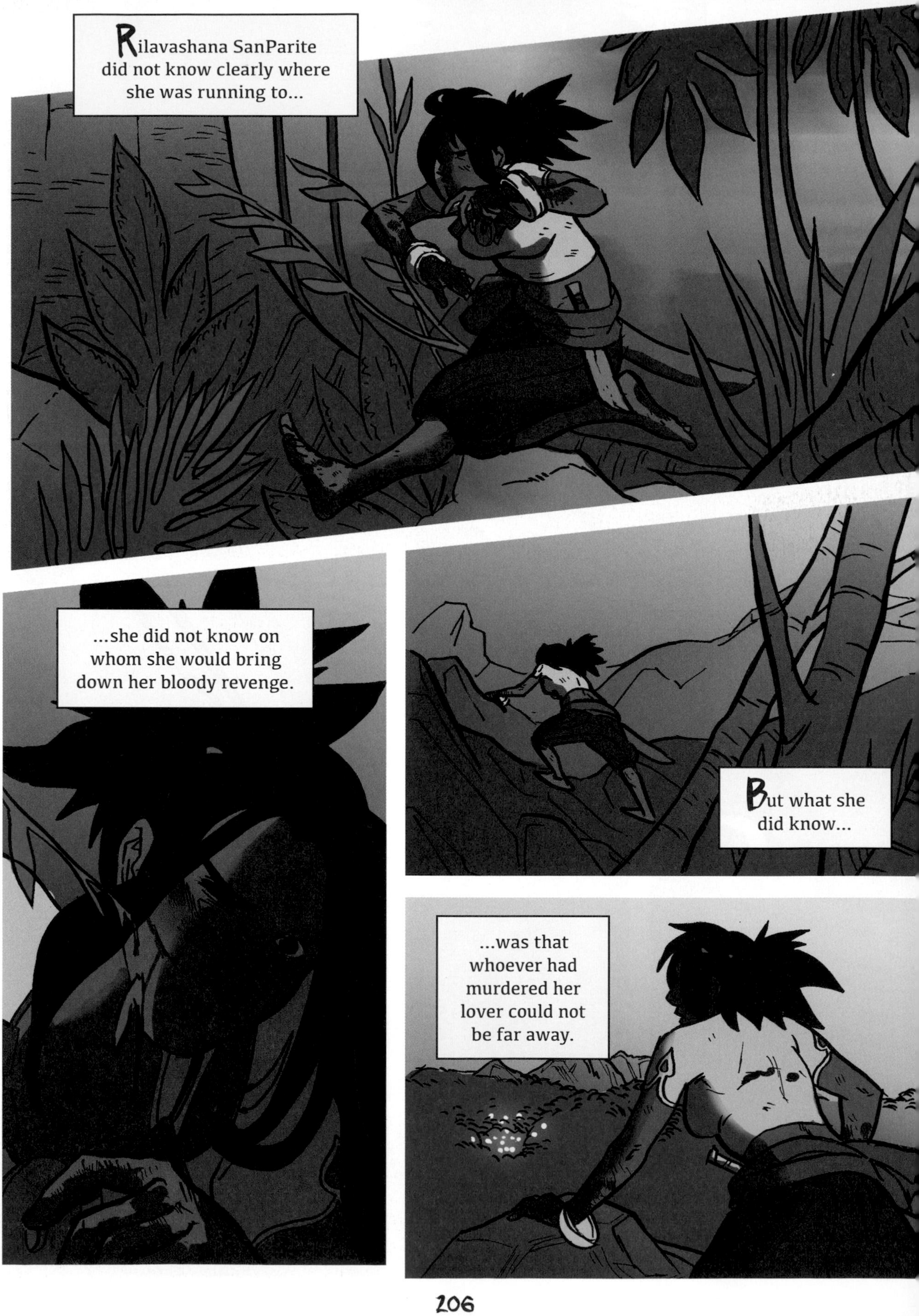
Rilavashana SanParite did not know clearly where she was running to...
...she did not know on whom she would bring down her bloody revenge.
But what she did know...
...was that whoever had murdered her lover could not be far away.

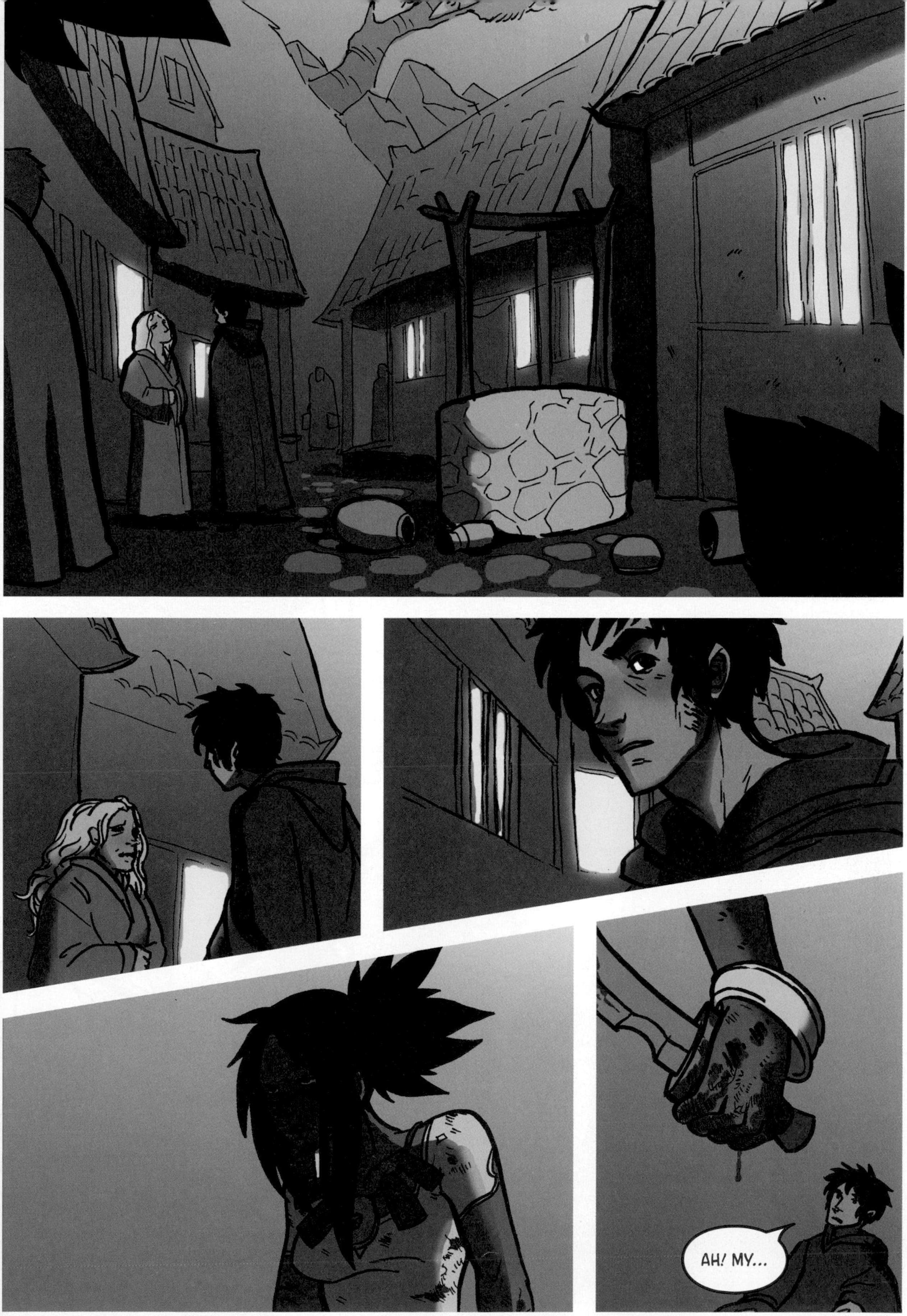
AH! MY...

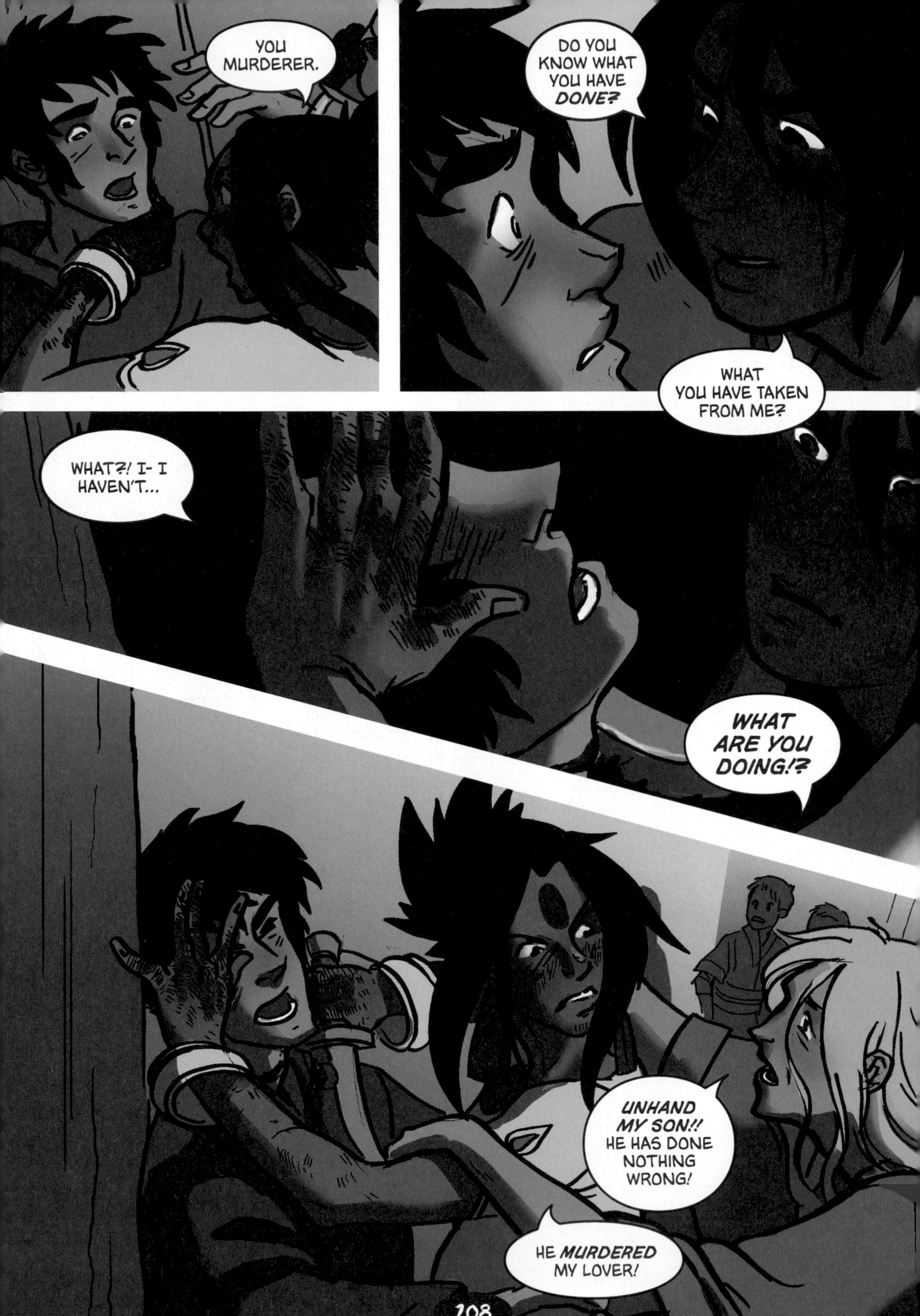
YOU MURDERER.
DO YOU KNOW WHAT YOU HAVE *DONE?*
WHAT YOU HAVE TAKEN FROM ME?
WHAT?! I- I HAVEN'T...
WHAT ARE YOU DOING!?
UNHAND MY SON!! HE HAS DONE NOTHING WRONG!
HE ***MURDERED*** MY LOVER!

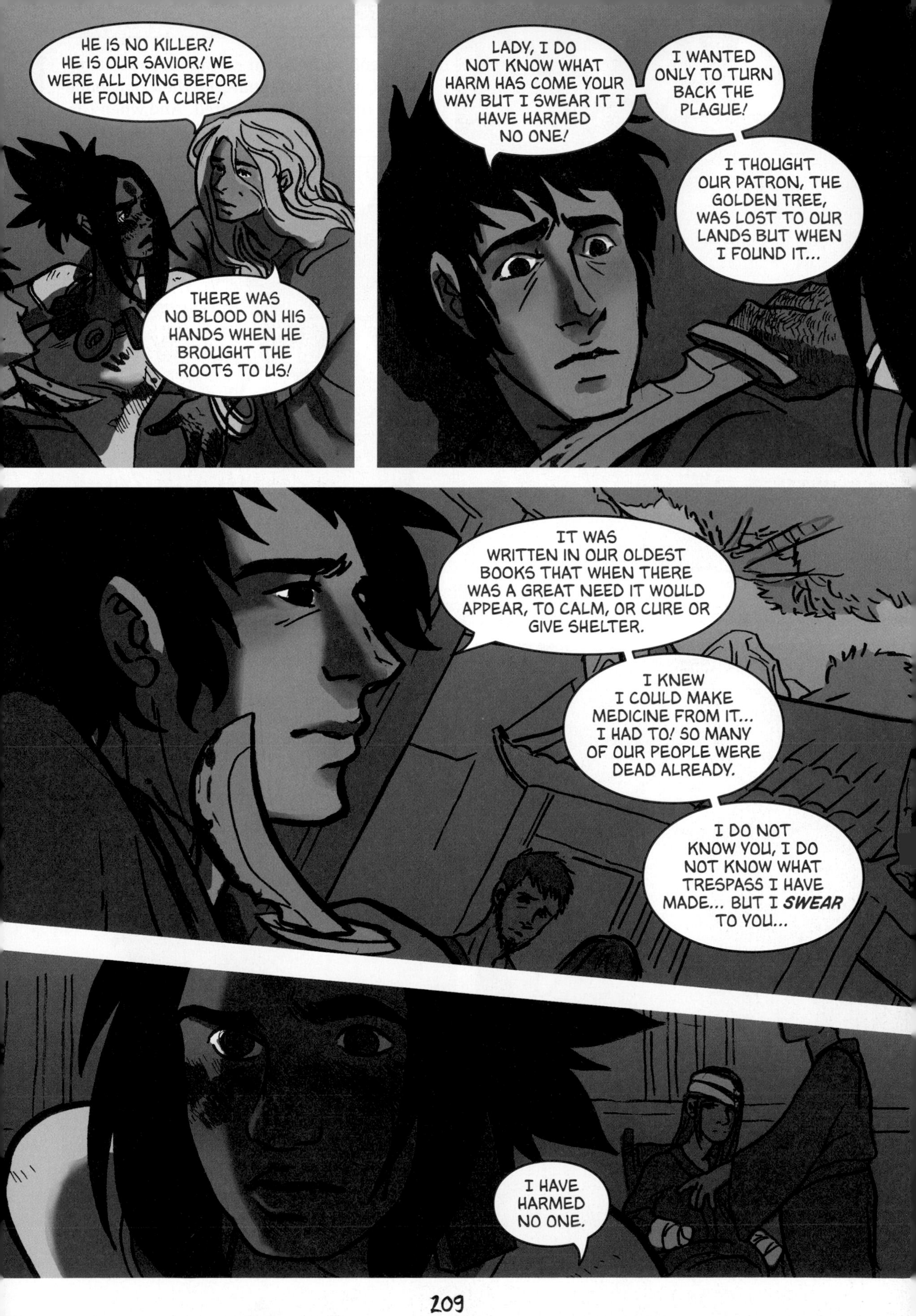
HE IS NO KILLER! HE IS OUR SAVIOR! WE WERE ALL DYING BEFORE HE FOUND A CURE!
THERE WAS NO BLOOD ON HIS HANDS WHEN HE BROUGHT THE ROOTS TO US!
LADY, I DO NOT KNOW WHAT HARM HAS COME YOUR WAY BUT I SWEAR IT I HAVE HARMED NO ONE!
I WANTED ONLY TO TURN BACK THE PLAGUE!
I THOUGHT OUR PATRON, THE GOLDEN TREE, WAS LOST TO OUR LANDS BUT WHEN I FOUND IT...
IT WAS WRITTEN IN OUR OLDEST BOOKS THAT WHEN THERE WAS A GREAT NEED IT WOULD APPEAR, TO CALM, OR CURE OR GIVE SHELTER.
I KNEW I COULD MAKE MEDICINE FROM IT... I HAD TO! SO MANY OF OUR PEOPLE WERE DEAD ALREADY.
I DO NOT KNOW YOU, I DO NOT KNOW WHAT TRESPASS I HAVE MADE... BUT I *SWEAR* TO YOU...
I HAVE HARMED NO ONE.

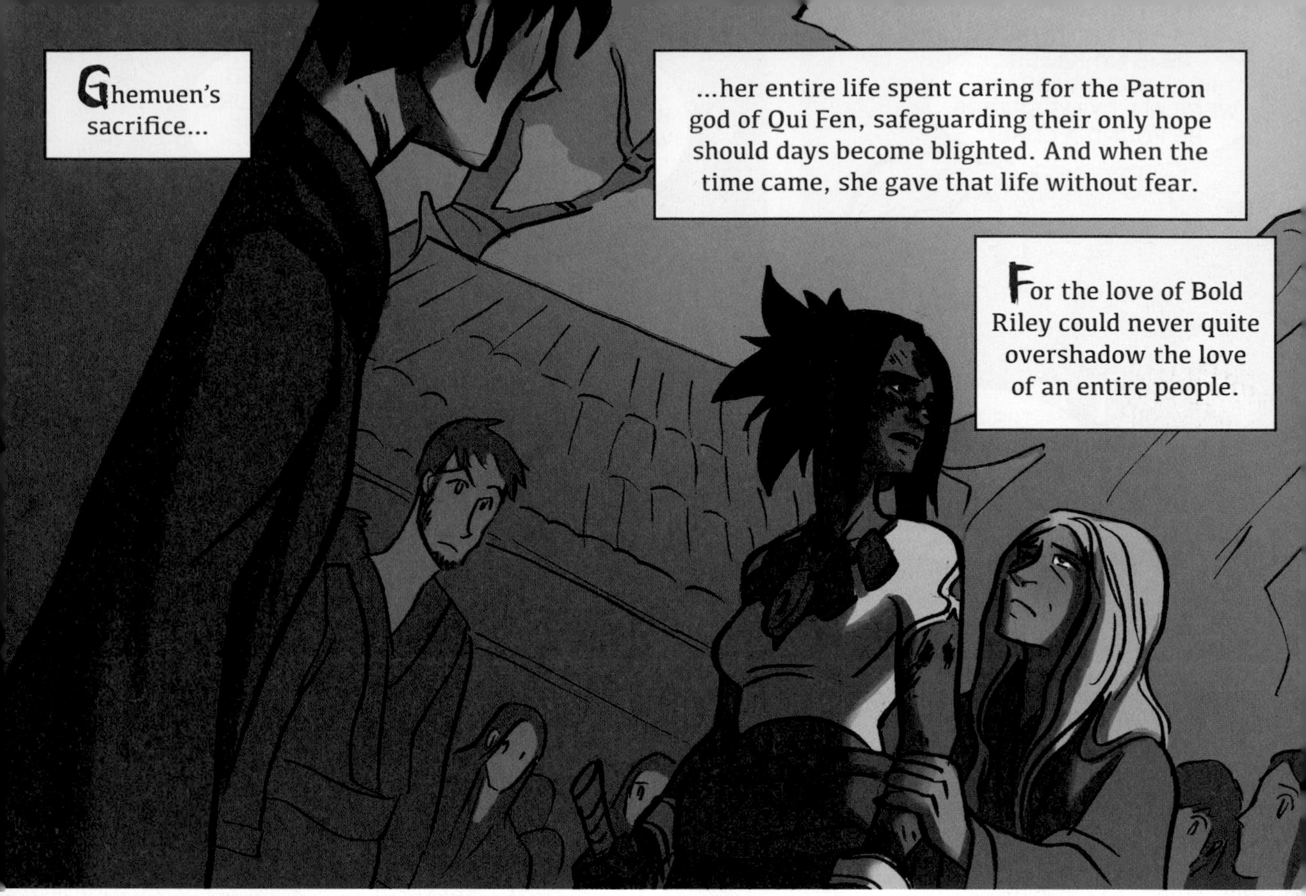
Ghemuen's sacrifice...
...her entire life spent caring for the Patron god of Qui Fen, safeguarding their only hope should days become blighted. And when the time came, she gave that life without fear.
For the love of Bold Riley could never quite overshadow the love of an entire people.

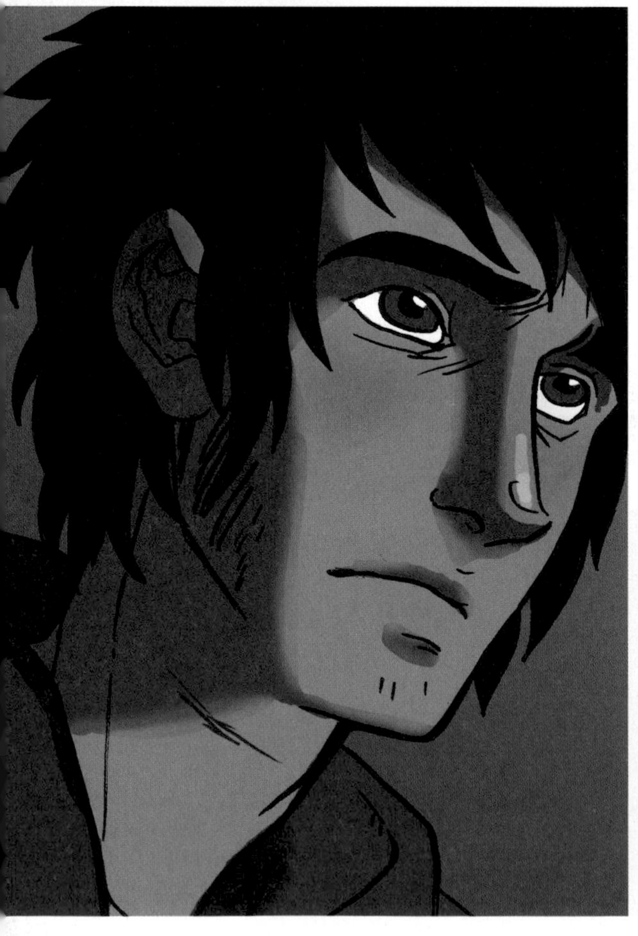

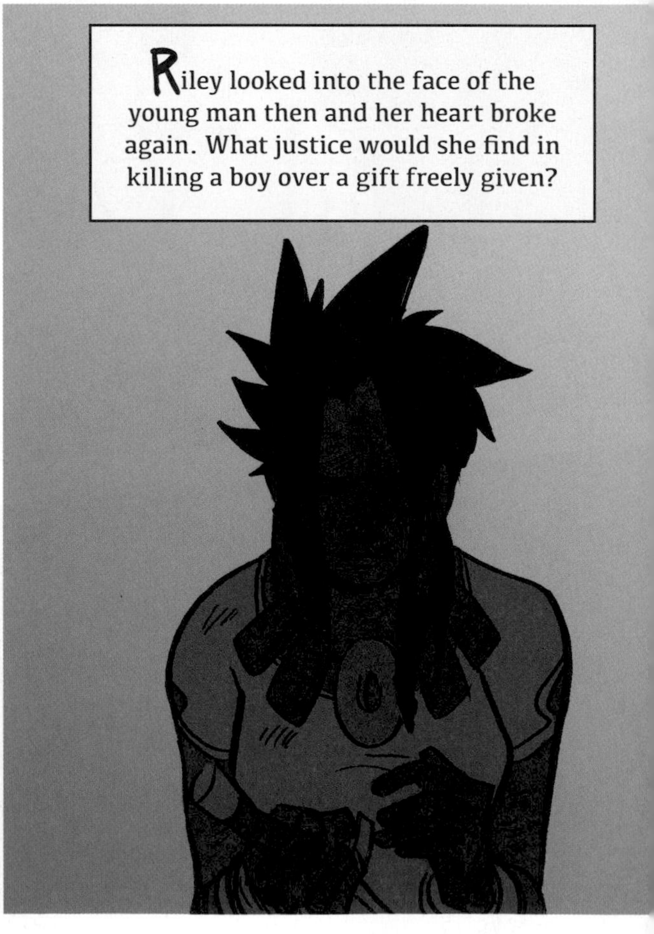
Riley looked into the face of the young man then and her heart broke again. What justice would she find in killing a boy over a gift freely given?

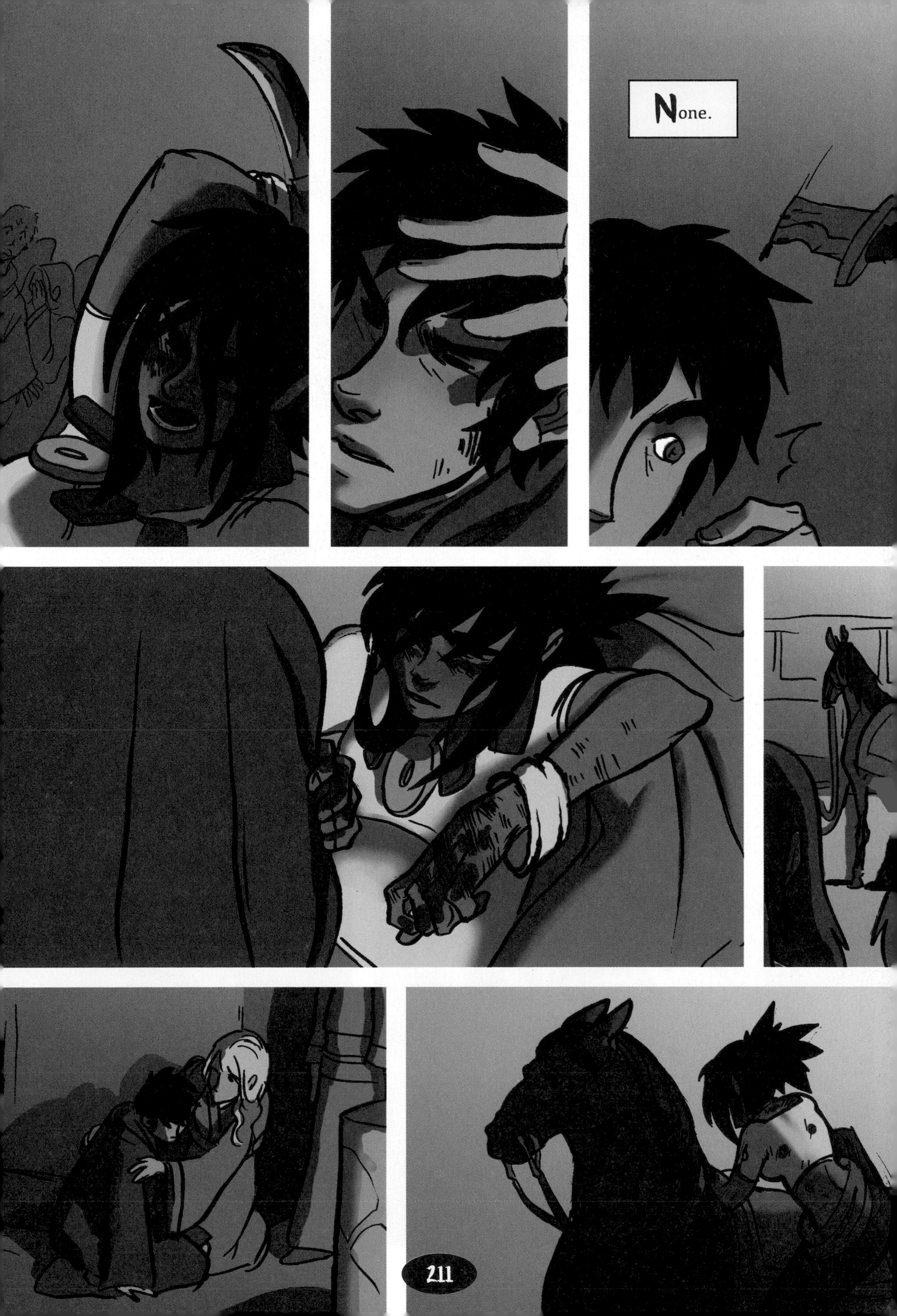
None.

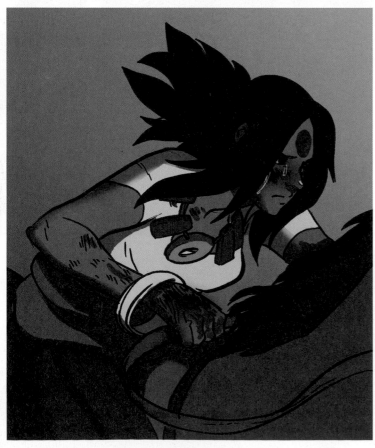

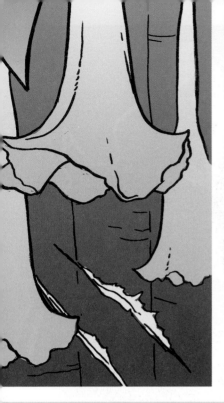
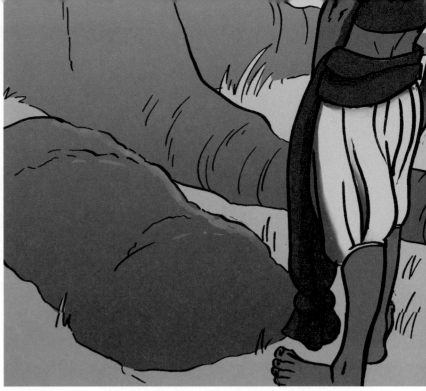

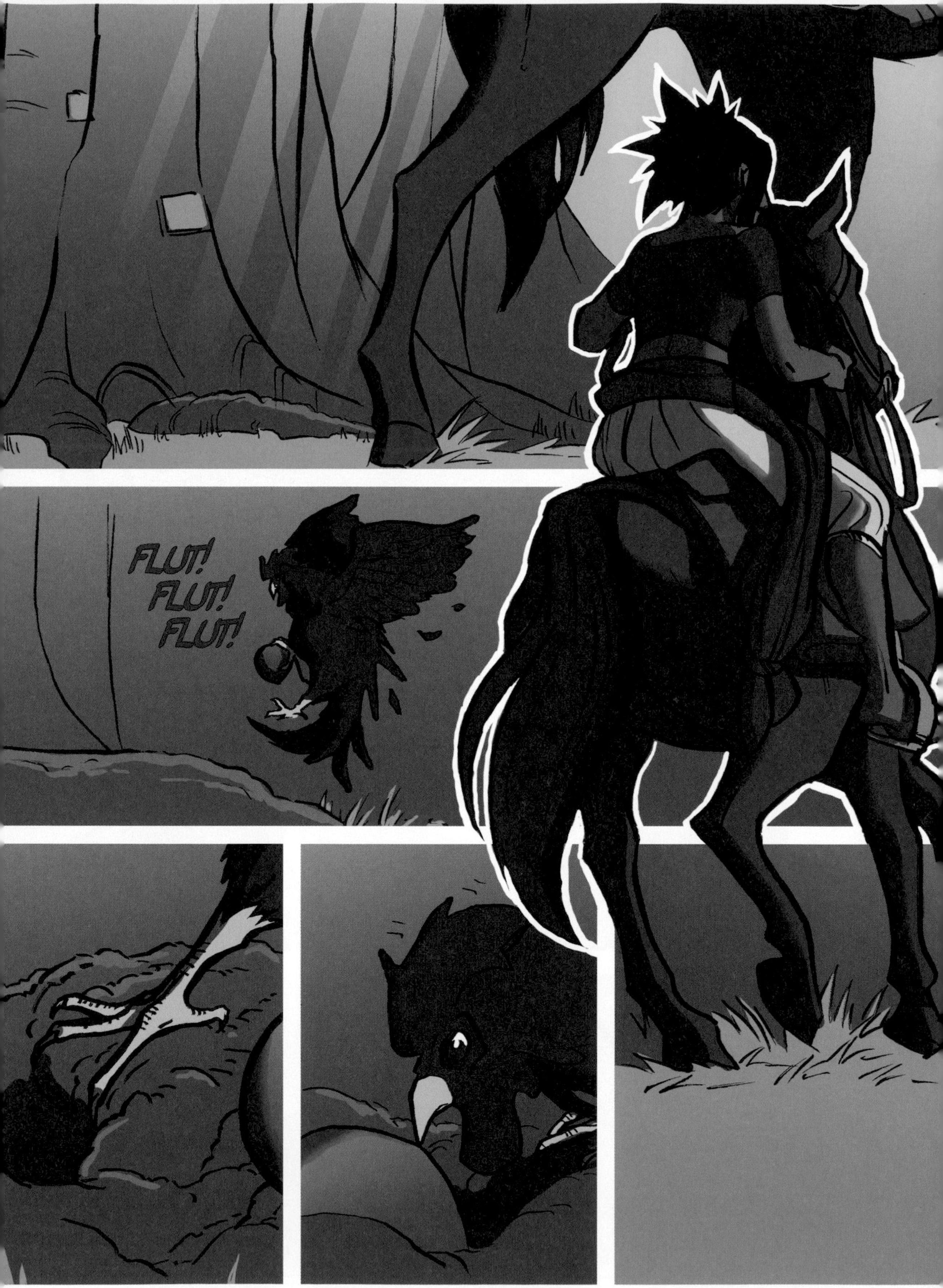
FLUT!
FLUT!
FLUT!

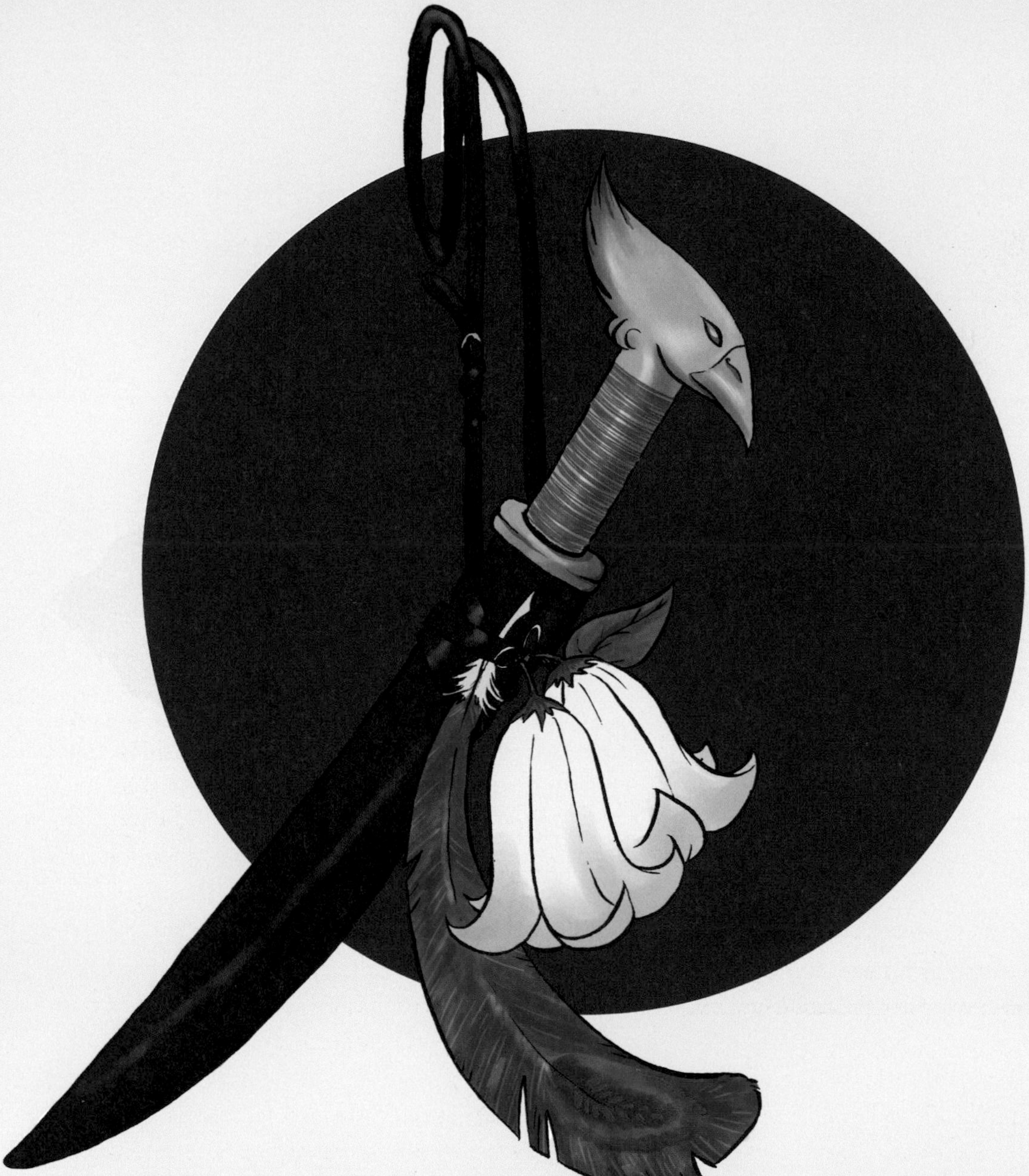

About the Creators

Leia Weathington is a writer and artist recently relocated to Portland, Oregon from San Francisco, California. She writes comics and cooks dinner in a little treehouse where she lives with her boyfriend. **The Legend of Bold Riley** is her first book. You can find more information at **boldriley.com** or read her crass humor blog at **ahappygoluckyscamp.wordpress.com**.

Marco Aidala works in the contemporary, jet-age world of advertising as an artist, and has enjoyed his foray into the storybook kingdom of Bold Riley. His offbeat concepts and characters may be viewed at **stbgogo.com**.

Vanessa Gillings is a comic book artist, writer, and graphic designer currently living in San Francisco. She was also a contributor to the anthology comic **Siren**. See more of her work at **vanessamakesthings.tumblr.com**.

Kelly McClellan is a hermit-y illustrator who spends most of her days talking to cats and hoarding hemp milk in west Sonoma county. She aspires to create graphic novels and illustrate board games, preferably ones involving sideburns and jet packs. Her website is: **kellymcc.com**.

Konstantin Pogorelov lives is San Francisco. He is 32 years old and has an MFA from the Academy of Arts University—where he became friends with the writer of this book—and 9 months later "The Wicked Temple" was... still being worked on. His website is **klumsyk.com**.

Brinson Thieme grew up in Florida and now lives in Los Angeles, California. She draws storyboards for animation and currently works on **Family Guy**. One day she hopes to draw and write her own comics... but until that day comes, she'll happily read, collect, and occasionally contribute to other peoples'. She has a Deviant Art page at **sairobi.deviantart.com**.

Jason Thompson is the artist of the H.P. Lovecraft adaptation **The Dream-Quest of Unknown Kadath and Other Stories**. He is also the creator of the graphic novel series **King of RPGs** (drawn by Victor Hao), **The Stiff**, **Hyperborea** (based on a Clark Ashton Smith story), and the Eisner-nominated manga encyclopedia **Manga: The Complete Guide**, published by Random House. He is currently working on an adaptation of **The Doom That Came to Sarnath** on his website, **mockman.com**.

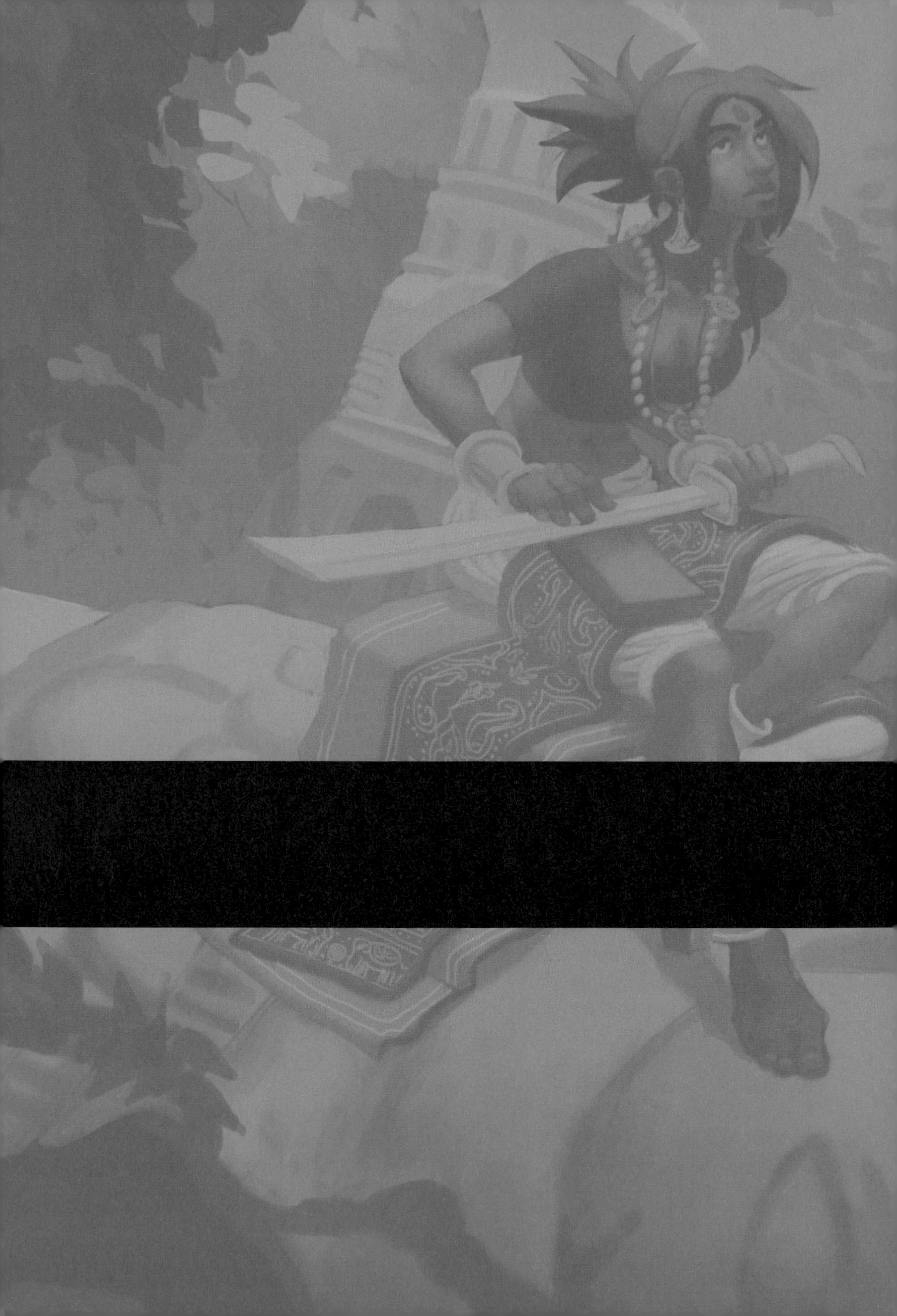

Gallery

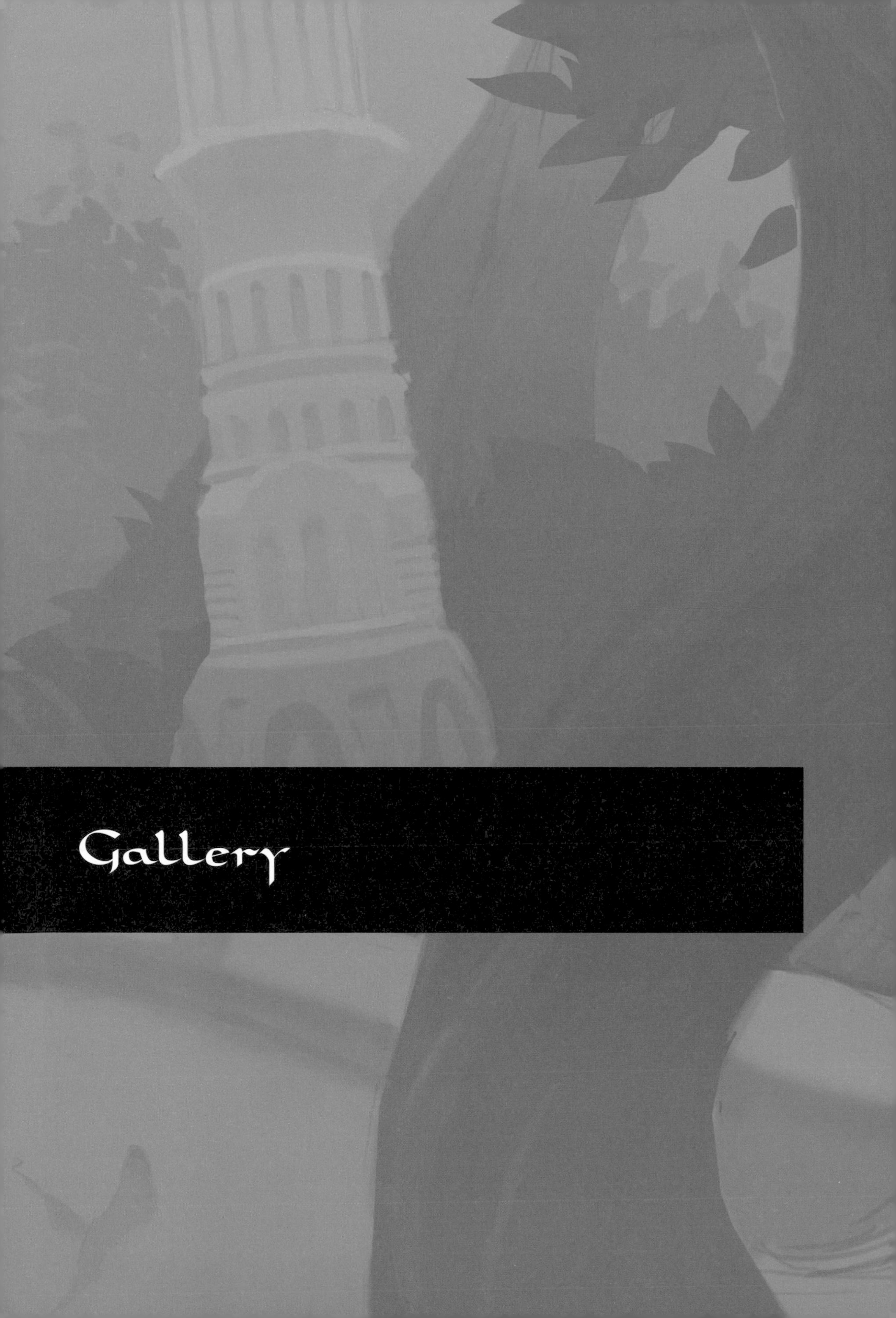

Jason Thompson painted this as the cover for "The Serpent in the Belly" back when they were being produced as single issues. The layout is loosely based off of a sketch I had done. I prefer his version much more.

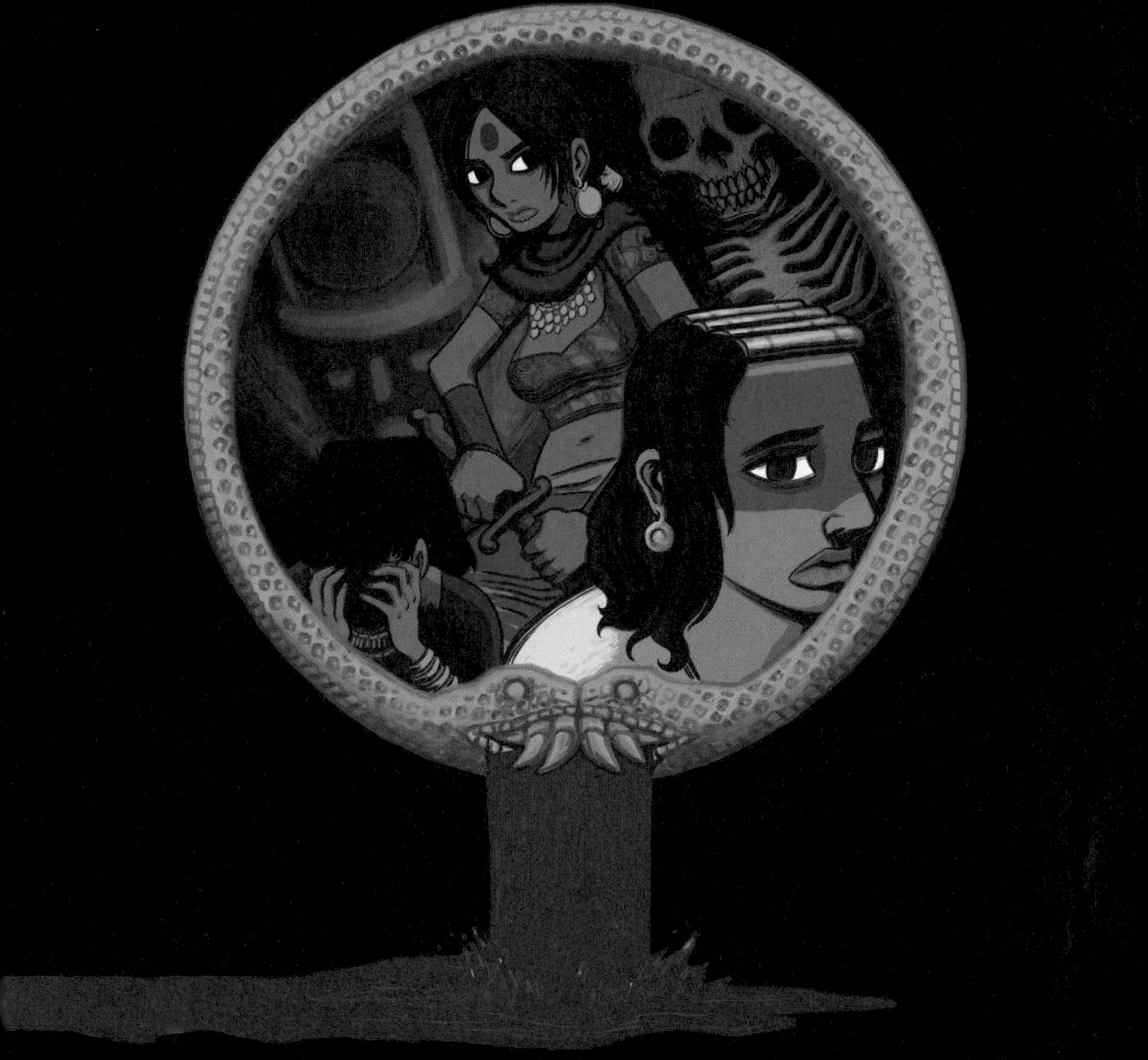

One of my illustrations of Riley at home in the royal palace in the capitol of Prakkalore.

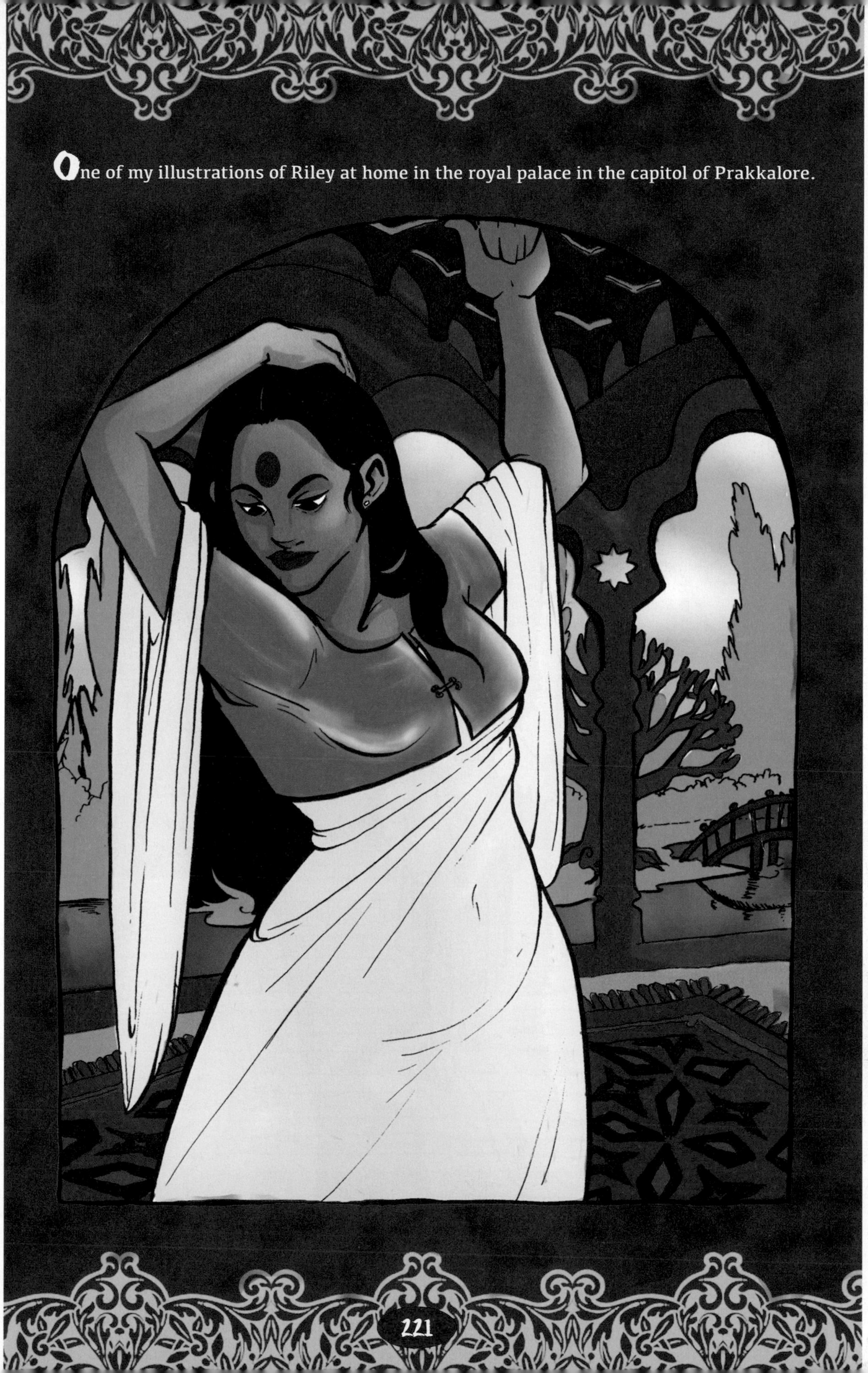

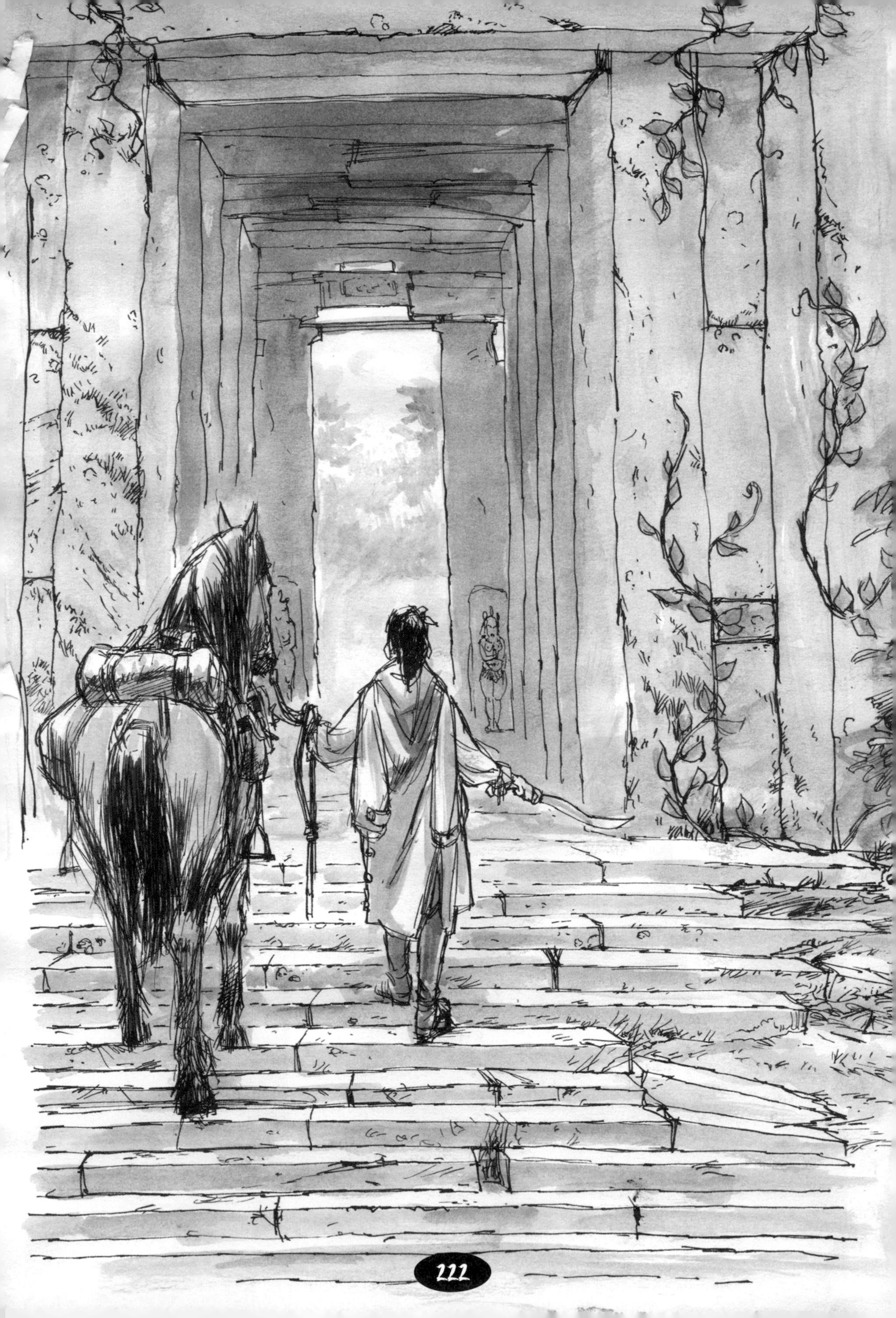

To contrast with Galliroh's haughty, superior dialogue in "The Wicked Temple", Konstantin Pogorelov drew him as a dopey looking sort of bird.

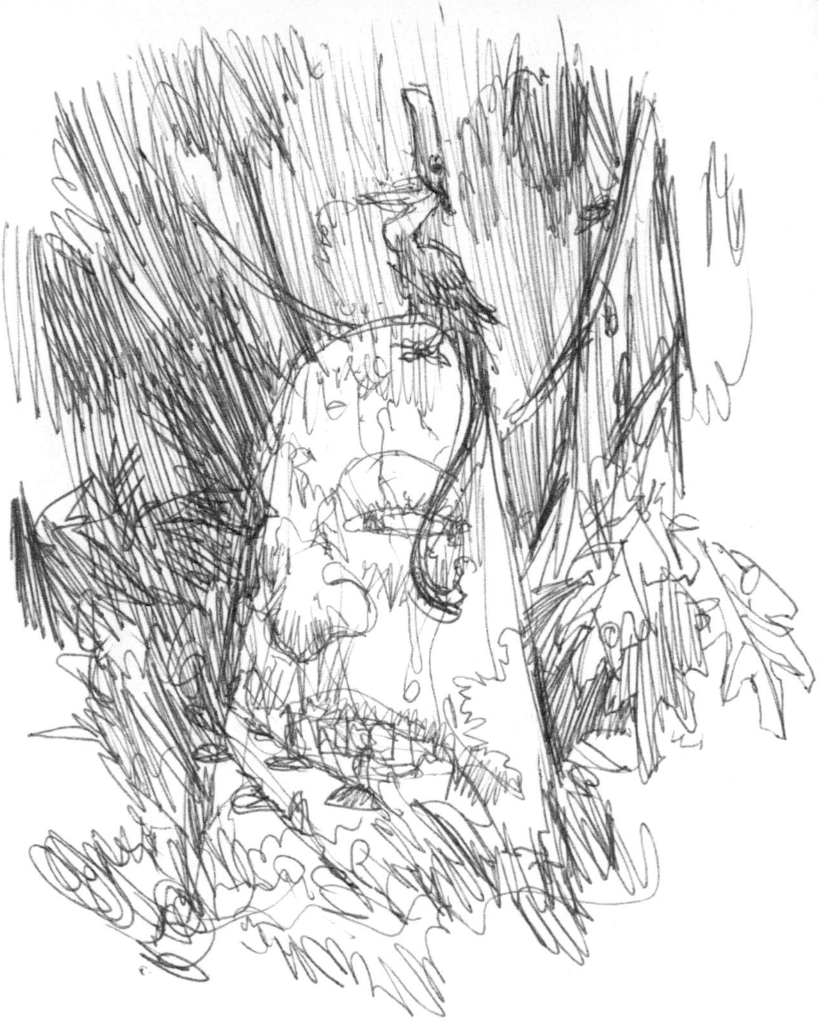

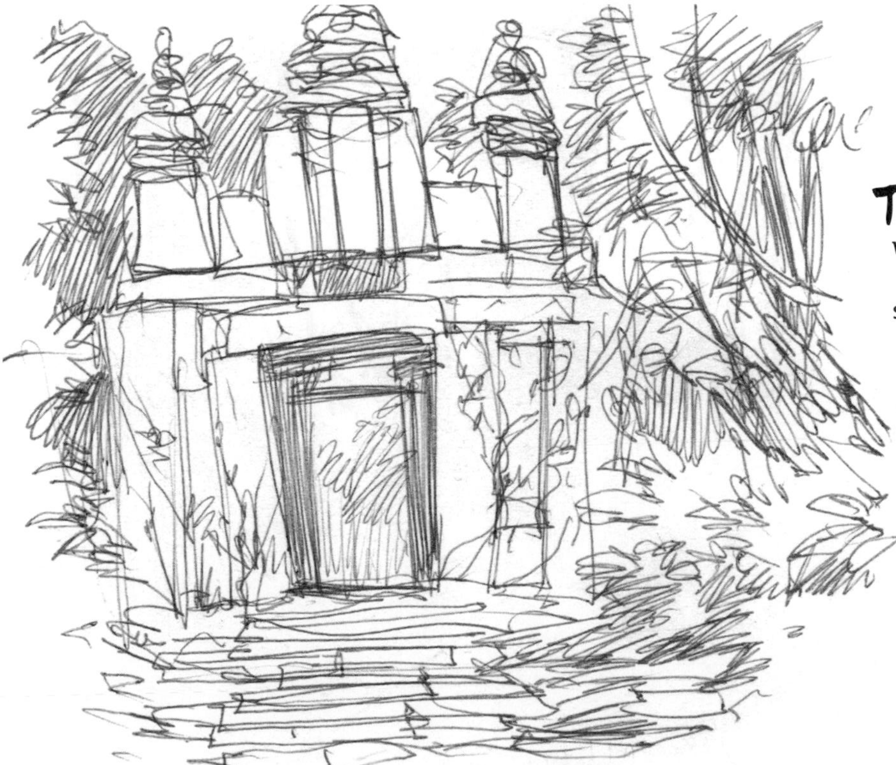

This sketch and the ink wash on the opposite page and the were some of Konstantin's early concepts for the temple setting.

Konstantin gets a handle on
how he wants to draw Riley
and her horse, Burlanni.

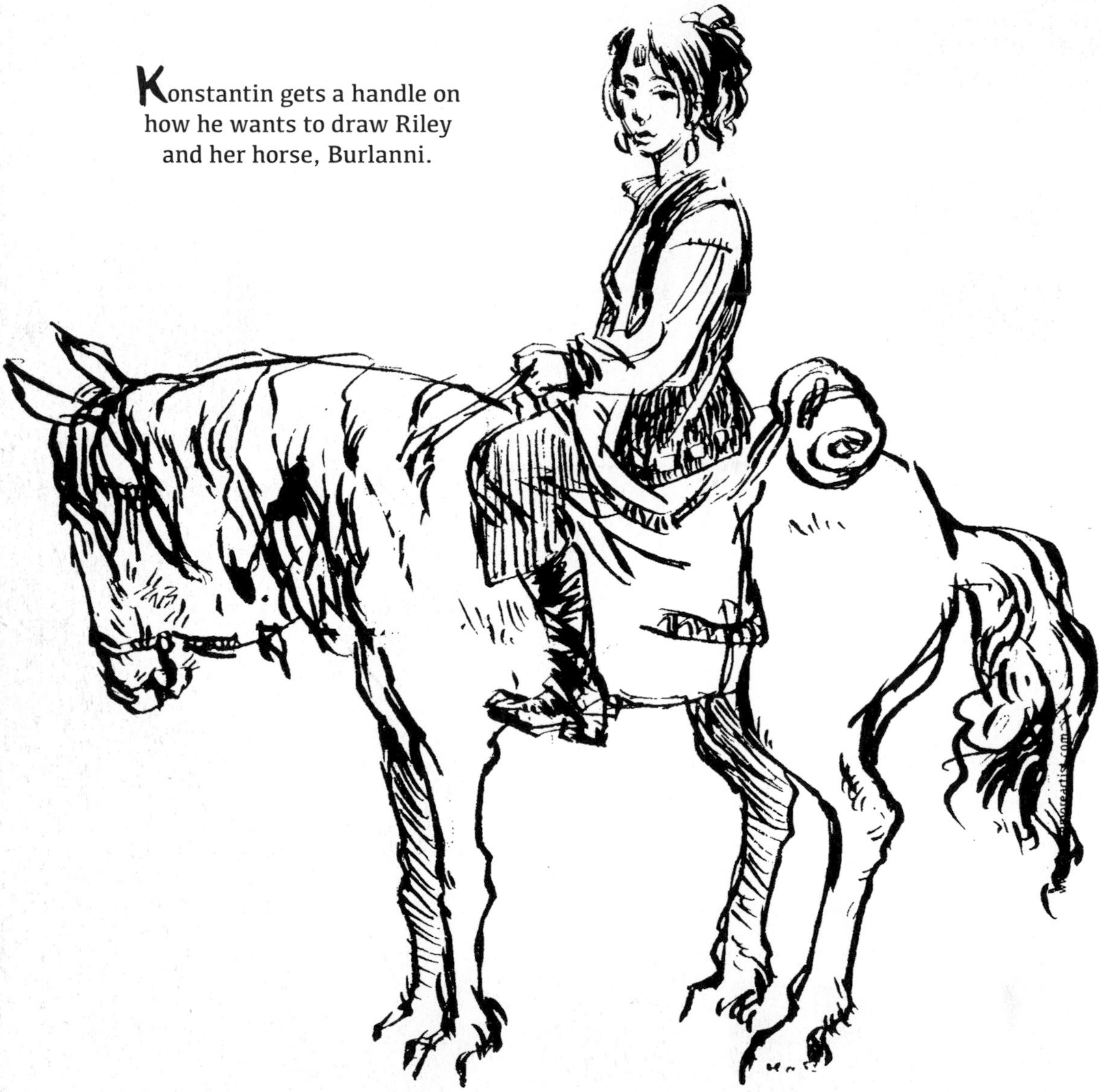

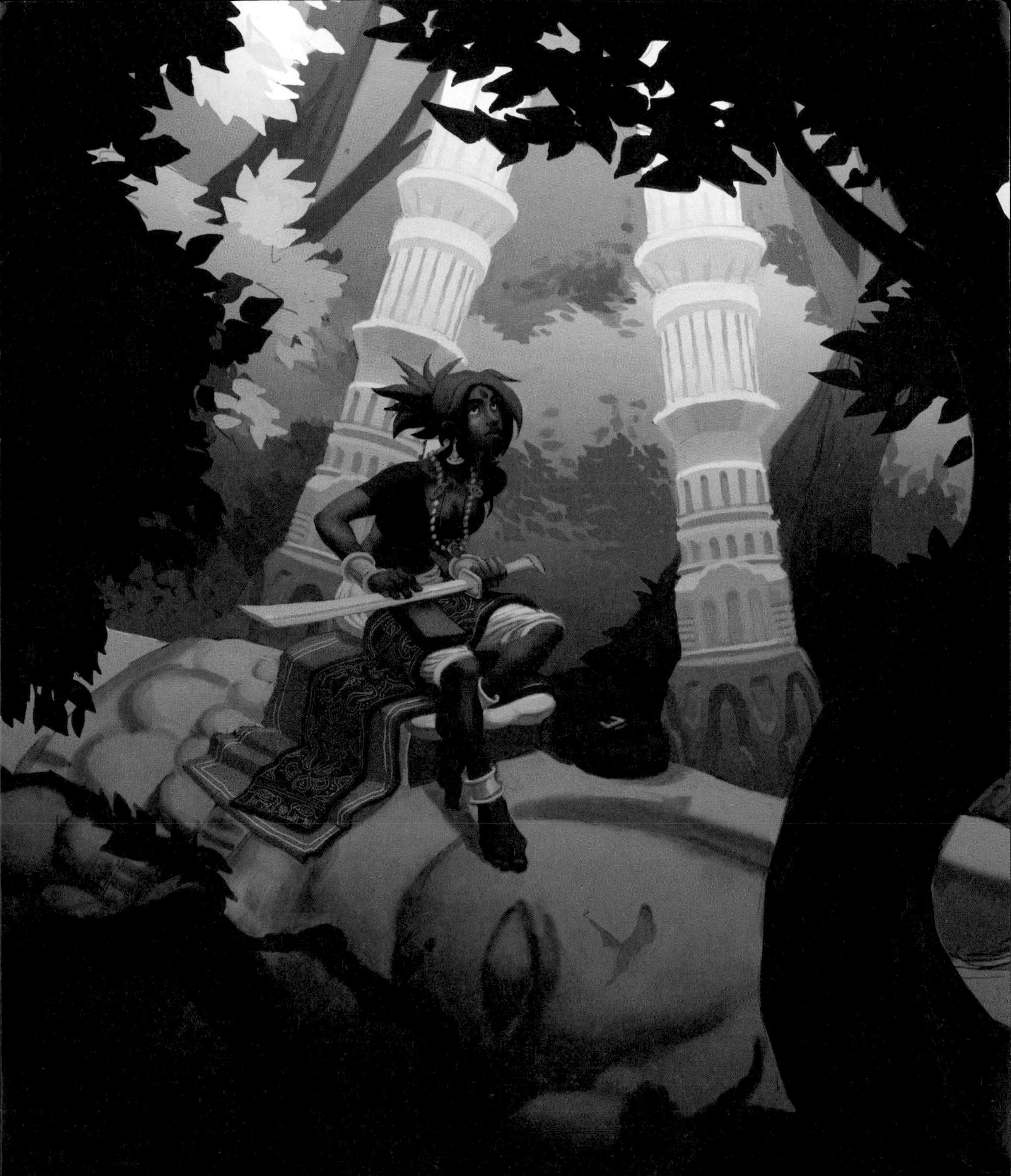

Kelly McClellan's beautiful illustration of Riley taking a moment to sharpen her sword somewhere in the jungles of Ang-Warr

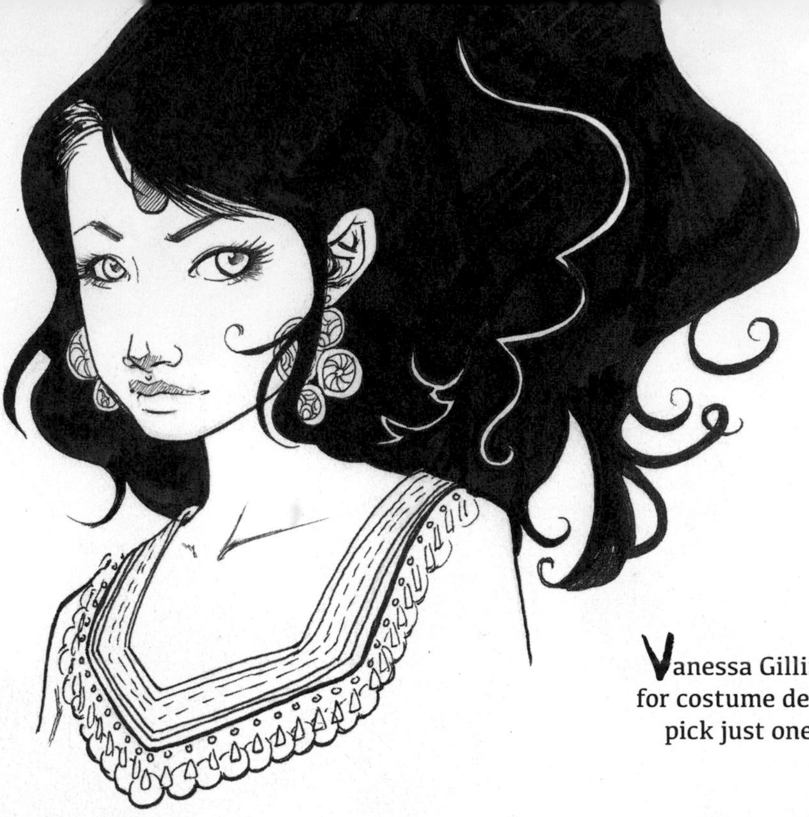

Vanessa Gillings has a fantastic eye for costume design. It was difficult to pick just one for "The Blue God".

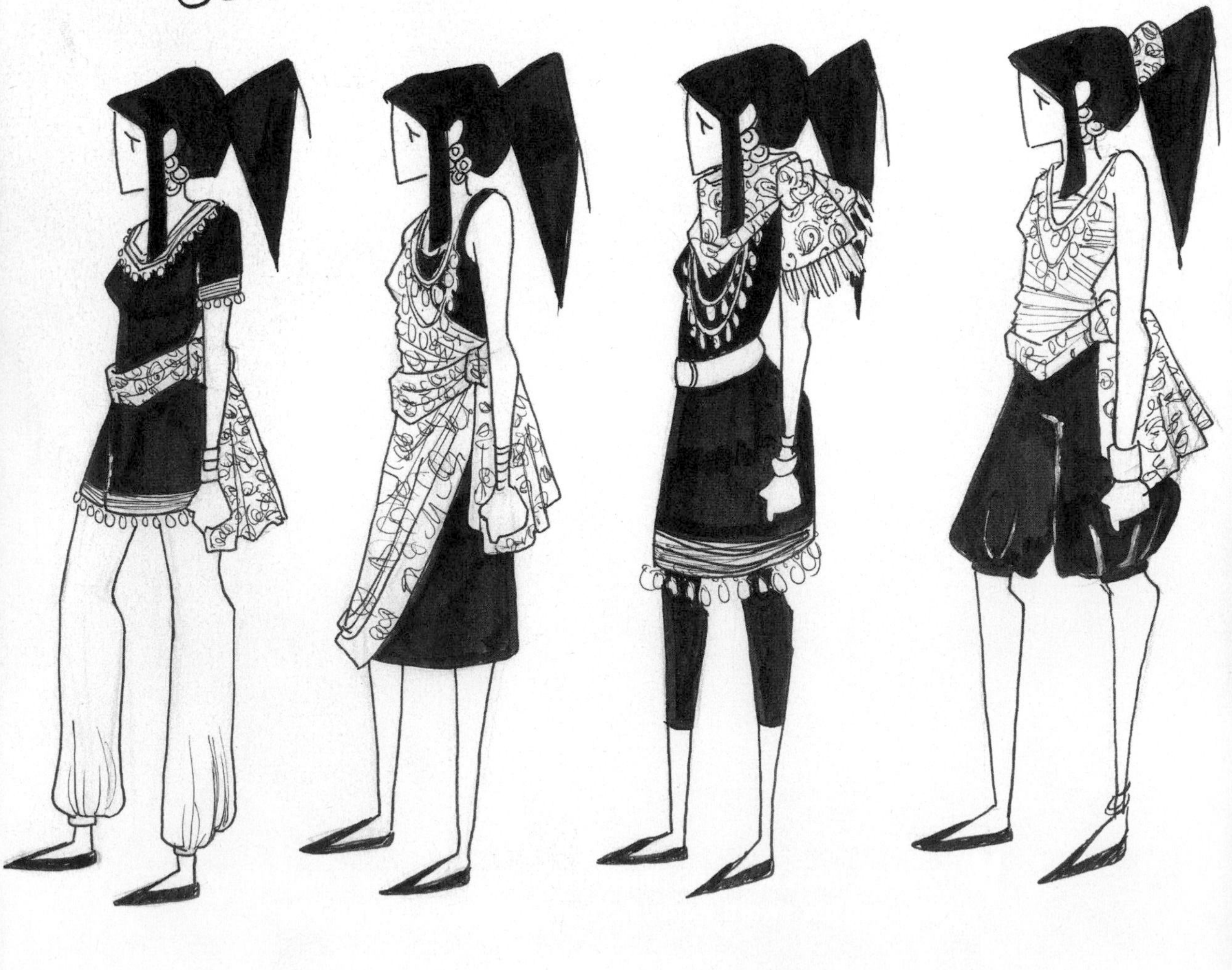

Vanessa also drew a more formally dressed Riley in a rare moment of serenity.

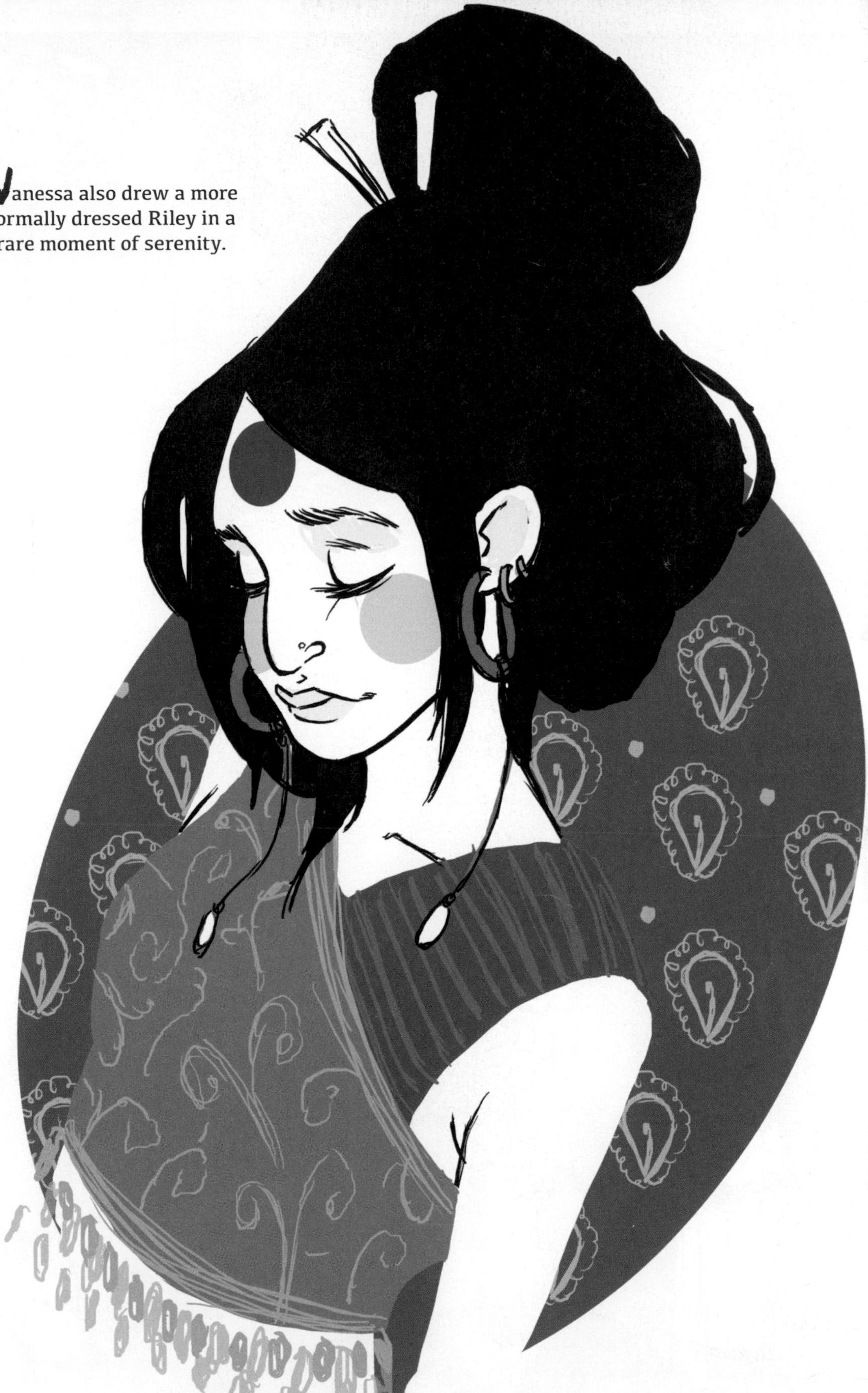

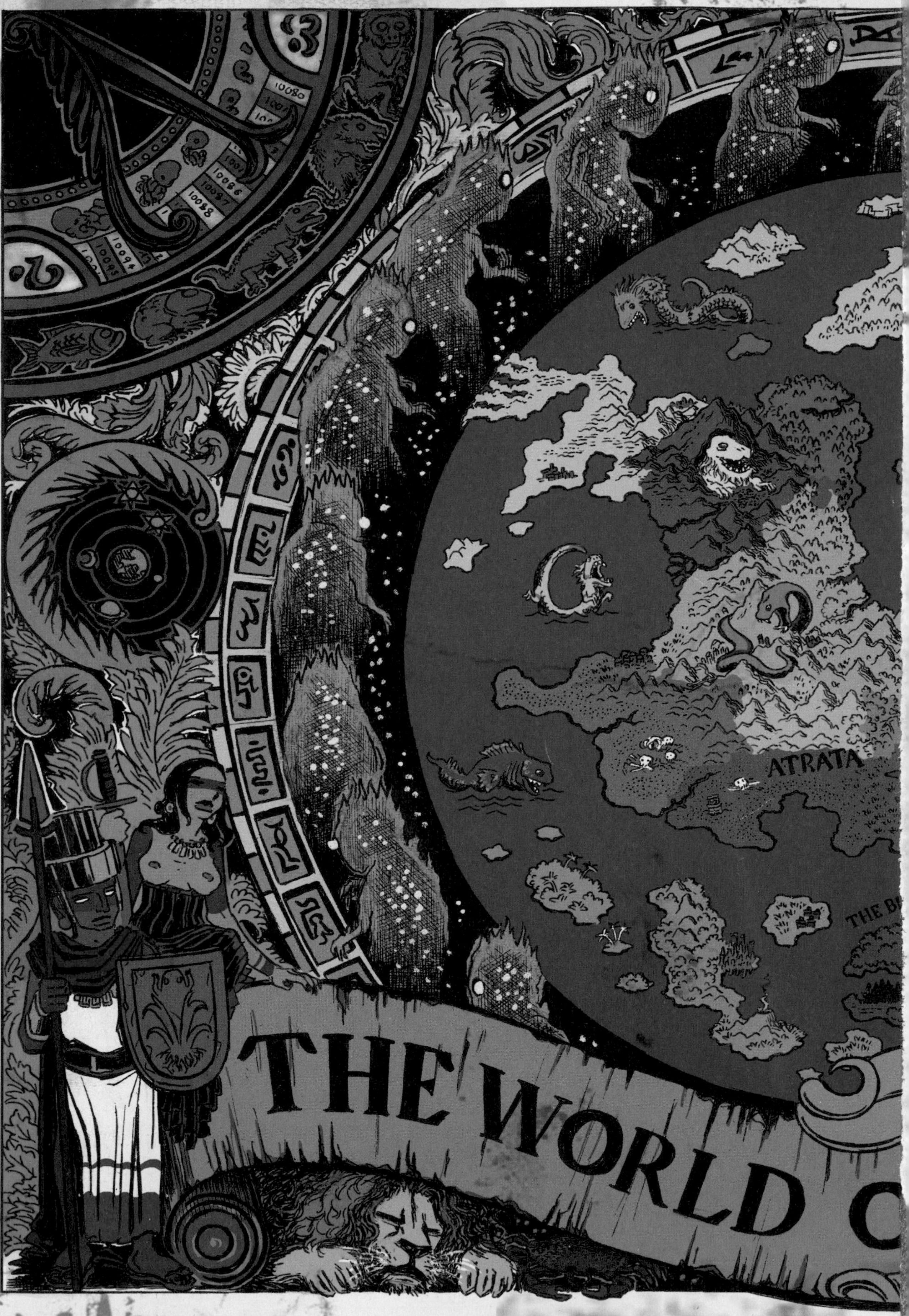
THE WORLD
ATRATA